NAPOLEON IN ITALY

C&C

CAMPAIGNS & COMMANDERS

GREGORY J. W. URWIN, SERIES EDITOR

CAMPAIGNS AND COMMANDERS

GENERAL EDITOR
Gregory J. W. Urwin, *Temple University, Philadelphia, Pennsylvania*

ADVISORY BOARD
Lawrence E. Babits, *East Carolina University, Greenville*
James C. Bradford, *Texas A&M University, College Station*
Robert M. Epstein, *U.S. Army School of Advanced Military Studies, Fort Leavenworth, Kansas*
David M. Glantz, *Carlisle, Pennsylvania*
Jerome A. Greene, *Denver, Colorado*
Victor Davis Hanson, *California State University, Fresno*
Herman Hattaway, *University of Missouri, Kansas City*
J. A. Houlding, *Rückersdorf, Germany*
Eugenia C. Kiesling, *U.S. Military Academy, West Point, New York*
Timothy K. Nenninger, *National Archives, Washington, D.C.*
Bruce Vandervort, *Virginia Military Institute, Lexington*

Napoleon in Italy

The Sieges of Mantua, 1796–1799

Phillip R. Cuccia

University of Oklahoma Press | Norman

Library of Congress Cataloging-in-Publication Data

Cuccia, Phillip R., 1967–
  Napoleon in Italy : the sieges of Mantua, 1796–1799 / Phillip R. Cuccia.
    pages cm. — (Campaigns and commanders ; volume 44)
  Includes bibliographical references and index.
  ISBN 978-0-8061-4445-0 (hardcover : alk. paper) 1. Mantua (Italy)—History—
Siege, 1796–1797. 2. Mantua (Italy)—History—Siege, 1799. 3. Napoleon I, Emperor
of the French, 1769–1821—Military leadership. I. Title.
  DC223.4.C83 2014
  940.2'7345281—dc23
                              2013042681

Napoleon in Italy: The Sieges of Mantua, 1796–1799 is Volume 44 in the
Campaigns and Commanders series.

Interior layout and composition: Alcorn Publication Design

To my mother, Mary

Contents

Illustrations

Maps

Figures

Acknowledgments

As a cadet at West Point, I remember Captain Paul Jacobsmeyer drawing on the chalkboard and describing Napoleon's great battles around the fortress of Mantua. Later, as a young officer, I liked to use those operations to explain some military concepts to my soldiers, but I had forgotten the name of that fortress city. My saying "somewhere in northern Italy" failed to convey the true extent of the campaigns. I told myself that if I ever came across the name of that city again, I would learn as much as possible about it and those campaigns. As I prepared to teach history at West Point I had that opportunity while studying under Dr. Donald Horward at the Institute on Napoleon and the French Revolution at Florida State University. To him I owe the greatest appreciation and thanks for his direction, guidance, encouragement, assistance, generosity, and especially friendship. He was like a second father to me during my time at FSU, and I am greatly indebted to him and can only hope to repay him by following his example.

Special thanks are due to the staff of the United States Military Academy Library, especially Alan Aimone and Faith Coslett of the Special Collections and the Interlibrary Loan office, respectively. Their assistance was a continuation of the superb support given by Florida State's Strozier Library Interlibrary Loan section and its personnel. Lucy Patrick and her Special Collections staff were quite helpful to my research on this topic. They were always accommodating and went out of their way to help with my frequent requests.

Other library staffs have been particularly helpful as well. The staff at the Service Historique de l'Armée de Terre at Vincennes as well as those at the Archives Nationales and the Bibliothèque Nationale in Paris were most professional in their assistance. The staff and director of the Museum of the Risorgimento and the State Archives in Milan directed me to documents concerning the sieges of Mantua and administration of the city from 1797 to 1799. The staff of the Biblioteca Nazionale Braidense in Milan helped locate manuscripts and maps and aided with microfilming. Special thanks go to Vittorio Scotti Douglas, who opened his home to me in Milan.

Likewise, the Ballerio-Porro family of Melegnano, who had relatives who served in the Napoleonic Milanese government, were very kind in their assistance and hospitality during my visits in Milan.

In Mantua, the staffs of the Biblioteca Comunale Special Collections, the Archivio di Stato di Mantova, and the Academia Nazionale Virgiliana were extremely courteous and helpful. In particular, Dr. Francesca Fantini d'Onofrio at the State Archives took a special interest in my work. She kindly showed me the research she had conducted in the archives into the 1797–99 period. Her knowledge of these years and her familiarity with the collection made my research more efficient. The director of the archives, Dr. Daniela Ferrari, and Raffaella Perini at the Biblioteca Comunale (Commune Library) provided much assistance and support. In addition, Mansueto Bassi and his daughter, Sara, were very helpful showing me manuscripts and books about the sieges that passed through their bookshop, Libreria Antiquaria Scriptorium. I must also thank Ms. Francesca Ferrari and her family for their assistance during my stays in Mantua. Their hospitality was greatly appreciated. I am also grateful to Ciro Paoletti for his many consultations. Many thanks are due to Dr. Peter Brouček at the Kriegsarchiv division of the Österreichisches Stattarchiv in Vienna for his guidance, and Bernhard Voykowitsch of Vienna for his assistance in pointing out the early military works concerning the Austrians in Mantua.

Several members of the Department of History at the United States Military Academy helped throughout my research. Colonels Robert Doughty, Cole Kingseed, and Lance Betros provided support and encouragement. While holding chairs at the department, the Frey sisters, Marsha and Linda, took time out of their busy schedules to read through the manuscript and provide suggestions. I am greatly indebted to both of them. Many of my colleagues at West Point and the Institute on Napoleon and the French Revolution at Florida State were extremely helpful with advice and assistance; in particular, Hal Blanton and Llew Cook of the institute, with whom I spent a summer in Paris conducting research. Steve Delvaux and Paul Reese were also very supportive. In addition, I wish to thank Professors Paul Halpern, Edward Keuchel, Jonathan Grant, and Antoine Spacagna for their support.

Most notably, I would like to thank my wife, Dr. Lenora Cuccia, for her continued support throughout this entire process and for her excellent work in translating the Russian documents used in chapters

9 and 10. She and our daughter, Maria, have been very patient and understanding throughout this endeavor. Finally, I especially thank my parents, Frank and Mary Cuccia, who have given continued support and encouragement in all of my academic interests.

Napoleon in Italy

PROLOGUE

Over the narrow flowing Rio in the center of the Lombardian city of Mantua, there is a covered bridge called the Ponte delle Pescherie where local vendors set up pushcarts and sell various kinds of fish just as they did more than two centuries ago at the time of the Napoleonic Wars.[1] As the present-day crowds of townspeople and tourists cross over the bridge, few if any notice the four cannonballs protruding out of the adjacent wall of the southeast corner. These unexploded shells, along with two small marble engravings and a religious painting, comprise the memorial to the sufferings of the townspeople of Mantua during the 1796–97 siege. Although this small tribute to the horrible siege is potentially seen by hundreds of people daily, little scholarly attention has been given to this series of historic events.

The sieges of Mantua in 1796–97 and in 1799 played a major role in the campaigns in northern Italy during the Wars of the First and Second Coalitions.[2] The sieges of Mantua effectively delayed invading armies, preventing a quick conquest in the region. The siege of Mantua in 1796–97 significantly slowed Bonaparte's earlier lightning movement across northern Italy whereby he rapidly subdued the Sardinian king and went on to capture the city of Milan. In 1799 Field Marshal Aleksandr Suvorov's combined army of Austrians and Russians was held up from continuing their victorious movement toward France because the Austrian emperor insisted on capturing Mantua first.

The first Napoleonic siege of Mantua is arguably the most important siege of the eighteenth century in terms of its outcome since it hastened the end of the First Coalition as Napoleon Bonaparte conquered the Austrians. Other significant eighteenth-century sieges include those of Turin, which ended operations in Italy during the War of the Spanish Succession; Yorktown, in North America, which effectively ended the American Revolutionary War; and Toulon, which propelled Captain Napoleon Bonaparte to the rank of general of brigade in the artillery.[3] What sets the siege of Mantua in 1796–97 apart from the others is that during this operation, the career of the most famous military figure in history was fully established: Bonaparte conquered four Austrian relief armies, all larger than his own, and solidified his position as leader of France in a period when France dominated Europe.

Mantua was besieged four times during the eighteenth century.[4] Its 1796–97 siege was, however, the first great siege of many that stretched from Cádiz in Spain to Danzig in Prussia during the Napoleonic Wars. With the surrender of Mantua in 1797, after eight long months of hardship for the inhabitants, two years of peace brought many changes to the city under the French administration. In 1799, however, the Austrians with their Russian allies returned to northern Italy, while Bonaparte was in Egypt, and they forced the French garrison to surrender the fortress after a much shorter three-and-a-half-month investment and siege. The 1799 Mantua siege during the War of the Second Coalition was a disaster for the French defenders. The glories of '96 and '97 were reversed when the French general François Philippe Foissac-Latour ignobly surrendered the city.

It is noteworthy that little has been published on the 1796–97 and 1799 sieges of Mantua in any language. To date, there is no complete treatment of these sieges in English. My intention in the present study is to fill that gap.

INTRODUCTION

In March 1796 Napoleon Bonaparte's talent and vigor breathed new life into a French army that had struggled for four years in a long-drawn-out war of attrition against Sardinian and Austrian troops in northwest Italy.[1] Bonaparte's juggernaut across northern Italy in 1796–97 brought an end to the War of the First Coalition on a secondary front.

Bonaparte's assignment to Italy followed a rapid chain of events during the French Revolution. After the French royal family's failed attempt to escape to the royalist fortress of Montmédy on France's northeastern frontier, Leopold, the Austrian emperor and brother of Marie-Antoinette, issued the Declaration of Pillnitz. The declaration obliged Prussia and Austria to prepare their armies for war and be ready to receive support from fellow monarchs. The revolutionaries initially did not react but instead focused on their new constitution, which created a new Legislative Assembly. Many in this assembly sought to renew the ancient contest of arms with Austria because they believed that war would help them achieve their domestic political goals.[2]

On 20 October 1791, the orator Jacques Pierre Brissot gave an exhilarating speech advocating for war. He repeated this theme often, citing the Declaration of Pillnitz as evidence the sovereigns of Europe intended to stop the Revolution. Eventually, in April 1792, Louis XVI was obliged to go to the Assembly and confirm that the allegations of Austrian aggression by Foreign Minister Dumouriez were also his own views. The king was compelled to ask for a vote for war. The proposal passed quickly.[3]

Bonaparte's rise to fame and glory during the Italian campaigns was preceded by a fortuitous sequence of events linking his life with the Revolution. When the war started with Austria in 1792, Bonaparte had been an officer for six years. He was born in Corsica on 15 August 1769, just over a year after France bought the island from the Republic of Genoa, which was relieved to be rid of the problematic Corsicans. Bonaparte's family fought against the French in the two attempts to subdue the islanders, who were led

by Pasquale Paoli. Bonaparte's father, Carlo, helped lead the resistance but eventually surrendered. Accepting his plight, Carlo
worked with the ruling French to eventually win for his two oldest
sons, Joseph and Napoleon, places at the seminary of Autun and the
military academy in Brienne, respectively. Napoleon left Corsica as
a nine-year-old and began his military career, initially hoping to join
the navy. In 1784 he entered into the École Militaire in Paris for his
primary military training and commissioning as an officer. He completed the two-year course in one year, graduating in 1785.[4]

Bonaparte reported to the La Fère Artillery Regiment in Valence,
and while a young officer he took a liberal amount of leave back to
his native island of Corsica. In June 1788 he traveled to Auxonne to
rejoin his regiment, and for the next fifteen months he studied there
at the artillery training school under the experienced Baron du Teil,
the great artillerist. Later, back in Corsica again in 1792, through a
cunning election campaign, he was voted lieutenant colonel of the
Ajaccio Volunteers at the age of twenty-one.[5] When war with the
coalition finally came in April 1792, Bonaparte found no employment for his talents in Corsica even after his election to lieutenant
colonel; meanwhile, his absence had cost him his commission in
the artillery. In May he left for Paris, where he witnessed the mob
attack on the Tuileries—a sight he remembered later, when called
upon to quell the mob to which he delivered a "whiff of grape."[6]

By the end of 1793, the Allies were driven from France, and in
1794 the French occupied the Low Countries and crossed into Germany. In 1795 Prussia, Spain, and the Netherlands made peace with
France, while the internal Vendée revolt was quelled. By 1796 only
Great Britain, Austria, and Sardinia remained in the alliance fighting against France.[7]

The campaigns in Italy against the southern armies of the First
Coalition began when France annexed the Sardinian provinces of
Savoy and Nice and sent in troops to claim the territory. From 1792
through early 1796 French soldiers fought on the foothills and slopes
of the Alps between Nice and Genoa but never won a decisive victory. The days of fighting indecisive battles in northern Italy would
not change until Bonaparte was placed in command of the army.

During the French struggle in the Alps, Bonaparte spent months
in 1794 as an artillery general of brigade with the French Army of Italy.
He owed this promotion from captain to artillery general of brigade
to his actions at the siege of Toulon, which resulted in the capture of

the city on 19 December 1793. With his promotion, he was named commander of the artillery in the Army of Italy. His special assignment was to reorganize the coastal defenses against the British to protect the southern ports. He worked in this capacity in early 1794, but in the spring he commanded his artillery in the French offensive along the Mediterranean coast. During this offensive, Bonaparte had the opportunity to work closely with Representative on Mission Augustin Robespierre, and indirectly with his brother, Maximilien Robespierre. More important, this offensive gave Bonaparte a first-hand view of the enormous problems the Army of Italy faced in the war in Sardinia-Piedmont. Although in Colmar in May, he was obsessed with Italy: he submitted a plan for an Italian campaign that gained the strong support of the Representatives on Mission. His detailed plan covered everything from army organization and lines of attack to how many cartridges and flints each soldier would need to carry. This plan was not accepted in Paris because the administration favored more limited operations in Italy.[8] A month later, from Nice, he submitted another equally detailed plan for the Army of Italy that apparently received the same response.[9]

On 27 July Maximilien Robespierre fell from power during the Thermidorean Reaction, and anyone thought to be one of his supporters was sought out and arrested. On 8 August Bonaparte, who fell into this category, was put in prison at Fort Carré in Antibes. The Representatives on Mission, however, understood his importance to the army, and since they had no condemning evidence, Bonaparte was released on 20 August and reinstated in the army. He then took part in a rather small but surprisingly successful operation against the Austrians in September.[10]

The following winter Bonaparte spent his time preparing for an expedition to Corsica, to drive the British from his former island home. The French fleet, which set sail on 5 March 1795, was forced to return after encountering the Royal Navy. In the meantime, Bonaparte's post in the Army of Italy was given to another artillery commander, leaving him temporarily unemployed. However, at the end of April he was summoned to Paris.[11]

At the end of May Bonaparte arrived in the capital and was assigned as an infantry brigade commander to fight against the Vendéean insurrection. He ignored the assignment and stayed in Paris on a plea of bad health. There he proposed various campaign plans for the Army of Italy and drew up instructions for its commanders.

In these plans, Bonaparte emphasized the importance of Mantua to the French forces in the capture of the Lombardy Plain.[12] In a plan written in late July 1795, Bonaparte explained: "In the present situation in Europe, the Army of Italy can be used in a grand way to deliver a decisive blow against the house of Austria in order to bring about peace."[13] He then described in intricate detail how that army could conquer northern Italy. He concluded by stating:

> Controlling Lombardy up to Mantua, the army will find all that is necessary to equip itself and will be able to take the gorges of Trent, cross the Adige and arrive at the interior of the Tyrol, while at the same time the Army of the Rhine can pass into Bavaria and also enter the Tyrol. Few campaign plans offer results more advantageous, at this time, worthy of the courage of our soldiers and the great destinies of the Republic.[14]

In his campaign plans he emphasized the movement through the traditional invasion route north of the Po River and south of the Italian Alps. This ancient invasion approach was guarded by the four fortresses of the Italian Quadrilateral (see map 2).[15]

The fortresses of Peschiera and Mantua on the Mincio River and those of Verona and Legnago on the Adige River formed the Quadrilateral. Legnago and Peschiera were small fortifications designed principally as bridgeheads that required large garrisons. Verona was a large walled town situated on both sides of the Adige, which had several outlying redoubts and fortifications. It was strategically valuable as a bridgehead since it had a formidable citadel, encompassed several bridges, and was capable of maintaining a strong defense. Mantua stood as a large walled town on the west bank of the Mincio, but as a fortress it derived its strength from the way it was situated on the river. The Mincio formed a lake around two-thirds of the city, and the other third could be flooded, making the city an island fortress. Bonaparte knew the importance of this powerful fortress, as evidenced by his writings.

Because of his study and work on operational plans through July 1795, Bonaparte found employment in August in the Topographical Bureau, the military planning section of the Committee of Public Safety, under Lazare Carnot.[16] This section drew up the operational plans for the field armies. Although dismissed from the bureau and cashiered from the army, in October he won the gratitude of the government by dispersing a Parisian mob that threatened the National

Convention during the famous uprising on 9 vendémiaire (5 October 1795). Following his appointment to command the Army of the Interior, Bonaparte continued to write letters proposing schemes for the Army of Italy to defeat Coalition forces there.[17] Mantua continued to preoccupy him as he felt it necessary for the government to order horse-drawn pontoons to cross the Mincio River.[18]

In March 1796 when General Barthélemy-Louis Scherer, the fifth commander of the Army of Italy in four years, requested to be relieved, Bonaparte was appointed to succeed him.[19] Bonaparte wasted no time assuming command of the army on 26 March at Nice. After diligently studying the situation and reorganizing his army as well as locating available resources, he confronted the Austrian enemy on 10 April at Voltri and, gaining the advantage, continued a relentless series of attacks, forcing the Sardinians to accept the Treaty of Cherasco on 23 April. The next day Bonaparte wrote to the Directory:

> I am sending the request for an armistice made by the Piedmontese general along with my reply. I hope this conforms to your intentions.
>
> This proposition for an armistice for one month, during which we retain control of everything the army has conquered and with two fortresses as a guarantee, would be very advantageous to the Republic. During this time I would be able to seize the whole of Lombardy up to Mantua and drive Beaulieu from Italy.[20]

After only a month and three days in command of the Army of Italy, Bonaparte wrote to Carnot from Cherasco: "With reinforcements, Italy is ours, as I then can simultaneously march on Naples and Mantua."[21] Thus, before attempting to capture the city and fortress of Milan, the capital of Lombardy, Bonaparte was determined to march to Mantua because he realized its strategic importance.

CHAPTER 1

THE IMPORTANCE OF MANTUA
TO AUSTRIA AND FRANCE

"[I have] to provide for the defense of Mantua, the *Key* of Italy."

GENERAL JOHANN PETER BEAULIEU

B ecause of its strategic position, Mantua became the focal point
of both French and Austrian efforts in northern Italy during the
Revolutionary period. The importance of the city was established by
its position within the Quadrilateral. Strategically, Mantua, along
with the other three fortresses of the Quadrilateral (see map 2), lay on
the traditional invasion route through northern Italy between Austria
and France. At the strategic level, any invasion between France and
Austria had to take place either in German lands or in northern
Italy, at the foot of the Italian Alps. The Apennines divide the Italian
Peninsula, from Naples in the south to the Po River at Stradella in
the north, and thus it would be difficult for an invading army to cross
an east–west route easily. The Po, which runs east–west, therefore
creates a natural southern boundary of this invasion route while
the foothills of the Italian Alps create the northern boundary. This
invasion route also provided the invading army with the subsistence
needed to survive—resources that were not readily available in either
the Alps or the Apennines. The fortresses of the Quadrilateral were
situated in the area where the distance between the southernmost
part of the Italian Alps and the Po was shortest. Both the French
Directory and the Austrian Aulic War Council believed that Mantua,
which is located on the Mincio River connecting Lake Garda and the
Po, had to be controlled for an army to cross the Mincio freely without a threat from the rear. To a certain extent this was true since
the garrison in the fortress could easily sally out and attack the rear
of an enemy army if the fortress were bypassed and the garrison
not contained. According to the views of the Aulic Council and the
Directory, Mantua appeared to be the key to the Quadrilateral.[1]

Controlling Mantua was the goal of any power that sought to control northern Italy. Lakes surrounding the city, established before 1,000 B.C. by the Etruscans, proved a natural fortification.[2] Mantua had withstood numerous sieges, with the most notable during the years 602, 924, 1090–91, 1114, 1236, 1256, 1367, 1629–30, 1703, and 1735.[3] Its location on the traditional invasion route between Austria and France made it vulnerable to attack and resulted in eighteenth-century sieges of the city during the War of the Spanish Succession and the War of the Polish Succession. It is not surprising, then, that Mantua would be the focal point for conquest during the Revolutionary period.

The city of Mantua is situated on a peninsula extending into a three-part lake, fed by the Mincio River (see map 4). In 1796 there were 2,650 houses, nineteen churches, and 25,000 inhabitants in the city. That year, this medieval fortress town still had the high stone walls and round bulwarks that were the predominant characteristics of most medieval fortresses. The high wall surrounding the city featured several large gates: Porta Molina, San Giorgio, the harbor gate Catena, Cerese, Pusterla, Pradella, and seven other small sally ports.[4] After the beginning of the sixteenth century, several newer outworks had been built around the older fortress. These newer works were continuously extended. Work on the great citadel to the north of the city began in 1533 under the Gonzaga Duke Federigo and was completed under his son Guglielmo in 1553. It formed a bridgehead and was connected to the town by a causeway called the Ponte Molina. The Ponte Molina causeway dammed the water of the Upper Lake to a depth of sixteen feet, and the water powered the twelve mills along the causeway known as the "Twelve Apostles." Each of these mills, built in 1198, lay below a statue of a particular apostle from which the group of mills derived its name. The mills provided all the ground flour and meal necessary for the city's residents (see map 5).[5]

To the south of the town were placed many newer Vauban-type bastions. On the south side, one bastion was constructed facing the west in front of the Porta Pradella. This one was called the Pradella hornwork.[6] One large structure was erected in the center, covering the Porta Pusterla, the Te Palace crownwork, and the Porta Cerese.[7] To the southeast, a bastion was situated to cover the Migliaretto entrenchments and the three San Carlo fleches.[8] Due to the thirty years of relative peace since the end of the Seven Years' War, these defensive outworks had been neglected, and by 1796 they were in severe need of repair. The northern and eastern sides of the town were flanked by the Upper, Middle, and Lower Lakes. Across the Upper Lake to the north was the Citadel with its five bastions. To the east of the Middle Lake was the suburb of San Giorgio. San Giorgio's only protection was a weak earthen wall. The suburb was connected to the city by the San Giorgio dam. The Ponte Molina and the San Giorgio dam both had drawbridges. The strongly built dams divided the waters of the Mincio River into the three Mantuan lakes. Water from the Upper Lake fell through the mills of the "Twelve Apostles" and into the Middle Lake, where it was held back by the San Giorgio dam; from there, the water moved into the Lower Lake and then downstream to the Po. The water from the Upper Lake supplied the moats of the outworks and the moats between the outworks and the city wall. A large part of the surroundings of Mantua, especially to the south, consisted of swamps and morasses that greatly hindered any approach of siege works.[9]

As the Mantuans received news of the treaty between France and Sardinia in late April 1796, they became worried about a French attack. On 2 May, the citizens of Mantua began a solemn three days of prayer in the Basilica of Saint Andrew for the safety of the city and the success of the Austrian army. For the solemn triduum, Bishop Giovanni Battista of Mantua had an Exposition of the Sacri Vasi, two sacred vases that, as legend had it, contained blood collected at the foot of Christ's cross by Saint Longinus (a Roman soldier of the Italic Legion), and brought to Mantua, where it was kept locked in the crypt of the basilica and only shown to the faithful on special occasions for veneration. That day a pastoral notice was posted throughout Mantua by Battista explaining when and why the exposition was taking place. In addition, the Congress of the State of Mantua hurried to send Marchese Luigi Cavriani, accompanied by half of the congressional deputies, to the imperial court in Vienna in order to explain the danger and to beg the court to deploy more troops to Italy.[10]

After Bonaparte's Treaty of Cherasco, the French troops continued to move rapidly across northern Italy, which served to cause even more excitement in Mantua. When Bonaparte crossed the Po on 3 May, the news even reached Paris that the young princess, archduchess, and government of Milan were on the road to Mantua.[11] Bonaparte did not rest on his laurels. He continued to push the

Austrian forces under Johann Peter Beaulieu eastward across northern Italy to entrap them.[12] Bonaparte won a vital victory at Lodi on 10 May 1796. It was after this Austrian defeat that the Austrians strengthened the garrison at Mantua with some of Beaulieu's field forces, fearing that they might be forced out of the Quadrilateral.

The day after the French victory over Beaulieu at Lodi, Bonaparte wrote to Lazare Carnot in Paris:

> You may, in making your calculations, consider me at Milan. I shall not, however, go there tomorrow because I wish to pursue Beaulieu and take the opportunity of his delirium to beat him one more time.
>
> It is possible that I will attack Mantua soon. If I take that city, there will be nothing to prevent my penetrating into Bavaria; in two *décades* I may be in the heart of Germany.[13]

Carnot replied in an agreeable manner to Bonaparte's stated objective of attacking Mantua declaring: "Their [the Directory's] intentions are conformable to the plan you have adopted, of no longer allowing the enemy to recover breath in Mantua: to postpone the defeat of a vanquished army is to jeopardize the event."[14] But Bonaparte was not willing to wait for the Directory in Paris to approve his plan. On 12 May, the day after he sent his letter to Carnot, his troops captured the town of Pizzighettone after an impetuous attack. The French captured four Austrian cannon and made the three hundred men in the garrison prisoners of war. As the Austrians retreated to Mantua, a strong detachment of French cavalry pursued them as far as Cremona.[15]

On 14 May Bonaparte wrote to the Directory again, informing them of his movements to invest the castle at Milan and of the activities of the Austrians at Mantua. He announced that Beaulieu was at Mantua and that the Austrians had flooded the surrounding countryside but would succumb there because it was the unhealthiest part of Italy. He concluded his letter by stating that their decision on this matter of command of the Army of Italy would be more decisive for the outcome of the campaign than the 15,000 reinforcements that the emperor might send to Beaulieu.[16]

Nevertheless, Bonaparte again did not intend to wait for a response from the Directory concerning his plan to capture Mantua and fully secure northern Italy for the Republic. On 15 May he entered Milan under the triumphal arch, surrounded by the large crowd that came out to see him. On the occasion the newly created national guard was present, with all the guardsmen dressed in Italy's new tricolor: green, red, and white. Commanding them was the Duke Giovanni Galeazzo Serbelloni, chosen by the men as their commander.[17] On the 16th Bonaparte sent a message to all of the Lombardian communes telling them that within twenty-four hours of receipt of his order they were required to send to his headquarters in Milan their act of submission and oath of obedience and fidelity to the French Republic.[18] These actions clearly show that Bonaparte was not going to be delayed in conquering northern Italy by waiting on the Directory's response. He was still set on getting to Mantua.

The next day he wrote to the French minister in Venice thanking him for the details about the Austrians' positions. Bonaparte sent him 6,000 livres to cover the expenses for spies whom the minister sent out daily to gather information. He told the minister specifically to "send spies to Trent, to Mantua and to the roads from the Tyrol, and let me know when the boats from Trieste have left for Mantua."[19] He knew the Austrians would send support by boats up the Po to the Mincio and the lakes of Mantua. While trying to come up with a plan to deal with this possible threat from the southeast via the river, Bonaparte also had to deal with the imminent threat of Austrian reinforcements coming through the Tyrol from their army on the primary front against the French in what is now Germany.[20] He was still concerned about the ultimate orders for the French armies, north of the Alps, facing the Austrians. On the 20th he wrote to the French minister in Switzerland informing him that the enemy had withdrawn to Mantua and that he was anxious to advance. He begged the minister to inform him of the movements of the Army of the Rhine and those of the Austrian army in Bavaria and Swabia. Bonaparte went on to ask specific questions of the minister, who was located at the critical point of observation in Switzerland: "Can the Emperor weaken his Rhine army to reinforce the one in Italy? What troops could he still send into the Tyrol?"[21] The general further encouraged the minister to give him any pertinent information about the subject and told him to send agents to discover precisely what forces could be sent to Italy.[22] By communicating with France's ministers to Venice and Switzerland, Bonaparte demonstrated foresight in gathering intelligence in preparation for his push to Mantua.

The same day Bonaparte dispatched his letter to Switzerland, officials in Mantua were posting a notice informing everyone in the Mantuan countryside not to flood into the city but instead to continue to cultivate their farms and collect their produce. It also stated that those who had already left their farms in the surrounding country must return.[23] The Austrian officials were concerned about the problem of feeding these additional people if the city were to be surrounded. Nevertheless, the fear demonstrated by these farmers was not shared by many within the city walls.

When Bonaparte and his invading army entered the Mantovano Province, many of the people felt relatively secure under the protection of the Austrian soldiers in the region. When Beaulieu left Piedmont, he did not stop until he reached Roverbella, just north of Mantua, where he established his headquarters.[24] The small town of Roverbella would later become the headquarters of Jean-Mathieu Sérurier, whom Bonaparte would charge with laying siege to Mantua.[25] Beaulieu limited himself to committing imperial troops only to the fortresses of Milan and Pizzighettone. He ordered the remainder of the troops around Mantua to garrison it in case of a surprise attack.[26]

The bad news that had reached Vienna since the end of April increasingly alarmed the emperor. The gains that Bonaparte was making in this secondary theater of operations forced him to focus much more attention toward the Lombardy Plain. Thus, by the day of the Battle of Lodi, 10 May, eleven battalions of Austrian infantry and ten squadrons of cavalry were on the march from various Hapsburg provinces to northern Italy.[27]

When the Austrian imperial army retreated behind the Mincio River in mid-May 1796, it became clear that Mantua would probably be left to its own defense. The condition of the post was appalling to Lieutenant Field Marshal Joseph Canto d'Yrles, the fortress commander, so he began repairs immediately.[28] Emperor Francis II had nominated him to the rank of lieutenant field marshal in March 1795 and assigned him to the fortress of Mantua, which he commanded after 17 April. With little pressure from any enemy force in the area, the manpower of the fortress was sent to fight in other places; this explains in part the more recent neglect of the fortress.[29] However, with the French moving eastward, the fortress curtains were refurbished and equipped with cannons and supplies.[30] The hurried retreat of the Austrian field army after Lodi did not leave enough time to finish the work.

On 14 May 1796 the fortress had only 2,154 soldiers, far short of the 14,000 men needed to garrison the city properly. Although plenty of cannon, ammunition, powder, and tools of all kinds was on hand, there were not enough artillerymen to serve the pieces; a lack of personnel was also true of the engineers, train wagoneers, administration officers, bakers, and *Tschaikisten*—the *Gränzer*, or frontier, riverboat men. The garrison did not have enough beds for the barracks or even the hospitals, the magazines seriously lacked provisions to fulfill the eight-month schedule for a full garrison, and the garrison had not yet received its allotment of money to sustain the city.[31] On the morning of 14 May, Beaulieu, from his new head-quarters at Castellucchio, sent orders to Canto d'Yrles. He stated that a commission of officials had confirmed his petition and that the garrison would be brought up to a strength of 12,000 men. He ordered Canto d'Yrles to expel all foreigners from Mantua, and the town residents to provide lists within twenty-four hours detailing their supplies of foodstuffs and the merchants all of their stock. He forbade the export of cattle and any foodstuffs. Beaulieu forbade Canto d'Yrles from surrendering the fortress except in the most dire circumstances, and he promised to address the concerns of the com-mission as quickly as possible.

On 14 May the floodgates of the Upper Lake dams were opened and the fortress moats were filled with water from the Mincio.[32] Anticipating that communications would be difficult, Beaulieu ordered the fortress commander to look for reliable messengers. Signals using several cannon to communicate with the field army were established between the two commanders on 16 May.[33] The same day Beaulieu crossed the Mincio and sent twenty-three battal-ions and three squadrons into the fortress, bringing the garrison to 12,779 men including artillerymen, engineers, and other specialty troops.[34] The Austrian troops entering the fortress had been weak-ened by the forced marches across northern Italy, from near Genoa to the Mincio during the previous four weeks. Within the next two weeks almost a thousand of these men would end up in the hospitals in Mantua. About 6,000 men, half of the garrison, were posted out-side the fortress to guard the Mincio, Tartaro, Oglio, and Po Rivers from the towns of Goito and Mariana near Marcaria to Torre d'Oglio to Borgoforte to Governolo. The remaining soldiers had the more difficult job of manning the fortress, which daily required 751 men to serve as lookout guards and 800 to man the ramparts.[35]

On 22 May eight of the garrison battalions and nine artillery pieces were detached from the Mantua garrison and sent to a camp at Marmirolo, before being moved to a position at Goito, where Field Marshal Baron Michele Angelo Colli-Marchei assumed command of them.[36] Immediately afterward, three additional battalions were sent to reinforce the field army. In all, the garrison of Mantua was reduced by 1,500 soldiers. However, on the evening of 30 May, after a short combat with the French on the Mincio, Colli sent the eight battalions back into the fortress while he followed the field army into the Adige valley with four squadrons of ulans (lancers).[37]

Beaulieu intended to occupy the entire line from Mantua to Lake Garda. He confided in the British liaison officer, Colonel Thomas Graham, that "on one hand he had to provide for the defense of Mantua, the *Key* of Italy, and on the other, to keep open his communications with . . . the Tyrol, [it] being the only way by which his reinforcements could come or his retreat be made."[38] Indeed, it was important for Beaulieu to hold the line from Mantua to Lake Garda in order to receive reinforcements. And although reinforcements were on the way, Beaulieu did not know that these additional troops would arrive with an additional commander who was ultimately to replace him. When the news of Beaulieu's continued losses in Lombardy reached Emperor Francis II, he decided to send a considerable number of troops to Lombardy from Germany. These troops were led by Beaulieu's replacement, Field Marshal Dagobert Siegmund Wurmser.[39] On 29 May Francis wrote to Wurmser in Mannheim:

> My dear Marshal, Count Wurmser! The war council has already told you of my order to change the plan of operations on the Rhine, which is indispensable, because the events in Italy make it necessary to send a considerable number of my troops from the Rhine to the Tyrol. According to the present situation in Italy, this theater of war is the most important to me where further enemy progress would bring about the devastation of my interior German provinces while success there promises the most important results with the retaking of the rich provinces I have just lost. I think in consequence I will give you a sign of my confidence and entrust you with command of the army destined to accomplish this great task. I hope that my choice of you remains confidential, as I have only told in confidence my brother, the Archduke Charles, who promises to keep this secret. I recommend you keep this a secret for several

reasons and because of the impression my decision might have on General Beaulieu whose physical strength and morale already suffered enough due to the reverses he has already suffered. . . .

The main thing is that Beaulieu can gain time, the French must be prevented from entering the Tyrol and thus prevented from marching through and looting Italy or laying siege to the fortress of Mantua which is to be supplied with everything necessary for a long and vigorous defense. I hope this will save time for the new army gathering in the Tyrol to advance and raise the siege of Mantua or if the enemy has taken a different approach, put us back in possession of the countryside surrounding Milan.[40]

Francis was clearly concerned about a siege of Mantua. Already the city of Milan had fallen to the Republican forces and Bonaparte had set up a new government there on 19 May.[41] Keeping Mantua was just as important to the Austrians as capturing it was to the French, and Francis had confidence that Wurmser could accomplish this goal.

At this point in 1796, Marshal Wurmser was not the symbol of military incompetence that he later became but instead was regarded as a successful and renowned general. Wurmser had defeated the newly combined French Army of the Rhine and Moselle under General Jean Charles Pichegru on 28–29 October 1795 outside of Mannheim. He then besieged Mannheim, shelling the city mercilessly for more than a month until it surrendered on 22 November with two-thirds of its buildings reduced to ashes. In this conquered city, he quartered troops in the houses still standing, confiscated the treasures belonging to the elector of the Palatine, and imposed a heavy indemnity upon the inhabitants. He arrested the elector's delegate and the elector's heir and threw them both in prison. Wurmser's successful maneuvers against Mannheim were prepared by Colonel Peter Duka, who would later play an important role in planning the upcoming relief of Mantua.[42]

The European audience expected that the seventy-two-year-old marshal would quickly destroy Bonaparte's Army of Italy. He was eager to set out and challenge the young French commander, who was born four years after Wurmser had attained the rank of general in the Hapsburg army.

CHAPTER 2

BONAPARTE'S INVESTMENT OF MANTUA

"I ought to have had Mantua by a plucky and fortunate coup."

BONAPARTE IN A LETTER TO JOSEPHINE

Once Beaulieu had evacuated Lombardy by crossing the Mincio River, he was determined to hold on to his position. After the Battle of Borghetto on the Mincio River on 30 May 1796, Bonaparte's forces crossed the river and forced the Austrian army into the Adige valley. Bonaparte then ordered General André Masséna to guard the southern approaches of the Tyrol with his division while General Pierre François Augereau and Jean-Mathieu Sérurier were sent to blockade Mantua.[1] It was the wish of both the French Directory and Bonaparte to capture this last Austrian stronghold in Italy before continuing any further operations into the Tyrol. The French considered it a simple task. They presumed they could take the fortress within a few weeks by blockade or bombardment. Yet these expectations would prove too lofty.[2]

The Austrian field army consumed much of the limited food provisions during the short time it camped in the vicinity of the fortress of Mantua. The command had made a liberal distribution of the garrison's food supplies to relieve the field army's suffering. Authorities doled out large quantities of bread, flour, and fruits to the soldiers and released stores of oats and hay for the horses. After the departure of the field army, there were a few days of low consumption, but this did not suffice to compensate. On 3 June, when the fortress was completely invested by the French, the magazines held only enough food provisions for 71 days, oats for 124, hay for 22, and wood for 56. Thus, the garrison could subsist for three months at best with its available resources. Although there were supplies of wheat, corn, and rice in the town magazines, other provisions such as wine, cattle, and fodder were lacking in the garrison's depots as well as the town magazines. In preparation for the siege, the fortress commander was forced to requisition all supplies of wine and fodder in the Papal town of Ponte Lago Scuro and its environs. During the final days before the fortress was surrounded, a large part of its treasury was spent to buy sheep and fruits from Verona and the Papal regions.[3]

To defend the fortress, Canto d'Yrles had stationed his subordinate commanders at the most strategic points around Mantua. General Fürst Roselmini was posted at the Citadel with 3,773 men.[4] General Mathias Ruckavina was given command of the Migliaretto works to the south of the city with 2,443 men.[5] Colonel Sturioni commanded the garrison troops defending the walls of San Giorgio Castle, the suburb of San Giorgio, and the dam connecting the two with 2,298 men. Meanwhile, Colonel Salisch commanded the Te Palace crownwork with 1,489 men.[6]

As Bonaparte prepared to make a reconnaissance of these positions, he gave orders for the movements of 2 June: Augereau was to go to Castiglione Mantovano and Sérurier was to make a predawn reconnaissance of the Austrian positions at Mantua and determine how best to invest the fortress.[7] During the next few days, Austrian soldiers vigilantly patrolled the approaches to Mantua and the surrounding countryside. For several days these patrols captured French soldiers who were making their reconnaissance of the fortress or who had straggled away from their main columns and were marauding in the area. As directed, Augereau advanced with his division to Castiglione Mantovano and later sent swarms of *tirailleurs* against the fortress while he reconnoitered the northern outworks. On the evening of the 2nd, his soldiers retired to Castiglione Mantovano, followed closely by Austrian hussars. The hussars captured two French engineer officers and six sappers to secure intelligence of their intentions.[8]

Although Bonaparte had intended to go to Mantua on 2 June, he spent that day at his headquarters at Peschiera coordinating supplies and the movement of troops.[9] At Peschiera, Bonaparte undoubtedly saw the gunboats the Austrians had on Lake Garda. Concerned about his own gunboat support, he ordered Lambert, the *commissaire ordonnateur en chef*, the person empowered to order disbursements for the Army of Italy, to send to the artillery general of brigade, Antoine-François Andréossy, the sum of 25,000 livres to pay the cost of arming galleys and other warboats on Lake Garda.[10] Arming these boats on the lake would pay off during the siege of the Mantua fortress. The man that was to command the French naval presence on the lakes of Mantua was the highly experienced naval officer Captain Pierre Baste.[11] He was attached to the Army of Italy on 11 June and sent to Peschiera the following day. On 18 June he was made commander of the half galley *La Voltigeante* on Lake Garda, and on 9 July was given command over the entire flotilla.

In the early morning of 3 June, Austrian patrols scouted toward Marmirolo. They learned that the French were again advancing by several roads against the fortress. General Baron Philipp Freiherrn von Vukassovich, with six battalions and one hussar squadron, in the Serraglio, was ordered to move into the fortress.[12] Soon thereafter, at approximately 8:30 A.M., a French trumpeter with a letter from Sérurier, requesting a prisoner exchange, approached the Citadel's gate and delivered a communique.[13] This parley was immediately followed by the advance of many French soldiers, who started to fire on the Citadel while their officers approached the ramparts to reconnoiter. The Citadel responded with heavy fire from the guns and *doppel-stutzen* muskets, forcing the French to move back.[14] The French then established their outpost line at a safe distance.

When the French attack began, the ramparts were occupied by garrison troops.[15] Although the force had been reduced by 1,500 men, the reduction was more than compensated for by the influx of convalescents, recruits, and especially by the men disembarking the transport boats that were destined for Giulay's Freikorps. Unfortunately for the garrison, many of these recruits were not drilled sufficiently to serve on the walls in combat. In addition to these various resources, Canto d'Yrles, to bolster his force, employed 233 men from the *Mantuanischen Landmiliz*, the local Mantua national militia; they were detached to serve as a police force inside the city, thus freeing more Austrian soldiers to serve on the walls.[16]

In addition to the troops manning the ramparts, other units were deployed around the city. The small suburb of San Giorgio was garrisoned by 100 Austrian infantrymen and ten cavalrymen from Colonel Sturioni's brigade. To the south of the city, the stone bridge at Pietole, which had been demolished, was guarded by fifty infantrymen, and the demilune at the Cerese mill was guarded by fifty infantrymen and ten cavalrymen. Later this force would be increased to one company and two 3-pounders. The Migliaretto entrenchments had 600 soldiers; the Te crownwork had 240 men; the Pradella hornwork, 400; and the Citadel's outworks, 500. Twenty horses and riders were positioned at the *Kaiserwirthshause*, the Emperor's Inn, with outposts on the roads to Soave, Marmirolo, and Bancole ready to dispatch messages at a moment's notice.[17]

At the same time the Austrian infantry and cavalry were preparing for the anticipated attacks, the artillery corps worked feverishly to produce fixed ammunition for the cannon, a tedious task because of the mixed calibers of fortress guns.[18] They also filled sandbags, bundled fascines, fabricated gabions, and repaired the outworks.[19] With this work complete, they tied up traffic in the town for over a day as they hauled the cannon from the artillery park to the ramparts.[20]

Meanwhile, outside the fortress on 3 June, Bonaparte ordered Sérurier to send to his headquarters in Roverbella an intelligent and resolute officer to take temporary command of the army's general headquarters.[21] He also wrote to Masséna hinting at an attack on Mantua on the 4th and requesting 1,500 soldiers be sent to Villafranca, where they would receive new orders.[22] Later that evening of the 3rd, Bonaparte decided to invest Mantua. Possibly he still intended a full attack if he encountered little resistance, but regardless, he did not countermand his earlier order to Masséna to send troops. At 10:00 P.M. Bonaparte sent orders to Augereau, Andréossy, Claude Dallemagne, Sérurier, and his engineer François Chasseloup-Laubat for the attack.[23] Bonaparte planned to make a reconnaissance of San Giorgio while Augereau was instructed to move his division at 5:00 A.M. to invest Mantua from the south at Cerese and send a detachment to reconnoiter the Upper Lake. Andréossy and Chasseloup were to accompany Augereau along with a company of sappers. This probe was definitely designed to be a reconnaissance in force. Bonaparte ordered Dallemagne to take the 10th Regiment of *Chasseurs à Cheval*, half of the 5th Battalion of Grenadiers, and six pieces of light artillery to San Giorgio. Likewise, Sérurier was ordered to take a demibrigade and two cannon to the old palace of the prince of Mantua, at La Favorita.[24]

The actual investment of Mantua commenced at 5:00 A.M. on the 4th. Bonaparte sent Dallemagne with his 600 grenadiers under General of Brigade Jean Lannes to attack the suburb of San Giorgio outside the town. Bonaparte himself went to the palace at La Favorita to direct the attack. At the same time Sérurier was ordered to support Dallemagne with his demibrigade.[25] Using the remaining houses for cover and concealment, the French force positioned field pieces on the commanding heights overlooking the village of San Giorgio and its surrounding low, incomplete earthworks. The French had no trouble overwhelming the detachment of one hundred infantrymen and ten cavalrymen from Sturioni's brigade. After a minor skirmish, the Austrians withdrew across the dam.[26] Dallemagne seized the entrenchment between San Giorgio and the Lower Lake, carried the suburb of San Giorgio, and secured the *tête de pont* (bridgehead) on the suburb side of the dam leading to the main fortress of Mantua. They boldly pursued the Austrian detachment across the bridgehead until the Austrians closed the outer gate on the eastern end of the dam. The French soldiers used tools they found in San Giorgio to break down the walls and the closed gate. The grenadiers were formed into a column; they advanced to the double drawbridge in the middle of the dam, firing at the Austrians who were trying to destroy this innermost wooden bridge. The Mantuan national militia, manning cannon in the main fortress of San Giorgio (not to be confused with the suburb of San Giorgio across the dam), fired scrap-shot from their guns and halted the French advance. A withering firefight began over the double drawbridge until 11:00 A.M., when Bonaparte put a stop to the futile efforts of his soldiers against the dam.[27]

Even as the dam of San Giorgio was being attacked, Vukassovich advanced from the Serraglio and entered the fortress with his troops through the southern entrances at 6:00 A.M. There Canto d'Yrles had him take a position at the Pradella gate with his 2,449 men. It was not long afterward, once the French generals had completed their reconnaissance, that the Austrians in the fortress could see the investing force digging earthworks at distances of 700–1,000 yards from the Pradella works and 500–1,500 yards from the Citadel.[28] That same day Augereau and his division marched from Castiglione Mantovano to the Mincio, crossed it at Rivalta, and continued marching to Cerese. His advance guard skirmished with the fortress outposts, and by 3:00 P.M. Major Moschlitz and his *Stabsdragons* retreated into the fortress.[29]

With this deployment of forces, the Mincio caused communication problems between Augereau, who was to the south of Mantua, and Sérurier, who was posted to the north and east of the city. Therefore, Bonaparte immediately ordered all of the boats found on the river to be collected and turned over to Andréossy. He also ordered that boats captured at Brescia be sent to Andréossy as well so he could use them to build a pontoon bridge over the Mincio.[30]

On 5 June the Austrian outposts in the south retired toward the fortress when French cavalry approached. As soon as the French infantry had caught up with the cavalry, Augereau launched an attack against the entrenchments near the Cerese mill, which was defended by 160 Austrian infantry, ten cavalrymen, and three cannon. The French deployed several cannon and two infantry battalions and kept up a continuous volley against the Austrians. After a determined defense lasting several hours, the Austrians abandoned the entrenchments.[31] Augereau's men then seized the entrenchments and the Cerese tower, which housed the mill over the Pajolo canal. During this action a twelve-year-old drummer distinguished himself when he climbed to the top of the tower under fire in order to open the gate.[32] The French pursuit was hindered by the swampy terrain and the destroyed bridges. They repaired the bridges and advanced to open fire on the outworks of the fortress. The Austrians responded with effective cannon and *doppel-stutzen* fire that forced the French to withdraw with some losses.[33] Augereau established his outposts 1,300 paces beyond the city walls—a safe distance, out of musket range. Meanwhile, north of the city at the Citadel, the Austrian infantry and sharpshooters pushed the French skirmishers back to La Fontana.

Early on the morning of 5 June, Sérurier's troops continued their efforts to probe Mantua's defensive strength and complete the investment by lowering the double drawbridge over the San Giorgio dam. Before the Austrians could bring fire to bear on the French, another French trumpeter approached the fortress from San Giorgio at 7:30 A.M. with a second letter from Sérurier to Canto d'Yrles concerning a prisoner exchange. In his letter Sérurier expressed his desire for the return of his aide Captain Bertrand, referencing his communique of 3 June on the matter. Canto d'Yrles responded the same day asking in turn for Lieutenant Girovano from the Alvintzy Regiment.[34]

At this point, action against Mantua was delayed. Bonaparte was convinced that the imperial army in the Tyrol would not be able to march to the relief of Mantua soon; therefore, he decided to fulfill his orders from the Directory and move against the Papal States and Naples. The unrest in Lombardy and the Genoese fiefs also called for his presence there.[35] For these reasons, on 5 June he ordered Sérurier to command the siege of Mantua while he departed for Milan to see to political considerations as well as matters concerning the entire army.[36]

Sérurier wasted no time. On 6 June he surrounded the fortress on all sides while General Alexandre Berthier, Bonaparte's chief of staff, started his two-day reconnaissance of the fortress.[37] Berthier improved the distribution of the siege corps and ordered that the bridge to be built over the Mincio be placed below the fortress to secure the link between Sérurier and Augereau in the most efficient location possible. Berthier considered the Cerese mill and the strip of land leading to the Pradella gate of such importance that he added 3,000 men to Sérurier's forces. These troops consisted of three grenadier battalions plus the 10th Chasseurs and the 10th Hussars.[38] Sérurier distributed his forces as follows: 3,600 observed the Citadel, 600 occupied San Giorgio, 600 more were posted at Pietole, 600 held Cerese, 1,000 guarded the Pradella works, and 2,000 men from artillery, cavalry, and infantry detachments formed flying columns around the lakes. In addition to these forces, Sérurier ordered at least a dozen gunboats to cruise the lakes.[39]

The French now had fully invested Mantua. On the morning of 8 June, Canto d'Yrles gave the previously arranged signal that the fortress was completely surrounded. The signal was six salvos fired within two minutes from 24-pounders in the Citadel. For the next week the pace of the action slowed down significantly.[40]

Meanwhile, at Milan Bonaparte was working to try to gain assistance for his soldiers at Mantua. He ordered *Commissaire Ordonnateur en Chef* Lambert to take steps to ensure the regular distribution of brandy and vinegar to the field troops. He explained that the blockade of Mantua forced the soldiers to bivouac in marshy areas, which was unhealthy, causing disease among the soldiers. Too many precautions, he said, cannot be taken to preserve them from the negative effects on their health from living in areas surrounded by marsh.[41] Bonaparte knew the reality of the situation and realized some of these "sick" soldiers were only feigning illness. Consequently, in his stern and practical manner, he followed up his letter to Lambert with an "Order of the Day" to the Army of Italy stating that he has been informed that many soldiers were not staying with their demibrigades on the march but were waiting in the rear to indulge and pillage, only to rejoin their units later. The army commander also acknowledged that many soldiers were admitted to the hospital faking sickness, only to remain there one or two days. For this reason, he expressly charged that the hospital directors, on pain of dismissal, refuse to admit any soldier, regardless of rank, unless they were presented with a certificate of sickness from the unit surgeon, countersigned by the company commander, and approved by the battalion commander.[42]

Bonaparte wanted to capture Mantua quickly, but he could see that his orders from the Directory to send troops to counter the pope and other commitments would create pressing problems for the siege. This, in part, explains his stern order to the army on 8 June, but that order alone would not alleviate his lack of manpower. The next day he wrote to General François Étienne Kellermann, in the Alps, expressing anxiety over his failure to send 1,800 urgently needed men to Cuneo.[43] To relieve some of the strain on his army, he slackened the pressure on the siege of Mantua by giving Sérurier responsibility for all of Mantovano Province.[44] Although the soldiers to cover this area would undoubtedly have to come from the siege force, Bonaparte was not giving up on the siege and he tried to make up for this necessary diversion of troops. On the same day that he increased Sérurier's responsibility, he discussed with Chasseloup a plan involving a hydrologic tactic. Since the Adige riverbed is higher than ground level around Mantua, then it might be possible to flood a great part of the Mantovano. He asked Chasseloup to visit the banks of the Adige from Badia to Verona and to inform him whether such flooding could be used to make the area between Mantua, the Po, and the Adige inaccessible to the enemy. He also asked specifically: "What effect would this terrible flood have on the fortress of Mantua?"[45]

On 12 June Bonaparte ordered Augereau to take the 4th and 51st demibrigades with their artillery to Bologna for a southern expedition. Dallemagne was instructed to take the 6th and 7th battalions of grenadiers to Cerese to replace Augereau and his troops blockading Mantua.[46] During this period of deliberate operations, the melting snow in the Alps caused the Po River to rise considerably, thus backing up the waters of the Mincio as far as Mantua. The rising waters increased the depth of the artificial moats of the fortress, but it did not delay the siege preparations of the French. Bonaparte's forces continued to construct batteries and improve trenches, while also accomplishing a critical objective: to cut all the roads leading out of the fortress.[47]

The citizens and the garrison soldiers inside Mantua were also active. The royal *Giunta* published a notice that day laborers, who could not leave the city to work the fields since the roads were blocked, were to be employed by the government to earn their keep.[48] Austrian soldiers together with these laborers repaired the ramparts and cut the reeds on the lakes in order to provide fodder for the cattle and an unobstructed view of the French positions. For the same reasons, the corn growing in front of the Migliaretto outworks was also harvested.[49] Indeed, food and fodder were already becoming short. On 13 June price controls were firmly established on meats, rice, flour, breads, wine, vinegar, eggs, oil, wood, hay, and candles.[50] The Giunta controlled anything with military value. Back in May it had already issued an edict that all boats in the area, including on the canals outside the city walls, were to be secured inside the city every evening as a precaution.[51] Although the Austrians collected ninety-four boats in Catena Harbor, the French constantly harassed Austrian navigation on the lakes, especially on the Upper Lake where the French commanded the heights of Belfiore and Osteria Alta (see map 4). Several times the imperial *Tschaiks* (armed river-boats) and the French outposts fired at each other.[52]

On 17 June Governor Canto d'Yrles received the first news from the Austrian field army since the end of May when his lines of communication were cut. He received two messages almost simultaneously, one written on the thirteenth and the other on the 14th. Both were from Beaulieu. They assured him of support as soon as reinforcements had reached the main army. The second message informed Canto d'Yrles that since cannon shots to signal the advance of the Austrian army might not be heard in the fortress, he wanted to signal instead with large columns of smoke by lighting fires on Monte Baldo.[53]

While Beaulieu was writing to Canto d'Yrles, explaining why he could not send support immediately, Emperor Francis II was communicating to Wurmser in Mannheim. Francis informed him that while he marched down the Rhine Beaulieu would be replaced temporarily by General Michael Melas.[54] On 21 June Beaulieu was recalled from command, and Melas reassured Canto d'Yrles of quick relief.[55] The fortress commander responded that as soon as he recognized the advance of the field army, he would give a signal by having six salvos fired every ten minutes starting at midnight.[56]

Meanwhile, preparations continued for the defense of Mantua. Because of the many trees blocking the view of the garrison defenders, Major Franz Orlandini suggested that a sortie be sent to tear down the houses and cut the trees and brush in the area south of the fortress.[57] On 16 June Canto d'Yrles called a military and civil commission together to debate this issue.[58] The next day he called a war council, which unanimously decided not to launch the sortie since the garrison was weakened with many sick, the enemy's strength was not known, and the French trenches and siege works were still far from the fortress. In addition, it was obvious that the Austrian field army could not advance in the near future to support the fortress, so the garrison would have to be preserved until the French trenches got nearer to the walls. Although the council decided not to make a major attack, it did decide that a limited sortie would be made in order to harass the French siege works.[59]

At 7:00 in the evening on 17 June, the garrison made the limited sortie agreed upon by the council. Three armed boats operated on the Upper Lake while the garrison soldiers kept up a withering fire beyond the Porta Pradella, on Osteria Alta, and on Belfiore in order to keep the French *tirailleurs* from sniping at the boats. At the same time twenty sharpshooters and fifty volunteers from Vukassovich's 52nd Erzherzog Anton Regiment drove away the French posts from the heights and the houses near the Pradella works. With this, the French expected a major attack and all French forces around Mantua were alerted. A large French contingent appeared in front of the Citadel but was quickly scattered by the heavy guns within. About four hundred soldiers advanced to confront the Austrian sortie on the left side of the Pradella hornwork, but the fire from the Te crownwork forced the French to withdraw. At dusk the Austrians returned to the fortress, having fulfilled their harassing mission. In order to determine if the French had reoccupied their former position in front of the Pradella hornwork, Canto d'Yrles had several sharpshooters sneak up to the heights to investigate. They encountered some French outposts, and after exchanging fire with them, the detachment returned.[60]

French forces were equally active. After he captured Fort Urban and the citadel at Ferrara, Bonaparte sent, on 19 June, one hundred of the captured Austrian cannon to the artillery siege train that was being collected at Borgoforte. When the citadel of Milan fell on 29 June, another one hundred cannon were floated down the Po for the siege of Mantua.[61] Meanwhile, the French continued to construct their siege batteries, and almost every day their efforts were disrupted by the Austrian artillery. On 20 June the French blocked the road to Roverbella with abatis, placed 150 yards north of the Citadel. The next day there was a combat between the French outposts and the Austrians occupying the Migliaretto works and the dam bordering the Lower Lake. To keep the French from crossing the Pajolo canal by the Pietole road, Canto d'Yrles reinforced the redoubt at the end of the dam with an additional two companies and two cannon.[62]

By this time Bonaparte, in Bologna, had discovered that Wurmser was coming to command the Austrian army in Italy. He learned this from an intercepted letter from Vienna. He quickly passed this information on to the Directory, informing them that Wurmser already had one division occupying the defiles of Graubünden and that it would be feasible for the Austrian army to enter Lombardy from that direction. Yet, concerned about his lack of troops, he informed the government that Beaulieu was receiving reinforcements daily in the Tyrol, some 10,000 since the Battle of Borghetto.[63] Bonaparte desperately needed more troops to hold the areas that he conquered, to invade the south, and to press the siege of Mantua.

Meanwhile, on 22 June, the French and Austrians skirmished in front of Migliaretto the entire day. The French approached the covered way (the area between the wet moat and the glacis) to the west of the Citadel and started a firefight with the defenders. The first salvo of canister, from one of the guns at the nearest bastion, convinced the French to withdraw.[64] On 24 June French troops advanced to the east of the Citadel, concealed by the tall cornstalks, but the Austrians pushed them back using hand grenades. During the next few days all the fortress outworks were continually probed by the French.

The initial French trenchworks surrounding the fortress were built more to serve as a defense from an Austrian sortie than to enable a French attack on the fortress ramparts. This was notably evident north of the city where the French cut and blocked all the roads and paths between fields around the Citadel so that sallying forth under the protection of the bastion guns would still be difficult. Nevertheless, the French continued to improve their positions, and by 26 June the siege works were ready for emplacement of the large cannon and mortars brought up from Borgoforte. That day and the next, Sérurier, Chasseloup, and General of Artillery Jean-Marie Sugny made a thorough reconnaissance tour. They started their mission near the Citadel and moved counterclockwise around Mantua. That evening they reached Cerese, where they spent the night of the 26th. On 27 June they continued the reconnaissance from the south of Mantua to San Giorgio to determine the best point of attack and sites for the heavy batteries. From his notes, Sugny drew up an elaborate plan of attack on the city, which he submitted to Bonaparte on 29 June.[65]

The rising and falling of the Mincio River played a major role in the operations around Mantua in terms of both offensive and defensive measures. By 26 June the continued melting of snow in the mountains caused the river to rise even more, and thus the three San Carlo fleches in front of the Migliaretto works were in danger of being cut off from the main fortress by rising water. Noticing this, the Austrians withdrew their two companies of infantry and two cannon from that location. This left only the dam across the Pajolo occupied by Austrian sharpshooters. Canto d'Yrles made changes on 27 June to the distribution of Austrian troops. The sectors of responsibility for each brigade were adjusted to match the strength of each unit. With this adjustment implemented, any time the French approached the outworks they were repulsed by musket and *doppelstutzen* fire. If they tried to advance in large numbers, perform siege works nearby, or enter neighboring houses, they were immediately fired upon by the fortress cannon and forced to withdraw.[66]

For the Austrian authorities in the city, the rural farmers who sought the protection of the fortress walls caused many problems. In order for the Austrian military to cope with the civilian situation, they decided to conduct a thorough census on 30 June. They wanted to get an accurate record of the number of civilians in the garrison and in particular what the civilians possessed in the way of foodstuffs. That day all nonmilitary persons in Mantua and their supplies were registered by Austrian officers. The number of civilian inhabitants regardless of age and sex was 23,837. The supplies in cattle, wine, wheat, and fodder were significantly scarce when compared to other foodstuffs. Earlier in the month, Canto d'Yrles had his commissariat, Antonio Maffei, mandate price controls on most all staples, but the situation was getting more critical with each passing day.[67]

The lack of fodder for the horses and cattle convinced Canto d'Yrles he would have to launch a sortie to secure additional supplies, but an even more important reason was to threaten the ever-nearing enemy trenchworks. A third reason to make an attack was to regain visual contact with the French that had been lost in some areas. Canto d'Yrles had posted officers in the five highest spires in the town and the Citadel in order to watch the French movements and monitor progress of the siege works. In the Torre della Gabbia spire, he placed a powerful telescope, furnished by the abate Mari, that was capable of observation as far as Verona for more accurate reports.[68] However, there were many trees and vineyards covering the surrounding terrain that were preventing a direct line of sight even for these elevated lookouts. In addition, there were houses yet standing that provided cover for the French. For these reasons, Canto d'Yrles decided to make a sortie. After a reconnaissance of enemy positions he planned to make the sortie from the Citadel despite the difficulty of achieving success in areas that were heavily blocked with abatis. Major Perrussy of the Nadasdy Regiment was charged with commanding the sortie. The plan of attack called for fire support from the guns of the Citadel and those of the Tschaiks positioned on the Upper Lake. Canto d'Yrles would place a hussar troop in the gate of the Citadel to be on call in case of an emergency, and five companies of infantry were positioned in the covered way to guard the retreat of the sally force.[69]

At 5:30 A.M. on 6 July 1796, the sortie began. Perrussy pushed the French out of the woods, the abatis, and the entrenchments around the Citadel. The forage party then began its work gathering fodder, cutting down trees, and destroying the French abatis and entrenchments. From the houses nearby, some French soldiers started to snipe at the forage party, so Perrussy directed an attack against the houses, seizing them and setting them on fire. Immediately, seven hundred French reinforcements arrived from La Favorita and advanced on the east side of the Citadel. The French fired on the workers and the covering detachment with two cannon and a considerable amount of musket fire. Although the heavy guns of the Citadel kept the smaller French field guns at a distance, Canto d'Yrles had Perrussy and his column withdraw a little since he did not want to sacrifice too many men in this limited sortie. The combat lasted two hours, but when the Austrians returned, they brought back twenty wagons loaded with hay. They successfully accomplished their mission: houses were destroyed and trees chopped down, making it easier for the lookouts to observe enemy activities and for the cannoneers in the Citadel to target the approaching entrenchments.[70]

On the evening of the 6th, Bonaparte and his staff arrived at the fortress and laid out their final plans for the siege works. He then wrote to the Directory informing them about the Austrian sortie that day, his reconnaissance for the siege, and his analysis that within four or five days he would have open trenches around the city. After investing a city by cutting off all the roads, the next step in a siege is to dig a series of trenches parallel to the main fortifications. Once dug to a sufficient depth to protect troops, and armed with artillery, the parallel trench is referred to as an "open trench." Communication trenches, connecting the parallel trenches, are dug in a zigzag pattern to prevent the fortress defenders from enfilading the trench with cannon fire. Bonaparte also reported to the Directory that Sérurier's division had a strength of 7,000 and that about fifty men a day in the division were becoming ineffective because of sickness. Bonaparte estimated the Austrian garrison to be 8,000 to 10,000 men strong. He informed the Directory that even with the enemy's numerical superiority, he had blockaded the fortress for more than a month and that the garrison was obviously aware of the French weakness since the Austrians had tried to make several sorties, albeit unsuccessfully since they were beaten every time. Encouraged by the defeat of the sorties and with his siege works nearing completion, Bonaparte was now more determined than ever to conquer Mantua and end the ordeal. He hoped to take the fortress as quickly as possible, before the French army lost even more soldiers to sickness owing to the unhealthy environment around the city. He explained that he was obliged to reinforce Sérurier's division because he would soon have open trenches around the fortress. At the same time, Bonaparte expressed concern about the Austrian threat coming from the Tyrol. Knowing that Wurmser was on his way south to relieve Mantua, he also informed the Directory of his scheme to check Wurmser's movements.[71]

As planned, at 6:00 P.M. on 8 July, the French started work digging the communication trenches for the two incendiary batteries that would fire hot-shot. One battery required a 540-yard trench near the Pradella hornwork at the Casa Michelli near the ruins of Belfiore Palace, while the other, which was to fire at San Giorgio Castle, required a similar 500-yard trench at Casa Zipata on the east bank of the Mincio (see map 6: G & H). Excavation also began on an additional communication trench east of the Citadel to fire on the bridge connecting the Citadel and the city (see map 6: J). By four o'clock the following morning the incendiary batteries' positions were laid out. Because this work was done in such close proximity to the Austrians, it continued slowly and only at night. The night of 9–10 July, four hundred infantrymen shoveled dirt from the trench leading to the Casa Michelli batteries while a 130-man company of sappers dug the communication trench for the guns at Casa Zipata.[72]

In the fortress Canto d'Yrles learned from Wurmser on 9 July that he had taken command of the field army and was assembling it in the Tyrol; Wurmser promised to march quickly to relieve Mantua.[73] Aware that the French ordnance in Borgoforte would soon be in position to start a bombardment, Canto d'Yrles informed Wurmser of the status of the siege and urged him to hurry. Nightly, the French dug zigzag approach trenches leading toward the fortress. During the night of 10–11 July, the Austrians fired illuminating cannonballs over the French trenchworkers to locate and thus bombard their exact positions.[74] The cannonade lasted until morning, but the French continued constructing approach trenches.[75]

Work on the communication trenches projected for the day of the 10th was interrupted because the sappers had to reassemble for a planned attack that night. At Casa Michelli, one hundred sappers and a detachment of four hundred miners were scheduled to dig about 280 yards of trench. At 10:00 P.M. the French were prepared for their attack but were ordered to stand down possibly because of the Austrians' use of illumination rounds. Regardless of the reason, this delay freed another one hundred sappers to work on enlarging the trench in front of the Porta Pradella. The next day, 12 July, the sappers began digging trenches during daylight hours.[76]

Bonaparte was determined to capture the fortress by direct attack to prevent a protracted siege. He had already made one attempt to seize Mantua on 4 June, and by mid-July he was planning another. This time he hoped to conquer Mantua by a surprise attack. In early July he told Andréossy to look for a point on the eastern shore of the Lower Lake where troops could board ships to be ferried beneath the outworks of the fortress. After a reconnaissance on 5 July, Andréossy suggested in his report the next day that the troops should embark near Casa Zanetti and land below the San Carlo fleches, south of the Migliaretto entrenchments.[77] On 7 July he reported to Bonaparte that he had gathered enough boats to transport three hundred to six hundred soldiers and that he had started construction of a bridge over the Mincio south of the Lower Lake where the river narrowed. The following day, at Roverbella, Andréossy informed Bonaparte that two sailors whom he had sent the night before by barge across the lake had landed north of the Migliaretto entrenchments and discovered that the San Giorgio dam was easily accessible. He closed by stating: "Order and silence provided, I guarantee success. Everything you [Bonaparte] have told me to prepare is ready."[78]

While Bonaparte's staff was making preparations for the French attack on the city, Canto d'Yrles called another war council on 11 July to decide whether an additional sortie should be made, this time to destroy the French trenchworks and delay the bombardment of the town. The council made the unanimous decision to launch a major sortie only when the bombardment actually started or Wurmser's main army reached the fortress. The council also decided, however, that with rations and fodder again running low, a limited foraging sortie might be needed by 16 July, the day their supplies were projected to run out. The plan called for Vukassovich to make the main sally at 3:30 A.M. with 2,200 infantry, 200 cavalry, and 400 workers, comprising all the carpenters of the fortress garrison. This 2,800-man force would be taken from the brigades of Vukassovich, Roselmini, and Sturioni. For a diversion to conceal the location of the actual assault, the Austrians planned to employ cannon fire from the Citadel, the Castle of San Giorgio, the Pradella hornwork, and the Giardino, Pompanazza, and San Nicolo bastions (see map 5). At the same time, from the Migliarctto entrenchments, Ruckavina was to demonstrate against Pietole and the Cerese mill while Colonel Salisch was to make a feint from the Te crownwork against the Belfiore heights south of the Pradella hornwork. Simultaneously, Lieutenant Redange, a pontonier with four Tschaiks, was to bombard Angioli while several other armed ships were to cruise on the Lower Lake attacking Pietole (see maps 4 & 6).[79]

As Canto d'Yrles and his staff hammered out their plan, for a foraging sortie on 16 July, Bonaparte completed his plan for a 16–17 July surprise attack on Mantua. On 12 July he related to the Directory that his primary concern was the siege of Mantua and that he was planning a bold operation. He explained that boats, incendiary batteries, and Austrian uniforms would be ready on 16 July and that any further prospects of such an operation would be in the hands of luck. Bonaparte's plan was to start the attack at 11:00 P.M. He would use the boats to move the Mantuan-born Colonel Giuseppe Lahoz and fifty grenadiers dressed in Austrian uniforms across the Lower Lake to below the San Giorgio Castle battery and bastion. There, they would disembark by 2:00 A.M. on 17 July and fall back into the fortress with the regular Austrian soldiers in order to later seize the Porta Poterna and lower the drawbridge of the San Giorgio dam. Consequently, they would allow the rest of the French army to enter the fortress from the suburb of San Giorgio.[80]

The Austrians launched their sortie on 16 July at 2:00 A.M. Ruckavina had Lieutenant Colonel Bisich with 600 men from the Karlstädter *Gränzers* and the 1st and 2nd Garrison Regiments attack toward the Cerese mill. Major Canciny advanced against Pietole with sixty sharpshooters, 260 men from the 16th Terzy Infantry Regiment and 2nd Garrison Regiment. With bayonets fixed, they pushed back the French advance guards and took the French entrenchments, advancing to within pistol shot of the French batteries. Holding the French entrenchments, they repulsed two attacks from a 600-man French column at Cerese. The combat was intense as Ruckavina's adjutant was shot and died instantly and Bisich fell with a head wound. Ruckavina then withdrew his troops back to the position behind the dam while Colonel Salisch with 150 men of the 44th Belgiojoso Regiment demonstrated against Casa Michelli and drove back the French sentries. Salisch paid dearly for the temporary gain of a small piece of ground, as the Belgiojoso Regiment suffered disproportionate losses.[81]

On the west side of the fortress, Vukassovich attacked from the Porta Pradella with three columns. The first column was commanded by Major Fegyeresty, who moved to the west against Angioli; the second column, under Captain Ivancovich, marched on the main road against Montanara; and the third, led by Lieutenant Colonel Mercandin, advanced on the Austrian left against Belfiore (see map 4). Each of the first two columns had one 3-pounder cannon, and the third column had two. With these artillery pieces, the Austrians started the combat by firing at the French hiding in the houses and behind the trees. The three columns then attacked down the three main roads that converged at the entrance to the Pradella hornwork. Although the French advance guards were driven off, several attempts to attack their entrenchments failed since every road and path was cut with entrenchments or blocked with abatis. Vukassovich then gained the upper hand. His soldiers brought into the town as much fodder as possible for several hours, and the line of fire was improved by burning down houses and cutting down trees. At the same time, Mercandin's third column attacked

Belfiore. They were counterattacked by the French 5th Combined Grenadier Battalion, which held the Austrian advance at bay until Generals Pascal Antoine Fiorella and Dallemagne committed their forces at about 4:00 A.M. in a vigorous attack that lasted two hours.[82] Vukassovich was forced to move his troops back into the fortress, but not before taking some French prisoners. The French then pursued the Austrians all the way to the palisades of the defensive works and, in turn, took approximately sixty-four Austrian prisoners themselves.[83] That day the French started emplacing six 24-pounders and six 12-inch mortars each in the two incendiary battery positions (see map 6).[84]

Inside the walls, the Austrians learned from their new French prisoners that the French siege corps had received reinforcements and that the French were pulling their guns into their newly constructed batteries. With this intelligence, Canto d'Yrles wrote immediately to Wurmser on 17 July asking for relief because of the poor condition of the ramparts, which was well known to the French, and dramatically rising numbers of sick among the army during the previous two weeks.[85]

On 16 July after the attack, Canto d'Yrles wrote to Fiorella asking for a prisoner exchange and accusing the French of using hacked shot, which he described as a crime against humanity.[86] Fiorella responded the same day, indicating that he had forwarded the exchange request to Sérurier, the siege commander, but denied the use of hacked shot. The next day Sérurier wrote to Canto d'Yrles stating that Bonaparte had given his approval for a prisoner exchange, and upheld Fiorella's position that the French soldiers had not used hacked shot. On the following day, 18 July, the prisoners were exchanged.[87]

The Austrian attack on 16 July was successful in securing fodder for the city magazines. The French attack launched against the Migliaretto works on 16–17 July, however, failed in its objective since the French were unable to lower the drawbridge and assault the town from San Giorgio. Bonaparte explained to the Directory that the Mincio River had dropped considerably, preventing the troops from crossing the lake.[88] During the night of 16–17 July, 100 of the 800 grenadiers making the river assault loaded the boats and prepared to move, but a sudden drop in the level of the Po had caused the water in the Lower Lake to fall as well. The mission had to be canceled for that day, and the grenadiers withdrew into the reeds on the eastern bank because they were fired upon by the imperial Tschaiks and the nearest ramparts of the fortress. Bonaparte intended to make the attempt again, but the waters continued to fall and when it was impossible to get the boats across the river during the night of 17–18 July, the river crossing operation was abandoned.[89] That day, from Marmirolo, a disappointed Bonaparte complained to Josephine in Milan: "I passed the whole night under arms. I ought to have had Mantua by a plucky and fortunate coup; but the waters of the Lake have suddenly fallen, so that the column I had shipped could not land. This evening I shall begin a new attempt, but one that will not give such satisfactory results."[90]

Having abandoned the river crossing operation on 18 July, Bonaparte was determined to continue with the attack on the San Carlo fleches in front of the Migliaretto works. That day he sent new orders to Sérurier and Joachim Murat for the evening's attack.[91] For several days, during the daylight hours, French sappers busied themselves making fascines and gabions. Four companies of sappers spent the day moving materials and entrenching tools across the newly constructed pontoon bridge, built by Andréossy, on the south end of the Lower Lake at Pietole, where the river was narrow.[92] On 18 July Generals Dallemagne and Murat and Adjutant General Martin Vignolle crossed over the bridge as well.[93] At 11:00 P.M. on the night of 18–19 July Sérurier ordered the attack on the San Carlo fleches and Migliaretto works. A half hour later Murat and Vignolle attacked the Migliaretto works with 2,000 men while Dallemagne attacked the works with a strong column on their left.[94] In concert Andréossy, on the Lower Lake with five armed sloops, fired furiously at the fortress in support of the main attack. The goal was to draw the Austrian cannon fire toward his boats on the Lower Lake. As a feint for this attack, the French had staged a mock attack against the Pradella hornwork but were driven back by grapeshot.[95] Dallemagne's column pushed Ruckavina's weakened advance posts to the back of the fleches and then to the main entrenchments of the Migliaretto works, where the Austrians had already brought up three cannon. About 1,000 French troops made the assault on the covered way; around twenty actually leaped over the palisades in a rage. Banding together, these few Frenchmen attacked, but they were swarmed by Austrians who clubbed them down with their muskets. Immediately upon the commencement of the attack, Canto d'Yrles reinforced Ruckavina's brigade with four hundred men. He also sent reinforcements to the Pusterla, Cerese, and Pradella gates.

Ruckavina repulsed the first attack, and the reinforcements allowed him to repulse the second and third onslaughts as well.

The fighting on Ruckavina's front continued throughout the following day, and later that night the Austrians could hear the French approaching for what at first appeared to be a fourth attempt to take the Migliaretto works. But it soon became apparent to the Austrians that in the darkness, the French were only coming to pick up their dead and seriously wounded.[96] Thus ended Bonaparte's second attempt to take Mantua by direct attack. The formal siege that Bonaparte had hoped to avoid would begin this same night after the French picked up their dead in front of Migliaretto.

During the initial investment of Mantua, Bonaparte's well-planned attack had enabled Dallemagne and Sérurier to gain control of the weakly defended suburb of San Giorgio. They did not, however, capture the city as intended because they were forced back east across the San Giorgio dam, but they held the suburb. Likewise, Augereau was able to capture the Cerese tower. After this first failure to capture Mantua by a coup de main, the French had begun fieldworks in earnest while continuing to make limited reconnaissance attacks on the fortress. In all, the Austrians conducted three limited but successful sorties to disrupt the French fieldworks and gather fodder. Once Chasseloup had the batteries prepared to receive the gun emplacements, Bonaparte ordered the second, and final, coup de main, which happened to take place simultaneously with the third Austrian sortie. Both sides fought doggedly, and although the French did not capture the city, they were quite successful in repulsing the sorties and establishing their fieldworks. By this time it was evident that the French were better organized for a siege than the Austrians were for stopping them.

CHAPTER 3

A CITY ON FIRE, A CITY AT PEACE

BOMBARDMENT AND RELIEF OF MANTUA

"We warmed it up from two batteries with red-hot shot and from mortars. All night long that wretched town has been on fire."

BONAPARTE IN A LETTER TO JOSEPHINE

Late in the evening of 18 July, the French started bombarding the fortress of Mantua from the north, east, and west. The incendiary batteries positioned at Casa Michelli and Casa Zipata were using glowing "red hot-shot" that had set fire to the monastery of St. Cantelma and the Carmelite monastery of St. Teresa, killing two of the nuns. The hot-shot caused many homes to catch fire, but the exploding shells prevented any attempts to fight the flames. Instead of combating the conflagrations, the citizens sought shelter in their basements, while shop owners locked up their stores to prevent looting. The rain of shells during the night was so intense in the center of town that Canto d'Yrles was compelled to relocate his headquarters. Twenty-seven bombs fell on St. Barnabas's Church alone during the day. One French cannonball passed through the cupola of the Basilica of Saint Andrew, shattered glass windows entering and exiting, and continued until it hit the Canossa Palace. Another shell exploded in a baker's shop, killing two women. Despite the heavy bombardment, the Austrian artillery was able to match the intensity of the attack.[1]

During the initial bombardment, the French engineers marked off their first parallel 200 yards from the Migliaretto bastion, sketching out 540 yards of trench (see map 6). Digging under the cover of darkness, they worked feverishly to get as much depth as possible before daybreak. During the night thirty-one sappers were killed or wounded, one engineer officer was killed, and another officer was wounded.[2] By the morning of the 19th, they had dug the trench to almost three feet in depth, but the fire from the San Carlo fleches became so concentrated that they were obliged to halt the project and withdraw temporarily.[3] During the day, after the sappers returned to work in the trenches, the Austrians launched a small sortie that resulted in the death of two more sappers and the wounding of three others.[4]

From Marmirolo, Bonaparte wrote to Josephine in Milan: "We attacked Mantua yesterday. We warmed it up from two batteries with red hot shot and from mortars. All night that wretched town has been on fire. The sight was horrible and majestic. We have secured several of the outworks; we open the first parallel tonight."[5] That same day, 19 July, Canto d'Yrles received an order from Wurmser to not conduct any further sorties until the main army arrived. He also promised aid soon and arranged for new signals to announce the arrival of his relief force. In acknowledging the dispatch, Canto d'Yrles appealed to Wurmser to hurry, emphasizing that the French were approaching closer to the Migliaretto works and that the bombardment had already begun.[6]

The shelling from all the French batteries renewed the night of 19–20 July. The Beltrami battery fired with exceptional intensity, trying to destroy the Mills of the Twelve Apostles and the locks of the dam, and to prevent communication between the city and the Citadel (see map 6: J). The French wanted to destroy the locks so that water held in the Upper Lake would quickly flow into the Middle Lake, thus lowering the Upper Lake level, and cause the flooding waters between the Pajolo canal and the outworks of the southern defenses of the town to subside. The French did not achieve their objective because the Beltrami battery was constructed too far from the dam and because earlier, the Austrians had secured the communication line and built up the dam with strong earthen breastworks. At 10:00 in the evening of the 19th, four hundred French grenadiers arrived to work on the trenches. They dug the parallel in front of Migliaretto deeper, increasing its length and strengthening its parapet. They also started a second parallel only 150 yards from the glacis of the Migliaretto works. On the east side of this parallel, they started to construct a battery of four 8-inch mortars (see map 6: C). After dawn, the heavy fire from the Migliaretto works once again prevented them from continuing. In this trench, as well as others around Mantua, the French were prevented from building batteries during the day by the fortress guns.[7]

During the day, on 20 July, the French sent in two companies of sappers and a company of miners, totaling 250 men, to continue to enlarge the trenches already under way. These trenches were enlarged to eight feet in width and three feet in depth.[8] That morning the bombardment continued with variable intensity. In the town, hot-shot again set fire to many houses, and exploding shells damaged many others. In the military hospital at the Capuchin monastery, a round shot from a 36-pounder crashed through the building, kill-ing a soldier in bed and wounding the hospital chief as well as two surgeons who were busy helping the wounded from the previous bombardment.[9] Later on, when the shelling was temporarily lifted, Canto d'Yrles received a letter from Berthier on behalf of Bonaparte, informing him that he was surrounded and that he should surrender the unfortunate town rather than let it be destroyed. Canto d'Yrles responded simply: "The laws of honor and duty oblige me to defend the place I am entrusted to the last."[10]

Bonaparte, now working out of his headquarters at Castiglione, did not expect Canto d'Yrles to surrender quickly, so he continued the siege in earnest. He sent word to the commissary chief, Denniée, ordering him to move vinegar and wine quickly to the trenches at Cerese for the besieging force.[11] In another letter that day, Bonaparte also told him to send 100,000 francs to Sucy, the commissary chief in Genoa, to enable him to meet the needs of the hospitals, to trans-port the artillery and siege equipment from Savona, and to send all the troops located between the Riveria and Genoa.[12] Bonaparte also sent a message to Nicolas Antoine Sanson, the engineer battalion commander, congratulating him on his successful efforts in tracing the trenches.[13]

By 11:00 P.M. on 20 July, the French renewed the bombardment of the town, killing one of the defenders and wounding four others. The French continued to fire until 3:00 A.M. the following morn-ing. During that night of 20–21 July, the French continued to extend and improve their second parallel in front of the Migliaretto works and connect it with the first parallel by a communication trench near the dike. That night three companies of sappers and a battalion of chasseurs, totaling six hundred men, sketched out and dug 540 yards of trench. While working, they lost seventeen men killed or wounded. In the second parallel they began to construct a new bat-tery emplacement, for two 8-pounder howitzers and one 8-pounder cannon, which came under fire from Ruckavina's forces at daybreak (see map 6: D). The guns of the Citadel shelled the Beltrami battery, but the French did not return fire. Soon all of the French guns became silent. On the morning of 21 July, the French trench commander in front of Migliaretto advanced to the Austrian outposts and asked to speak with Ruckavina. The word quickly reached Canto d'Yrles, who gave his permission for a meeting between the two subordinate commanders. The French officer, in an effort to alleviate some of the suffering, proposed to mark the Austrian hospitals of the town so that the French cannoneers would not train their guns on them. They agreed that the hospitals would be identified by black flags. By that afternoon all of the designated hospitals were displaying protective banners. From that time on the French officially no longer fired at the old military hospital or the civil hospital.[14] Despite the black flags flying over the new military hospital set up in the university in the center of town, the French hit it with more than one hundred cannon projectiles, demonstrating their inability or unwillingness to judge distances and direction properly; fortunately, none of the patients were harmed.[15]

All day long on 21 July three companies of sappers and a detachment of miners, about two hundred men, enlarged the trenches begun the previous night.[16] At 10:00 P.M. the French started their evening bombardment, which by this time was becoming familiar to the citizens and defenders of Mantua. That night of 21–22 July the French south of Migliaretto lengthened their trenches to the west by a hundred paces. On the east side of the Mincio, they began to build new batteries at Zipata and Zanetti that could enfilade the Migliaretto outwork (see map 6: I & K). They also dug a 130-yard communication trench toward the battery on the east side of the Migliaretto trench. That night two sappers were wounded along with their battalion commander Sanson, who had recently been congratulated by Bonaparte for the fine work his sappers had done. The besiegers suffered from the heavy shelling throughout the night until 5:00 A.M. 22 July. From then until noon, the French continued with only limited firing. The Austrians lost one dead and six wounded during the attack. After the shelling had subsided, the Austrian lookouts observed several flashes on the mountains between Monte Baldo and Verona, which they understood to be cannon shots and rockets signaling the advance of the Austrian army from the Tyrol.[17]

At 4:00 A.M. on the 22nd, the night shift of trenchworkers was relieved by three companies of sappers and a detachment of miners amounting to 180 men. The new contingent worked in conjunction with 300 infantrymen to enlarge the left side of the Migliaretto parallel using a sap roller.[18] The bombardment that evening started at 11:00 P.M., but only from the Zipata and Michelli batteries. That night the French continued to extend their trench farther to the west toward the flooded plain of the Pajolo stream. At 3:00 in the morning, 23 July, they climbed out of the trenches and for an hour kept up a strong musket fire against the covered way of the Migliaretto outworks, killing one of the Austrians and wounding three others. At daybreak the Austrians in the observatory as well as on the ramparts realized that the French in the trenches in front of Migliaretto had been strongly reinforced. In reality, what they saw was a group of 300 men coming to relieve the 300 infantrymen and 180 sappers and miners. This new crew's purpose was to enlarge the communication trench from the first parallel to the second parallel. Realizing this, Canto d'Yrles ordered two companies of the Warasdiner *Gränzers*, six companies of the Nadasdy Regiment, and one company of the 1st Garrison Regiment to leave the less threatened areas of the fortress and support Ruckavina at the Migliaretto outwork. The cannon duel between the French and Austrians continued throughout the day with the former firing an extraordinary amount of large-caliber artillery projectiles and mortar bombs into the town. Later that evening the French reduced their rate of fire on the town.[19]

In the afternoon of 23 July, Canto d'Yrles received a letter from Wurmser stating that the main army would relieve Mantua by 2 August. The same promise was repeated in another letter the next day. Canto d'Yrles responded with a series of letters, continual appeals to Wurmser to hurry the relief and appraisals of the perilous situation inside the fortress. Just as Beaulieu and Melas had, Wurmser promised several times that help was coming and urged that the fortress must continue to hold.[20] The Austrians under Wurmser were confident of success, and judging from a letter from John Trevor, the British minister at Turin, to the British liaison officer Thomas Graham at Wurmser's headquarters, even the Sardinians expected Bonaparte to be soundly defeated:

> I am glad to hear of the very respectable state of the Austrian Army, which I have the fullest confidence will effectually overcome any obstacle which the enemy will be able to oppose. There are the

strongest reasons for believing that Bonaparte, once thoroughly beaten, will never be able to recover from the blow—the whole country through which he must retreat is exasperated against him.[21]

During the night of 23–24 July the French Michelli battery was inactive for repairs. The following day the battery was firing again. When it was silent, the French bombarded the town with the other batteries as usual from 11:00 in the evening until sunrise. The Austrians returned fire from the heavy fortress guns so effectively that many of the French guns were silenced. Every day the Austrians destroyed some of the French earthen field battery positions and were often successful in dismounting the French guns. According to an Austrian survey, the French bombardment averaged 300 bombs and 400 round shot per day with the Austrians answering with 325 bombs and 2,767 round shot. Although the French directed a large part of their fire against the bridge of the Twelve Apostles, trying to cut the Austrian communications to the Citadel, the firing had little effect because the Austrians had reinforced the dam.[22]

The night of 24 July the French batteries did not fire and at daybreak on the 25th the Austrians observed them repairing the destroyed embrasures of the Michelli battery with sandbags. Before dawn the French also hurried to lengthen their trench in front of the Migliaretto works and to align it with the flooded part of the Pajolo stream, in the face of heavy bombardment from Ruckavina's large-caliber guns. At noon the Zipata battery fired round shot and bombs into the town for two hours, while the Beltrami battery fired round shot at the causeway mills. Later that night the Austrians observed from the Citadel the firing of six to eight rockets in the east toward Legnago.[23]

During the night of 25–26 July, the Beltrami battery was silent while the other French batteries fired more intensely. Despite the hot-shot and exploding shells, no fires started that night as they typically did when the French employed hot-shot. On the 26th 250 infantrymen and two companies of sappers filed into the trenches to continue the digging work. The French altered their schedule—firing only a few guns during the day, and bombarding the town only at night. The fortress artillery often succeeded in quieting the French batteries; once achieved, firing from the fortress stopped. The lull gave the French a chance to repair the batteries and renew the bombardment the following night. To disrupt the French from repairing their batteries during the day and bombarding at night, Canto d'Yrles ordered attacks on the French batteries to begin in the evening. This adjustment forced the French to repair the batteries at night, delaying their bombardment until the morning, when the defenders could more effectively respond to the French fire.[24]

The intended effect was achieved. The French were prevented from bombarding the town the night of 26–27 July because they were busy repairing their batteries shelled by Austrian guns. On the morning of the 27th, the French tried unsuccessfully to storm the covered way of the Migliaretto works. The fully exposed attacking infantrymen were driven back with heavy losses while the Austrians, firing from the covered way, received only seven casualties. During the day occasional shots were fired from the fortress at the French entrenchments, and the French momentarily halted their bombardment. That night and all the next day the two opposing sides faced each other in silence.[25]

Both sides were ready for a respite after ten days of active fighting, but just as quickly as the silence descended upon Mantua, it was shattered: before daybreak on 29 July, the French resumed bombardment of the town from all their batteries. It became apparent to the defenders that the French had spent the previous day retraining their batteries and bringing up more artillery and ammunition. By noon they had fired some five hundred shells and six hundred round shot into the fortress. The House of the Congressional Delegation caught fire and burned down, and several Austrian cannon were damaged by direct hits. Hot-shot set the old Gonzaga Ducal Palace on fire along with many other structures. Many bombs fell in the center of the town on the ghetto where the Jewish community lived. One civilian was hit in the head with a shell fragment, and another was hit in the leg. More critical for Ruckavina, the French batteries near Zipata and Zanetti across the Lower Lake now enfiladed the Migliaretto works, killing nine Austrians and wounding thirteen. The fortress returned fire until the French bombardment died away in the afternoon, more likely due to a scheduled lapse than to the efforts of the defenders.

At about 8:30 P.M. the entrenched French suddenly opened heavy musket fire against the covered way of the Migliaretto outwork. The volley was answered by the garrison of the covered way with musket fire and by the lunette with cannon fire that forced the attackers emerging from their trench to storm the covered way to withdraw.

After about fifteen minutes the fighting subsided. Nevertheless, Canto d'Yrles decided to withdraw the garrison from the western part of the covered way because the position required a strong force whose retreat was endangered by the distance back to the rampart. That evening the Austrians vacated the covered way, leaving behind some sharpshooters to cover the withdrawal of the main body, while the artillerymen repositioned the guns in the main lunette. During the night the French continued the bombardment, and many houses were damaged as usual, though few fires resulted.[26]

By 5:00 A.M. on 30 July, the French renewed the bombardment with a furious shelling, especially from the Michelli and Zipata batteries. The intensity slackened until midnight when the French stopped firing. During the bombardment a French shell fell into a small ammunition magazine in the Pompanazza redoubt causing the explosion of twenty Austrian shells stored there (see map 5: e). Fortunately for the Austrians, the only casualty was a head wound to a captain standing nearby. That day the Austrians counted six dead and twenty wounded—the heaviest daily loss from shelling during the entire siege. The observers in the towers stated in their morning reports that fires had been observed in the direction of Verona and Valeggio during the night and that fifteen cannon shots were heard from the direction of Villafranca.[27]

The cannon shots were, no doubt, signals from Wurmser, who intended to inform Canto d'Yrles of his advance. On the morning of 31 July, Wurmser had his second column march from Calmasino via Colà and the third column from Campora by Sandrá to Castelnuovo (see map 2). General Baron Adam Bajalich moved south of Peschiera. When Bajalich approached the east bank of the Mincio, he encountered and engaged Masséna's rear guard. By 1:00 P.M. at his headquarters in Castelnuovo, Wurmser detailed his progress to Canto d'Yrles in Mantua. Because he suspected that a considerable part of the French army remained at Roverbella to cover the siege of Mantua, he thought it necessary to position a corps to protect his left flank and rear.[28]

On 31 July at daybreak, the French opened their bombardment, but only from the Michelli battery; they continued until 6:00 P.M. Sérurier ordered the day's final shelling of the city at ten o'clock that evening, but it tapered off by midnight. The French launched infantry attacks against the Migliaretto works throughout the day, ending along with the cannon fire around midnight.[29]

While Wurmser was moving from Castelnuovo to Valeggio on 31 July, patrols gave him two reports at 4:00 P.M. One confirmed that the French were marching toward Brescia and the other stated that Bonaparte had not abandoned the siege of Mantua and was preparing for battle at Roverbella. Indeed, even at the time Wurmser received the reports, the shelling of Mantua was ongoing. The report prompted Wurmser to order General Johann Meszaros to cross the Adige River at Legnago and to head for Mantua by way of Nogara, while maintaining constant contact with the Austrian force at Villafranca.[30]

During the night of 31 July–1 August a messenger from Wurmser in Castelnuovo handed over a letter to Canto d'Yrles telling of his imminent advance. But Sérurier had already received warning of the Austrian movement earlier on the 31st when he was ordered to retreat south of the Oglio River by way of Marcaria (see map 2).[31] At 10:00 P.M. Sérurier once more had the town bombarded with hotshot and bombs from the Zipata battery. After an hour the shelling gradually ceased and was replaced by musket fire until around midnight.[32]

Unknown to Canto d'Yrles and his garrison, Bonaparte had ordered Sérurier to abandon the siege on 31 July in order to move toward the Oglio and join the rest of the French army for a major attack on Wurmser's force. The same night, as the fighting around Migliaretto was ending, the Austrian outposts heard only muffled rattling in the enemy trenches as the French discreetly withdrew from their positions. That same night Canto d'Yrles received a message informing him of Wurmser's impending arrival at Mantua.[33]

The Austrian advance was indeed nearby. On 1 August Wurmser sent four infantry battalions and an equal number of cavalry squadrons under General Anton Lipthay to form an advance guard of the Austrian center from Castelnuovo to Roverbella.[34] Lipthay's patrol reached Mantua and realized that Sérurier had lifted the siege; he then returned to Roverbella and then Goito, where he arrived that evening. He sent Lieutenant Piaczek back across the Mincio to pursue the weak French rear patrols toward Guidizzolo. In Goito the French had left five large cannon; many French stragglers were also taken prisoner there. From Valeggio, Wurmser wrote to Canto d'Yrles thanking him and his troops for their defense of the fortress and informing him that Bonaparte was moving with his entire army against Brescia and the Austrian right wing. At the same time Wurmser sent General Karl Funk from the artillery corps and General Franz Lauer from the engineer corps with several officers to Mantua to do whatever was possible to expedite the necessary repairs to the fortifications.[35]

On the morning of 1 August 1796, there was an eerie silence around the city as Canto d'Yrles sent out patrols to investigate.[36] The shouts of joy from the patrols quickly announced to the garrison and inhabitants of Mantua that the French had departed. Immediately Canto d'Yrles sent detachments from the garrison to pursue the French. Several of the Austrian detachments reached the retiring French soldiers, inflicting losses on some units and capturing stragglers. At San Benedetto the Austrians captured a French war chest. Captain Mentegazza with the Mantuan militia and twelve dragoons took three hundred prisoners at Governolo, while Captain Barco of the Archduke Josef Hussars took sixty prisoners at San Michele del Bosco.[37] Twenty-six Frenchmen fell into the hands of Captain Mack's dragoons.[38] First Lieutenant Koslousky, of the Meszaros Ulans, attacked the flank of a five-hundred-man French column at Goito;[39] this caused a panic and led to the capture of five cannon, many prisoners, and several wagons loaded with flour and hay. Lieutenant Klein with a troop of the Erzherzog Joseph Hussars and some *Gränzers*, aided by local Italian farmers who took up arms, captured at Borgoforte the whole French artillery reserve. Also at Borgoforte they took prisoner a commissar, a colonel, nine other officers, and three hundred rank and file. Including the reserve artillery park, the Austrians captured 177 cannon, howitzers, and mortars, the vast majority of which were Austrian made, having been captured earlier during Bonaparte's previous campaigns and shipped to Borgoforte to be carried overland to the siege works (see appendix C).[40]

The Austrians brought into the fortress 775 prisoners.[41] The people of the city praised the garrison for its seemingly overwhelming success. In addition to the forty pieces of artillery in the batteries immediately surrounding Mantua, the French left behind mass stores of small arms and siege equipment, which the Austrians gathered up. Realizing the struggle was far from over, Canto d'Yrles then ordered his men to fill in the French entrenchments (see appendix C).[42]

Canto d'Yrles immediately sent a message to Wurmser explaining this great capture of stores from the "fleeing" enemy, failing to realize that it was not his sorties and counter-artillery fire that drove the French away. Wurmser forwarded this letter to Emperor

Francis II the following day.[43] When the emperor received Wurmser's communication, he responded, congratulating him on his "brilliant success," and sending along a Commander's Cross of the Order of Maria Theresa for Canto d'Yrles and a small cross of the Order of Maria Theresa for General Ruckavina for his defense of the Migliaretto. The letter from Canto d'Yrles describing the Austrians' raising of the siege of Mantua was interpreted as a great victory in Vienna, since it apparently proved that Wurmser had accomplished his mission.[44]

The departure of the French from Mantua caused various reactions throughout the countryside. Those in Italy loyal to the Austrian crown, hearing the news about the successful Austrian defense, did not doubt they would eventually obtain a victory over the French. They ardently cherished the hope that a counterrevolution would complete the destruction of the French in Italy. In the towns and villages the counterrevolutionaries fostered this sentiment by spreading rumors. When Pope Pius VI heard that the siege of Mantua was raised, he sent a vice legate to retake possession of Ferrara.[45] Cardinal Mattei, the archbishop of Ferrara, spoke out joyfully about the raising of the siege. The pope hoped to avoid paying the balance of the enormous requisitions placed upon the Papal States by Bonaparte with the 23 June armistice. Some of those requisitions included one hundred pictures, busts, vases, or statues and five hundred manuscripts selected by French commissioners, 21 million livres in French money—15.5 million of which would be in specie or ingots of gold or silver and the remaining 5.5 million in commodities—merchandise, horses, and cattle according to the agents of the French government.[46] The pro-Austrian citizens of Cremona and Pavia could not contain their excitement about the French expulsion from Mantua. Other cities like Reggio and Bologna that were pro-French were dumbfounded and alarmed by the situation.[47]

On the morning of 2 August, Wurmser ordered Canto d'Yrles to send Generals Vukassovich and Ruckavina with seven infantry battalions and three cavalry troops to the main army at Goito and one cavalry squadron to Meszaros's fourth column. This order was not executed to the letter by Canto d'Yrles, who argued that he had already sent numerous detachments to Governolo and Borgoforte; he reasoned further that the French siege corps was still in the vicinity of Marcaria and remained a viable force.[48]

At 11:00 A.M. on 2 August, Canto d'Yrles sent Ruckavina and the engineer Major Orlandini to pay respects to and thank Wurmser as well as report on the siege. After speaking with the officers, Wurmser decided to visit Mantua. The marshal met with Canto d'Yrles and dined with some of the more important officers and city officials. They then conferred with Canto d'Yrles's headquarters staff and the whole entourage went toward the Porta Molina, where they were greeted by cheering civilians and the discharge of a seventy-two-cannon salute. Crowds gathered wherever Wurmser went, praising him for relieving the city. He then sent Orlandini, who departed that night, to Emperor Francis II with an account of the blockade and the siege.[49] That evening Wurmser left Mantua for Goito.[50] Between 4:00 and 5:00 the next morning, on Wurmser's order, Vukassovich started marching to Goito with four battalions and four companies, consisting of not more than two thousand men all together. Wurmser also had the reserve artillery that was sheltered in Mantua sent to the field army on 3 August. Meanwhile, the remaining garrison troops continued hauling the captured cannons and ammunition into the fortress and leveling the French trenches.[51] With this ongoing task in mind, Canto d'Yrles protested against Wurmser's decision to detach more troops from the fortress. Because of the number of soldiers suffering from illness, he feared he would hardly be able to man the fortifications.[52]

On the same day Wurmser entered Mantua, 2 August, Bonaparte wrote to the Representative on Mission Antoine Christophe Salicetti: "I shall seize the first occasion to deliver battle to the enemy: it will decide the fate of Italy. Beaten, I will retire to the Adda; victorious, I will not stop at the marshes of Mantua."[53] The following days proved disastrous for Wurmser. Bonaparte defeated the Austrian field army during three days of battle near Castiglione delle Stiviere from 2 through 5 August, giving the French a crowning victory. By daybreak that morning, the French occupied the heights of Castiglione.

Sérurier's division of five thousand men had received orders to leave Marcaria, march all night, and attack Wurmser in the left rear at daylight. Wurmser's forces, just southeast of Castiglione, were on line facing northwest. The firing by Sérurier's division was to signal the start of the battle. Sérurier, who was ill, was temporarily replaced by Fiorella to lead the division. The French made a feint by falling back from Wurmser's position, but when Fiorella's cannons fired on the Austrians' left rear, the French to their front marched toward them and attacked. Augereau attacked their center and Masséna, north of Augereau, attacked their right. The light cavalry surprised the Austrian headquarters and nearly captured Wurmser, who was forced to retreat back across the Mincio River.[54]

Wurmser sent General Joseph Alvintzy von Berbereck to Mantua on 6 August.[55] There Alvintzy gave Canto d'Yrles a formal letter on behalf of Wurmser ordering him to collect the necessary provisions to secure the fortress until lines of communication could be reopened with the field army. With the siege lifted, the Austrians were able to collect enough foodstuffs, cattle, corn, and fodder in the vicinity to support the fortress for two months.[56] Alvintzy left Mantua during the night and arrived in Verona early the next morning. In the evening of the 6th, Canto d'Yrles received Wurmser's letter from the 5th informing him that the army was retiring to the Tyrol and that the fortress had to expect a second attack. Wurmser assured him that he would do everything he could to free the fortress after gathering his forces together and joining with General Peter Vitus Quosdanovich, who a week earlier led a column of 18,000 Austrians southward between Lake Idro and Lake Garda to attack French outposts there.[57] Still later that night Generals Karl Spiegel, Ferdinand Minkwitz, and Sturioni sent six battalions of infantry, one squadron of cavalry, and the detached field artillery into the fortress;[58] these reinforcements gave Canto d'Yrles a total of 15,513 men, of which more than 80 percent was fit for service.[59] During the night of 6–7 August, the Austrians pushed pickets beyond the Gambari canal, which runs from Curtatone to Borgoforte.[60]

Bonaparte had ordered a pursuit of Wurmser's army on 6 August.[61] Augereau's division marched to Borghetto and Masséna's to Peschiera, where General Paul Guillaume and his four hundred men were besieged by fresh Austrian troops. General Louis Suchet's 18th Line of Masséna's division broke the Austrian formations, taking eighteen pieces of artillery and many prisoners. Bonaparte marched with Sérurier's division, still commanded by Fiorella, in pursuit of Wurmser up to the gates of Verona, arriving there on the night of the 7th. Wurmser had the gates secured, but the French artillery battered them down and the French army captured the city.[62] Meszaros covered the retreat of the Austrian columns with his cavalry but ordered his four battalions of infantry under Minkwitz to Mantua. Meszaros positioned hussars on the roads leading to the main gates of Mantua in order to prevent them from being prematurely opened.[63]

On 8 August Fiorella, with Sérurier's division, left Verona and marched back to Marmirolo with instructions to blockade Mantua. Another French siege at this point was impossible without siege artillery. The French had to content themselves with observing the fortress at a distance, since the Austrian garrison still held the Serraglio. The next day a report from Chasseloup in Verona stated that Fiorella was sick and had relinquished command of the 2,700-man division.[64] On the 10th Bonaparte ordered General Jean Joseph Sahuguet to take Fiorella's place as commander at Mantua.[65] Bonaparte gave Sahuguet specific orders: "General of Division Sahuguet, commander at Milan, will transfer the command to General of Brigade Beaurevoir along with all of the papers concerning that city and go to Marmirolo, between Goito and Mantua, to take command of the division of General Sérurier, provisionally commanded by General of Brigade Fiorella." Fiorella was to communicate to Sahuguet further instructions.[66]

The French gained a series of minor victories as they pursued the Austrians to Verona and beyond. The following letter from Bonaparte to the Directory relates his triumphant march:

> The enemy, after retreating, strongly occupied La Corona and Montebaldo, and showed a desire to keep possession of them. Masséna began his march 11 August, carried Montebaldo, La Corona, and Preabolo, took seven pieces of cannon, and made 400 men prisoners. He praised the gallantry of the [18th] demi-brigade of light infantry, and the brave conduct of his aide-de-camp Rey, and his Adjutant-General Chabran. . . .
>
> Augereau has passed the Adige, pursued the enemy to Rovereto, and made several hundred prisoners.
>
> The enemy has 4,000 sick at Mantua. This month the environment of that place is pestilent and I am confined to placing observation camps around [the city] to hold the garrison within.[67]

Bonaparte did not have much to report to the Directory concerning Mantua. He was getting impatient with the new commander Sahuguet, who had not yet reported to his new station or at least had not communicated to Bonaparte if he had done so. Five days after ordering Sahuguet to Mantua, Bonaparte wrote to him again and, as before, gave him specific instructions:

The General of Division Sahuguet will take command of the division formerly commanded by the General of Division Sérurier, and currently by the General of Brigade Lasalcette, in the absence of the General Sérurier. General Sahuguet will receive from General Lasalcette the instructions and information concerning this division. He will correspond with the General in Chief [Bonaparte] for all which he will report concerning this service. The headquarters of the Division is in Marmirolo, in the Mantovano.[68]

Inside Mantua the military government was working to recycle unexploded artillery ammunition and cannonballs by buying what the townspeople would bring into the royal arsenal. On 7 August prices were set for shells and cannonballs.[69] Now that the Austrians had brought in the cannon that were previously firing these twenty-six different-sized munitions into the city, it only made sense to round up the salvageable ordnance to reuse. The response must have been favorable because on the twelfth, the royal Giunta had to publish another *avviso*, or notice, explaining the enormous expenses of the military treasury and the necessity of lowering the price for cannonballs and shells.[70]

On 19 August Wurmser established his headquarters north of Trent, after evacuating Riva and burning the vessels on Lake Garda. The rapid flight of the Austrian army gave the French time to restore order to their divisions and to send away the numerous enemy prisoners.[71] After a few skirmishes, the blockade of Mantua recommenced under Sahuguet's command. Bonaparte informed the Directory from his headquarters at Milan on 26 August:

The division of General Sahuguet now blockades Mantua. On 24 August, at three in the morning, we attacked all at once the bridges of Governolo and Borgoforte, to obtain the garrison admittance within the walls. After a smart cannonading, General Sahuguet, in person, gained possession of the bridge of Governolo, at the time that General Dallemagne made himself master of Borgoforte. The enemy lost five hundred men, either killed, wounded, or taken prisoners. The 12th demibrigade, and Citizen Lahoz, eminently distinguished themselves.[72]

With the attack on 24 August, the Austrian garrison troops holding land on the east side of the Mincio were forced to cross to the west side into the fortress. The Austrians retained the soldiers in the Citadel and in San Giorgio. Sahuguet also occupied the Serraglio and began to tighten the blockade. He then proceeded to build redoubts and other fieldworks around the fortress. Since all of the siege materials had been brought in by the Austrians and the siege works destroyed, Bonaparte was compelled to resort to investment alone. However, the investment in late August was limited, though supplies continued to arrive from the south.[73]

After the two attempts to take Mantua by a coup de main, the French began bombarding the city while simultaneously opening the first parallel trench south of the Migliaretto works. After a severe initial bombardment, Bonaparte invited Canto d'Yrles to surrender the city, but the defender pinned his hopes on Wurmser's approaching relief force. The French constructed batteries that could enfilade the side and rear of the Migliaretto works. Instead of immediately withdrawing from the exposed position, Canto d'Yrles reinforced it in an effort to hold the position until Wurmser arrived. The French advanced their trench to within 150 yards of the works and made two attempts to take it by force. When Wurmser's army neared the area of operations, Bonaparte boldly lifted the siege, risking his heavy guns, in order to mass his forces to confront the Austrians. Consequently, because of their rapid withdrawal from Mantua, the French left behind their siege artillery, which was captured by the Austrians. Although Bonaparte defeated Wurmser at Castiglione, the loss of the siege guns had a profound impact on the French attempts to capture the city. It forced Bonaparte to implement a protracted blockade.

CHAPTER 4

THE SECOND AUSTRIAN ATTEMPT TO RELIEVE MANTUA

THE BATTLE OF SAN GIORGIO

"The siege of Mantua is more disastrous for humanity than two campaigns."

BERTHIER TO WURMSER

E arly in September 1796 the French military situation in northern Italy was complicated by the reprovisioning and regarrisoning of Mantua by the Austrians. Bonaparte could not make a total commitment with his available resources to pursue the main Austrian army outside of the Quadrilateral with the Mantua garrison in his rear. The garrison, fighting for survival at Mantua, also posed a dilemma for the Austrians, who wanted to relieve the fortress in order to regain the Quadrilateral as a stepping-stone to capture Lombardy. This quest to relieve Mantua would lead Wurmser into another major battle with Bonaparte and leave the Austrian field army trapped inside the fortress city.

By mid-September the Austrians had 15,746 soldiers in the fortress of whom only 9,004 were fit for duty; sickness had taken its toll.[1] On 5 September the Giunta issued an avviso explaining that even with the extraordinary resistance demonstrated by the gallant defenders, more hardships were to be expected. Because of the large number of wounded and sick soldiers inside the city, the military could not provide beds for all of them. The Giunta asked that the people of Mantua bring their straw mattresses to the house of Monsignor Abbate of St. Barbara's Church for the officer in charge of quartering to collect and distribute.[2] Bonaparte was also having problems with illness in his army. On 1 September he ordered his chief commissariat to establish a 200-bed hospital at Lonato and a second hospital with 400 beds at Saló, to make 300 beds available at the hospital in Soncino, and to evacuate the sick soldiers besieging Mantua to Cremona.[3]

In addition to the problems the fortress presented to the opposing armies in Italy, Mantua influenced the overall strategic situation in France and the German lands. The withdrawal of 25,000 troops by Wurmser to reinforce the Austrian army's attack to relieve Mantua had so weakened the Austrian armies along the Rhine River that the French were able to cross the river and invade Germany again. The French Army of the Sambre and Meuse, under General Jean-Baptiste Jourdan, crossed the Rhine north of the Main, and the French Army of the Rhine and Moselle, under General Jean-Victor Moreau, crossed the Rhine at Strasbourg. The citizens of Mantua were aware of this crisis. On 9 September the *Gazzetta di Mantova* reported the movements of the French armies. The paper also reported that Canto d'Yrles had received a letter from Wurmser on the 1st declaring that Jourdan was on the march to Nuremberg.[4] The Directory told Moreau that in order "to free Mantua absolutely," he must move to Innsbruck in order to threaten Wurmser's line of communication and thereby allow Bonaparte to stay on the offensive. The Directory incorrectly believed that Moreau's operation would cause Wurmser to retreat from the Tyrol and rejoin Archduke Charles in Germany.[5]

The Directory detailed to Bonaparte the same plan they had given to Moreau. They insisted that Bonaparte take the offensive in the Tyrol. In addition, they commended Bonaparte for his success in rapidly raising the siege of Mantua, collecting his forces, and defeating the enemy in the battle that followed. Their new advice to him was to "abandon the project of trying to take Mantua by a well-organized siege and leave the garrison to die of sickness."[6]

While the Directory was making strategic plans for the French army commanders, General Lauer, Wurmser's new chief of staff, was developing a new operational plan for the Austrians; he recommended dividing the army into two equal corps. Wurmser would place one corps in the upper Tyrol, where General Michael von Fröhlich would guard the passes to the north and General Johann Ludwig Loudon would observe the sources of the Inn River.[7] The other corps would be commanded by General Paul Davidovich, who would remain in the lower Tyrol and defend the passage from Legnago to the Upper Adige.[8] Wurmser would advance with his corps in the north to Bassano, where he would reassemble his forces and start offensive operations with the objective of relieving Mantua. Each corps could then advance cautiously, and if Bonaparte attacked one, the other corps could relieve Mantua and attack the French line of communications. Wurmser's corps, moving toward Bassano, departed on 1 September 1796.[9]

In the French theater of operations, Bonaparte had 10,000 men, in three brigades, under General Charles-Henri Vaubois, west of Lake Garda.[10] Two of these brigades were north of Lake Idro, and one was at Saló. Masséna had a 13,000-man division between Lake Garda and the Adige River. Augereau's division of 10,000 men was at Verona, as was General Charles Edward Kilmaine's mixed brigade of 2,000 men.[11] Sahuguet was renewing the investment of Mantua with a force of 8,000 men.[12]

Bonaparte informed the Directory and Moreau that he would advance on Trent on 2 September; after reaching Trent on the 4th or 5th, he would then decide on his next move.[13] When the campaign started, one division of Wurmser's corps was at Bassano, one was in the valley of the Brenta near Primolano, and one was just east of Trent (see map 1). Davidovich was compelled to detach two brigades to protect his communications from Moreau's army. His main body was at Ala, and his reserve was at Trent. Bonaparte intended to advance in three columns. Vaubois with two brigades of his division would advance to Torbole, on the northeast bank of Lake Garda (see map 2). There he would meet his other brigade at Saló under the command of General Jean Joseph Guieu, who would be transported up the lake in boats on the night of 1 September.[14] The same evening, Bonaparte ordered Masséna to advance up the Adige valley toward Ala and Augereau to move up the valleys north of Verona. Kilmaine was to hold Verona with the fortress guns and the 1,200-man garrison while covering it with his newly assembled and attached cavalry brigade.[15] Bonaparte, however, was very concerned about maintaining his investment of Mantua. In fact, he sent more instructions to General Sahuguet regarding his deployment at Mantua than he sent to Masséna, Augereau, Kilmaine, Guieu, and Jacques Charles Dubois combined.[16] Sahuguet received additional forces from Milan and was told to prepare for a withdrawal followed by a counterattack if the Austrians were to march on Mantua. However, he was also instructed to send a cavalry outpost to Legnago, thereby counterbalancing his reinforcements from Milan.[17]

On 2 September Masséna crossed the Adige and arrived at Ala on the 3rd as Vaubois advanced to Torbole. At two o'clock that morning, they drove back Davidovich's Austrian cavalry outposts. On 4 September Masséna captured Rovereto, taking twenty-five cannon and seven colors (see map 2).[18] The next day at 8:00 A.M. Masséna entered Trent while Wurmser left that village seeking refuge at Bassano. Vaubois's division pursued Davidovich's troops to Lavis, on the Adige River north of Trent.[19] Bonaparte wasted no time setting up a new government for Trent; the following day, 6 September, he established the new governing body by issuing ten articles to the city council.[20] He then ordered Vaubois to secure the towns of Trent, Torbole, and Rovereto while he pursued Wurmser into the Brenta valley.[21]

The situation in Mantua was changing. At 6:00 P.M. on the 6th, Canto d'Yrles ordered detachments of fifty-seven cavalrymen and more than fifty infantrymen to attack Sahuguet's blockading forces when some French soldiers were noticed moving back toward Marmirolo. The sortie turned back once the French formed up in a battalion formation. This venture was only a small version of several major sorties launched by the Austrians during the preceding two weeks.[22] Informed by Kilmaine from Verona about the daily sorties taking place at Mantua, Bonaparte was clearly worried.[23] On 6 September Bonaparte wrote to the Directory stating that he thought it was now necessary to move three battalions of Milanese soldiers to join the army blockading Mantua.[24]

The next morning Augereau's advance guard encountered the Austrians entrenched at Primolano. With the 4th and 5th demibrigades Augereau and Masséna took the town and captured the Austrians. Bonaparte then decided to rest his army that night at Cismon (see map 1).[25]

Meanwhile, Wurmser had united his army at Bassano with the exception of General Johann Meszaros's corps, which was marching on Verona to confront Kilmaine. From 4:30 until 11:00 on the morning of 7 September, the people of Mantua could hear the shelling from Meszaros's attack on the Verona fortifications.[26]

On 8 September at 2:00 A.M., Bonaparte resumed his pursuit of Wurmser from Cismon through the defiles of the Brenta valley. By seven o'clock Augereau's division attacked the Austrians near Solagna, in the foothills of Bassano. Masséna attacked the Austrian right. Both the Austrian and French armies were split in two by the Brenta River, but the two French commanders coordinated their attack better than the defending Austrians. The French then marched toward Bassano, where Wurmser was establishing his head-quarters. The French attacked with Augereau and the 5th demibri-gade on the east side of the river and Masséna at the head of the 4th demibrigade on the west side. They captured Bassano after defeat-ing several battalions of Austrian grenadiers armed with fixed bay-onets. Wurmser himself narrowly escaped. Compelled to abandon Bassano, he personally led his two wrecked grenadier battalions to Montebello, located between Vicenza and Verona (see map 2). There he joined a division that had escaped the attack at Bassano. The Austrian army was now in three parts. Davidovich had been forced northward into the heart of the Tyrol, Quosdanovich was retreating eastward, and Wurmser was at Montebello.[27]

Bonaparte made the following triumphant announcement to his superiors:

> In six days we have fought two battles and four combats. We have taken from the enemy twenty-one colors; we have made 16,000 prisoners, among whom are many generals; the rest have been killed, wounded, or scattered abroad. We have, in six days, always fighting in inexpugnable gorges, marched forty-five leagues, taken seventy cannon with their caissons and horses, a part of their grand park, and considerable magazines spread along the route.[28]

Although Bonaparte's claims about what the French had cap-tured are exaggerated, his letter still demonstrates both the incred-ible speed of the French army that pursued its enemy in the field and the culminating effect of his victory at the Battle of Bassano.

On 9 September Wurmser decided to move on Legnago, cross the Adige River, and march to Mantua. He spent the day reorga-nizing and resting his troops near Arcole, then sent a cavalry force to the fortress of Legnago. The French garrison there was forced to immediately evacuate. Bonaparte had begun his pursuit of Wurmser after the battle on the 8th by putting his divisions in motion. He and Masséna pursued the Austrians to Montebello, while Augereau moved to Padua to cut off their retreat into the Friuli region (see map 1). On 10 September Wurmser reached Legnago and later in the afternoon crossed the Adige. Masséna's advance guard crossed at Ronco that night as Augereau continued his march toward Legnago. Since the fighting at Trent, Bonaparte had anticipated

Wurmser's making a run for Mantua. On 10 September, he explained to Josephine that Wurmser now had no alternative but to attempt to reach the fortress.[29]

At the same time, Sahuguet at Mantua was worriedly reporting to Bonaparte that the Austrians were at Porto Legnago with 7,000 men. Reminding Bonaparte of the constant sorties made by the Mantuan garrison, he also noted that three new battalions had arrived from the Vendée.[30]

The next day Sahuguet received instructions from Bonaparte to destroy all the bridges over the Molinella River, guard the river, and place a brigade at the town of Castellarrio, on the main road Wurmser was taking to Mantua.[31] Kilmaine was assigned to assist Sahuguet in stopping Wurmser's column.[32] Masséna was ordered to march to Sanguinetto in order to intercept Wurmser's column, while Augereau was directed to take Legnago if possible.[33] Wurmser left a strong force at Legnago and began moving to Sanguinetto with his main body. Bonaparte's plans went astray on 11 September as Sahuguet did not destroy all the bridges as ordered and Masséna's guide took him through Angiari and Cerea, instead of directly to Sanguinetto.[34] Masséna, with only two brigades, both of which were considerably weakened because of stragglers, ran into Wurmser's main force at Cerea and was defeated by General Peter Karl Freiherr Ott. During the combat at Cerea, Bonaparte galloped up to the village just as the French advance guard was routed and had just enough time to turn around and depart. Wurmser arrived at the same spot a few minutes later and, after learning about the French general's appearance from an old woman, sent soldiers in pursuit saying he should be brought in alive. Back at Mantua, Sahuguet abandoned his investing lines, as ordered, and moved his soldiers north to the river-crossing site at Goito, where he prepared to strike against the Austrians.[35]

Having won a small victory, Wurmser quickly continued his march to Sanguinetto. Upon reaching the town, he discovered that Sahuguet's and Kilmaine's reserves were waiting for him on the Molinella River near Castellarrio. Guided by a native, Wurmser marched all night on 11 September, moved off the main road to Mantua, and crossed a small bridge at Villimpenta south of the main road. Wurmser's cavalry surprised the small detachment of Frenchmen who were guarding the bridge. General Charles-François Charton moved quickly with five hundred men of the 12th Light Demibrigade from Sahuguet's besieging force in front of Mantua to defend the bridge but could not reach it in time. Forming a square on the road, Charton's troops vigorously resisted an Austrian cavalry attack, which left the general dead on the field and his detachment routed.[36]

The same day, 12 September, Augereau's division arrived at Legnago and with the help of some of Masséna's troops he invested the city. Augereau's adjutant, General Auguste Belliard, was wounded in the fighting, but victory was close at hand.[37] The Austrian commandant of the fortress sent a letter to Augereau with an offer to surrender, but the Frenchman refused most of his requests. For example, the commander requested that the garrison be able to keep their colors, cannon, arms, and ammunition along with their wagon train and horses. Augereau's response was simply that "all [such] belong to the French army."[38] Augereau then sent an infantry battalion and a troop of cavalry up the Adige to Ronco, where Bonaparte was to secure the line of communications. He also sent cavalry down the Adige to Castelbaldo, just south of Legnago, to get information about the Austrians' movements.[39]

The Mantua garrison poured out of the fortress to unite with Wurmser's force once his army arrived outside of San Giorgio. Wurmser deployed his army between the suburb and the Citadel. Together with the reinforcements from the fortress, Wurmser's command comprised a total of 33,000 men. Leaving 5,000 men to guard the city walls, he encamped with 25,000 soldiers outside the fortress, occupying the countryside.

Augereau fell sick and had to give over his command to General Louis-André Bon.[40] On 13 September Bon entered Legnago with Augereau's division, and the Austrian fortress commander was induced to surrender his garrison, withdraw to Trieste, and serve no more during the war. At Legnago the French took twenty-two cannon and 1,673 prisoners and liberated the five hundred French soldiers taken prisoner during the combat at Cerea. With this obstacle removed, Bonaparte could again concentrate on blockading Mantua. He quickly set Augereau's division, under Bon, on the march to Governolo.[41]

Occupying the east bank of the Mincio, Wurmser set up a position in front of San Giorgio, with an advanced post at the village of Due Castelli, which was actually an ancient country manor of the Gonzaga dukes. At 2:00 A.M. of 14 September, Sahuguet's division, consisting of the 12th and 6th Line Regiments, departed Goito with orders to march on San Antonio.[42] Masséna, coming from Castellarrio the same day, marched toward Due Castelli and caught the Austrian infantry and cavalry outpost off guard, cooking rations; he quickly captured the old ducal château.[43] The 5th *Légère*, under General Jean Pijon, led the French column. General Karl Ott and Colonel Johann Klenau attacked the advance guard from San Giorgio, forcing them to abandon their cannon. It seemed as if the Austrians would soon win the fight, but the French 32nd Line arrived on the field and pushed back Klenau's men, who abandoned the cannon they had seized just two hours before.

Wurmser then sent nine battalions of grenadiers against the 32nd Line. Six times the 32nd formed squares on the plateau in order to defend themselves on all sides. Finally at 4:00 P.M. the French placed two 12-pounder cannon on the Austrian right flank to rake Ott's line with canister while Kilmaine charged with the 20th Dragoons. Held down by the French fire, Ott called up cuirassiers, hussars, and ulans along with 3,000 infantry. A French battalion was cut off and lost three hundred men when it was attacked by two regiments of Austrian cuirassiers.[44]

Bonaparte would not accept defeat. He immediately set to work dispatching orders to his commanders calling for a well-organized attack for the next day, 15 September, against the 18,000 men Wurmser had deployed in San Giorgio and the surrounding area north to La Favorita. Sahuguet was directed to move down the Roverbella road on the Austrian left wing.[45] Sahuguet, who had yet to experience much military success, was at first pushed back with severe losses, but bringing up all his available units, he forced the Austrians to withdraw into the palace at La Favorita.[46] Meanwhile, Bon moved up the east bank of the Mincio from Governolo. His force reached San Giorgio and marched on the right flank of the Austrians located south of the suburb. Pijon at the head of the 18th *Légère* and Nicolas Bertin with the 5th Line attacked Ott. Wurmser attacked Bon's force, thinking that he was dealing with both Augereau's and Masséna's forces. In order to repel the French at San Giorgio, Wurmser employed part of the battalions from the center of his line, which extended from the La Favorita palace to the suburb of San Giorgio.

Sahuguet launched a new attack on Wurmser's position at La Favorita, so Wurmser sent 6,000 reinforcements there, at the expense of thinning his center even more. Bonaparte, who had kept Masséna's force in reserve and out of view, seized this moment to strike in column formation at Wurmser's weakened center. Masséna's generals—Claude Victor, Joseph Chabran, and Antoine-Guillaume Rampon—gallantly leading their men, debouched upon the suburb to the front and the flank. Victor attacked San Giorgio with the 8th Battalion of Grenadiers, the 8th Line Regiment, and the carabineers of the 4th and 29th *Légère*. Rampon commanded the reserve which was made up of chasseurs, the 29th *Légère*, and the 32nd Line. Pijon's 18th *Légère* stopped the Austrian cavalry as Chabran attacked into San Giorgio. Victor arrived in time to support Pijon and occupy San Giorgio. Masséna then ordered an attack en masse. The right wing of the Austrian army, south of San Giorgio, heard the fierce storm of cannon and musketry in their rear and gave way to Bon's attack. Withdrawing, they came upon two French battalions of Sahuguet's division, which were holding the bridgehead of the San Giorgio dam that divided the Middle and Lower Lakes and connected to Mantua. Sahuguet had not been quick enough with his reinforcements to support his two forward battalions, but Rampon, seeing the danger they faced, led his regiment into the fray against the Austrian defenders. Rampon's 32nd Line, a mere 900 men of the French reserve, held off 3,000 Austrian soldiers, most of whom were Croatians. Much of the Austrian force was killed. Some soldiers were driven into the Mincio River; others were captured. Many on the Austrian right flank at San Giorgio were forced back across the dam into Mantua. In their center and left flank, the Austrians moved into the protection of the Citadel. Wurmser was now trapped in the fortress he had marched to relieve. That night the French bivouacked at San Giorgio and celebrated their successes by singing the Marseillaise.[47]

Losses were high on both sides, but the Austrians suffered greater casualties. The French captured an Austrian regiment of cuirassiers, completely mounted, with three standards and eleven pieces of artillery. The French retook the most favorable positions for making the blockade effective. Wurmser now had, in and around the fortress, about 30,000 men, of whom nearly 4,000 were cavalry. Of these men, only 18,000 were ready for service, which left about 12,000 sick or wounded.[48] At first Canto d'Yrles refused to admit the field army into the fortress, since he did not have provisions or quarters for them. He eventually relented, aware that Wurmser's army would be destroyed by the French if it was not given shelter.[49] For administrative reasons, however, as late as 17 September, the garrison command under Canto d'Yrles was still only reporting the regular garrison soldiers. On the morning report that day, the garrison listed 16,993 soldiers, with only 9,555 fit for service.[50]

After the battle, Bonaparte and his commanders bestowed awards and laurels on their men. Masséna said that he owed the most praise to the bravery with which Victor and Rampon had led their brigades. Victor was wounded twice, once severely, Masséna reported, and after having his wound dressed, he still led his men into San Giorgio. He also commended Bonaparte's aide-de-camp Auguste-Frédéric-Louis Marmont for having checked the cavalry that was charging part of the 18th. He requested the promotion of Adjutant-General Chabran, who had led the column into San Giorgio.[51] Bonaparte, in his report to the Directory, echoed many of Masséna's comments, with some additions and omissions. Bonaparte began by saying that it was the coolness of Victor in leading the courageous 8th Battalion of Grenadiers that contributed to their survival during the combat at Cerea on 12 September. Victor was also named among the wounded, along with Murat, Suchet, Lannes, and others.[52] Enraged upon reading the report, Masséna wrote to Bonaparte: "I read your report of the battle of San Giorgio, my general, and of the affair at Cerea. I was surprised that you gave praise to some generals who, far from contributing to the success of that happy day, are at fault for failing a column of my division intended for an attack on Favorita, and you did not say a word about me or Rampon." Masséna went on to say that he deserved the justice that he merited and that "the victory of the Battle of San Giorgio was due to his military disposition, his activity, and his cold blood for all to see."[53]

The day after the battle, Bonaparte made General Kilmaine the siege commander at Mantua. Bonaparte also reaffirmed Kilmaine's command of the army's cavalry, which was divided into two brigades. The first brigade, commanded by General Marc Antoine Beaumont, would assist in blockading Mantua; the second, commanded by Murat, would be conducting field operations. Bonaparte gave very detailed instructions to Kilmaine. He was to blockade the Citadel and occupy San Giorgio as well as the Pradella and Cerese gates. The major problem for Kilmaine was that the French did not control these gates at this time. Bonaparte informed Kilmaine that occupying the gates was "very essential" and that he would give the new siege commander three to four days to accomplish the task.[54]

After a quiet day following the Battle of San Giorgio, several minor combats erupted and continued for the rest of the month as

Kilmaine sought to fulfill his orders from Bonaparte. Before 7:00 A.M. on 17 September, French troops, on the east bank of the Lower Lake, fired muskets on boats laden with food supplies destined for the Catena Harbor to resupply the Austrian troops. Soon the fortress erupted with three volleys from the large cannon, which halted the French harassing fire.[55] The French could not contest the Austrian boats on the lakes because their own flotilla was scuttled a month earlier. Captain Baste gallantly held his fleet together through the French evacuation in early August and continued to fight the Austrians on the lakes. Ultimately, however, on 18 August he blew up the vessels in order to keep them from falling into Austrian hands. He returned to Peschiera and again took command of his former half galley *La Voltigeante*.[56]

Wurmser ordered 2,000 infantry and six hundred cavalry to forage outside the fortress on 17 September. He also wanted to occupy the Serraglio in order to disperse his troops and move as many soldiers as possible out of the town. General Karl Spiegel moved to Madonna delle Grazie and Montanara with a combined force of 2,600 men. Another 1,100 troops was sent to a position south of Montanara. Wurmser ordered 1,200 infantry and 200 hussars from the Cerese mill to Governolo and Borgoforte to observe the French.[57] That night they brought 200 wagons loaded with provisions into the city. The next night another 80 wagons full of supplies rolled into Mantua.[58]

Kilmaine was having difficulty executing Bonaparte's orders quickly because the Austrian cavalry dominated the Serraglio. On 19 September the Austrians sent five hundred cavalrymen to Castellucchio, and the French advance guards in that area fell back, as ordered.[59] The night of 20 and 21 September the city of Mantua was alive with activity: Austrian troops moved throughout the town preparing to relocate to the countryside. At 6:00 A.M. 6,000 infantry and cavalry began marching out of the Pradella and Cerese gates.[60] Colonel Klenau took three companies of *Jägers*, almost four battalions of infantry, and seven squadrons of hussars to occupy Curtatone, Montanara, Buscoldo, Ponteventuno, and Borgoforte. General Ott moved to Cerese with the Alvintzy Regiment and three squadrons of hussars in order to prepare to march on Governolo.[61]

The march to Governolo started on 22 September with Generals Ott and Ferdinand Minkwitz leading the advance along the west bank of the Mincio. Minkwitz had 800 infantry and 600 cavalry, while Ott had 1,000 infantry and 600 cavalry.[62] Between 3:00 and

4:00 A.M. on 23 September, they ran into Kilmaine's forces, reinforced by Augereau's division, which fired at the Austrians rapidly
with six howitzers and two large field guns; following the barrage,
the French attacked with their infantry. It was a bitter struggle for
the Austrians. Minkwitz was wounded in the hand with a saber.
The Austrians were driven back, and the French captured five cannon and many supply wagons. The Austrians retreated to a position
below the Migliaretto works.[63]

While the Austrians occupied the Serraglio, locals were free
again to enter and leave the fortress through the southern gates.
On 18 September the Giunta issued an avviso stating that for the
next eight days anyone entering the city with wine, new or old,
would enjoy an exemption from the wine tax that was normally
paid upon entry.[64] This measure was taken because of the need to
get as many provisions into the fortress as possible. If the officials
could get more wine vendors into the fortress by suspending the
wine tax, they would not have to send people looking throughout
the countryside for this highly demanded commodity. On the 26th,
when the eight days of tax exemption were up, the Giunta issued
another notice stating that the earlier avviso exempting the wine
tax would be extended until St. Francis Day, 4 October—in honor
of Emperor Francis II.[65] However, by the time this new avviso was
published, the French troops had reestablished their investment of
the city. As before, the Austrians appealed to the townspeople for
military goods as well as foodstuffs. A 24 September avviso promised 50 Milanese scudi for every firearm turned in to the authorities.
They also offered to buy disassembled musket parts and gun bar-
rels.[66] This appeal to the residents demonstrated the pressing need of
the Austrian authorities to rearm the soldiers who had lost so many
weapons during their retreat into the fortress.

On 28 September a French trumpeter approached the fortress
from San Giorgio.[67] Bonaparte's aide-de-camp Joseph Sulkowski
entered the city to talk to Wurmser about an exchange of prisoners.
The old field marshal's response was entirely dutiful: he would wait
until they were fully surrounded before making a prisoner exchange.
Nevertheless, Sulkowski was taken, blindfolded, to visit the French
officers being held prisoner. The Polish aide-de-camp, who spoke
German, was able to listen to the conversation of the Austrians
without their knowing his facility in German, but he did not gain
any significant information. Of the one hundred French officers he

visited, sixty were sick. It was clear that the area's unhealthy conditions were much worse for the Austrians inside the fortress than for the French outside. From the prisoners, Sulkowski learned that the Austrians had about 7,000 sick of their own inside the fortress.[68] After Sulkowski's visit, Wurmser left the city to make a personal reconnaissance of Borgoforte.[69]

Bonaparte had departed for Milan after entrusting Kilmaine with the blockade of Mantua. From Milan he continued to press the Directory and subordinates alike for soldiers and equipment to force the Austrians in Mantua to capitulate. On 28 September he issued a series of instructions to reduce the Mantua fortifications quickly. He ordered Chasseloup to make the situation even worse for the Austrians inside Mantua by flooding the city. Bonaparte told him simply: "You will please, citizen, cut the dikes at Governolo so that when the Po floods, it will back up the water of the Mincio into the city of Mantua which will do much damage to the besieged. There is not a moment to lose in carrying out this operation because the Po will soon rise."[70] Bonaparte also ordered the same instructions to be sent to Kilmaine to ensure that the order was carried out.[71] To assist Kilmaine with the blockade, Bonaparte ordered Berthier to provide four army commissaries for Kilmaine's forces: one each for Dallemagne's and Sahuguet's divisions, one for Beaumont's cavalry brigade and the final one for the artillery and engineers assigned to Mantua.[72]

Bonaparte then ordered General Augustin Lespinasse to send, as quickly as possible, a large army boat down the Mincio to the Upper Lake at Mantua and recommended that Andréossy command the ship. The purpose of the vessel was to prevent the Austrians, who then had complete control of the Mantua lakes, from making a sortie by boat across the lakes.[73] The French still had a fleet on Lake Garda. The plan worked well, and on 12 October Captain Pierre Baste was again assigned as commander of the French fleet at Mantua. He remained in that command until well after the siege in 1797.[74] Bonaparte also gave Lespinasse instructions on where to place the artillery around Mantua. He wanted to collect all the French pieces in the artillery park and use only foreign cannon to fire on Mantua.[75]

Kilmaine remained in the same position he held after the fight at Governolo, hoping that the Austrians would launch another sortie to gather forage. Instead, the Austrians encamped outside the Pradella and Cerese gates.[76] On 29 September Kilmaine attacked in three columns against Pietole, Cerese, and Belfiore. The Austrians fell back under the protection of the fortress guns. The column attacking the Pradella gate from Belfiore was fired upon from across the Upper Lake by the guns of the Citadel facing southwest as well as the guns on the Te crownwork. However, the worst cannonade for the attacking French was the canister that poured on them from the Pradella works and the San Alessio bastion of the main fortress. Dallemagne, who attacked the Porta Pradella, pushed his troops forward. Despite the heavy fire, they took the Osteria Alta and Belfiore. That night the French started digging trenches near the Cerese mill, and by 1 October 1796 they occupied the same positions they had held in July.[77]

Bonaparte, back in Milan, thought this was a significant victory; he also thought that Kilmaine's attack on 29 September, which carried Belfiore, had gained the Pradella gate. Because of this satisfaction, and the patriotism spreading daily among the people of Lombardy, he saw no reason to continue the wartime custom of taking hostages as a guarantee of public tranquility in and around Milan and Cremona. He ordered the commander at Antibes and Nice to release hostages that had been taken in those regions.[78]

Because Bonaparte had finally closed Wurmser off in the "island" fortress of Mantua, the Army of Italy again enjoyed an interval of comparative rest. Kilmaine's soldiers remained around Mantua, albeit breathing the foul air of its marshes and performing the cheerless duties of a blockading force. His two divisions under Sahuguet and Dallemagne each had about 4,500 troops. Vaubois was sent into the Tyrol to watch the valley of the Adige and cover Trent with 8,000 troops. Masséna with 5,500 men and Augereau with 5,400 were ordered first to Verona, and afterward to the Brenta valley. Meanwhile, the Austrians within the fortress settled in for another siege.[79]

Having arrived in Milan on 19 September 1796, Bonaparte remained there until 12 October, when he crossed the Po to deal with the leaders of Modena, the Legations, and Rome.[80] By 23 October he was again at Verona, preparing for another anticipated conflict with the Austrians. While in Milan, he worked tirelessly, delving into politics and requisitioning provisions, troops, and cannon for the siege of Mantua. He made inquiries into the civil administration of the army and began to create a Lombard Legion, which he intended to employ in the blockade at Mantua. On 29 September he authorized the popular Mantuan Giuseppe Lahoz, his aide-de-camp, to admit those French officers who wanted to enter the legion and allow the Lombard administration to give brevet ranks to officers employed by the legion, subject to approval by himself and Lahoz. The Directory agreed to Bonaparte's plan for the new legion, which would fly the famous red, white, and green tricolor, closely copying the French flag.[81]

The Directory wanted Bonaparte to end the siege of Mantua quickly and make war on the Papal States and the king of Naples.[82] Bonaparte advised the Directory on 2 October 1796 that for political and military reasons, it was not prudent to confront several enemies at the same time. All his efforts in writing to the Directors in Paris and Pope Pius VI in Rome were focused on maintaining peace between the two. He tried to coerce the papal court and to show the Directory the madness of waging war on too many fronts simultaneously. He told the Directory that Mantua was not yet taken and that if he set out on other tasks with his army, all would be lost. Bonaparte had 9,000 of his 27,900 soldiers committed to the siege at Mantua, one-third of his operational force. So he advised the Directory against making war with Naples or breaking negotiations with Rome, until the moment came to march upon that "superb city."[83] The Directory in Paris took his advice in both cases: France made peace with Naples and continued deceptive talks with Rome. The Directory likewise agreed with Bonaparte that the two main concerns for the Army of Italy were the new Austrian army forming in the Friuli and the siege of Mantua.[84]

In order to appease the Directory, Bonaparte had to threaten the pope and the papal troops with a possible invasion as he worked to counter the designs of the Papal States government. When Wurmser made his second advance on Mantua, some Italian authorities evidenced a stronger propensity to overthrow the pro-French governments imposed on them. Conversely, other Italian states that had not yet felt the exacting demands of French rule waited with anticipation for the French to free them from Austrian rule. Modena was one such state that could not wait for the French, however. On the night of 25–26 August, the pro-French citizens of Modena took up arms, overthrew the Austrian garrison, planted a tree of liberty, and proclaimed their independence. On 4 October Bonaparte, by solemn proclamation, declared that the overthrown Modenese leader, Hercules Rinaldo, had forfeited his regency by violating his sworn neutrality to the French and Austrians; that is, he was accused of providing supplies for Wurmser's garrison in Mantua in September when the Austrians were gathering forage. Thus Bonaparte laid the foundations of another Italian republic, which would receive its baptism of fire the very next day when the Modenese National Guard attacked and took as prisoners 150 Austrians who had been cut off from Mantua at Borgoforte in late September. Now that Wurmser was blocked inside of Mantua, Bonaparte could deal with the smaller Italian states that were rebelling.[85]

By October the government in Paris was just as determined as Bonaparte to force the capitulation of Mantua. To expedite the process, a council was convened to decide on a new strategy to secure the fortress. After coming to a decision on 1 October, Carnot sent Bonaparte a decree stating that Wurmser was to be treated as an émigré, because of his having been born in Alsace and having served in the French army early in his career. The Directory intended this as an inducement to Wurmser to surrender the fortress since he could extract himself honorably as an émigré. This was just one in a succession of bizarre schemes Bonaparte was expected to carry out. The Directory allowed Bonaparte to use his own discretion as to whether or not to present the decree to Wurmser.[86] In another scheme, Bonaparte was instructed to write to Emperor Francis II telling him that he has orders from the Directory to march on Trieste and destroy that harbor if the emperor did not send plenipotentiaries to France to begin peace negotiations. He sent the communique on 2 October.[87]

The same day Carnot sent his letter to Bonaparte concerning Wurmser, the general in chief of the Army of Italy informed the Directory that he had 14,000 sick soldiers in his army.[88] Malarial fever caused by the pestilence in the marshes around Mantua was spreading, to the detriment of both warring armies. When Wurmser withdrew to the Tyrol in August, he had left 15,000–17,000 men in the fortress. The number of Austrian troops affected by intermittent bouts of malaria continued to increase as fall approached. At the beginning of October, Wurmser had about 28,500 men in the fortress, of whom about 11,500 were not healthy enough to perform duties. Although the additional soldiers that Wurmser brought inside the fortress helped to lighten the burden of the weakening garrison, they quickly consumed the small stock of cattle.[89] Canto d'Yrles was correct in his concern about the strain put on the provisions stored in Mantua. Even with the provisions that Wurmser was able to bring into the fortress in September, by the beginning of October the troops were reduced to eating rationed horseflesh.[90] After the Battle of San Giorgio, Wurmser brought in more than 4,000 horses. The amount of fodder available could not support the great number of horses, so inspections took place twice a week to identify those animals that seemed to be weakened by the meager rations. The weak were slaughtered, and a daily distribution of a quarter pound of horseflesh was made to all soldiers choosing to accept it. At first many declined, especially men of the artillery corps, but eventually they became eager and competitive to get this provision.[91] By the end of the month the number of horses was reduced by half.[92]

Inside the fortress, sickness took its toll on civilians and soldiers alike. Between 100 and 150 civilians died in Mantua each day during the worst period of the siege.[93] The lack of medical supplies, particularly of bark, accelerated the death rate among the troops to an alarming extent. Certain types of bark were commonly boiled and served as a tea that acted to relieve pain. Illness affected the military as severely as the civilians. On some days as many as 150 soldiers died; the number rarely fell below 75 deaths.[94] The problem became so critical that on 3 October fifteen additional buildings were designated as military hospitals. To meet this need for hospital space, the Austrians converted churches, convents, schools, and suitable houses into hospitals.[95] Nevertheless, the lack of supplies for these new hospitals undercut efforts to care for the men. So few men who entered the hospitals ever returned to their units that many Austrian soldiers preferred to conceal their sickness in order to avoid being condemned to the hospitals, which they considered a death sentence. As a result, many Austrians died at their posts.[96]

In this desperate state the Austrian army waited for information from the outside on whether there would be an attempt to relieve the city. Quite often, hired spies and soldiers in disguise would slip through the French patrols and outposts to carry messages to and from the fortress. In this manner, the Austrians in Mantua finally learned that Francis II appointed General Alvintzy to command an army collecting at Gorizia to relieve Mantua.[97]

On 3 October Kilmaine sent a letter from Borgoforte to Canto d'Yrles asking if he had a French officer of equal rank to exchange for Colonel Baron Anton Zack. The French delivered the letter at the Porta Cerese. Canto d'Yrles, who remained the fortress commander while Wurmser commanded the entire army in the city, quickly wrote a response to Kilmaine and dispatched his agreement to the individual prisoner exchange.[98]

On 4 October the president of the Mantua Council and Austrian commissary, Count Luigi Cocastelli, informed Wurmser of the ever growing need for grain, flour, and wood. As early as May, Cocastelli had issued a notice to the citizens of Mantua to chop down to the root all trees located within a half mile of the city.[99] Wurmser's situation was critical. Cocastelli had all of Mantua's magazines inspected to find out exactly what provisions were available to the army and began sending daily reports on their condition to Wurmser. On the 6th he sent a detailed matrix that enumerated how many sacks of flour and wood were available, how many rations they would make, and how long they would last at the current rate of consumption. In addition, through his local contacts, Cocastelli was able to keep Wurmser abreast of the military situation of the French forces surrounding the fortress.[100]

On 6 October Cocastelli issued an avviso that brought much delight to the desperate citizens of the city. It promised that the government at Mantua would start printing paper cedole (vouchers) that upon redemption would be worth three times their present value. However, the cedole had to be held for at least three months—at which time, Cocastelli projected, foodstuffs would run out in Mantua.[101]

While work on the siege progressed, the French continued the usual bombardment of the fortress. On 5 October they opened up with their cannons from morning until about noon. They set up a battery on the road leading north out of the Citadel, which the Austrians pounded using cannons in the Citadel bastions. On the south side the French fired at the San Carlo fleches to provide cover as they again dug trenches below the Migliaretto works. The French shelling caused the Austrians to round up all of the horses from the cavalry units stationed in their town. They corralled the horses in the open court of the Ducal Palace, in the nobles' expansive gardens, and in specially built stables or anywhere they could contain and guard them. Penning the horses would serve two primary purposes: (1) to shelter the animals during the shellings, and (2) to make it easier to pick out and slaughter the weaker horses for soldiers' rations.[102]

All day on 6 October the Austrians moved about the town assembling for a sortie that was to take place the next night. Wurmser ordered the troops conducting the sortie to forage northwest of the Citadel toward Marmirolo and Soave with 8,435 infantry and cavalry, six cannon, and six howitzers. The men were to move out in three columns commanded by Generals Meszaros and Ott and Colonel Klenau to gather as much wood and food as possible. The first column departed on the night of 7 October, marching toward Soave. The other two columns followed the first down the road to Soave and then turned north toward Marmirolo. Along the road they attacked the Prada castle, which was defended by the 11th demibrigade. The Austrians were able to gain enough of an advantage to cut down several trees and bring in the wood along with more than a hundred wagons loaded with hay. The Austrians captured two French officers and 119 soldiers. In the action, the Austrians lost eight killed and twenty-four wounded. A French officer, with only a small detachment of men from the 69th demibrigade, captured 117 of the Austrians. The total number of missing Austrians from the columns returning on 8 October was two officers and 153 men.[103]

The garrison leadership was concerned not only about food supplies running low but also about the massive consumption of powder by the fortress cannon. In order to provide ammunition for the large fortress guns and cartridges for their muskets, the Austrians established a gunpowder laboratory under the Church of Saint Marta. Much of the gunpowder, charcoal and sulfur captured from the French in early August was moved there. Daily work producing powder and assembling ammunition called for a lieutenant, a sergeant and corporal of artillery, twelve cannoneers, and fifty-four infantrymen. On 9 October around 9:00 A.M., a terrible disaster struck the Austrian garrison. The laboratory caught fire and exploded. The blast was so powerful that it shook the casements of the castle at Borgoforte more than seven miles away. Bricks and stones and whole pieces of wall from the Church of St. Marta went flying into the air, causing damage to nearby houses. Forty-five people were killed, and many of the bodies were so mangled that they could not be identified. The entire structure was destroyed. The ground floor no longer existed. In addition to the bricks and stones, a shower of musket balls and cannon shells rained down on the surrounding area. A massive column of black smoke rose up from the burning ruins. The French outside the fortress who heard it thought the explosion signaled another sortie. The frequent sorties by the Austrians made them come to expect the attacks. Although they were wrong about the signal, they were correct about the sortie. That night Wurmser called for a small sortie to be made by 150 volunteer hussars. During the night, while engaging the enemy only slightly, they were able to slip through the lines and bring back about forty wagons of hay into the fortress.[104]

Throughout October the small forage sorties continued as Wurmser tried to provide for his sick soldiers and hold off the French long enough for Alvintzy to bring relief. News and rumors trickled into the fortress about the reverses of the French armies in Germany. Now, more than ever, Bonaparte, also realizing that another Austrian force would soon be sent to relieve Mantua, wanted to move his forces out of the unhealthy swampy area. If he could force Wurmser to surrender, he could continue his offensive campaign in northern Italy. He decided to act on the Directory's suggestion to offer Wurmser émigré status. Apparently unwilling to lower himself to begging the enemy to surrender, Bonaparte allowed Berthier to write to the Austrian commander offering to let his troops withdraw if he would surrender the city. On 16 October Berthier wrote: "The siege of Mantua is more disastrous for humanity than two campaigns: brave men should face danger, not the pestilence of a marsh. Your cavalry has no fodder, your garrison is lacking rations, thousands of sick require a change of air, medicine and healthy food."[105] Wurmser was even offered the opportunity to ascertain the situation and strength of the French army in order to encourage a positive response. But the old marshal did not even send a reply to the French entreaty.

The Austrians had to keep a constant watch on the activities of the French in order to curtail any buildup for a major attack. On 18 October from Porta Pradella the Austrians noticed considerable French activity in the direction of Montanara. That night they fired illuminating cannon rounds in that direction to highlight French activities. The Austrians noticed that during the night the French were working on the road from Pradella to Montanara. While continuing to fire illuminating rounds, they directed artillery fire on the French workers and forced them temporarily to abandon their project.[106]

On 24 October Wurmser finally received positive information from Alvintzy about his plans. He responded explaining his situation inside the fortress. Wurmser informed Alvintzy that the French army around Mantua was not a particularly strong force, but that the French army of observation around Verona was formidable.[107]

The same day he posted a notice throughout Mantua that gave the citizens and soldiers alike hope for relief soon. In the lengthy notice, he shared the details that Alvintzy had provided. The notice advised the populace that official word had been received that Emperor Francis II had commissioned, and the Aulic Council had so ordered, that General of Artillery Baron Alvintzy be sent to free Mantua and all of Lombardy. The notice also detailed the names of the various commanders of the Austrian columns, totaling 30,000 soldiers being sent to their rescue. In addition, it gave an account of the battles of Archduke Charles against Moreau and Jourdan.[108] It was a grand attempt to bring hope and encouragement to the garrison, which had been completely contained by Kilmaine's forces. The reality for the forces inside, however, was horsemeat rations at best and sickness at worst.[109]

As Wurmser resisted the French investing forces, he had to continue to send out foraging sorties in order to survive. After he set his staff to work on a course of action, General Lauer presented Wurmser with a plan for a grand sortie to be made on 28 October. The plan called for four columns to attack the French and force an opening out to the countryside. The first column was to be led by Adjutant Major Mohr. He was to take 455 men at 3:30 A.M. across the Lower Lake in boats, land near San Giorgio, and attack the French there. The second column was to be led by Colonel Klenau with 2,212 men including 850 cavalry. They would have seven cannon and use four portable footbridges to cross the San Giorgio dam and attack the suburb. Once they broke out of San Giorgio, they were to press on to Montata, La Favorita, and San Antonio. The third column, commanded by Major Josef Radetzky of the pioneer corps, was to have 606 men, including 108 cavalry, and two cannon. This column would follow Klenau's column and then take the route to Governolo. The fourth column, under General Ott, was to have 1,494 men, of which 570 were cavalry. They were to assemble in the Citadel with four cannon and four portable footbridges, and when Klenau made his move, they were to attack out of the main gate and from the glacis of the Citadel using the footbridges to cross the water. Once they broke through the French line, they were to mount an attack toward Marmirolo and Roverbella. A reserve of 1,661 men, including 156 cavalry, was to be held at the Citadel ready for Ott's commands.

The plan was doomed to fail from the start when the boats of Mohr's column were not able to cross the lake by 3:00 A.M. They

were delayed getting under way for about an hour, and the first soldiers did not disembark south of San Giorgio at Casa Zipata until
5:00 A.M. Klenau's column, therefore, began its attack unsupported.
Met with a hail of musket fire from San Giorgio, they turned back
and returned to the city. Ott's column never got started, and thus
ended the great sortie. The Austrians lost one officer and 23 men
wounded, in addition to two officers and 125 men captured in their
boats by the French.[110] Wurmser was now definitely trapped inside
the "island" fortress, haunted by sickness and starvation. By the
end of the month, as supplies of flour diminished, each soldier was
given one-half pound of horsemeat per day as the wait for Alvintzy
dragged on.[111]

September 1796 had promised to be the month for the successful relief of the Austrian garrison at Mantua by Marshal Wurmser.
That hope died when Bonaparte successfully employed an economy of force with Sahuguet blockading Mantua while Augereau
and Masséna dealt with Wurmser in the field. After Wurmser's ter-
rific losses at Rovereto and Bassano, he had no choice but to go to
Mantua in the hope of raising the siege. His efforts failed when
his forces became trapped at Mantua—and thus part of the problem instead of the solution, as his troops consumed provisions at
an enormous rate. October marked the beginning of the worst hardships for the garrison and the city's inhabitants. The troops were
feeling the effects of food rationing as Cocastelli tried to manage the
city's resources to serve both the civilians and the army. In addition,
he issued the cedole so he could buy whatever food and wood were
still available for sale. While the garrison inside suffered from depri-
vation and fever, the French outside, also suffering, tightened their
hold. Bonaparte, anxious to end the siege, offered Wurmser a chance
for survival, but the old marshal would have none of it and settled
in for a long siege.

CHAPTER 5

ALVINTZY AND THE THIRD
ATTEMPT TO RELIEVE MANTUA

"I rely on his [Wurmser's] valor and zeal, he will defend Mantua
to the last extremity."

FRANCIS II TO ALVINTZY, 5 DECEMBER 1796

"In a word—everything depends on the fall of Mantua."

BONAPARTE TO DIRECTORY, 6 DECEMBER 1796

B y the beginning of November 1796, the political situation did not
look promising for Austria. At the end of September the British,
concerned about the major military setbacks in Italy, informed
the Austrians that they were opening peace negotiations with
the French.[1] The Austrians needed to change the British equation
and so pinned their hopes on the sending of a new army to relieve
Mantua. The commander in chief selected for the new army was
Baron Joseph Alvintzy von Berbereck. The imperial appointment
took place on 24 September. Alvintzy was born in 1735 and was
therefore only ten years younger than his predecessor. He had taken
command of a division in 1790 and four years later was appointed
Feldzeugmeister, or chief of ordnance. In 1795 he was assigned to
the upper Army of the Rhine and soon thereafter was appointed a
member of the upper war council. The emperor intended to organize an army to strike again to relieve Wurmser's army at Mantua.
Major Franz von Weyrother was responsible for the plan, which
would employ two corps: the Tyrol corps under Baron Davidovich
(18,500 men) and the larger Friuli corps under Baron Quosdanovich
(28,700 men). In the Friuli corps, Quosdanovich would take the
right wing across the Piave and the Brenta while General Giovanni
Marchese di Provera marched with three brigades on the left wing.[2]
Davidovich was to march down the Adige and reconquer Trento
and Rovereto and then seek to reunite with Quosdanovich's Friuli

corps. Alvintzy wanted the two corps to unite in the vicinity of Bassano and Vicenza so that he could march on Verona to confront Bonaparte. After the two armies united and defeated Bonaparte at Verona, they were to sweep the French across the Mincio River and march southward to relieve Mantua. To assist in the relief, Alvintzy expected Wurmser to break out of Mantua and support the attack. Alvintzy's plan to relieve Mantua was simple in concept yet difficult to carry out with a newly established army since he was operating along two separate lines of communication. The plan looked feasible to the Austrians, because they outnumbered the French, and they were confident that it would succeed.[3]

Bonaparte had a plan of his own. From Verona in late October, he wrote to Carnot that the enemy was beginning to move. The desperate situation in Mantua required the Austrians to move quickly to try to relieve the fortress. Mantua was in its last gasps, and indeed its occupants were at the point of starvation. He went on to state that he intended to blockade Mantua until 15 December, then defeat the Austrian army, and bring up his siege artillery to besiege Mantua. He calculated that Mantua would be in French hands before the end of January. There was every reason to believe that if the Austrians did not succeed, Mantua would not be able to withstand the blockade for a month.[4]

On 1 and 2 November Alvintzy crossed the Piave, and Masséna, losing a secure footing in his advanced position, withdrew back to Bassano. On Bonaparte's orders, Masséna moved through Padua to Vicenza.[5] On 3 November Davidovich advanced his left in order to cut off Vaubois from the Brenta valley and sent his right wing along the west bank of the Adige while Alvintzy advanced in two columns to Bassano and Cittadella (see map 1).[6]

While Alvintzy and Bonaparte maneuvered their main armies, Kilmaine continued his tight siege of Mantua. In response, on the morning of All Saints' Day, the Austrians opened fire with the larger fortress cannon on the newly constructed French positions. The French artillery at Belfiore responded with similar ferocity, prompting the Austrians in the trenches before the Te Palace to concentrate their fire on the Belfiore battery. The heavy firing continued until noon, and a sporadic fire from both sides lasted for the rest of the day.[7]

In early November the lakes were at the point of flooding the city because of the excess water flowing down the Mincio coupled with the damming projects that provided water to the artificial moats. The rapidly rising water started to flow over the Cerese road, which was built up and served as a dike across the Pajolo stream. Consequently, Ruckavina announced on 2 November that he had abandoned the embankment to the left of the Cerese mill. He withdrew the troops and abandoned the two cannon that overlooked the Cerese mill since they could not be transported across the dike, which was being quickly washed away. As the Austrian soldiers left Cerese, cannon on the east side of the fortress and the Citadel fired on French troops and wagon trains moving near the San Giorgio suburb, and the cannon at the Te crownwork and the bastion of San Alessio opened fire on the Belfiore positions once again. Simultaneously, the cannon at the Migliaretto works fired on the French at Pietole and Cerese. The Austrian cannon attack lasted until 5:00 P.M. The next day, the fortress guns continued firing on the French troops, who marched in formation to new positions outside of musket range. The Austrians likewise continued to fire their cannon on the ever approaching French trenches. The fortress guns also provided covering fire for small bands of Austrians that would go out as foraging parties to gather as much wood as they could carry.

Wood was extremely important to the garrison; it was sorely needed for heat but even more so for cooking. Most of the available wood inside the fortress had been burned up, and the authorities had already ordered all trees within the city to be "cut down to the roots" to harvest as much wood as possible.[8] The little bit of flour and meal still available had to be baked, so the wood was precious. Unfortunately for the garrison officials and citizens, the wheat or corn that they did have was difficult to mill because the mills on the upper dam ceased operations in early November once the water level got too high to turn their undershot waterwheels.[9]

Flour was not the only staple that was being consumed at a rapid pace inside the city. Butter, oil, lard, and pig fat were also needed. Beef was only a memory, and wine, eggs, and tallow for candles were scarce and high priced. Because of the consumption rate, the authorities issued a price list for all foodstuffs on 4 November to control inflation and hoarding. Prices were set on everything (and given in several currencies). Snakes and peacocks cost 4 Milanese scudi; a pair of geese was worth a royal Austrian gold piece; twenty eggs could be sold for 60 Mantuan soldi; one hen was worth a Spanish peso, and a pair of chickens cost a French franc.[10]

Within the walls, the soldiers sought escape from their plight. Many of the troops even clamored for a major sortie just to investigate the situation and determine the intentions of the French besieging force. At the same time, the cannonade from the fortress continued daily upon the French trenches and troop concentrations.

During the afternoon of 6 November, Wurmser went out of the Porta Cerese to visit his forward posts at Migliaretto. As he encouraged his soldiers, fully exposed to hostile fire, the Austrian marshal was nearly hit by a French cannonball that landed within a foot of him—*un palmo solo distante dalla sua persona*. Neither Wurmser nor anyone else standing nearby was injured. The fortress guns carried on an intense bombardment of their usual targets, which consisted of the more threatening French positions, batteries, marching troop columns, and equipment train formations. The French guns did not respond with equal vigor; the garrison leadership interpreted the restrained response as evidence the French were conserving their resources to challenge Alvintzy's relief army.[11]

The next day, 7 November, Wurmser received word from Alvintzy that the relief army was on the march. Alvintzy, writing on 29 October, explained his attack plan to the besieged marshal and enclosed, as usual, some intricate cannon signals for when his army was crossing the Adige River.[12] It did not take long for news of the imminent arrival of Alvintzy's force to spread throughout the city. Meanwhile, Austrian artillerymen inside the fortress were immediately ordered to transport many of the large mortars, captured in early August when Sérurier lifted the siege, to the fortress walls in preparation to support the relief army.[13]

The Austrian gunners began a heavy bombardment on the San Giorgio suburb on 8 November precisely at 11:00 A.M., probably to register their newly positioned mortars since Alvintzy's force would approach from that direction. On the following day, the French and Austrian guns fell silent and a pall draped the city. Meanwhile, much to the delight of the citizenry, the lake level dropped to a point that the Mills of the Twelve Apostles were able to start grinding wheat and corn again and thus provide some flour and meal to those who could afford them.

Word of the mills' renewed operations was well received by the Mantuans, but they were even happier on Thursday, 10 November, to hear the rumor that the relief force would arrive in three days. The forecast created a tremendous anticipation, which was felt by civilians and soldiers alike. Amid the celebration on Thursday, the cavalry mustered for inspection and the artillery heightened preparations. The next day hopes were still high as outposts strained to hear the expected cannon signal. That night, at 11:15 P.M., reports were received that the signal had been heard, and the fortress began a massive cannonade in anticipation of the arrival of the relief army. The next morning a terse calm engulfed the city as the realization set in that it had been a false alarm. When Sunday passed without any sign of a relief army, the population was further disappointed.[14]

The false alarm may in fact have been caused by someone actually hearing cannon shots—from the battle at Caldiero. Bonaparte considered Caldiero, located on the east–west road between Vicenza and Verona and between the mountain spurs to the north and the swamps of the Adige valley to the south, to be the best place to hold off Alvintzy's force attacking from the east. But he could not readily occupy the position since he had to contend with Davidovich's column advancing down the Adige. On 11 and 12 November he launched Masséna's and Augereau's divisions to stop Alvintzy's columns advancing on Verona at Caldiero, but the French were greatly outnumbered and were forced to fall back to Verona. To buoy the spirits of his soldiers after the first day's fighting, Bonaparte issued a proclamation informing them of the state of affairs in the besieged fortress:

> Soldiers! Mantua is without bread, without meat, without forage. Wurmser, the remnant of the army which you destroyed at Bassano, San Giorgio, and Governolo, is ready to fall into your hands. The liberty of Italy, the happiness of France, depend on your courage. . . .
> Soldiers! Remember then to be worthy of yourselves. I will only say two words to you, they will be sufficient for Frenchmen: Italy! Mantua! The peace of Europe, the happiness of your families, will be the result of your courage. Let us do once more what we have done so often, and Europe will not contest our right to the title of the bravest and most powerful nation in the world.[15]

On 13 November Bonaparte warned the Directory of the dire straits of his army, telling them he had withdrawn his exhausted, barefoot troops to Verona while General Loudon advanced with a column on Brescia and another Austrian column moved on Chiusa. Both columns were on the move to join the main Austrian army.

Bonaparte only had Masséna's 6,000 men, Augereau's 5,000 and Vaubois's 7,000 to resist the Austrian army, which he estimated to total at least 50,000 soldiers. Bonaparte informed the Directory that his troops were resting, but that on the following day he would respond according to Alvintzy's movements. In the process, Bonaparte made sure the Directory understood that he despaired of being forced to abandon the siege of Mantua, since he calculated he could subdue it in a week's time. He then warned the Directory that if he had to raise the siege again and did not receive any new troops, it would be a disaster for his army, which would be forced to retreat behind the Adda and beyond.[16]

Although the people of Mantua expected a lightning attack from Alvintzy's relief column, the timid Austrian corps and division commanders marched along slowly and cautiously. Davidovich remained inactive on the Upper Adige, while Alvintzy was constrained by secret instructions from the Aulic Council not to attempt anything hazardous, but rather to remain on the defensive in order to facilitate the secret negotiations that were about to begin.[17]

On 14 November the Directory wrote a letter to Emperor Francis informing him that they would like to start peace negotiations under two conditions: (1) that both sides suspend fighting simultaneously, and (2) that plenipotentiaries of the two sides and their allies meet to work out a definite peace.[18] The next day the Directory appointed General of Division Henri Clarke as envoy to Vienna to propose a general armistice between the two powers and to investigate the possibility of a negotiated peace.[19] Alvintzy thus squandered his best opportunities of defeating the French and relieving Mantua by his repeated halts, which he felt compelled to make because of the impending negotiations. Bonaparte knew that his opponent's headquarters was plagued by indecision over such things as upcoming secret negotiations. He complemented Alvintzy's timidity by privately dispatching intelligence to him from Verona of Clarke's upcoming mission, of the meetings that opened at Paris and in Great Britain, and of the possible success of those conferences. By delaying his movements in order not to upset the negotiations, Alvintzy lost the advantage of his initial success by not moving rapidly to join forces with Davidovich.[20]

On 14 November Bonaparte ordered Kilmaine to keep Wurmser in Mantua and send 3,000 troops to Verona. At 10:00 P.M. the French started a bombardment of the fortress from Belfiore to distract the garrison while Kilmaine moved his men. The shelling was the worst the city had received since the July bombardment under Sérurier. Several buildings caught on fire, and many people, fleeing their burning homes, ran to the Basilica of Saint Andrew for protection. Kilmaine and his 3,000 troops, as ordered, arrived at Verona and successfully covered Bonaparte's preparations to strike at Alvintzy's line of communication near Arcole.[21]

On 16 and 17 November Wurmser's observers with their telescope could see columns of smoke from near the marshes formed by the confluence of the Adige and Alpone Rivers, where Bonaparte was locked in battle with Alvintzy's forces. While Vaubois's troops prevented Davidovich from reinforcing Alvintzy, Bonaparte gathered all of his available forces and crossed the Adige at Ronco, south of the Austrian main body, in order to turn Alvintzy's left flank. While Masséna fought off Provera at Porcile, Augereau tried to take the town of Arcole. After three days of constant French assaults at Arcole, Alvintzy decided to leave the field to the victorious French just as Davidovich finally routed Vaubois to the north. But it was too late for Davidovich to come to the aid of Alvintzy and thus Bonaparte dispatched his cavalry toward Vicenza to pursue the retreating Austrians, then moved to Verona to meet Kilmaine's 3,000 troops; they marched together to support Vaubois, who had been forced out of Rivoli by Davidovich. Davidovich's occupation of Rivoli was a major concern to the French. Bonaparte described Rivoli as "a very important position since it covered the blockade of Mantua."[22] The close run battle at Arcole is one of Bonaparte's more famous victories.

Davidovich began a promising campaign but did not follow up on his initial successes. Had he pressed the French, Bonaparte would have been compelled to cross the Adige and raise the siege of Mantua.[23] On 18 November the citizens of the besieged fortress could hear cannon fire in the direction of Legnago as they continued to await the relief army. It was not the signal they had been waiting for since the 13th, however, and was most likely cannon fire from Bonaparte's pursuit of Davidovich.[24] During those few days, even after the appointed day passed, anxiety was high as they listened with great impatience for the signal from the relief army crossing the Adige. In the evenings Colonel Zach, Colonel Klenau, Major Count Radetzky, and Colonel Thomas Graham would spend several hours at the edge of the Lower Lake anticipating the signal.[25]

The garrison and people of Mantua were not the only ones anxiously waiting for the siege to end. Bonaparte was also eager to conclude the siege, as he reestablished his positions around Rivoli. Although the Austrians may have felt confident in the arrangements they had made for the continued defense of the city, Bonaparte was convinced of its imminent surrender. On 19 November, from Verona, he wrote to Josephine as if to say that once he captured Mantua he would finally be able to rest. "In a week," he told her, "Mantua will be ours, and then your husband will clasp you in his arms, and give you a thousand proofs of his ardent affection."[26] The same day he wrote to the Directory to give the highlights of his victory at Arcole. He explained that he rallied and reinforced Vaubois's division before sending it to Castelnuovo, 8,000 strong, while Augereau took his position at Verona and Masséna marched to Villanuova. He proposed to attack Davidovich, chase him into the Tyrol, and then undertake the reduction of Mantua, which would not cost him more than fifteen days.[27] Later that day, encouraged by the tactical developments, Bonaparte wrote to Carnot exclaiming: "The face of affairs in Italy begins to assume smiles. We promise another victory tomorrow, and I hope, before ten days have passed, to write to you from our headquarters in Mantua."[28] The news resonated with the officials in Paris, and the letter was published, like many others from Bonaparte, on the front page of Le Moniteur Universel.[29]

On 21 November Davidovich, learning that Masséna was moving to attack him, and that Augereau was marching toward his line of communication, decided to withdraw as quickly as possible. The next day he sent word to Alvintzy, who had reoccupied Caldiero and Arcole, about his decision to withdraw. He felt his soldiers were in no condition to continue the campaign. On 23 November Alvintzy decided to withdraw as well since he did not dare face Bonaparte's force alone.[30]

The same day that Alvintzy ordered his troops to withdraw, Wurmser made a sortie, on the (mistaken) assumption the relieving armies were nearby. The massive sortie of four columns consisted of 7,917 men, including 2,005 cavalry. The first column of 2,259 men, commanded by General Minkwitz, quietly exited the Porta Maggiore of the Citadel at 2:00 A.M. and moved toward La Favorita concealed by a dense fog. For the early morning assault, 1,700 infantrymen led the way. They launched a furious attack, followed by 568 cavalrymen. From the windows of the Ducal Palace inside the city, one could see the French troops level their muskets and blast these five squadrons of Hungarian cavalrymen. Minkwitz still managed to take Montata, but his reserve placed at San Antonio reported enemy in their flank. He then sent a detachment from Montata to San Antonio to keep watch, and if need be, counter any French retaliation.[31] The second column, commanded by General Spiegel, was about equal in size and composition to the first. His column followed Minkwitz out of the Porta Maggiore and moved toward San Antonio. He took the town and then continued on to capture Mantovana and Drasso. He then looked for a way to reach La Favorita, but the French had the path cut off. General Ott led the third column of 2,200 men toward Maldinaro, turned west, and took San Girolamo and Bettola. The fourth column was led by General Heister, who took his 1,200 infantrymen over the wet moat on the west side of the Citadel using footbridges placed there by the engineers. Attacking under the cover of the Citadel's guns, Heister's men quickly took the French positions and then proceeded to capture San Giovanni Bono, Cammino, and Prada di Sopra.[32]

When the sortie began, Canto d'Yrles made a feint against San Giorgio to draw the French away from the main attacking force leaving the Citadel. Reserves were left in the Citadel to reinforce any success the Austrians achieved, while limited sorties departed out of the Pradella gate toward Belfiore and from the Migliaretto works toward Cerese and Pietole. These smaller sorties, designed to keep the French from concentrating their forces on the Citadel, were quickly beaten back, but the larger sorties departing the Citadel to the north gained an advantage. Each of the major columns was supplied with thirty ladders to scale the French breastworks. Initially successful, they captured a French cannon and three ammunition wagons and took prisoner sixteen officers and 197 soldiers. The Austrians, however, were spread out after these successes, which could only spell disaster if the French counterattacked.[33]

Just when Wurmser's sortie had succeeded, Kilmaine, returning from Verona with his forces, drove an assault against the center of Spiegel's second column. The French pushed Spiegel back to San Antonio, where Ott provided a small reinforcement of three hundred men. But the French continued to push forward, forcing Spiegel and then Ott back to the glacis of the Citadel. Ott made an attack toward Bettola, thinking he would be supported by Spiegel's men, but Spiegel's column had retreated, forfeiting any opportunity to assist and the attack failed. Minkwitz's first column could not help either Ott or Spiegel since it turned south to attack San Giorgio. Heister's fourth column was too far west to support Ott and was busy the whole day fighting engagements at two separate locations. The advantages won by the Austrians were quickly lost because of a failure to mass forces and concentrate on a single objective.[34]

Although the Austrians still occupied many small villages, Wurmser's hopes for a victorious breakout to unite with Alvintzy and Davidovich diminished when he learned from the French prisoners that the Austrian relief army had been defeated. Hoping against hope, he decided to hold his position that evening and again listen for the cannon signal that announced Alvintzy's crossing of the Adige. When no signal was heard, he ordered his men back into the fortress; the columns returned under the cover of darkness, having lost that day two cannon and 789 casualties. Of 789 losses, about 200 were taken prisoner by the French. The French then returned and reoccupied their entrenchments.[35]

During the foraging expeditions earlier in the month and the temporary breakout on 23 November, Wurmser's troops were able to bring in some wood, hay, and provisions, but any gains in food provisions were diminished by the arrival of many peasants entering the fortress when the four columns temporarily occupied their villages.[36] During a chilling violent rain on 25 November, Wurmser wrote to Alvintzy giving the details of the failed sortie and explaining the grave situation inside the fortress.[37]

Bonaparte, elated with his successes against Davidovich, wrote from Verona on the 24th telling of the great victories of Vaubois, Masséna, and Augereau. He ended his letter to the Paris officials by applauding Kilmaine and his efforts. Bonaparte explained:

> Wurmser attempted a sortie from Mantua. A cannonading was kept up the whole day. General Kilmaine made him retire again much faster than he came out. He also took a hundred Austrian prisoners, and captured two cannon and a howitzer. Wurmser headed the sortie in person. General Kilmaine writes that this is the third time Wurmser has tried his success at sorties, and invariably failed. Wurmser conquers only in the journals which the enemies of the Republic fabricate in Paris.[38]

Having followed up his victory by positioning troops at Vicenza, Bassano, and Padua, Bonaparte reestablished the blockade

at Mantua. At the same time he met with General Clarke to discuss the envoy's peace-seeking mission, in particular how Clarke
was to handle the issue of Mantua in the negotiations for an armistice that was supposed to last until June 1797.[39] They had a lengthy
meeting in Milan at Bonaparte's headquarters on 30 November.[40]
Clarke first proposed to Bonaparte a cease-fire of three months,
but Bonaparte vehemently objected to an armistice until Mantua
surrendered, considering its capture of paramount importance to
holding Italy. Clarke, however, continued to argue for a truce and
presented his letter from the Directory.[41] The Directory had hopes of
obtaining an armistice in which France would retain Huningen and
Kehl, both of which Archduke Charles was besieging, and Austria
would preserve Mantua. The sieges of Huningen and Kehl were to
be raised and Mantua was to be placed in status quo. Austrian and
French commissioners were to be allowed to send provisions daily
into Mantua for the troops and inhabitants. Bonaparte argued to
Clarke that the fortresses of Huningen and Kehl were less important than Mantua, that it would be impossible to prove the number
of inhabitants and troops in the city, and that by reducing them to
half rations, Wurmser could accumulate provisions for six months.[42]
Later, Bonaparte wrote to the Directory as well explaining why an
armistice should not be conducted without first capturing Mantua:

> Masters of Mantua, the enemy will be too happy to leave us the
> position on the Rhine. But if an armistice is concluded, we must
> abandon that fortress [Mantua] until May, and then find it com-
> pletely provisioned, so that its fall cannot be accomplished before
> the unhealthy months of fall. We will lose the money we expect
> from Rome, which cannot be influenced but by the fall of Mantua:
> and the Emperor, being closer to the scene of action, will recruit his
> army much more effectively than we can, and in the opening of the
> campaign we shall be inferior to the enemy. Fifteen days' repose is
> of essential service to the army of Italy; three months would ruin
> it. To conclude an armistice at this time is to cut ourselves off
> from all chance of success—in a word, everything depends on the
> fall of Mantua.[43]

The Directors understood Bonaparte's position, and they clearly
endorsed it.[44] In a letter to Clarke signed by Carnot, Reubell, and
Révellière-Lépeaux, they informed him that an armistice without the possession of Mantua would be disastrous.[45] However,

before the Directory's letter arrived, Clarke had already written to Emperor Francis II and met with the emperor's aide-de-camp Baron Karl Vincent on 3 January at Vicenza, where they had two conferences. Vincent informed Clarke that the emperor could not receive in Vienna a plenipotentiary from the French Republic, which he did not recognize; that he would not act separate from his allies; and finally, that if he had any communication to make, he should apply to the Austrian minister at Turin. Thus, the quest for a cease-fire was effectively crushed by the Austrians themselves.[46]

The French were not alone in their diplomatic maneuvering for control of Mantua. Emperor Francis II informed Alvintzy of Clarke's mission but told him to attend to his own, which was the greatest goal: the deliverance of Mantua, either by force or by armistice negotiations.[47] Clarke had barely reached the Adige, on his way from Vicenza, when Alvintzy moved to relieve Mantua.[48]

Active campaigning slowed down during the last month of 1796, but the soldiers received no reprieve as December marked the beginning of an abnormally cold winter for Mantua. As the soldiers settled in for the winter siege, there was a marked decrease in the fighting during the month, but military planning for operations continued as usual. For the Austrians, this meant that more risks would be taken as spies and messengers attempted to slip correspondence into and out of the fortress so that Alvintzy and Wurmser could coordinate their efforts. For the French, this meant continued surveillance to try to capture these messengers while finding ways to tighten the blockade. Because of the torrential rains, Bonaparte had apprised the Directory in early October that an active siege was impracticable before January.[49] His prediction in October turned out to be more valid than his more recent prediction in November that he would take Mantua in ten days;[50] the mud turned to ice in December, and the lakes started to freeze, but they did not remain frozen long enough for the French to attack over the ice.

During December 1796 three men in particular, who would later become famous, made names for themselves at Mantua: the French general Alexandre Dumas, the Austrian major Count Josef Radetzky, and the English colonel Thomas Graham.[51] General Thomas-Alexandre Davy Dumas, a Creole from Jérémie, Saint Domingue (present-day Haiti), arrived at Mantua from Milan on 18 December to take command of one of the two understrength divisions in Kilmaine's command. Dumas's 1st Division was positioned on the north bank of the Mincio, while General Claude Dallemagne's 2nd Division blockaded the city on the south bank. The day after Dumas reached Mantua, Kilmaine was given leave to recover from a sickness he contracted in the unhealthy environment around Mantua. Dumas, as senior general of division, was given command of the siege operations, temporarily replacing Kilmaine. He was given this assignment before he could even unpack at his division headquarters in Roverbella. Although he knew the position was a temporary one, he would not settle for mediocrity and instead insisted on making improvements to the siege operations.

Indeed, Dumas took this position seriously. Each day he wrote to his two division commanders giving them instructions. To familiarize himself with the situation, Dumas visited all of the besieging force units and inspected the French defensive positions facing the Austrian garrison. He doubled the guard on all roads leading into Mantua, an important precaution that led to an incident that gained him Bonaparte's praise.[52] On the night of 24 December, three men who were trying to get through the French lines to the fortress were stopped by Dumas's sentries. The new blockade commander had them brought to his headquarters where he interrogated them. He wrote to Bonaparte: "I paid the most attention to one of them because I believed him to be charged with the most important mission."[53] Convinced he was a spy, Dumas had him strip-searched. When that proved fruitless, he accused the man of having swallowed the dispatch. Dumas summoned a pharmacist to obtain an emetic, which the man was forced to drink. After several hours of vomiting, a small ball coated with wax was produced. It contained a message from Alvintzy to Wurmser. Alvintzy, who had received instructions from Francis II, consolidated the plan and was passing it on to Wurmser with his refinements.[54] Dumas made a copy of the letter and forwarded the original to Bonaparte.[55]

According to Baron Paul Charles Thiébault, Dumas had summoned the camp butchers with their blood-stained hands, aprons, and cleavers and had them strip the man and tie him by the feet and hands to a table. In a terrible voice he gave the order to cut him open if he did not immediately say where the dispatch was that had been given to him. The man, fearing for his life, admitted that he had swallowed the dispatch.[56] Bonaparte forwarded the dispatch to the Directory and told them that it was an Austrian cadet, sent from Trent by Alvintzy, who had swallowed the dispatch and that after a great deal of coercion, he confessed that he had the dispatches. Bonaparte told the Directors that the Austrian threw up for twenty-four hours before the capsule was retrieved and that if this method was unknown to them, he was including the details so other French generals could be informed since the Austrians frequently made use of this method. Bonaparte went on to tell them that the spies would keep the dispatches in their stomach for several days and that if their stomach became upset and they vomited, they would retrieve the capsule, soak it in elixir, and then swallow it again. He also pointed out that the capsule was soaked in Spanish wax, which could be dissolved by vinegar.[57] The wax protected the paper inside the capsule from being digested by the stomach acids. Interestingly enough, the news of this event did not reach London for two months, but when it did, the British journalist's perception of Bonaparte's character was presented to the public. Even though he was not even present at Mantua when the dispatch was captured, the *London Times* article concerning the event stated otherwise:

> Buonaparte is said to have obtained the information of one of the most important plans of the Austrians, during the late attack in Italy, in the following manner—An Austrian officer was taken prisoner in attempting to reach the garrison of Mantua. Upon his being seized he was observed to swallow something; and not giving a satisfactory account of what he had swallowed, Buonaparte commanded him to be put to death immediately. This command was obeyed; the body of the officer was opened, and out of the stomach was taken a ball of wax, inclosing written orders to General Wurmser.[58]

Francis II's message instructed Wurmser to hold out as long as possible. If necessary, he was to destroy everything that could be of use to the enemy and break out of Mantua toward the south. Then he was to cross the Po and retire to Ferrara or Bologna or, if necessary, move toward Rome or Tuscany. Alvintzy had added that he could not move toward Mantua for three to four weeks, and he told Wurmser to update him on the situation in the besieged city. He added a postscript stating: "In all probability, the movement that I will make will be around 13 or 14 January. I will advance with thirty thousand men through the plains of Rivoli, and I will send Provera with ten thousand men along the Adige to Legnago with a considerable convoy [of supplies]. When you hear the cannon, make a sortie to facilitate his movement."[59] The information provided in the intercepted dispatch was very helpful to Bonaparte in formulating his plan to battle Alvintzy. Knowing when Alvintzy would attack, Bonaparte made his plan accordingly. He was very pleased with the Creole general's work and sent him a letter stating, "It is impossible to have received more essential information. . . . I am happy with your success and your good omen."[60]

General Sérurier, the first commander of the siege, returned, with his health restored, to resume his position as siege commander on 29 December 1796. Dumas briefed Sérurier on all his military operations concerning the siege and then returned to his division command on the north bank of the Mincio, where he set up his new headquarters at San Antonio. He would continue to command this division, which played a major role when the Austrians made their final attempt to relieve Mantua.[61]

Although Dumas had been outside the fortress while Colonel Thomas Graham, commander of the British 90th Foot, and Count Josef Radetzky were inside, their actions intertwined. Dumas's policy of doubling the guard around Mantua in December had a significant impact on a plan Graham and Radetzky made to escape from the fortress "prison." Earlier that year in May, the prime minister of Britain, Lord William Grenville, informed Graham that King George III had appointed him to a special mission to the Austrian army in Italy.[62] On 21 May Graham joined Beaulieu's headquarters at Valeggio, where he befriended Count Josef Radetzky.[63] In June Graham attached himself to Wurmser's army and entered Mantua along with Radetzky when Wurmser's forces were forced into the city in mid-September.

Graham did not feel he was of particular use to his government or the Austrians confined to the fortress of Mantua. Therefore, he decided to try to escape from the city. In December the ditches on the side of Porta Cerese and some parts of the lakes froze over. The Austrian soldiers took pains to break the ice wherever the French might have had the opportunity to attack the weak ramparts over the ice on the south side of the fortress. The hard freeze was followed by a heavy snow that stayed on the ground for several days. It was during the freeze that Graham made his plan to escape from Mantua. He described it as such:

> The marshy edges of the lake were now rendered capable of bearing horses, and in concert with my friend Radetzky, I formed the plan

of making my escape across the lake, between Borgo San Giorgio and the bridge of communication . . . which the enemy had below Pietole. A considerable platform, laid across two large flat-bottomed boats, was prepared, capable of containing 12 or 14 horses. The Marshal [Wurmser] approved of my request, and Colonel Klenau promised to give me an escort of eight or ten of Wurmser's Hussars, under an intelligent officer. Colonel Radetzky was, at my request, appointed to be the bearer of dispatches from the Marshal to the Court of Vienna.[64]

Graham first got the idea to try to get out of Mantua and escape to the Tyrol while accompanying Wurmser and Ott during the sortie on 23 November. As the sortie was pushed back into the Citadel by the French, Graham thought otherwise since he had not made prior preparations for such a journey. His revised plan included two companies of cavalry to clear the way of any enemy pickets on the east side of the Lower Lake so that he and Radetzky could make their escape to Venetian territory. Graham claimed that one of Wurmser's aides-de-camp foiled his plan. The individual allegedly resented the fact that Radetzky was picked to undertake the mission. Two nights before they were to depart, Wurmser told Graham that the attempt would not be necessary since he had learned from a spy that Alvintzy would arrive in a few days to relieve the town. On 18 December the word spread throughout the city, just as it had in the past, that Alvintzy would arrive to free them. This time the date of relief was set at 24 December. Graham, who thought that Wurmser informed the city of this imminent relief for the sole purpose of blocking his attempt to escape, claimed to have "positively ascertained that no spy had entered the town." However, he was too timid to advance his theory, conveniently stating instead: "Of course neither Colonel Radetzky nor I ever betrayed our knowledge of the fraud practiced on the whole garrison to defeat our project."[65] It was a good thing for Graham that he did not "betray" his knowledge as he was sadly mistaken—Alvintzy had a deliberate plan for the relief of Mantua, and messages to that effect did in fact reach Wurmser.[66]

Graham then decided to make his attempt alone, so he went to visit Canto d'Yrles. After conferring with him, he went to Wurmser, who remonstrated with him about the imprudence of the attempt, but he finally relented and signed a letter ordering the pontoon commander to furnish Graham with a boat. Radetzky advised Graham to take a local guide; he did so at the cost of leaving behind

Mr. Russell, the surgeon of Graham's 90th Foot. During a pelting rainstorm at midnight on Christmas Day, Graham and Radetzky embarked on an Austrian gunboat and floated down the Lower Lake where they anchored. A pontoon sergeant floated out on a smaller boat to meet them but also brought the bad news that there was a French guard boat positioned where the Mincio flows out of the lake. They waited there for four hours. Finally the French boat floated out of the way and down the Mincio toward the French engineers' bridge, which connected Pietole to the east bank, Graham and his guide left Radetzky, departing in a smaller boat that belonged to the pontoon sergeant and paddling to Pietole, where they disembarked and hid in the house of the guide's father. Dodging French sentries along the river and in Pietole, they made their way through the half-melted snow. Moving parallel to the main road for fear of running into a French cavalry patrol, they reached Borgoforte at dawn, and for the next day and a half, Graham continued his daring escape down the Po River to the Venetian town of Polesella, coming close to being captured on several occasions.[67]

Succeeding in his self-appointed mission to find Alvintzy's headquarters, Graham later wrote to Lord Grenville:

> My Lord, I had the honor of acquainting your Lordship by my note of the 28th from Brondolo of my having escaped from Mantua, and of my intention to join Gen Alvintzy as soon as possible: having found him at Padua I represented to him in the strongest manner the urgent necessity of resuming his operations for the relief of Mantua as soon as possible. . . . I despatched my guide to Marshal Wurmser with such directions as I trust will enable him to elude the vigilance of the enemy and with the promise of a high reward if he got quickly back to Mantua. I did not hesitate to incur this additional expense, knowing under the present circumstances, of what consequence it may be that the Marshal should be informed of General Alvintzy's intentions and that he had not heard from him in a month.[68]

Although Graham was well intentioned when he sent his guide back to inform Wurmser about Alvintzy's plans, his efforts were not needed since Wurmser had heard from Alvintzy. Graham was still under the impression that it was almost impossible to get a message through the French lines and that Wurmser had made up the story of an imminent relief. But the commanders were in contact—albeit disjointedly when they tried to coordinate signals and attacks. Commonly, the same messages were sent by more than one courier to ensure that the recipient received the correspondence. When Dumas intercepted one of the messages with Alvintzy's plan, and forwarded it to Bonaparte, it spelled disaster for his relief effort. On 30 December Wurmser, responding to a letter from Alvintzy, described his desperate situation. He told Alvintzy that so long as there was a horse, a dog, a cat or a piece of bread in the fortress, he would hold on waiting for the relief force.[69]

In November 1796 General Alvintzy boldly divided his forces in order to march on Verona and then relieve Mantua. Although he met with some initial successes, interference from the authorities in Vienna caused him to delay capitalizing on those successes. Bonaparte, in contrast, consolidated his troops and reduced the number besieging Mantua to the bare minimum; he then moved his forces quickly to the most threatened areas along his line of defense and soundly defeated the Austrians at Arcole. In Mantua, Wurmser continued to wait for Alvintzy to relieve him and in so doing lost an opportunity to attack the French investing forces when they were the weakest. Spies continued to deliver messages into and out of the fortress, but the capture of a spy by Dumas and the dispatch that was obtained allowed Bonaparte to prepare for the next Austrian attempt to relieve Mantua. As a result of Alvintzy's failure to reinforce and resupply the fortress, Mantua remained tightly blockaded. The resources expended on the effort to relieve Mantua achieved little and demonstrated the weakness of the Austrian strategy.

CHAPTER 6

THE FOURTH ATTEMPT TO RELIEVE MANTUA

THE BATTLE OF LA FAVORITA

"The fruit of the battle is 7,000 prisoners, colors, cannons, all the baggage of the army, a regiment of hussars, and a considerable convoy of grain and beef that the enemy intended to bring into Mantua."

BONAPARTE TO DIRECTORY, 17 JANUARY 1796

T he extremely cold month of January 1797 added to the misery of the citizens and garrison of Mantua. At the beginning of the new year, the garrison was down to 18,493 men, of whom only about 9,800 were fit for duty.[1] Food and fuel were in very short supply. By the end of the month, all would be consumed. Wood was so scarce that Commissary General Cocastelli included special reports on wood availability in his daily ration reports to Wurmser. Cocastelli's reports and matrices, supplied to Wurmser on large two-foot-by-three-foot cardstock, tracked the amount of the remaining hardwood as well as freshly cut green wood, in addition to all available foodstuffs for the garrison. Cocastelli also had his local spies bring in information about different locations of wood in the surrounding areas; Wurmser would send out armed forage parties throughout the winter to gather the precious resource.[2] On 8 January Cocastelli drew up a huge matrix and sent it to Wurmser indicating that on 4 January the garrison had 13,607 sacks of flour remaining and that at the current consumption rate of 498 sacks a day, the garrison could only be fed for twenty-three and one-half days. To Wurmser, this meant that he had to be relieved by Alvintzy before the end of 27 January.[3]

Alvintzy knew of Wurmser's desperate situation and planned once again for a rapid relief of Mantua. After his first campaign, Alvintzy concentrated the bulk of his army, about 28,000 men, at Rovereto, leaving Baron Adam Bajalich with 5,000 at Bassano and Provera with 10,000 at Padua. Alvintzy and his chief of staff, Weyrother, drew up a new plan to divide the Rovereto force into six brigade columns. The first column, under Colonel Franz Joseph Lusignan, was to follow the eastern shore of Lake Garda and join the others south of Rivoli; two columns, under Lipthay and Köblos, were to follow the mountain road through La Corona; two, under Generals Joseph Ocksay and Quosdanovich, were to follow the west bank of the Adige; and the sixth column, under Vukassovich, would travel along the east bank of the Adige. The latter brigade was to build a bridge across the river south of Rivoli. Alvintzy's artillery and cavalry were to follow the river roads. To deceive the French, Provera was to move on 7 January and seize Legnago on the 9th. Alvintzy provided Provera with a bridge train so that he could cross the Adige quickly and relieve Mantua, whose garrison was, if necessary, to retire across the Po and join the papal forces. Bajalich's job was also to move on the 7th and to capture Verona on the 12th to prevent its garrison from moving to either flank.[4]

Bonaparte took the opportunity between Alvintzy's two advances to organize and rejuvenate his army. He relieved the inefficient officers, replaced them with competent ones, and promoted those who demonstrated talent, skill and bravery.[5] On Christmas Day Bonaparte ordered a reorganization of the field artillery and siege artillery serving at Mantua. The field artillery of the 1st Division serving at Mantua under Dumas was divided into two artillery divisions—the first of which had four 5-pounder cannon and two 5 1/2-pounder howitzers completely harnessed to be moved rapidly; the second of which had two 5-pounder and four 3-pounder cannon without harnesses to conserve the gear for the field army, which needed it more than did the stationary siege pieces. Dallemagne's 2nd Division serving at Mantua had two 12-pounder cannon, three 4-pounder cannon, and one 5 1/2-pounder howitzer fitted with harnesses and two 5-pounder, three 3-pounder, and one 5 1/2-pounder howitzer employed without harnesses. Bonaparte also stipulated that four 3-pounder cannon at the reserve park at Goito were to be used on the boats on the Mantuan lakes. The heavy siege artillery surrounding Mantua was organized into four divisions and two reserves.[6] To implement changes in the artillery structure, Bonaparte sent Lespinasse to Milan to reorganize and reequip the field and horse artillery for the entire Army of Italy.[7]

Reorganizing the artillery was important for Bonaparte because he wanted to ensure that the heavy guns were concentrated at the siege of Mantua and that his lighter guns were available for his mobile forces. He also used his artillery to implement cannon signals similar to the Austrians, but he modified and adapted this method of command and control much more effectively than his adversary. Bonaparte positioned his cannon at intervals along his front between Porto Legnago and Verona; they were arranged so that warnings could be transmitted from one division to another when the Austrians approached. Additional signals were arranged to indicate whether or not assistance was desired.[8] To promote and expedite clear and concise communication among his divisions, he established a network of courier posts in order to transmit his orders rapidly in all directions.[9]

At the beginning of the campaign, Bonaparte assigned General Barthélemy-Catherine Joubert to command a division of 10,300 men at Rivoli, with outposts guarding all the lines of approach to the town.[10] Masséna with 8,500 men was stationed at Verona, and Augereau with over 8,000 men was to guard the Adige with his forces spread out from Verona to Legnago. Rey's 4,000 men were positioned at Desenzano, Brescia, Peschiera, Lonato, and Saló. In addition to these forces, cavalry brigades were placed in front of Augereau at Legnago, in the rear of Verona, and at Villafranca. A demibrigade of 2,000 infantry under Victor was also at Villafranca. Blockading Mantua, Sérurier had about 10,000 men in two divisions, under Dumas and Dallemagne, to contain Wurmser.[11]

The Austrian force under Provera departed Padua on 7 January and marched toward Este while Bajalich left Bassano. The next day Provera's men engaged the advance guard of Augereau's division commanded by General Mathurin-Léonard Duphot. Augereau's men retired to Legnago on 9 January, and in the north Bajalich continued his march to Verona. Augereau sent word of the attack to Bonaparte, which reached him in Bologna on 10 January.[12] At once he sent Lannes, with his force of 2,000 men that had been assembled to hold Bologna against advancing papal troops, to defend the Adige below Legnago. That same day Provera threw away his advantage by waiting for his wagon trains to join him. Masséna's cavalry attacked Bajalich's outposts in front of Verona, causing the Austrians to fall back to Caldiero. Consequently, Alvintzy's plans began to go awry as the first three brigades, which were to move along Lake Garda and the plateau, initiated their march for Rivoli.

On 11 January Provera ordered a reconnaissance of the Adige at Angiari, where he decided to cross, but he continued to be non-committal to an all-out advance. The next day he ordered a bridge built across the river, but later he retracted the order. Meanwhile, the more confident Bonaparte arrived at Roverbella that morning and began to direct his operations against Alvintzy. First he met Sérurier at the siege headquarters and detailed what the siege troops were to do if Alvintzy advanced on the city.[13] From the reports he received while at Roverbella talking to Sérurier, he thought that Provera commanded the main attacking force. He ordered Masséna, who had just stopped an advance by Bajalich's forces, to be ready to move to Legnago.[14] Bonaparte then went to Verona, where he arrived just in time to witness Masséna's counterattack against Bajalich.[15]

At last Provera made a decision to cross the river and, to his credit, even showed some finesse in accomplishing the task. On 13 January he concentrated his forces near Legnago in a feint, then sent a force several miles down the Adige as if intending to secure a crossing. After dark he moved back upriver to Angiari and sent a small detachment across in boats to drive out the French garrison guarding the town. He then began constructing a pontoon bridge.[16]

While Provera was busy on the Adige, Bonaparte decided that he would concentrate his forces against the Austrian columns moving toward Rivoli. He considered neither Provera or Bajalich to be strong enough to cross the Adige. Familiar with the topography, Bonaparte knew that during this season of the year, only infantry columns with a few small mobile guns could cross the mountains. Because of the dispatch intercepted by Dumas, Bonaparte knew the direction of the Austrian attack, so he concluded that the heavy field guns and the cavalry could only reach Rivoli by the river roads. He decided to use Joubert's division to hold the road between the river and the plateau to prevent the Austrians from securing it. If this were accomplished, he could defeat Alvintzy.[17] To reinforce Joubert, he ordered Masséna at 5:00 P.M. on the 13th to march with the 18th, 32nd, and 75th demibrigades from Verona to Rivoli.[18] He also reinforced Sérurier at Mantua in the event that Provera did cross the Adige. He ordered Rey to leave Valeggio immediately and take two battalions of the 58th demibrigade, the artillery and the cavalry to Roverbella to be placed in reserve, specifically under the command of Sérurier.[19] That night Bonaparte went to Rivoli and reached Joubert by 2:00 A.M.[20]

On 14 January Provera crossed the Adige River and marched toward Sanguinetto. The brigades of Bon and Guieu and a reserve of cavalry from Charles François Joseph Dugua attacked Provera and delayed his movement. The French force of 1,500 men, however, could not do much to stop Provera's 10,000-man force. The French troops were reinforced by a column of Lannes's troops that Augereau, headquartered in Legnago, sent to assist them. The fight continued and the French took three hundred prisoners. Determined to reach Mantua, Provera pushed on through the French force all the way to Cerea.[21]

Alvintzy's attack at Rivoli that same day did not rival the success Provera had in crossing the Adige. Alvintzy delayed his attack until the afternoon since he wanted to concentrate one of his brigades at a position south of Rivoli to control the heights. The delay was all Bonaparte needed. He decided to attack with Joubert's weaker force. Bonaparte took this risk knowing that it would buy him time until Masséna's forces could arrive to reinforce Joubert. Bonaparte concentrated his forces and soundly defeated Alvintzy at Rivoli, and Joubert started the pursuit by nightfall. After Bonaparte received word at 2:00 P.M. that Provera had crossed the Adige, he ordered the tired troops of Masséna's 18th, 32nd, and 75th demibrigades and Victor's two battalions of the 57th demibrigade to make a night march to Villafranca to assist Sérurier. He left the pursuit of Alvintzy to Murat and Joubert.[22]

The night of 14 January, Bonaparte himself arrived in Castelnuovo to inform Sérurier that Provera was marching down the Legnago road to Mantua. He told his siege commander to defend San Giorgio and all the approaches to the Citadel. He also ordered the cavalry units of Charles Emmanuel Leclerc and Dugua to join forces with Masséna and Victor at Roverbella. Bonaparte then recommended to Sérurier to concentrate all of his available forces into San Giorgio for forty-eight hours and to put General Sextius-Alexandre Miollis in charge of the suburb.[23] Miollis quickly occupied San Giorgio and by the next day had 1,200 men positioned and ready for Provera's approach.[24]

While Miollis prepared for an attack the morning of 15 January, Provera continued his night march to relieve Mantua by way of Castellarrio. Augereau reacted by falling upon the rear guard that Provera had left to protect his bridge. The 2,000-man rear guard attempted to join the main body but was cut off and captured along with sixteen artillery pieces. Forty of the prisoners were officers. The French then burned the floating bridges erected by the Austrians across the Adige. Nevertheless, Provera continued to move forward.[25] He sent his advance guard, the Hohenzollern Hussars, to communicate with Wurmser, but this small force was quickly repulsed by the more powerful blockading force. At sunrise on the morning of the 15th, the hussars reached the gate of San Giorgio. Because of their white-cloaked uniforms, the Hohenzollern Hussars were mistaken for the 1st French Hussars and were about to be admitted to the suburb. As they approached closer, an old French sergeant gathering wood near the gate noticed what was happening and told a drummer boy nearby to sound the alarm. The drawbridge was suddenly drawn up before their commander, Prince Friedrich Hohenzollern, advancing at a gallop, could reach the gate.[26] A blast of grapeshot from a nearby cannon ended their attempt to seize the gate. At 7:00 A.M. a strong column of Austrians arrived outside of San Giorgio and sent a message to Miollis that he had five minutes to surrender the place. Miollis refused. An hour later the Austrians launched an attack on San Giorgio that lasted throughout the day. Miollis, supported by the guns from the main castle fortress of San Giorgio on the west bank of the Mincio, continued to repel attacks from Provera's advance guard during the day, giving time for Victor's and Masséna's troops to arrive from Rivoli. Fortunately for the Austrians, Provera was able to send a boat across the lake to inform Wurmser of his approach and to coordinate an attack on the blockading force the next day.[27] The atmosphere inside the city became festive as people rejoiced on hearing the news that Provera had brought grain and cattle with his column to bring inside the fortress. Wurmser ordered the cavalry to attack from the Citadel and join up with Provera's forces. Canto d'Yrles rejected the logic of attempting a sortie due to the strength of the French positions, so Wurmser called off the immediate cavalry attack in favor of a planned attack the following day that would utilize the entire garrison.[28]

During the night of 15–16 January, when Wurmser planned his sortie, Bonaparte marched to San Antonio, where he prepared to attack Provera on the 16th. Bonaparte prepared to repel an attack from Provera at San Giorgio as well as an assault from Wurmser out of the sally ports of Mantua. Bonaparte in fact anticipated exactly what Wurmser would do on the 16th. He sent Dumas to reconnoiter in front of the Citadel. Sérurier, with a column of

1,500 men, began a march at an early hour toward La Favorita while Victor, leading the 57th and 18th demibrigades, was positioned to turn Provera's column.[29]

Determining from the reports of the advance guard that San Giorgio was too strong to attack, Provera decided to attack instead near La Favorita to gain access to the Citadel. He sent a second summons to Miollis to surrender, which again was refused.[30] At about an hour before daybreak on the 16th, he attacked. At the same time, 5:00 A.M., Wurmser made a sortie with 5,000 men under Generals Ott, Spiegel, and Minkwitz toward La Favorita to link up with Provera's troops. The sortie was attacked by the lead elements of Sérurier's column and could not take La Favorita nor link up with Provera. The garrison sortie therefore opted to withdraw to San Antonio. General Ott led the column that attacked Dumas's six hundred men at San Antonio, and briefly he held the few houses there. But Victor, at the head of the 57th demibrigade and the lead element of Masséna's division, pushed Ott back, forcing Wurmser to withdraw to the fortress leaving four hundred Austrians prisoner. Minkwitz was wounded, and the Italian colonel Count Paolo Sola Milanese was killed. Ott's brief possession of San Antonio was the only real Austrian success of the day. Provera, advancing near La Favorita, was attacked on the right by Victor's 57th demibrigade and the 25th Chasseurs, supported by Masséna's 18th demibrigade and Dugua's cavalry. The 57th made a furious attack, carrying the Austrian artillery on one side and turning back a regiment of hussars on the other. When Masséna arrived with the rest of his division, he intensified the attack on Provera's right, near La Favorita, while Miollis, from San Giorgio, attacked Provera's left and Lannes came up on his rear. It was here that the 57th demibrigade earned its sobriquet "the Terrible" for the valorous fighting of its soldiers throughout the day. Wurmser, who had already retired into the fortress, could not support Provera. Augereau and Lannes approached Provera's rear and compelled him to capitulate.[31] Bonaparte reported to the Directory that the fruit of the Battle of La Favorita was 7,000 prisoners, numerous flags and guns, as well as the Austrian army's entire baggage train, a regiment of hussars, and a large convoy of wagons laden with corn and cattle destined for Mantua.[32]

Again an ill-coordinated Austrian attack allowed Bonaparte the precious time he needed to defeat the separate Austrian forces in detail. At 11:30 A.M. in front of the walls of San Giorgio, Provera surrendered to Sérurier twenty cannon, 6,000 infantry, and seven hundred cavalry—almost all volunteers from Vienna. He hoped to get generous terms from the French with his surrender, and his foe obliged him. In total, three generals, five colonels, ten majors, and 211 company-grade officers surrendered.[33] This surrender gave Bonaparte the flexibility to propose a prisoner exchange to get back two of his generals who had been captured earlier by the Austrians. The day after the Battle of La Favorita, he sent a letter to Alvintzy proposing to exchange Major General Count Hohenzollern for General of Brigade Pascal Antoine Fiorella and the Austrian general Johann Rudolph Sporck for Adjutant General François Lanusse.[34]

Although Sérurier and Miollis appeared to work well together to defeat Provera, jealousy over the surrender soon became apparent. Feeling that it was he who should have been given credit for the defeat of Provera, Miollis wrote a lengthy letter to Bonaparte on 29 January explaining that Provera initially surrendered to him verbally and that Sérurier and Victor did not really know what was taking place during the battle. Miollis complained that the other forces did not arrive until after Provera had given up and spoken with him about surrendering.[35] In his report of the battle, Sérurier explained to Bonaparte that Miollis had performed well and that the Austrians did turn to Miollis to capitulate. Sérurier praised Victor for driving the Austrian soldiers back into Miollis's concentration of forces. Sérurier also praised many other individuals by name down to dragoon and infantry lieutenants and two sergeant majors. His letter did not carry the same tone of arrogance as Miollis's.[36] Bonaparte was not impressed with Miollis's letter and did not react immediately. When the fortress finally surrendered, Bonaparte made Sérurier the fortress commander but quickly passed the command on to Miollis in order to give Sérurier another field command. Bonaparte appointed Miollis to command the fortress while his contemporaries went on to win additional laurels in the field. It was, however, a very important fortress, and Miollis at least retained enough of Bonapart's confidence to get that command position eventually.

After his defeat of Provera, Bonaparte rushed to Verona to follow up his series of victories with a pursuit. The remainder of Alvintzy's corps withdrew in opposite directions. One unit retreated toward Trent and the other toward Bassano. General Loudon, with 8,000 men, tried to hold Rovereto, but Joubert pushed him back to the city of Trent, taking 500 prisoners. Masséna, with a rapid march over the mountains to Primolano, turned the enemy position at Bassano, taking another thousand prisoners and driving the Austrians through the Treviso Pass to the east bank of the Tagliamento River. Provera's surrender ended Alvintzy's second, and the Austrians' fourth and final, attempt to relieve the besieged fortress of Mantua.[37]

With the capitulation of Provera's troops, Bonaparte was confident of the imminent surrender of Mantua. Knowing that Wurmser was desperate but still capable of launching sorties, Bonaparte informed Beaumont on 17 January that his three regiments of cavalry would remain at Mantua ready to respond to any sorties Wurmser might attempt.[38] The same day he ordered General Louis Chabot to Marmirolo to take command of the 1st Division, which Dumas commanded, and sent Dumas to Masséna's division.[39] He later posted more troops in towns near Mantua and gave operational control of them to Sérurier. On 20 January he ordered the 3rd Battalion of the 64th demibrigade from Bergamo to Goito, just north of Mantua. Sérurier already had the other two battalions of the 64th with him at Mantua. Bonaparte also sent the 1st battalion of the 13th demibrigade from Milan to Goito to await orders from Sérurier.[40] Bonaparte did not, however, concentrate forces at Mantua. He simply maintained the presence of forces there while he rotated out some units to other assignments. On 22 January he ordered Sérurier to send one of the two battalions of the 45th demibrigade to Tortona and the other battalion to follow whenever the 1st Battalion of the 13th reached Goito.[41] On 27 January he ordered Sérurier to send a battalion at Mantua to Tortona in two days.[42] In addition to reassigning forces, Bonaparte also pushed out his courier posts using various cavalry units, including those at Mantua under Beaumont.[43]

The Austrians' plan and Alvintzy's execution of the campaign to relieve Mantua were seriously flawed because of the way his forces were dispersed over the countryside. Alvintzy tried to compensate for the dispersion by reuniting his army south of Monte Baldo. But he did not stick to his plan, thereby giving Bonaparte time to react. Bonaparte and his generals were quick to capitalize on Alvintzy's mistakes. Armed with valuable intelligence obtained by Dumas at Mantua and led by aggressive generals like Masséna and Joubert, the French army defeated Alvintzy at Rivoli, leaving Provera unsupported in his attack on the French forces besieging Mantua.

Although Wurmser attempted a major sortie to join forces with Provera, he waited an entire day to coordinate the attack, which enabled Bonaparte to move his forces from Rivoli to Mantua to support Sérurier. The much needed grain provisions and cattle that Provera was bringing for the Austrian garrison therefore fell into French hands. It was now just a matter of time before the Austrians would consume the remaining provisions and be forced to capitulate.

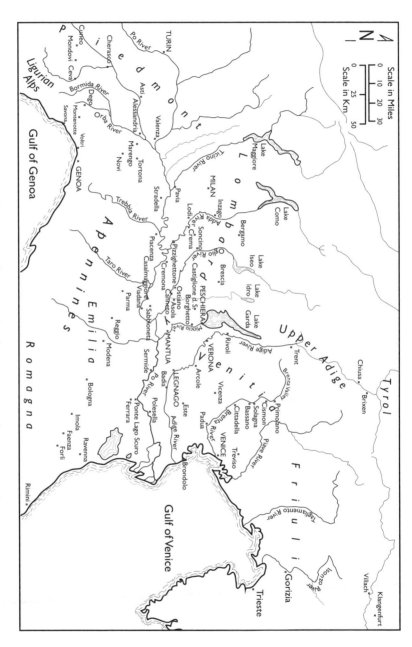

Map 1. The Lombard Plain was the center of activity for the 1796–97 and 1799 campaigns.

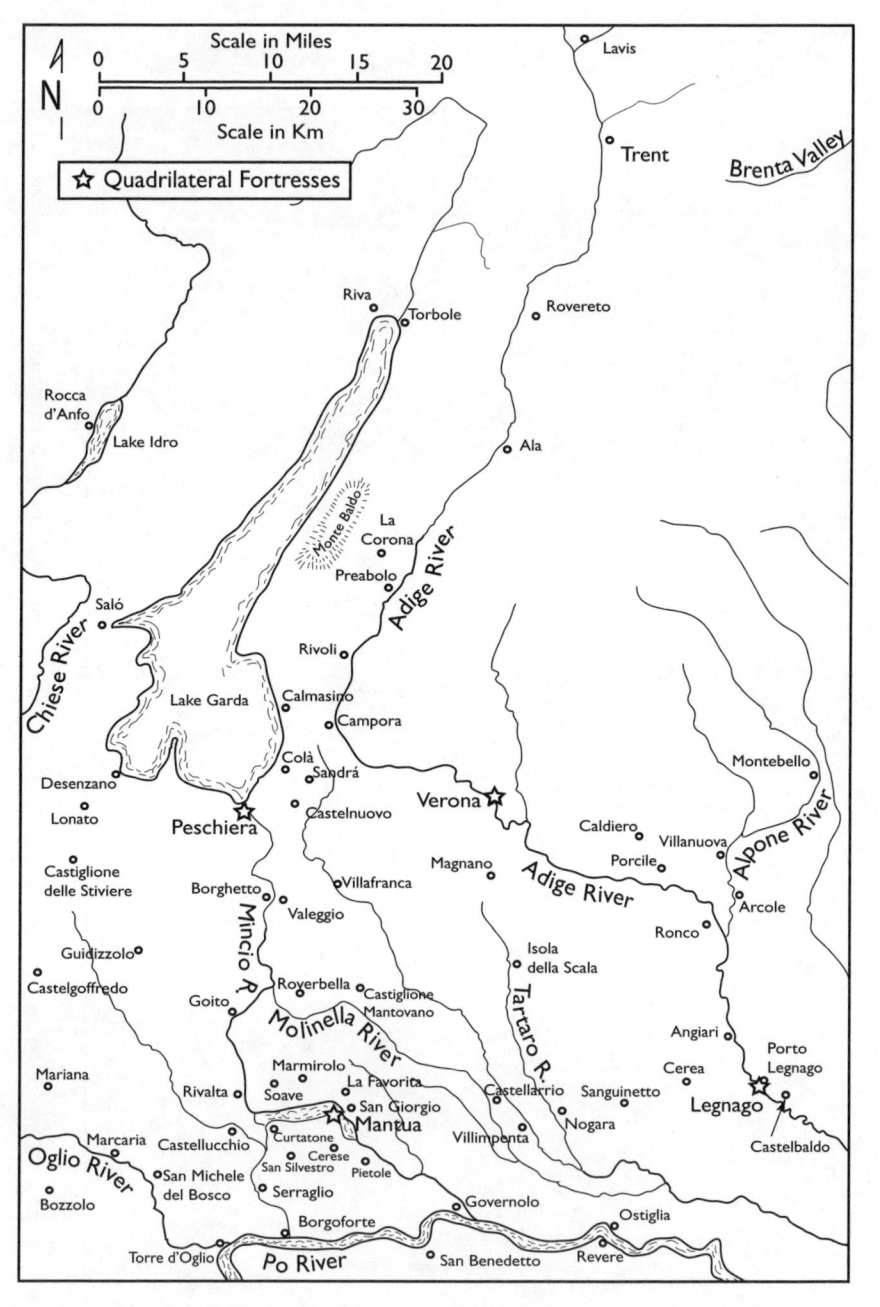

Map 2. The Quadrilateral is formed by the four fortress cities of Mantua, Peschiera, Verona, and Legnago.

601

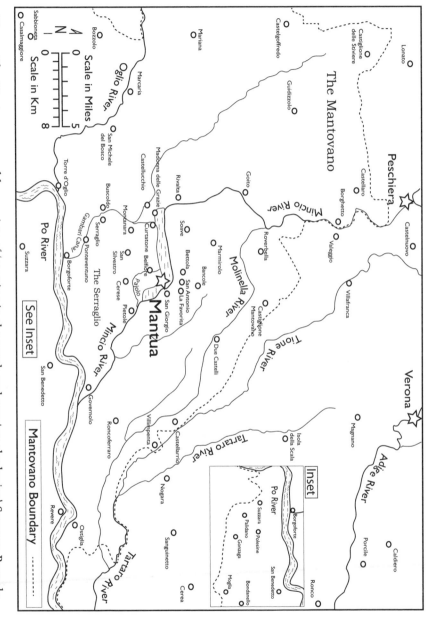

Map 3. The Mantovano roughly consists of (starting in the south and moving clockwise) Suzzara, Bozzolo, Castiglione delle Stiviere, Castellaro, Castiglione Mantovano, Castellarrio, and Ostiglia, with the land extending farther east and south of Ostiglia.

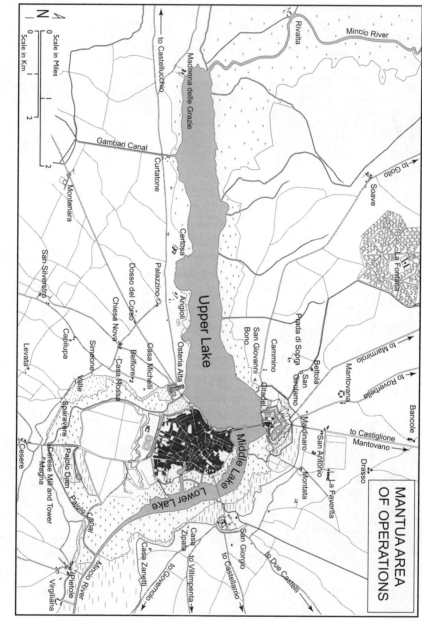

Map 4. Mantua area of operations.

N

Scale in Miles
0   2

Scale in Km
0   2

MANTUA AREA
OF OPERATIONS

Upper Lake

Middle Lake

Lower Lake

Mincio River

to Castellucchio

Madonna delle Grazie

Gambari Canal

Curtatone

Certosa

Palazzino

Angioli

Osteria Alta

Dosso del Corso

San Silvestro

Chiesa Nova

Casa Micheli

Belfiore

Casa Rossa

Capilupa

Levata

Simeone

Valle

Sparavera

Cesere

Cerese Mill and Tower

Magna

Pajolo Dam

Pajolo Canal

Mincio River

Casa Zanetti

Pietole

Virgiliana

Montanara

Citadel

San Giovanni
Bono

Cammino

Prada di Sopra

San
Girolamo

Bettola

Mantovana

to Marmirolo

to Roverbella

Bancole

to Castiglione
Mantovano

San Antonio

Maldinaro

Montata

La Favorita

Drasso

to Castellaro

to Due Castelli

San Giorgio

Casa
Zipata

to Villimpenta

to Governolo

La Fontana

Soave

to Goito

Mincio River

Rivalta

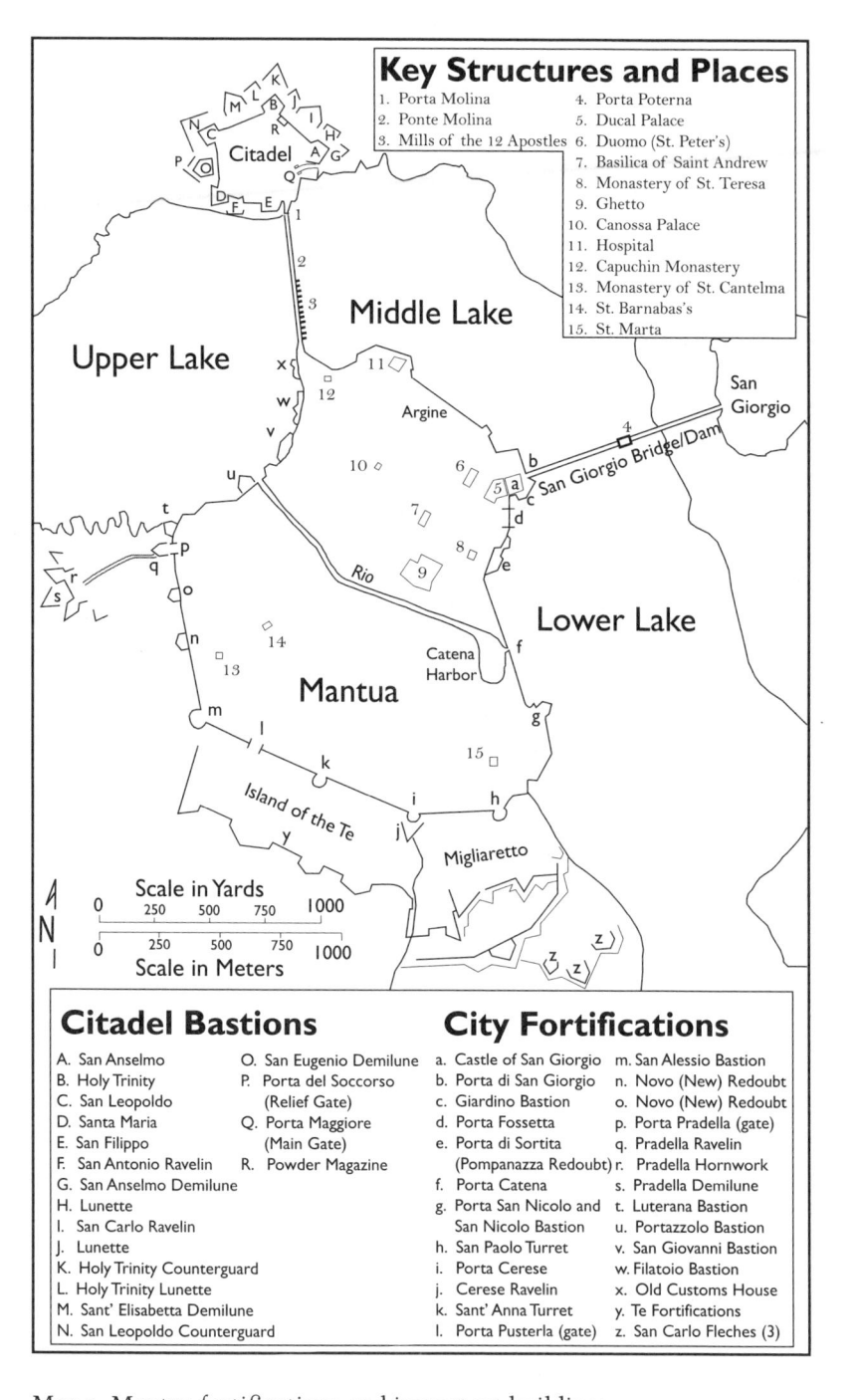

Key Structures and Places

1. Porta Molina
2. Ponte Molina
3. Mills of the 12 Apostles
4. Porta Poterna
5. Ducal Palace
6. Duomo (St. Peter's)
7. Basilica of Saint Andrew
8. Monastery of St. Teresa
9. Ghetto
10. Canossa Palace
11. Hospital
12. Capuchin Monastery
13. Monastery of St. Cantelma
14. St. Barnabas's
15. St. Marta

Citadel

Upper Lake

Middle Lake

San Giorgio

Argine

San Giorgio Bridge/Dam

Lower Lake

Rio

Mantua

Catena Harbor

Island of the Te

Migliaretto

Scale in Yards
0   250   500   750   1000

Scale in Meters
0   250   500   750   1000

N

Citadel Bastions

A. San Anselmo
B. Holy Trinity
C. San Leopoldo
D. Santa Maria
E. San Filippo
F. San Antonio Ravelin
G. San Anselmo Demilune
H. Lunette
I. San Carlo Ravelin
J. Lunette
K. Holy Trinity Counterguard
L. Holy Trinity Lunette
M. Sant' Elisabetta Demilune
N. San Leopoldo Counterguard
O. San Eugenio Demilune
P. Porta del Soccorso (Relief Gate)
Q. Porta Maggiore (Main Gate)
R. Powder Magazine

City Fortifications

a. Castle of San Giorgio
b. Porta di San Giorgio
c. Giardino Bastion
d. Porta Fossetta
e. Porta di Sortita (Pompanazza Redoubt)
f. Porta Catena
g. Porta San Nicolo and San Nicolo Bastion
h. San Paolo Turret
i. Porta Cerese
j. Cerese Ravelin
k. Sant' Anna Turret
l. Porta Pusterla (gate)
m. San Alessio Bastion
n. Novo (New) Redoubt
o. Novo (New) Redoubt
p. Porta Pradella (gate)
q. Pradella Ravelin
r. Pradella Hornwork
s. Pradella Demilune
t. Luterana Bastion
u. Portazzolo Bastion
v. San Giovanni Bastion
w. Filatoio Bastion
x. Old Customs House
y. Te Fortifications
z. San Carlo Fleches (3)

Map 5. Mantua fortifications and important buildings.

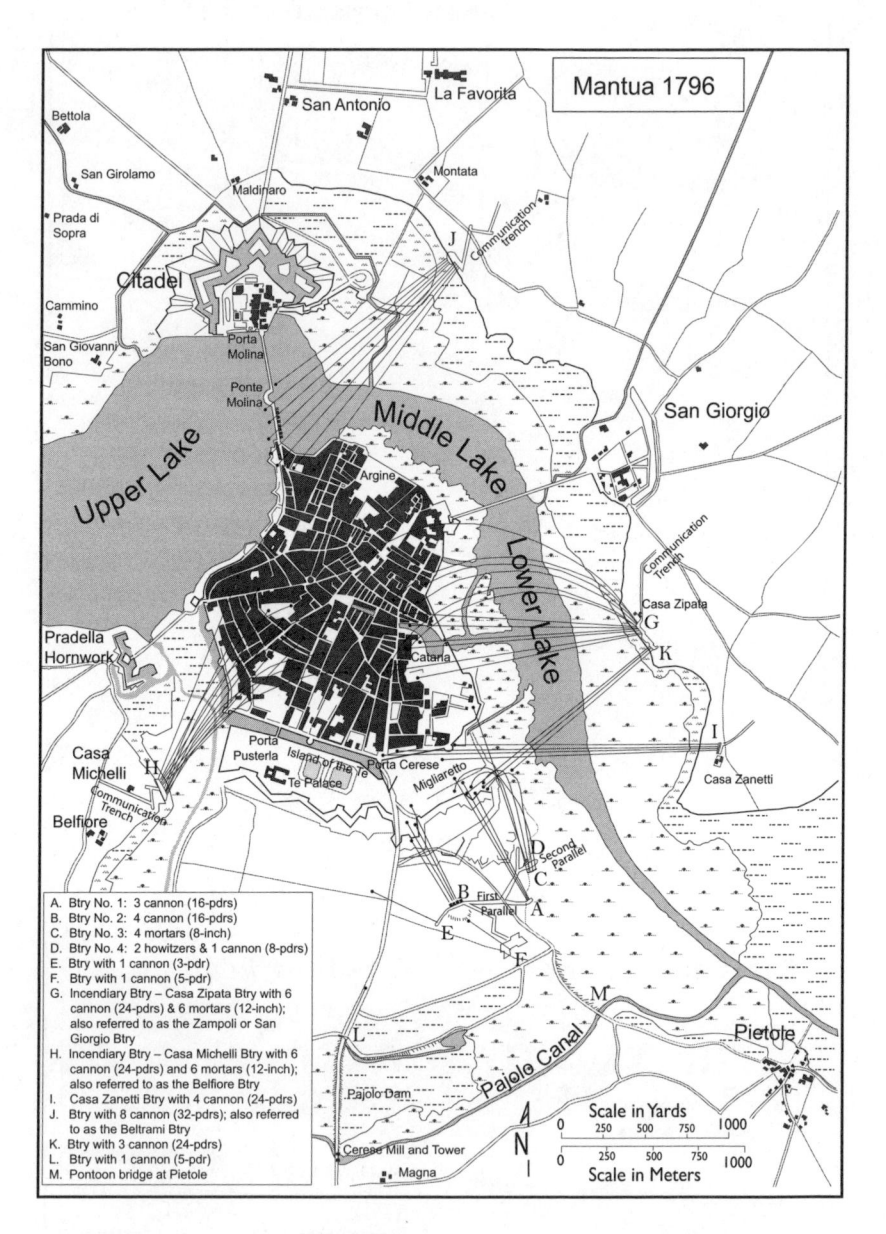

Map 6. This map shows the placement of French batteries before the siege was lifted at the end of July 1796.

The following labels appear on the map:

Mantua 1796

Bettola
San Antonio
La Favorita
San Girolamo
Montata
Maldinaro
Prada di Sopra
Communication trench
J
Citadel
Cammino
Porta Molina
San Giovanni Bono
Ponte Molina
Middle Lake
San Giorgio
Argine
Upper Lake
Lower Lake
Communication Trench
Casa Zipata
G
K
Pradella Hornwork
Catara
Casa Michelli
H
Porta Pusterla
Island of the Te
Porta Cerese
I
Te Palace
Migliaretto
Casa Zanetti
Belfiore
Communication Trench
Second Parallel
D
C
B First
Parallel
A
E
F
M
L
Pietole
Pajolo Canal
Pajolo Dam
Scale in Yards
0   250   500   750   1000
Cerese Mill and Tower
Magna
N
Scale in Meters
0   250   500   750   1000

A. Btry No. 1: 3 cannon (16-pdrs)
B. Btry No. 2: 4 cannon (16-pdrs)
C. Btry No. 3: 4 mortars (8-inch)
D. Btry No. 4: 2 howitzers & 1 cannon (8-pdrs)
E. Btry with 1 cannon (3-pdr)
F. Btry with 1 cannon (5-pdr)
G. Incendiary Btry – Casa Zipata Btry with 6 cannon (24-pdrs) & 6 mortars (12-inch); also referred to as the Zampoli or San Giorgio Btry
H. Incendiary Btry – Casa Michelli Btry with 6 cannon (24-pdrs) and 6 mortars (12-inch); also referred to as the Belfiore Btry
I. Casa Zanetti Btry with 4 cannon (24-pdrs)
J. Btry with 8 cannon (32-pdrs); also referred to as the Beltrami Btry
K. Btry with 3 cannon (24-pdrs)
L. Btry with 1 cannon (5-pdr)
M. Pontoon bridge at Pietole

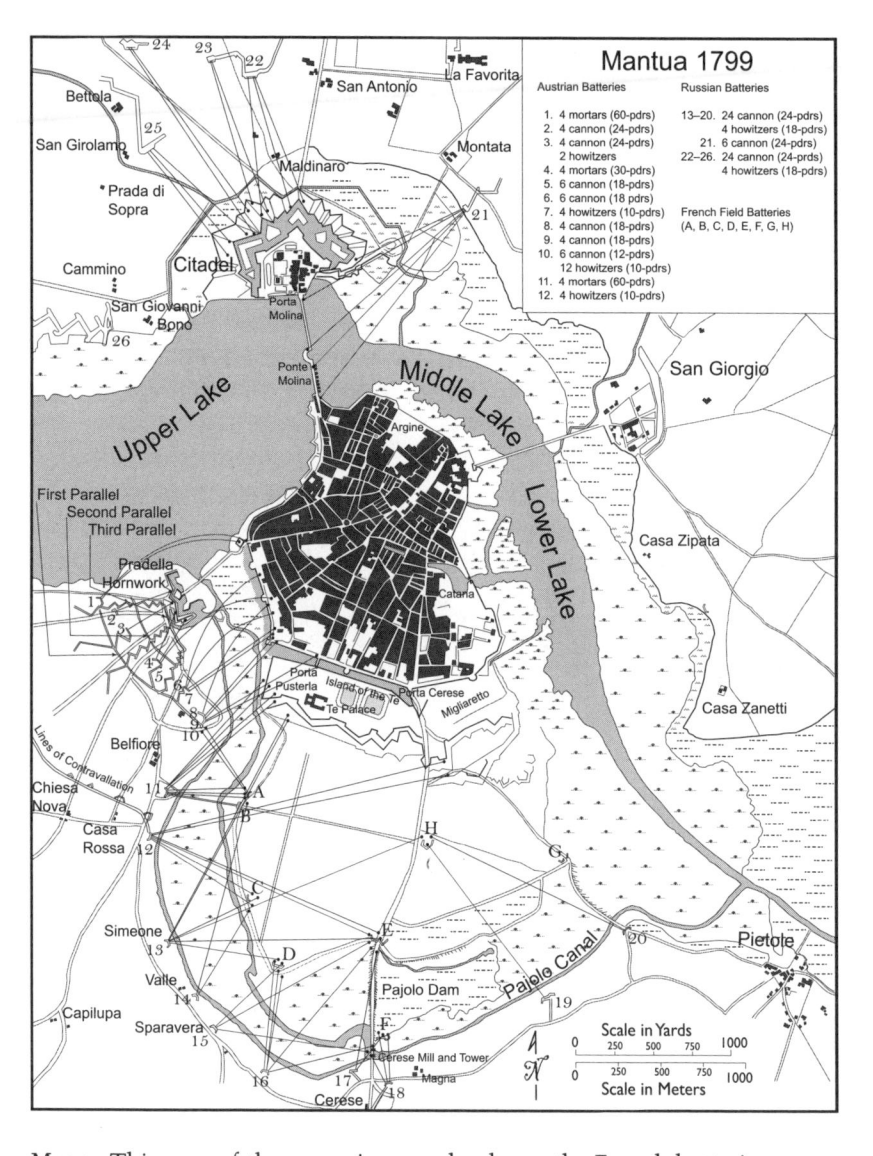

Map 7. This map of the 1799 siege works shows the French batteries as presented by Foissac-Latour. A contemporary Italian map indicates that the French did not have batteries at B, C, and H.

Figure 1. *Bataille de St. George, Près Mantoue* (Battle of San Giorgio, near Mantua), 15 September 1796, by Carlo Vernet.

Figure 2. *Fête de Virgile, à Mantoue* (Festival of Virgil, at Mantua),
15 October 1798, by Carlo Vernet.

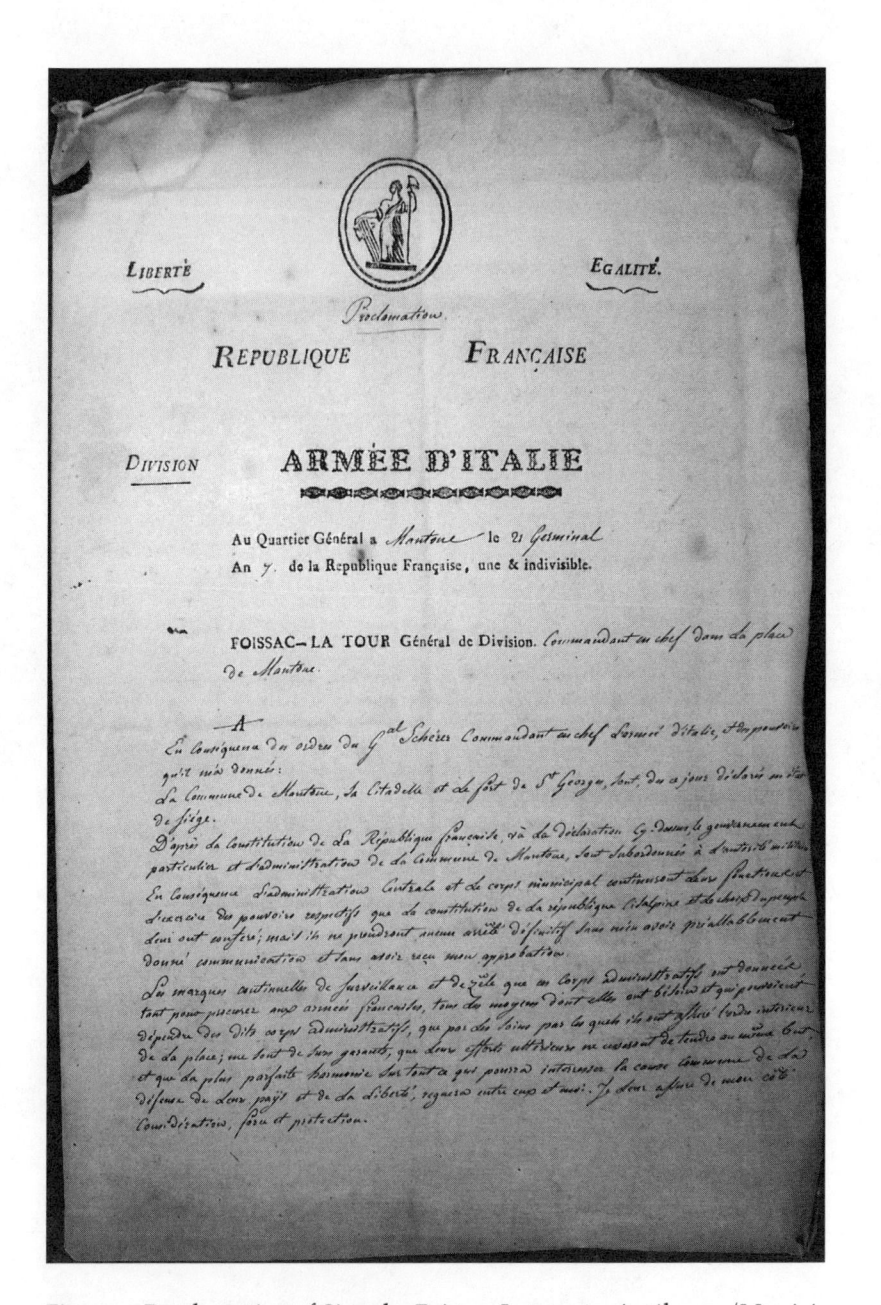

Figure 3. Proclamation of Siege by Foissac-Latour, 10 April 1799 (Municipalità, Busta 208, Archivio di Stato di Mantova).

A. 3-Lire Austrian *Cedola*, 1796.

B. 1-Soldo Bronze Republican Coin, 1799.

C. 5-Soldi Silver Republican Coin, 1799.

D. 5-Soldi (1758) Silver Austrian Coin, 1799.

E. 1/2-Soldo (1777) Austrian Coin, 1799.

Figure 4. *Cedola* and coins of the sieges: The paper *cedola* (pl. *cedole*) used at Mantua in 1796 was a type of voucher to be used as real money. The local government promised that it could also be redeemed at three times its value after three months. The four coins were all minted by the French during the 1799 siege.

CHAPTER 7

CAPITULATION AND BONAPARTE'S RISE

"A military reason has determined me to offer you the fortress of Mantua, on the preliminary condition of my being permitted to march out freely, with my garrison and all the artillery and munitions, to the imperial army."

WURMSER TO BONAPARTE, 29 JANUARY 1797

E ven with Provera's surrender and Alvintzy's inglorious retreat, the authorities in Vienna were determined to continue the war with vigor. In Paris, however, the Directory was concerned with the risk the Army of Italy had run at Arcole and Rivoli as well as the fate of the Republic should Bonaparte's army sustain a loss. They also envied the rising popularity the young general was gaining with all of his victories. For these reasons, the Directors were determined to try once again to end the war through negotiations. They continued to encourage Clarke to obtain an armistice that would stipulate that France retain Mantua.[1] They renewed their proposals because now they wanted Clarke to conclude a peace provided it gave France not only Mantua, but also Belgium and the frontier region of the Rhine.[2]

The other powers of Europe were interested to see what the negotiations between Clarke and the Austrians would yield. In particular, Pope Pius VI was concerned. The French intercepted a letter from Cardinal Antonio Busca, the papal secretary of state, to Prelate Gianfrancesco Albani, the papal nuncio at Vienna. Through it, Bonaparte learned of the Papal States' interests in Clarke's negotiations. In the letter Busca informed Albani: "I do not doubt that you have taken measures to get to the bottom of the negotiations that Clarke is holding at Innsbruck. The details which I expect from you on this subject will serve as a guide to my conduct."[3] The treaty between the pope and Bonaparte signed in June 1796 was becoming tenuous, especially after Dumas intercepted the message indicating the Austrian intentions to relieve Mantua and join with the papal forces then arming. The more recent letter also captured by the French addressed the same scheme. Busca informed Albani that he should have learned from the last courier from Rome that the cardinal was contemplating the possibility of papal forces uniting with the Austrian troops invading Romagna. He raised the issue of whether it would be more expedient for the Austrian troops to embark at Trieste and land at Ancona or march overland to meet the papal forces. Busca told Albani to cultivate this project, which would be most helpful to the emperor and the pope should it succeed because they then would be able to influence the inclinations of the king of Sardinia.[4] But Albani never learned of Clarke's intentions. Bonaparte had again intervened and effectively stopped Clarke's negotiations. Bonaparte knew Mantua was about to fall, and he did not want any interruption of the operations that would give the defenders a chance to recover.

In the meantime, by the end of January all provisions in the fortress were consumed, the garrison was surviving on the remaining horses, and after four months of reduced rations, half of the Austrian military was hospitalized. By the 24th the troops had consumed almost everything available. That day Cocastelli issued an appeal to the citizens to sell any flour, meal, rice, grain, or firewood to the government to supply the soldiers.[5] The next day the supreme commander himself sent out a similar appeal. Wurmser asked the people to bring food to the royal military magazines, with the promise that those who were selling the goods would get a handsome price for their sacrifice.[6] Cocastelli and Wurmser sent out these appeals because the end of the ration stores was only two days away, even after putting the garrison on half rations. Wurmser had continued to receive his daily reports from Cocastelli concerning the consumption of flour. According to Cocastelli's earlier projections, at the current consumption rate the supply of flour would last just a few days more.[7] But because of the appeals, conservation, and soldiers dying, the garrison had managed to survive until 29 January with 28 sacks of flour and 46 sacks of whole grain remaining—far below the 498 sacks of flour needed to provide the garrison with that day's allotment of half rations.[8] On the morning of 29 January, Wurmser wrote a message proposing a possible capitulation and forwarded it to Sérurier at Roverbella. He stipulated two preliminary conditions:

that the entire garrison go free and not be made prisoners of war; and that all of the field artillery, with its equipment and ammunition, also be allowed to be taken freely from the fortress.[9] Klenau delivered the message, and Sérurier notified Bonaparte in Verona about Wurmser's proposals.

Years later, while in exile at St. Helena, Napoleon Bonaparte stated that he arrived at Sérurier's headquarters where the capitulation talks with Klenau were taking place. He recalled that he stood in the corner of the room wrapped in a blanket while Klenau discussed the final terms of surrender with Sérurier. Finally, growing tired of Klenau's attempts to get better terms by arguing that Mantua could still hold out for three more months with its wealth of resources, he went to the table, took pen in hand, and spent nearly half an hour writing his decisions in the margins of the document with Wurmser's proposals while Klenau and Sérurier continued to discuss the terms. When he finished, Bonaparte said to Klenau:

> If Wurmser had provisions for eighteen or twenty days, and talked of surrendering, he would not deserve an honorable capitulation, but I respect the Marshal's age, his bravery, and misfortunes. Here are the conditions I will grant him if he opens the gates tomorrow. If he delays fifteen days, a month, or two, he shall still have the same conditions. He may therefore hold out to his last morsel of bread. I am about to set out instantly to pass the Po and I will march on Rome. You know my intentions, so go and communicate them to your general.[10]

According to Bonaparte, Klenau at first did not know who was addressing him but soon realized it was the French commander in Italy. The Austrian colonel examined the decisions and was pleased with the unexpected and generous terms Bonaparte offered. Realizing that he could not obtain better terms, Klenau acknowledged that the Mantua garrison could not hold out more than three days.[11] Bonaparte did not date this event, but any meeting near Mantua involving Bonaparte's presence would have occurred in the afternoon of 29 January at Roverbella (Sérurier's headquarters) or at San Antonio, where a third meeting with Klenau was to take place.[12] Whether he met with Klenau, as he claimed years later, or gave his instructions directly to Sérurier, as he reported to the Directory as well as to Clarke on 1 February, it is clear that Bonaparte's response to Wurmser's proposals was that he could not grant the capitulation as requested, but would allow Wurmser to leave with five hundred men of his choice on condition that they would not serve against the Republic for three months; the remainder would become prisoners.[13]

Bonaparte departed for Modena early in the morning on 30 January.[14] That same day, with no hope of immediate relief, Wurmser held a council of war and made the decision to surrender since the provision would only last one more day.[15] He then sent Klenau to meet with Sérurier to finalize the agreement. Wurmser insisted that his entire garrison be included in the release and not confined to only five hundred as offered by Bonaparte. He no doubt believed his request would persuade those in Vienna to see the capitulation favored all of his soldiers, not just himself. He promised Sérurier that the garrison would not serve for one year against France, but he desired that the article so stating not be included in the capitulation. The French general kept to the terms that Bonaparte offered the Austrians on the 29th but still forwarded the proposal to Bonaparte. Klenau was astonished to learn that Bonaparte had actually left, and that it would take four days to receive an answer. This he found out because he had a captured dispatch from the Directory to Bonaparte that told the French commander not to leave until the business at Mantua was terminated.[16] What Klenau did not realize was that insofar as Bonaparte was concerned, the affair at Mantua was finished. Klenau was also surprised that the French seemed to be willing to wait an additional four days to conclude the capitulation. Waiting an additional four days would have had a significant effect on the Austrians since the garrison did not have enough provisions to subsist that long. Bonaparte received Sérurier's letter and from Bologna informed the Directory of the latest news. He also told them that he would instruct Sérurier to hold to his first proposal and that if Wurmser did not accept before 3 February, he would not allow the marshal any capitulation other than that of prisoner of war for himself and his garrison.[17] However, the letter to Sérurier, which Bonaparte had Berthier send on 1 February, stated: "The General in Chief desires to know, my dear general, where you are in the negotiations with General Wurmser. Please send news right away."[18]

On 31 January and 1 February Klenau and Sérurier continued to negotiate as Wurmser tried to improve the terms.[19] On the 1st Sérurier addressed a few of the terms of Wurmser's proposal. Sérurier promised that the garrison would have the honors of war that Wurmser requested through Klenau. Sérurier agreed to allow Wurmser to select 500 individuals plus 200 cavalrymen to accompany him to freedom, along with six field pieces and their respective equipment. Sérurier indicated that all of the remaining troops would be held prisoners of war, but they were to leave the fortress with the honors of war and then deposit their weapons, colors, and standards on the glacis of the fortress. He also stated that those troops not being made prisoner were not to fight against the French army for three months after their return to Austria.[20] As Sérurier and Klenau talked, several copies of Wurmser's fourteen articles were drafted by Sérurier and his staff.[21] An agreement was completed on the 1st, and Wurmser retained the small gains he had made in the negotiations. The following morning at 9:00 the armistice was declared.[22]

With the preliminary provisions complete, 2 February was a busy day for the Austrian staff officers as they worked out march tables and the allocations each unit would receive for their share of the five hundred individuals and two hundred cavalrymen who would not be made prisoners. Each unit was allocated a varying amount—Wurmser's Hussars were allowed to take twenty-two officers; the Erzherog Joseph Hussars and Alvintzy Regiment, ten each; the pioneers, sixty; and the Tschaikisten, thirteen.[23] The same day Wurmser wrote to Ott in the Citadel informing him that Klenau, Adjutant General Auer, and Wurmser's aide-de-camp Captain Count Degenfeld were authorized to sign the impending capitulation.[24] More refinements were made to the proposed articles, such as the size of caliber of the cannon that would be brought out of the fortress and the exact number of horses allowed per officer.[25]

The final terms of surrender were signed on 2 February 1797 at 10:00 P.M. at San Antonio by Klenau, Ott, and Wurmser (see appendix A).[26] That day the garrison had 13,266 officers and men, fit for service, remaining in the fortress.[27] Wurmser did hold out to the last piece of bread, but not to the last horse as he promised Alvintzy in late December. There were, however, only 200 cavalry horses that survived, along with 1,153 officers' horses. In addition to the military personnel, there were 1,110 noncombatants and their 201 horses attached to the army, all of which would be surrendered.[28]

The next day, 3 February, the imperial garrison of Mantua marched out of the Citadel gate with all the honors of war, drums beating, colors flying, and the cannoneers' matches lit. The column marched out to the glacis where they laid down their arms, colors, standards, and every piece of military equipment belonging to them.[29] There was an

enormous amount of matériel. The fortress artillery that was surrendered totaled 364 pieces: 126 brass 18- to 52-pounders, 175 brass
12-pounders, 56 brass mortars, and 7 cannon adapted for boats. The
French also captured 43 brass field artillery pieces, 16 brass howitzers, 17,115 muskets and carbines (not counting the muskets
laid down on the glacis of the fortress by the departing soldiers),
1,214,000 musket cartridges, 80 tons of lead, 264 tons of powder,
14,746 cannon cartridges, 184 caissons and wagons, and equipment
for 25 pontoons.[30] On 3 February Wurmser wrote to the Emperor
informing him of the fall of the fortress city. In this lengthy letter,
he listed the many reasons that drove him to his decision to surrender but emphasized the scarcity of provisions; since November
his men had been living on horsemeat.[31] Sérurier likewise wrote to
his commander. He sent Bonaparte the original copy of the surrender document and informed him that General Miollis and his command, the 69th demibrigade, entered the Citadel. Sérurier informed
Bonaparte that there were 15,000 men at arms and 6,000 in the hospitals at Mantua. Knowing that it would take a long time to organize and form the 1,000-man columns stipulated in the capitulation
terms, and because there were only 20,000 rations remaining with
no means of making any more, Sérurier allowed the Austrians to
depart in three groups of 5,000 each over the course of three days
rather than let them starve. The first column, he told Bonaparte,
would leave on the 4th; the second, on the 5th; and the third, on the
6th. Wurmser would depart in the morning with the first column.[32]

On 3 February Sérurier wrote to Wurmser in regards to his passport and added that he was honored to have made his acquaintance
and that he could rest assured that he held the marshal in esteem.[33]
Passports were indeed important as the three Austrian columns had
to move through French-held territory while making their way from
Mantua through Legnago to Padua. The next day Meszaros led the
first of three large columns that departed from Mantua on consecutive days. Wurmser and Ott marched with this column, which consisted of nine companies and twenty-eight squadrons totaling about
4,000 men and 800 horses. The following column departed on 5
February; it consisted of about 4,000 men and 300 horses and was led
by General Karl Philipp Sebottendorf.[34] The last column, made up
mainly of the regular garrison soldiers who had manned the fortress
walls since the beginning of the first blockade in May 1796, were led
out by their redoubtable commander, Canto d'Yrles, on 6 February.

Spiegel, Minkwitz, and Ruckavina accompanied him as they departed with the remaining 4,500 soldiers and 300 horses toward Gorizia.[35] In total, 13,266 officers and men marched out of the fortress.[36]

The French forces monitored the prisoners as they moved with one day's march distance between columns. The columns rested every third day. Wurmser was in Padua on 8 and 9 February, where he received letters from Augereau and General François Desponai.[37] On 12 February Guieu reported to Bonaparte that Wurmser had just arrived in Treviso with his entire headquarters and about 6,000 men, 1,200 horses, and the six artillery pieces and caissons he had been allowed to take out of the fortress. Wurmser informed Guieu that the columns were on the way to Gorizia and, by the terms of capitulation, they should have a French commissary accompany them. Wurmser had requested French commissaries to supply the Austrians as they marched. However, the capitulation called for the columns to march in 1,000-man units so they could forage in the countryside; that decision was altered because no provisions remained at Mantua and Sérurier had to evacuate the fortress as quickly as possible. Guieu told Bonaparte that his commander, Augereau, had departed two days earlier to take the news of the capitulation of Mantua to Paris. As a result, Guieu had no instructions, so he did not send an escort with the Austrians.[38] Wurmser's first column reached Gorizia on 21 February, and his last column arrived there on the 24th, thus ending his campaigns in Italy (see map 1).[39]

Once Bonaparte responded to Wurmser's initial capitulation terms of 29 January, he left Sérurier to see to the details and departed to Bologna, the site proposed by Cardinal Busca for the possible rendezvous of papal and Austrian troops.[40] After eight months of toil to bring about the fall of Mantua, Bonaparte left in haste to pursue new victories, leaving the honors of surrender to Sérurier, who had conducted the blockade and siege very effectively.

On 3 February Bonaparte wrote to the Directory to tell them that Sérurier and Wurmser were to have met on the 2nd to determine the day of the execution of the capitulation of Mantua and to organize the train for that purpose. Even though the capitulation had already been signed, Bonaparte could not give the Directory a definitive confirmation that Mantua had been taken or even when it would be taken (he was over eighty miles away when he wrote his letter on the 3rd and the capitulation was signed at 10:00 in the evening of the 2nd). In the same letter to Paris he spoke of Wurmser's ill fate and expressed his sympathy. He wrote that he was "anxious to show French generosity toward Marshal Wurmser, a general seventy years of age, toward whom fortune has been, in this campaign, very cruel: but who has, nevertheless, not ceased to show a courage and constancy of which history will keep account."[41] Bonaparte went on to describe all of the problems with which Wurmser had to contend, from his loss of his army and a part of the Tyrol at the Battle of Bassano, to his decision to flee for refuge in Mantua. Bonaparte continued with an account of Wurmser's exploits in reaching Mantua and the sorties that he led from that fortress. Reflecting on Wurmser's situation, Bonaparte advanced the notion that all those who rush to sneer at the unfortunate would not fail to persecute Wurmser.[42] Bonaparte was kind to Wurmser in many respects. Wurmser was an Alsatian and thus on the list of émigrés, and Bonaparte spared his life by sending him back to Austria and not France. Wurmser returned the gesture by warning Bonaparte of a conspiracy to poison him with *aqua tofana* in Romagna.[43] Although Bonaparte told the Directory he was anxious to show French generosity to Wurmser, he was not present at Mantua to personally act on these sentiments. Instead, he had Sérurier act in his behalf.

Sérurier acted with honor and generosity toward Wurmser and his army at the capitulation. One of the articles requested by Wurmser called for the sick and wounded to be treated humanely and stipulated that surgeons and attendants be left in the hospitals to administer to them. The request stated that the people who had to stay at Mantua because of certain circumstances, such as the surgeons, be given passports so that they could leave later. The French response was to grant these terms "without the least exception."[44] Bonaparte was content with the capitulation Sérurier had accepted.

On 7 February, five days after the surrender, Bonaparte, then in Ancona, finally received the copy of the capitulation that Sérurier sent on 3 February. He forwarded it to the Directory on the 10th, thereby confirming his letter of 1 February indicating the imminent fall of Mantua.[45]

The Directory did not receive word of the surrender of Mantua until 11 February 1797. Although that information was unofficial, it did not stop them from celebrating and passing the information to the Council of Five Hundred. Upon reading the notice, Villetard, a member of that council, declared to the Assembly:

The superb city of Mantua has fallen into the hands of the Republicans! Thanks to that army of heroes, whose success has astonished Italy itself—once the scene of most glorious feats, which will collapse all sinister plans of the enemies of freedom of the people. . . . I propose for the council to declare that the Army of Italy, newly victorious at Mantua, never ceases to merit the praise of their country.[46]

The motion carried unanimously. When the Directory passed the news of the capitulation of Mantua to the Council of Ancients, Lacombe-Saint-Michael went to the rostrum and announced:

The clouds that obscured the dawn of liberty in Italy have finally dissipated in recent months and the promise of freedom is advancing! Mantua is taken. Yes, you will be free successors of Camillus and Cato. . . . May the conquest of that happy shore which gave birth to Virgil be the omen of your happy fate. Take advantage to learn from our mistakes, which caused divisions, so a common enemy will not take advantage of those mistakes. If you ever want to wield the torch of discord between our two republics, remember what we did for you. And you, brave Army of Italy, it belongs not to us to order festivals for the celebration of your victories, but to the government. Yet we all feel impatience to publicly declare, in this forum, that the Army of Italy has invariably deserved the thanks of their country.[47]

The news of the capitulation of Mantua was proclaimed all over Paris to the sound of beating drums. Detachments of troops accompanied the officer who posted the good news as shouts of joy filled the air throughout the city. The festive scene was remarkable. The local national guardsmen and other corps vied with each other to show who could exhibit the most appreciation to the "victors of Mantua." General François Pommereul, a contemporary who took part in the campaign, stated: "The continued extraordinary displays of gratitude and delight were a continuous testimony to the victories of the defenders of Italy."[48] Although official confirmation of the victory was not made until a few days later, Parisians delighted in the news and citizens of all classes gave banquets in honor of the Republican triumph.[49] Before the courier arrived with the official word of the reduction of Mantua, deliberations were under way by the authorities to determine the most efficacious mode of testifying to the gratitude of the nation to the Army of Italy. A few days prior to the arrival of the courier, it was discovered that the father of General Augereau lived in the city. Officials quickly decided to express the respect of the nation for the Army of Italy by honoring the father of Augereau—a man of seventy-five years. A deputation was appointed to invite him to a fraternal banquet, and a magnificent chair was prepared for him at the head of the table. A wreath of laurel decorated with a tricolor ribbon was humbly presented to him while patriotic songs accompanied the festivities.[50]

Before the end of February numerous songs were published commemorating the event. The most popular one, titled "The Capture of Mantua," set to the music of an earlier military song, related the exploits of Bonaparte and his great conquest of the fortress city.[51] Another, "The Popular Song of the Siege of Mantua," had nineteen verses.[52] Dozens of songs and odes were also published throughout northern Italy lauding the magnificent French victory. One written in the Mantovano was titled "The Liberty Tree," and another was titled "Lombardy"; both were published on broadsides at Mantua.[53]

On 18 February the Directory received fresh trophies from the Army of Italy. The colors taken in the final combat around Mantua at San Giorgio and La Favorita were carried into the hall of the National Assembly amid the animating cries of "Vive la Republique!" They were presented by the minister of war and General Jean-Baptiste Bessières, whom Bonaparte had sent to present them to the Executive Directory.[54] After a few preliminaries, the minister of war addressed the Directory and confirmed that Mantua—"that superb fortress, the last hope of the enemy"—had fallen into their hands. After he spoke at length, Bessières addressed the Directors. Ultimately, the president of the Directory rose and delivered yet another lengthy speech. All three of the speeches applauded the success of the Army of Italy in capturing Mantua, and all three sounded as if the war were indeed over.[55] For all intents and purposes, it was. As Bonaparte expressed to his army on 10 March: "The capture of Mantua has ended a campaign which has given you titles to the eternal gratitude of the nation. You have won victory in 70 actions and 14 pitched battles; you have taken more than 100,000 prisoners, 500 field pieces, 2,000 heavy guns and 4 bridging trains."[56] Bonaparte had defeated one Piedmontese and four separate Austrian armies. Emperor Francis II would send yet another Austrian army to Italy, to try to take back what Beaulieu, Wurmser, and Alvintzy had lost there. Although he expected the commander, his brother

Archduke Charles, to be successful, this expedition, too, would end with a French victory and would serve to further catapult Napoleon Bonaparte to power.

CHAPTER 8

BONAPARTE'S ADMINISTRATION
AND PREPARATION FOR WAR,
1797–1799

"You have sent 30 million to the Minister of Finance to assist the public treasury. You have enriched the Museum of Paris with more than 300 masterpieces of ancient and modern Italy which it took thirty centuries to produce."

BONAPARTE TO HIS SOLDIERS

When the Austrians departed Mantua in early February 1797 and the French troops entered, the government administration underwent a change on a scale that had not been seen in that city since the War of the Spanish Succession (1701–14) when Duke Ferdinand Carlo Gonzaga fled the city and the Austrians entered in 1708. The Gonzaga dukes had ruled Mantua for 379 years (from 1328 to 1707), and the Austrians for 89 years.[1] The French established in Mantua a republican form of government modeled after their own. Initially, this government worked well, but as time passed the excessive French demands upon the Mantuans undermined the administration.

The bureaucratic machine established by the French was well organized and complex and included an archive for the governmental correspondence that rivals modern archives in the registration and classification of documents.[2] These documents reveal the fascinating history of the French occupation of Mantua.

On 1 February 1797, two days before the French entered the town, while capitulation terms were still being negotiated, the president of the royal governing Giunta, Luigi Cocastelli, called a meeting of the Congressional Delegation of Mantua: Dr. Leopoldo Micheli, Count Anselmo Freddi, and Count Antonio Cantoni.[3] Along with the director of finance, Dr. Antonio Gobbio, and the two councillors

Dr. Luigi Tonni and tax lawyer Luigi Trenti, Cocastelli received the delegates according to normal procedures. The delegates were to legitimize Wurmser's capitulation. Political authority was represented by the Giunta, thus Cocastelli delegated the Giunta's managerial powers to the Congressional Delegation.[4]

President Cocastelli, aware of his own responsibility in light of the current situation in Mantua, wanted to guarantee that the administration would continue to function although the delegates were reduced from twelve to three individuals. In the wake of the French invasion, many nobles and property owners had fled.[5]

Cocastelli was concerned about the needs of the people. On 2 February, during the session called to prepare for the French takeover, the delegation examined the problem of the filthy prison cells. They discussed the requests for subsidies from the women whose husbands were killed in the siege and the anticipated requests for restitution for damages sustained during the siege. Their ability to deal with these issues expeditiously illustrates their determination.[6]

After taking care of the most pressing issues, on 2 February the Giunta selected eight internal delegates to join the current three delegates to complete the council, including the lawyer Leopoldo Camillo Volta, famous for his opening of the library at Mantua and later for the publication of a massive work on the history of Mantua.[7] This delegation oversaw the transformation of the old Austrian wartime government of the Giunta into the new French administration. From 2 February until 13 March the Congressional Delegation carried out the orders of the French and represented the city and the state of Mantua, while the French organized their new government.[8]

On the morning of 3 February, three of the delegates, Leopoldo Micheli, Angelo Petrozzani, and Amadio Basilia, took a list of four objectives decided upon by the entire delegation to General Sérurier, who was temporarily residing in the Citadel. The objectives were:

1. To bring in supplies immediately to sustain the people living in the city and the French troops entering;
2. To attend to the public health by disposing of the massive heaps of manure and restoring order to the hospitals abandoned by the Austrian troops;
3. To implement a procedure for receiving the new garrison;
4. To seek a solution concerning the local economic situation in regard to the cedole to ensure they did not lose their value.[9]

That same day Sérurier responded to this request on a sheet of paper with *BLOCUS DE MANTOUE* printed as the letterhead, the same stationary he had been using at his headquarters at Roverbella during the previous months of the "blockade of Mantua." He drew a single line through the words *BLOCUS DE*, thus leaving only the title *MANTOUE* for the letterhead. In his letter, Sérurier ordered the *Municipalitè*, which was the new French name of the royal governing Giunta, to prepare on the following day appropriate lodgings with 1,200 beds, each furnished with chairs, straw mattresses, a pair of sheets, and a blanket for the partial French garrison that would enter the city on 5 February. The Municipalitè was to also prepare stables for the horses of one French regiment, as well as shelter for the horses turned over by the Austrian garrison, possibly as many as six hundred. He recommended that the area designated for the French troops be in the highest state of cleanliness. In addition, he wanted them to provide the French commissary with a sufficient number of boats to evacuate the 6,000 sick Austrian soldiers and carriages necessary to take them to the boats. In conclusion, he told them that the strict execution of this order would prove the sincerity of the city to the French soldiers, who in turn would respect the people and property of the city.[10] Thus Sérurier answered the requests of the delegation by making demands of them.

Sérurier did not address the financial problem with the cedole in his letter to the delegates. The creator of the cedole, Luigi Cocastelli, now ex-president of the former Giunta and commissariat of the Austrian army, had departed with the Austrians, leaving the delegation to handle the transfer of power to the French. He had apparently been respected in the town until he introduced the cedole.[11] On 7 February the delegation tried to solve the cedole problem by issuing an avviso stating that the paper cedole would continue to be used as actual money at their face value. This violated Cocastelli's promise—that later a cedola could be redeemed for three times its face amount.[12] Eventually the cedole were abolished, making the paper money held by many citizens totally worthless (see fig. 4).[13]

As a transitional government, the Congressional Delegation worked hard to maintain order in the city as the government of the Austrian royal governing Giunta was replaced by the French system of the Municipalitè (or *Municipalità*, as it was locally called). The Giunta had been led by a president and three councillors with three sections of government (see appendix F). Within the ministers' section, which was further divided into four parts, the General Congregation comprised the largest body. The head of this congregation, the prefect, was institutionally one of the three councillors in the executive branch who worked with the president of the Giunta. The Ministry of the General Congregation traditionally consisted of 100 property owners: sixty members, selected as a block, included thirty nobles, fifteen lawyers, and fifteen merchants; the remaining forty represented the sixteen districts of the Mantovano—thirty for the fifteen districts of the Mantovano outside the city of Mantua, and ten for the city proper.[14] The General Congregation nominated from their numbers the twelve delegates who became the Congressional Delegation. The newly elected delegation managed to transfer governmental authority in a peaceful manner. Many members of the delegation in turn served in the government of the Municipalità.

In order to accomplish the most urgent tasks, establishing order in the city after the siege and meeting Sérurier's demands, the Congressional Delegation organized ten departments as an interim government. The first department handled public administration and district chanceries and the second dealt with military lodging. Other departments were responsible for sanitation, roads, embankments, religious foundations, hospitals, schools, orphanages, and dowries. The new Municipalità, which consisted of a president and twenty-one *municipalisti*, in turn, established six committees. These six committees were in reality a rearrangement of the ten interim departments of the Congressional Delegation. In keeping with French priorities at the time, the first committee provided for the needs of the military. Some of the committees combined many of the functions of the departments under the former regime, but the French did add one new function and established it as a separate committee. The newly established sixth committee was a vigilance committee to monitor the academy and public education, religious discipline, and public entertainment. The prefect of the Congressional Delegation, Angelo Petrozzani, became the president of the Municipalità, and Leopoldo Camillo Volta as well as three others who served in the delegation became municipalisti. The new government, which would carry out the orders of the French civil and military leadership in the Mantovano, included many Jacobins, such as Giuseppe Lattanzi and Teodoro Somenzari, who became municipalisti.[15]

Bonaparte, who was concerned about the rumors that Archduke Charles was moving toward Italy from the Rhine, wanted to prepare to counter the new Austrian threat in the field and at the same time prepare Mantua for an Austrian siege. Bonaparte ordered Lespinasse, commander of the artillery, to transport all of the artillery not being used for the defense of Mantua to Pizzighettone and to name a senior artillery officer to command the fortress artillery and put its defenses in the best state of defense. To ensure that the siege works dug earlier by the French would be unusable to a future enemy, he ordered the engineer commander to destroy all the blockade works immediately.[17]

In preparing Mantua for an attack, Bonaparte once again showed his prudence, foresight, and military competence by ensuring the city was quickly provisioned and prepared to endure a siege. He ordered the chief of commissaries to provision Mantua for 12,000 men and 2,000 horses for one year and to establish a pharmacy with drugs for the fortress. He also advised that since it was normal to put additional men in the fortresses, the chief of commissaries should plan for a one-year siege with a garrison of 36,000 men. He stated that it was absolutely necessary that the magazines were stocked before 5 March, and that half of the necessary supplies be delivered to the fortress by 19 February. He ordered that an inventory of the provisions, signed by the chief of commissaries, be sent to the general headquarters, and that under penalty of death, nobody would be able to use the stored provisions unless ordered by the general in chief. Every month, the fortress commander and the commissary of war, who were solely responsible for the provisions, were to visit the magazines and note what was about to spoil, and to add these items to the bottom of the official report. Those items were to be replaced within twenty-four hours. Bonaparte also required that each branch of service have an employee to supply the magazines. These men would be replaced only in the event of death or a direct order from him and would be forbidden to leave Mantua without an order from the fortress commander. Bonaparte also mandated that there would be salted meat rations for 12,000 men, in addition to the fresh meat held in the fortress. He ordered enough wine, brandy, and vinegar to be available to supply every soldier in the garrison with a daily ration. He also required that half of the grain supply be ground into flour and that special care be taken to establish sites for firewood storage.

Bonaparte mandated that 800,000 rations of biscuit be readily available in the magazines.[18]

Upon receiving these instructions from Bonaparte, the interim government, on 6 February, issued an avviso stating that the long blockade of the city had deprived the citizens of the most necessary articles to sustain life, such as every type of livestock, food, firewood, hay, straw, wine, and spirits. The delegates explained in the avviso that in order to remedy this situation, the people and soldiers alike had to gather quickly these items into the fortress. To accomplish this, magazine directors with the best credentials were assigned to establish contracts. The administration allowed the people to obtain a reasonable profit by exempting the goods from local taxes and eliminating the weight limit on their goods brought into the city.[19] The avviso stated that General Sérurier would allow the exemption to last from the 7th until the 11th of February.[20]

The tax break was intended to assist the administration in meeting Bonaparte's first deadline of 19 February to acquire half of the provisions for the magazines. Frustrated that Mantua was not being provisioned quickly enough, Bonaparte issued an additional order, on 13 February, detailing what he wanted stored in the magazines. Because of Mantua's strategic importance, and certain impact on the other Italian states if lost, he ordered the Congress of the State of Milan to take whatever measures were necessary to pour into Mantua 10,000 quintals of corn, 50,000 pints of brandy, 200,000 pints of wine, and 2,000 quintals of rice.[21] Bonaparte also extended the deadlines for getting the provisions into Mantua. He ordered that one-third of the new provisions be sent to Mantua before 5 March; the second third, by 20 March; and the last third, by 4 April. Bonaparte emphasized the importance of this endeavor by ordering that General Miollis officially receive the supplies, in addition to the quartermaster and inspector in charge of provisions of Mantua. To assist in gathering provisions, the newly established revolutionary government of Modena was ordered to send 100,000 pints of brandy and 500,000 pints of wine; the government of Ferrara, 10,000 quintals of corn, 100,000 pints of brandy, 200,000 pints of wine, and 1,500 quintals of rice; and the provisional government of Bologna 3,000 quintals of corn, 27,000 pints of brandy, and 100,000 pints of wine. Rudolf Emanuel de Haller, the commissary general of the Army of Italy at Milan, was ordered to send 16,000 quintals of corn seized in the countryside of the various Papal States along with all the wine and brandy he could draw from those same regions.[22] In addition, those regions were ordered to supply all the salt necessary for 40,000 men for one year. These requirements were established to prevent Miollis from sending troops to try to gather provisions in the same areas. Bonaparte ordered Haller to have the administration of Mantovano send all of the wood that belonged to the abbey of San Benedetto, and if that were not enough, to gather more from different private individuals in the Mantovano, especially in areas closest to the Mincio and the Po, so that it could be transported quickly to Mantua. The commissary of Mantua was to bring into the city 80,000 quintals of hay and 200,000 bushels of corn for animal fodder. Miollis was to insure that there were quartermasters available to receive the food and fodder that would be flowing into Mantua. To emphasize even more the importance of his order, Bonaparte decreed that the newly established time line must be met and that any generals, officers, commissaries of war, employees, or others who impeded this provisioning would suffer the pain of death.[23]

Miollis, as commander, was to ensure that all of these orders were followed, but with his increased responsibility, he also received some additional benefits. When Bonaparte was informed of abuses from his commanders demanding table money, a military allowance for entertaining visitors, he established a standard payment schedule for commanders in the conquered territories. Bonaparte ordered that towns with fewer than 10,000 people did not have to pay the commanders any money; the officers could claim only housing. For towns exceeding 10,000 people, such as Mantua, the municipality was required to pay 6 French livres per day to assist their commanders in the execution of their daily tasks.[24]

The same day that Miollis was ordered to take command at Mantua, Bonaparte informed Sérurier that he intended to give him an active division of the army that would be made up of five regiments complete with a horse artillery regiment of six pieces of light artillery and an additional six pieces of foot artillery, a regiment of light infantry and a regiment of line infantry that was presently on its way down from the Rhine. The 12th, 64th, and 69th Regiments would complete his field division but would form the garrison at Mantua for the time being. The 25th Regiment of Chasseurs were also destined for Sérurier's division, and two of its squadrons were to operate as dispatch riders at Mantua in the meantime. General Beaumont would command Sérurier's cavalry, and General Chabot would head the division's units in Verona. Sérurier would stay in Mantua to command the Mantovano until the French army began to advance against the Austrians. Sérurier was rewarded for his effort during the eight-month siege of Mantua with a significant field command of a powerful division once hostilities started again.[25] In the meantime, Sérurier remained at Mantua to command the Mantovano, prepare himself for his field command, and participate in the extraordinary changes that took place upon the French entry into the city. However, on 13 February Bonaparte ordered him to send the 12th and the 64th demibrigades and the two squadrons of the 25th Chasseurs with Chabot into Venetian territory to establish an advance guard at Cittadella. This arrangement effectively gave Chabot field command of the entire division designed for Sérurier. Bonaparte explained to Sérurier that his presence in Mantua "could" be necessary.[26] Sérurier continued to remain in Mantua, while Miollis commanded the fortifications, and waited for Bonaparte to send him to replace Chabot at the head of his division.

When the French entered the fortress of Mantua, the first to celebrate were the Jews, who circulated a broadside praising the Republicans. They affixed the document to the columns of the plaza and distributed other papers recounting the inequities they had suffered.[27] The emancipation of the Jews by the French came at a time when debates in Mantua had taken place on that very issue. In 1770 the Austrian authorities had taken strong measures against government officials who were anti-Semites. The central authorities in Milan sent a message to the authorities in Mantua that if the notary, who had incited the bishop against the Jews, did not stop his activities, he would be banished from the state. The officials in Milan in 1770 stressed that they would not tolerate injury to the Jews in the Austrian Empire. On the eve of the French Revolution, the debate on the question of the status of Jews in Italy was centered in Mantua. The reforms of Joseph II came into effect in the 1770s, during the early part of his reign while his mother, Maria Theresa, was still alive. In the 1780s, as the sole ruler, Joseph extended them. Both Jews and Christians reacted to the reforms with mixed feelings as each community perceived positive and negative impacts. The reforms had granted Jews limited civil rights and abolished many of the discriminatory laws, while at the same time Jews were required to give up some of their most cherished rights, specifically in the area of communal independence. In a debate during the 1780s on this topic, the physician Benedetto Frizzi of Ostiano represented the Jews and the nobleman Giovanni Battista Gherardo D'Arco of Mantua represented the Christians. Although D'Arco welcomed the emperor's reforms, he nevertheless took the opportunity to attack the Jews in general and their economic endeavors in particular. But neither Frizzi nor D'Arco ever thought of giving the Jews equal civil rights. That only became a reality after the French entered the city in February 1797. A month later, however, in early March, the Jewish community asked the French commander not to accelerate the emancipation of the Jews, especially in the area of appointments of Jews to official public positions. Despite the equality guaranteed by the French, the Jewish community argued that there remained social differences between the two communities and that the Christians were not able to divorce themselves easily from prejudices of centuries. Consequently, they requested that the gates of the ghetto be retained. The Municipalità responded that the Jews would be forbidden to close the gates of the ghetto. It was not until 21 January 1798 that the ghetto gates were destroyed in order to eradicate that visible symbol of differences between Jews and Christians. At the same time, the ghetto square was renamed the Piazza Concordia, or Brotherhood Square. The Jewish petition to the French to exclude them from the Municipalità was to no avail. Two Jews were added to the Municipalità, and others were appointed to help keep order in the city. Jews who enlisted in the local militia had to carry a sword and musket—a task that caused a conflict between the fulfillment of their civic duties and the precepts of Judaism. Rabbi Ishmael Cohen permitted the Jews of Mantua to bear arms on the Sabbath, but he forbade the two members of the Municipalità to join the procession of carriages of the council members to the Council House, which also took place on the Sabbath.[28]

Along with the liberation of the Jews, other major changes took place in Mantua when the French took over. The press was affected greatly. The only newspaper in the city at the time, which was printed under the license of the emperor, ceased to exist after the Austrians departed. On 8 February 1797 a "prospectus of a newspaper" with the title *Giornale degli Amici della Libertà Italiana* (Journal of the friends of Italian liberty) was circulated throughout the city. The prospectus promised a sort of free press by presenting the people's interest twice a week, on Tuesdays and Saturdays. The price was 20 Milanese lire for one year. The advertisement introduced the people to a new calendar along with a new year for the people of Mantua. The date on the prospectus, 8 February, was given as 22 *piovoso* of Year V of the French Republic and Year I of Italian Liberty (using the Italian spelling for the French revolutionary month of pluviôse).[29]

On 18 February the first issue of *Giornale degli Amici della Libertà Italiana* was published. Unlike its Austrian counterpart, this newspaper had a name and, more distinctively, a symbol printed on the front. The symbol was a circle encompassing a liberty cap and two crossed swords. Under the swords were the words "Democracy or Death," and around the circumference of the circle were the words "Liberty—Virtue—Equality—Justice." The press translated the Republican calendar month into Italian but eventually dropped the French calendar year V, replacing it with Year I of Italian Liberty. The press, however, continued to put the Gregorian date in parenthesis following the Republican date.[30] The structure of the paper was consistent throughout the first year, but in its second year the liberty cap, crossed swords, and patriotic words in Italian were replaced by a printing of Lady Liberty, and "Year II of Italian Liberty" gave way to "Republican Year 6" thus signifying the Cisalpine Republic's link to France.[31] The paper was run by Jacobins and published odes, sonnets, and songs praising the successes of the French. The articles were understandably pro-French, but the *Giornale* differed in another way from its pro-Austrian counterpart: it published much more local news of Mantua, the Mantovano, and Lombardy than did the earlier Austrian paper, which had focused on events in Austria, France, German lands, and the Papal States. The journalists described the many festivals and celebrations in Mantua under French rule. The last printing of the *Giornale degli Amici della Libertà Italiana* was 4 April 1799 when the city was surrounded by Austrian forces during the War of the Second Coalition.[32]

Besides dealing with the new social issues presented by the emancipation of the Jews and publishing a new newspaper, Miollis and the interim delegation of the Municipalità had much work to do in the war-torn fortress town. The delegates issued notices reminding the townspeople that they were responsible for cleaning up the street in front of their homes or places of business.[33] In continuation of the preparations for war, everyone who owned a horse was required to register it with the commissary of war and no citizen was allowed to leave the fortress with any type of military arms, including guns, pistols, swords, or bayonets.[34] In addition, no out-sider was allowed to remain overnight in the home of a resident without written permission from General of Brigade Antoine François Barthelemi, commander of the piazza. The penalty for violating this rule was time in jail and a 50-lire fine.[35] Despite all the work to be done and the new rules and regulations to be codi-fied, the new administration still found time to celebrate. On 14 February the patriotic citizens of Mantua were invited to celebrate their independence and the "regeneration" of Italy and to recog-nize the brave French army that had made it all possible. In the first French civic function in Mantua, patriotic songs were sung and a military ball was held in the city's grand theater.[36] Another celebra-tion was planned for Bonaparte's arrival in Mantua.

Bonaparte had left Mantua in such a hurry after discussing capit-ulation terms with Klenau that he failed to make a triumphant entry into the city as he had done in Milan. He spent all of February 1797 between Bologna and Tolentino concluding his operations against the papal troops. The day the Treaty of Tolentino was signed, 19 February, Bonaparte informed the Directory that he would return to Mantua.[37] Although he stopped over in Bologna until the end of the month, he wanted to return to Mantua to oversee the establish-ment of the new government and to prepare the fortress to with-stand another possible siege. Extensive preparations were made for Bonaparte's arrival at Mantua.[38] The city administration posted an avviso on 1 March asking everyone to illuminate their houses for the arrival of the general in chief that evening and to greet him in the Piazza di San Pietro in the city center.[39] The same day a five-page prospectus on the illumination of the house of Girolamo Coddé, a member of the Municipalità, and his brother Pasquale Coddé was distributed.[40] Jewish leaders were asked to inform their community so that they would illuminate their houses as well. In addition, the representatives of the Jewish community were asked to participate in the official celebration honoring Bonaparte.[41]

The whole city was illuminated with candles in the windows of the houses when Bonaparte finally arrived at 2:00 A.M. on 2 March 1797.[42] Miollis assembled the garrison in the Piazza. The soldiers, as well as the citizenry, greeted Bonaparte with loud shouts and clap-ping. The people recited sonnets and poems in his honor, and one devotee presented to Bonaparte a laurel wreath with the inscription "THE FRIEND OF THE PEOPLE: THE TAMER OF THE KING."[43] Bonaparte, who fittingly enough stayed at the old Gonzaga Ducal Palace, which faced the Piazza di San Pietro, remained in Mantua for a week while he set about giving new orders and reiterating old ones.[44]

Although Bonaparte was up all night traveling and was greeted with a grand celebration upon his arrival in the early morning, he spent his first day in Mantua working to improve the fortifications. He ordered Berthier to renew his command that all the directors of the service departments could not leave the general headquarters of Mantua without the permission of the chief commissary of the army. He ordered the paymaster general of the army to send his funds from Milan to Mantua and to establish his office there on 5 March. He also ordered the commissary in charge of contributions to transport his funds and his office to Mantua. The 22nd Regiment of Chasseurs, then at Rovereto, was ordered to go to Mantua, where they were to be outfitted in uniforms and given new mounts. The quartermaster and the uniform inspector also were summoned to Mantua.[45]

Bonaparte revised the command structure of the Mantovano. Miollis was ordered to control not only the city of Mantua but all of the Mantovano, from the Po to the Oglio.[46] Meanwhile, Sérurier departed to command his 4th Division in the field, and subsequently took part in the Battle of the Piave on 12 March.[47] Bonaparte assigned Adjutant General Touret to work with Miollis stipulating that the latter was authorized to have two aides-de-camp. He further stipulated that the fortress commander of Mantua would have the rank of a colonel, and that there would be four adjutants for the city. Bonaparte mandated that the Citadel be commanded by a general of brigade, and he designated General Claude Marie Lebley for the position. Miollis was to confer with Bonaparte regarding selections to fill the other newly established positions including the one for Lebley's adjutant. Furthermore, Bonaparte chose General Nicolas Bertin as the general of brigade to command the island of the Te; he was charged with commanding all the fortifications and outworks of the Te and Cerese as well as supervising the reconstruction and maintenance of the works. San Giorgio was also to have a highly qualified officer in charge of its fortifications. Bonaparte also ordered that the Citadel, the island of the Te, and San Giorgio would each have an engineer and an artillery officer, who were to reside at their respective locations. Bonaparte further mandated that in the Citadel there should be artillery and food magazines, separated from those of the city, and that the employees in charge of those magazines were to reside in the Citadel.[48]

After establishing a clear command structure for the fortress city, Bonaparte worked on the specifics of the fortress defenses. He accomplished all of these tasks on 2 March 1797—with minimal sleep, if any. He ordered the commander of the city and the commander of engineers to cut down all the trees within 1,300 yards of the fortification outworks so that enemy attackers could be seen and engaged more easily. Fruit trees were the only exception to the rule. All of the cut wood was brought in and stored for use in the city. In addition, all of the houses outside of the fortress that could provide the enemy with cover were to be demolished without exception. Bonaparte reserved the right to compensate all individuals who suffered losses from these orders. The Municipalità was charged with creating a commission to present accounts of individual damages.[49] A week later Bonaparte suppressed the abbey of San Benedetto, ordering that half of its property be made available to the Municipalità to compensate the individuals who suffered losses from these orders to improve the fortress defenses.[50]

Bonaparte took great pains to ensure that the best engineers were working on the fortifications of Mantua. He put Chasseloup in charge of all engineers to begin a massive construction project to improve the fortifications, especially the weaker sides facing Porta Pradella and Pietole.[51] Earlier he wrote the Directory requesting the rank of brigadier general for Chasseloup and general of division of artillery for General Lespinasse, both of whom had signed the Mantua capitulation document. In the same letter, he also had requested the rank of colonel for Nicolas Antoine Sanson and André Etienne Maubert, two engineers who played important roles in fortifying Mantua.[52] Sanson, in particular, served as the engineer battalion commander at Mantua working on the fortification construction project. To begin this project, Girolamo Coddé and Gaetano Arrivabene issued an avviso asking for 1,200 workers to report to Sanson for employment.[53] The project generated work for the inhabitants and improved the fortifications at the same time.[54] Maubert would later play an important role during the French defense of Mantua against the Austro-Russian siege in 1799.[55] Bonaparte also gave detailed orders for arming the fortress.[56]

The status of the navy at Mantua also concerned Bonaparte. He ordered Berthier to ensure that there was a naval officer in Mantua to control the Lower and Middle Lakes. On the Lower Lake, he was to have three small armed boats and twelve small boats capable of carrying five or six men each; in addition, five boats, each able to carry one hundred men, were to be established on the Lower Lake. On the Upper Lake, a naval officer was to command six armed boats, twelve small sloops able to carry six or seven men each, and finally fifteen boats able to carry one hundred to two hundred men. Captain Pierre Baste was the obvious choice to command the naval effort on the lakes of Mantua. Bonaparte ordered the fortress commander and the commander of the engineers to establish a port for the boats and to provide the marines with a barracks nearby.[57] Establishing and arming a navy imposed a significant burden on the Municipalità because Bonaparte did not assign a special fund to support it.[58] Baste, however, worked quickly and within a month he had rigged out the first of the two required flotillas of the Mantuan navy and had begun work on the second.[59] Within the next year, boats operating on the Mantuan lakes would bear the names *Buonaparte*, *Berthier*, *Miollis*, *Masséna*, *Dallemagne*, *Kilmaine*, *Augereau*, and *Fiorella*, while other boats went without names.[60] (Curiously, the name "Sérurier" was not used. If Miollis had anything to do with naming the boats, he clearly was still holding a grudge for his perceived slight during Provera's surrender to Sérurier.)

Already in early 1797 Bonaparte was demonstrating his unique ability for propaganda. Although he was imposing heavy taxes and requisitions on the Mantovano, outsiders would not have been aware. He ensured the publication of an avviso, on the day of his arrival, that exempted the town of Pietole, the home of the ancient poet Virgil, from every form of tax as a means of showing his admiration for the renowned Roman poet.[61] The gesture of exempting the people of Pietole from taxes, which received wide publicity in Italy and France, amounted to very little loss to the government since so few families lived in that town.

To provide more money to the Municipalità's treasury, Bonaparte ordered the Administrative Commission of the Mantovano to manage both public revenues and religious funds until the new administration had settled with the French Republic on how such monies would be handled. The commission was also charged with confiscating superfluous silver ornaments in the churches on behalf of the French Republic. However, Bonaparte ordered the Administrative Commission of the Mantovano not to remove the treasures of the Municipalità, the hospital, and the charitable lending institution known as the *Monte di Pietà*.[62]

The Municipalità paid 100,000 francs as its first installment on reparations. The administrative commission executed Bonaparte's order and stripped the churches of anything that contained silver. The commission even attempted to remove the sacred vases in the Church of St. Andrea that were claimed to contain the blood of Christ as well as the silver statue of St. Anselmo. These latter actions aroused such resentment among the people of Mantua that the commission agreed to a settlement whereby several citizens volunteered to pledge the necessary sum to redeem the items' value. The pledge, loaned by the *Monte di Pietà*, amounted to 6,000 Milanese lire.[63] In addition to the initial installment of 100,000 francs, the Municipalità was required to pay 500,000 francs more.[64] If that were not enough financial strain on the Mantovano, Bonaparte established, in addition, a 100-franc pension, to be paid by the Mantovano, for each officer to whom he presented a saber. He also awarded monetary gifts of 5,000 to 20,000 livres to thirty-eight officers, again paid for by the Mantovano.[65]

The money and silver contributions were not the only valuables demanded by Bonaparte from Mantua and the Mantovano. Many other things that he saw and liked during his visit to Mantua ended up in Paris. He explained this to his Army of Italy in one of his more famous proclamations:

> The capture of Mantua has ended a campaign which has entitled you to the eternal gratitude of the nation.
>
> You have won victory in 70 actions and 14 pitched battles; you have taken more than 100,000 prisoners, 500 field pieces, 2,000 large-caliber guns, and four pontoon trains.
>
> The contributions levied on the lands you have conquered have fed, paid and maintained the army throughout the campaign; in addition, you have sent 30 million [livre] to the Minister of Finance to assist the public treasury. You have enriched the Museum of Paris with more than 300 masterpieces of ancient and modern Italy which it took thirty centuries to produce.[66]

Some of the masterpieces to which Bonaparte alluded came from Mantua. The *Giornale della Libertà* in Mantua published Bonaparte's letter to the army in full and made no attempt to conceal the fact that many of these contributions were coming from Mantua.[67] Bonaparte sent to Paris many fine paintings from Mantua. The French art commission scoured the area for art treasures, and at the Te Palace they were excited to find the frescoes of the "Chamber of the Giants" by Giulio Romano, a student of Raphael. Undeterred by their size, the commission devised several plans for removing and transporting them to Paris, including one that would involve cutting them. In the end it was decided not to risk their destruction.[68] They instead searched the city for other artistic and scientific objects of value; Leopoldo Camillo Volta, the city librarian, was forced to turn over ten incunabula, several collections of academic memoirs, and a dozen or more rare manuscripts.[69]

After establishing a clear command structure, beginning to rebuild the fortifications, attending local celebrations, and trying to stimulate the economy of Mantua, Bonaparte turned his attention once again to the provisioning of the city. He was very protective of the stores that were already placed in the magazines that were to be used only in case of a siege. His concern was evident when he asked Berthier why some troops had passed through Mantua when he had ordered that all troops pass by Brescia. Bonaparte considered it essential to spare the town of Mantua as much as possible.[70] In order to wring out all of the supplies left by the Austrians, Bonaparte ordered that all inhabitants of Mantua declare any stores or unspecified equipment that had belonged to the Austrians. Those inhabitants who did not make such a statement within forty-eight hours had to pay a fine equal to the value of the objects they had concealed and were condemned to one month of prison.[71]

Bonaparte was determined that, in the event of a blockade, the fortress of Mantua would not have to face the same problems that the Austrians endured in providing for the local inhabitants. He held the individual citizens responsible to provide themselves with contingency supplies in case of a siege. On 6 March he issued an order containing fourteen articles, which the Municipalità in turn published on 9 March.[72] The articles stated that all religious and secular congregations whose members had a total worth of 100,000 lire were required to supply enough bread, wine, vegetables, oils, salted meat, wood, and so on to sustain their families for one year. The University of the Jews, in the center of the ghetto, was required to supply all of the Jews' needs for one year. All individuals possessing up to 50,000 lire had to prepare enough provisions to last six months; those with up to 10,000 lire had to do the same for three months; and those with up to 3,000 lire, for two months. The Municipalità was charged with taking measures to ensure that it could feed the

poor who could not store provisions for themselves. Bonaparte mandated that the provisions had to be stored in the homes of the private individuals. Again he set deadlines. Each citizen was to acquire
half of the necessary provisions by 21 March and the rest by 4
April. Bonaparte required the Municipalità to name commissaries
to ensure that the order was carried out. Those citizens who were
delinquent were given a fine equal to the value of the food products
lacking. He ordered the Municipalità to give a list to Miollis by 18
March of all citizens, divided by classes, noting the provisions each
lacked. The administrators of the hospitals were required to have in
store a supply of medicines and the provisions necessary to sustain
the number of patients and nurses that the hospital was designed
to accept and employ. The Municipalità was authorized to take all
necessary measures for the execution of Bonaparte's order, after first
securing the consent of the French general commanding the city.
Bonaparte also ordered that those citizens who left Mantua were to
pay an absence tax to the Municipalità, which was scaled propor-
tionally to the wealth of each citizen in question. The absence tax
was used to provision the city. In the event of a siege, any individual
who wanted to leave the city with his family was required to immediately render to the Municipalità the monetary sum equivalent to
the provisioning that he would have held to provide for his family.
And finally, Bonaparte ordered that any private individual who followed the imperial army, or moved to a country at war with the
Republic, was to pay triple the amount of the absence tax.[73]

Bonaparte wanted to unite the region's small Italian states to
make them more defensible in case of a future Austrian incursion.
At the invitation of Bonaparte, Teodoro Somenzari made a motion
in the National Assembly on 7 March that Mantua be united to the
Cispadane and Transpadane Republics and to all the cities of Italy.
The fervor of a united Italy was clearly present in the assembly hall
as all agreed upon the motion. This was but one step in the creation
of the Cisalpine Republic.[74]

During his visit to Mantua, Bonaparte encouraged the local
officials in their government. He confirmed the provisional
Municipalità as the official governing administrative body. He
stayed in Mantua through 8 March and then departed for Bassano,
leaving the Municipalità of Mantua to complete the so-called quest
for liberty and equality. Two days after Bonaparte left Mantua,
Somenzari proposed to the Municipalità that the nobility and all

of their emblems be abolished. Building on Somenzari's proposal, Carlo Franzini motioned to permanently eliminate the titles of count, marquis, baron, and prince. The measures failed to pass the first time, but on the following day Franzini recommended they be printed and distributed throughout the town. After the distribution, Bishop Giovanni Battista of Mantua departed for Milan.[75] Finally, after much deliberation and lobbying from many people, the proposal to abolish all titles of nobility in Mantua passed on 15 March.[76]

Within a month after his departure from Mantua, Bonaparte defeated the 5th Austrian army sent by Francis II to the Italian front. Bonaparte rapidly defeated Archduke Charles in northeastern Italy and began to march his army to the gates of Vienna when the Austrians sued for peace. Bonaparte's armistice with the Austrians at Campo Formio on 18 October 1797 effectively ended the War of the First Coalition. Back in Mantua, as the Jacobins continued to make the city more Republican with each passing day, Bonaparte used the opportunity to substitute Italian and foreign soldiers for French soldiers in the garrison. During Bonaparte's visit in March, Giuseppe Lahoz had issued an appeal to the people of Mantua to join the Lombard Legion, which ultimately stationed a battalion in the Te Palace fortifications.[77] Bonaparte ordered most of the French regiments out of Mantua and sent the first battalion of the 2nd Polish Legion to the city.[78] This Polish battalion, which had recently been raised at Mantua, would return once more in 1799 to the city where the unit would meet its unfortunate end.[79]

The Mantuans had gained new freedoms from the French, but the contributions required of them by their liberators were enormous. Leopoldo Camillo Volta, representing the Municipalità, wrote in Italian a bold letter to Bonaparte stating: "After many calamities suffered by the people of the Mantovano for over a year, one can resort to nobody but you, Citizen General, because you desire justice for them although it is an impossibility since unfortunately they must support additional weights and burdens."[80] Volta's lengthy letter explained in intricate detail the many problems faced by the people of the Mantovano and the impossibility of the Municipalità's tasks—to collect the required taxes, pay the annual contribution of 1 million lire, and meet the other requisitions. Bonaparte's response was laconic and unsympathetic. He simply wrote in French on the same letter under Volta's signature: "Send back to citizen Haller to take measures to sell what is necessary."[81] With Bonaparte's reorganizing of the Cispadane and Transpadane Republics into the Cisalpine Republic on 29 June, Haller's job of collecting taxes and contributions was simplified.[82]

On 30 June 1797 the Constitution of the Cisalpine Republic, to which Mantua would belong, was proclaimed.[83] Two weeks later Haller ordered Franzini to increase taxes to collect the necessary finances required of the Mantovano.[84] Ignoring this fiscal strain, the Jacobins in Mantua organized more public festivals, thus adding to the local debt. On 18 July a large celebration commemorating Bonaparte's 12 April 1796 victory in Sardinia-Piedmont at the Battle of Montenotte took place at Mantua; it started at 10:00 A.M. when the entire garrison with twenty cannon commenced a march to the suburb of San Giorgio under the eyes of Miollis and the entire administration. The parade consisted of the French 29th Light Regiment, stationed at Mantua, as well as the battalions of the Lombard and Polish Legions. As the soldiers marched over the bridge to San Giorgio, Captain Pierre Baste, with his marines, passed under the bridge firing volleys from the cannon on his boats. In the middle of San Giorgio, a four-sided pyramid was erected with the names of the heroes LaHarpe, Stengel, and Dubois inscribed upon it along with the names of all the officers, noncommissioned officers, and soldiers who died in the Battle of Montenotte. The fete consisted of music, patriotic songs, and musket and cannon firing demonstrations. Then Miollis and Lattanzi gave energetic speeches to the troops. Afterward the troops marched back from the suburb into the main fortress of Mantua, and the citizens illuminated the town as the celebration continued with a military ball in the piazza.[85]

During the summer, Bonaparte devoted considerable effort to provisioning Mantua and to working out the details of the new Cisalpine Republic. On 10 October he wrote to the Directory to inform them that negotiations with the Austrians were at the point of concluding and that either a definitive peace would be signed or talks would be broken off. He also outlined the principal conditions of the projected treaty—specifically, that the Cisalpine territory would have good military frontiers and be composed of Lombardy, Bergamo, Crema, Brescia, Mantua, and Peschiera and all of the fortifications up to the west bank of the Adige and the Po with Modena, Ferrara, Bologna, and the Romagna. Bonaparte, demonstrating the vast impact of his victories, explained that in the treaty 3.5 million inhabitants of the new Cisalpine Republic would gain liberty as would 4 million more within the new boundaries of France. The Austrian Empire would gain 1.9 million inhabitants with the addition of the Venetian territory but lose 1.5 million in Lombardy, 300,000 in Modena, and 2.5 million in Belgium.[86] Articles 6, 7, and 8 of the Treaty of Campo Formio, signed on 17 October 1797, solidified Bonaparte's assurance to the Directory concerning the Cisalpine Republic and established the new military frontiers.[87]

In addition to these changes in the secular realm, the French made significant ecclesiastical changes in Mantua. Over the course of 1797, French troops occupied the Convent and Church of the Holy Spirit after driving out the Reformed brothers of Saint Francis. The French abolished the following Roman Catholic orders: the Clerics of the Congregation of Saint Paul, the Benedictine brothers at the Church of All Saints, the Benedictine nuns of St. John, the Dominican brothers and Dominican sisters of St. Catherine of Siena, the Lateran brothers of the Annunciation in the suburb of San Giorgio, the priests of the Oratory of St. Philip Neri, the friars minor of St. Francis of Paola, the ministers to the infirm at St. Thomas, the Olivetans of St. Christopher, and the Servants of Mary at St. Barnabas. The French also abolished the Servants of St. Mary of Mercy in Breda on the Water, the Teatine clerics at St. Maurizio, and the Third Order Franciscans on the *via degli Stabili* (street of stables), whose church with the name "St. Louis, King of France" was left in ruins. They desecrated the church of Our Lady of Victory, where they stole the famous painting by Andrea Mantegna that portrayed Mary and the infant Jesus seated on a tall pedestal with Francesco Gonzaga IV and his wife, Isabella d'Este, and other figures, courtiers, and warriors kneeling in adoration. In addition, the French seized the beautiful bronze head of the painter Mantegna, which had been in the Chapel of St. John the Baptist in the Church of St. Andrew. They took the famous picture by Rubens depicting the Transfiguration, styled after that of Raphael; the painting *Temptation of St. Antonio Abate*, attributed to Paolo Veronese, which hung in the main hall of the duomo of St. Peter's; and the picture of the Apostles Peter and Andrew being called by Jesus, which was a prized work of the Mantuan artist Fermo Guisoni, a student of Giulio Romano. The theft of these artistic treasures, and many others, greatly contributed to the Mantuans' growing hatred of the French.[88] The local *Giornale della Libertà* published a list of all the artistic treasures the French art commission sent from Rome to Paris but never mentioned the losses in Mantua.[89]

The tensions between those favoring and those despising the French continued to grow. Many were upset with the constant celebrations paid for from public funds. The Municipalità sponsored a large festival on 15 October to honor Virgil in Pietole, where earlier a large pyramid and bust of the poet had been erected in the woods commemorating him.[90] Two days later Bonaparte ordered the army to honor the fallen hero of the campaigns in Germany, General Lazare Hoche, on 31 October.[91] In response, the Municipalità of Mantua sponsored yet another major civic festival to honor Hoche, Virgil, and Italian liberty. Bonaparte visited Mantua for the celebration and was received by Lattanzi and Franzini, the leading Jacobins, who spoke to him about the organization of the new local Mantuan National Guard. Similar to the 18 July festival, the garrison, consisting of French, Polish, and now Cisalpine troops, passed in review for Miollis and Bonaparte in honor of Hoche, in the central plaza at 10:00 A.M. and then marched to the San Giorgio suburb to the *Campo di Marte* (Field of Mars) to hear patriotic speeches. In addition to this celebration, Bonaparte inspected the Citadel, the newly constructed fortifications and the fleet that Baste had assembled. Baste then transported Bonaparte and a party of government officials to Pietole to join the celebration honoring Virgil. That evening Mantua was illuminated and Bonaparte attended the festival and a ball held at the theater. The following morning he visited the Migliaretto fortifications and met with several of the officers and adjutants, then spent the afternoon meditating on the topographical maps of Mantua with such intensity that he delayed his scheduled 2:00 P.M. departure until 8:00 P.M.[92]

On 11 November Bonaparte addressed the people of the Cisalpine Republic in a proclamation telling them that on 21 November their constitution would be in force and that their Directory, Legislature, Court of Appeals, and subordinate administrations would be in operation. He warned them that to be worthy of their destiny, they must pass only wise and moderate laws, execute them with force and energy, respect religion, and promote the spread of education. He ended his address with a farewell saying that he would be leaving in a few days and that only the orders of his government or some imminent danger to the Cisalpine Republic would bring him back. Finally, he declared that wherever the service of his country would take him, he would always have a lively interest in the welfare and glory of their republic.[93] The next day Bonaparte informed the Directory that he was working night and day to complete the organization of the

Cisalpine Republic and arrangements for the Army of Italy, so that his absence would not be felt when he returned to France.[94] In the process, Mantua was garrisoned with three French regiments that were no longer needed in the field army. Although Bonaparte tried to ensure his absence did not adversely affect the fledgling republic, he was far from successful in that endeavor.

Once Bonaparte left Milan for France on 17 November, the discipline and morale of the French army in Mantua began to collapse.[95] The 14th Regiment had not been paid in five months, and the 12th and 64th in four months. On 11 February 1798 these regiments marched toward the Pradella gate threatening to abandon the defense of the city and leave for France. With his adjutant and the commander of the piazza, Colonel Voix, Miollis persuaded the soldiers to return to their posts by promising them they would be paid. At eight o'clock that evening, in an effort to correct the situation, Miollis wrote to the Central Administration of the Department of the Mincio requesting 400,000 francs to pay the soldiers.[96] Even as the administration struggled to collect enough money to pay the army, it continued to stage large civic celebrations. As recently as 21 January 1798, the Municipalità held yet another festival, this time recognizing the citizens of the Cisalpine Republic.[97] Even though many were excited about the new Cisalpine government, the new administration encountered the same problems that the previous administration faced. The burden of taxation made the people weary. Moreover, many in Mantua were upset that their city was placed under the authority of the new capital of Milan in the restructured Cisalpine Republic.[98] The influence of those who favored the Austrians grew in towns of the republic after Bonaparte left. From Paris, the French government tried to exert additional pressure on the Cisalpine Republic, which led to some unwise decisions, such as the arrest of Citizens Paradisi and Moscati, two members of the Cisalpine Executive Directory. Bonaparte, who had personally selected both men at the moment of the republic's creation, now protested to the Directory. He noted that, during the first campaign when the Austrians still held Mantua, Paradisi had dared to lead two hundred of his compatriots against two hundred Austrians who had withdrawn into a castle and succeeded in taking the Austrians prisoner; and that afterward he and his family, and their entire town of Reggio, became the target of threats by the Austrians. After also speaking well of Moscati, Bonaparte argued that disparagement of the Cisalpine government at the very moment of its birth and the loss of its best citizens would be a real misfortune for France and a triumph for Emperor Francis and his partisans.[99]

The citizens of the Cisalpine Republic were not the only ones growing discontented with the administration. Friction within the French garrison of 6,774 stationed at Mantua continued to grow as well.[100] Soon after the February 1798 mutiny, General of Brigade Jacques Chambarlhac was assigned to replace Miollis.[101] The change in command of the fortress did not improve the situation, however. In September many soldiers deserted from the Mantuan National Guard.[102] Later in 1798 a French requirement to conscript soldiers from the city exacerbated the situation further. The government passed laws on 30 November and 31 December mandating that all male citizens eighteen to twenty-six years of age be enrolled in the military. On 26 January 1799 the first forty-seven young men from the commune of Mantua left the city as soldiers; only three were volunteers, while the rest were conscripts.[103] The hatred of the conscription order caused riots in other towns. At San Benedetto, even though the town had sent many recruits, the local municipality imposed an order proposed by a self-proclaimed "Representative of the People" that all men had to be subject to conscription or none at all. The result was that the conscript law in San Benedetto caused the people of Gonzaga, Bondanello, Moglia, Palidano, and Polesine to riot from 2 to 4 February. They burned all of the papers and registries of the commune offices, threatened the local municipality leaders, and destroyed food supplies. At Moglia and Bondanello, they burned the church registries as well to ensure there were no records of who lived in the town. They claimed their actions were justified since they had willingly paid numerous taxes and filled numerous requisitions and therefore were exempt from military service. When the commandant of San Benedetto learned about the riots, he immediately sent to Gonzaga two companies of French grenadiers. The troops had only to beat their drums to quell the disturbance and disperse the crowds. Commissariats Somenzari and Brochetta and the military agent Franzini went immediately to San Benedetto and deposed the municipality, enforced the conscription order, and arrested the self-proclaimed "Representative of the People" and his associates on 5 February. The next day at Gonzaga, working with the commandant, they identified the leaders of the mutiny and sent them to Casalmaggiore to stand military trial.[104]

Such was the condition of the fortress and the status of the government when the War of the Second Coalition broke out. At the end of February 1799 the Directory sent General Barthélemy-Louis Scherer, who was the minister of war, to assume command of the Army of Italy. Upon arriving in Mantua on 21 March, Scherer ceremoniously reviewed the troops destined to march to the border on the Adige to counter the Austrian force buildup around Verona.[105] On the same day, Scherer ordered a new commander, General François Philippe Foissac-Latour, to take command of Mantua.[106]

The departure of the Austrians from Mantua and the arrival of the French brought many changes to the city. Bonaparte rebuilt a powerful fortress at Mantua and provisioned it to endure a year-long siege. He and the government granted to the people new freedoms, emancipated the Jews, abolished titles of nobility, and incorporated Mantua into the Cisalpine Republic. But these liberties came at a heavy price exacted by Bonaparte and the French government. The government levied taxes, confiscated works of art, stripped churches of valuable objects, and conscripted young men. These exactions led the Mantuans to change their attitude toward the French army between 1797 and 1799 from a generally positive view to a more negative one.

CHAPTER 9

ENTER KRAY AND SUVOROV

THE SECOND COALITION IN ITALY

"Mantua, Turin, and Tortona are besieged. I hope that the first of
these places will hold out until November. I hope, if luck is with
me, to arrive in Europe at the beginning of October."

BONAPARTE TO KLÉBER, 1799, WHILE IN EGYPT

B Y 1798 the French Directory concluded that an aggressive foreign
policy was necessary to expand French political and economic
hegemony as well as sustain their fragile financial system at home.
French ambitions in the Middle East, as manifested in Napoleon's
Army of the Orient, and military actions in Switzerland, Italy, the
Low Countries, and on the Rhine led Austria, Great Britain, Russia,
Turkey, and the kingdom of Naples to form the Second Coalition.
Given its financial resources, Britain was the glue that held the
coalition together. Coalitions that are formed easily can also come
apart easily, because of differing war aims, but this coalition was
determined to defeat the expanding French Republic. During this
war the Austrians and Russians besieged and captured Mantua in
1799. Nevertheless, because of the divergent interests and goals
of the Austrian Aulic Council and the Russian command regarding the importance of capturing Mantua, the siege acted as a wedge
to divide the alliance. The Austro-Russian siege of Mantua caused
much concern for France and the Directory. Bonaparte was with his
Army of the Orient in Egypt during the siege, but he cited the siege
as one of the reasons for his prompt return to Europe.[1]

Bonaparte had started to form his army for the expedition to
Egypt after the Directory named him general-in-chief of the Army
of the Orient on 12 April 1798.[2] Many of the individuals who helped
him capture Mantua in 1797 accompanied him to Egypt. While on
board the *Orient* from 22 June to 1 July during the trip across the

Mediterranean, he organized his army. He brought Andréossy to command the pontoon train, Dumas to command the cavalry, and Rampon to command the 18th and 32nd demibrigades, which had ensured Provera's defeat.[3] He brought his favorites as well: Berthier, his ever present chief of staff as well as Lannes, Marmont, and Murat. Coincidently, some of the men and equipment were transported to Egypt on a ship named in honor of the famous 1796–97 siege—the *Mantoue*.[4] Sérurier and Miollis were not chosen by Bonaparte to go to Egypt, so they remained in Italy. However, neither were at Mantua when the 1799 siege began. The drain of many of the best French generals, save Masséna and Joubert, from northern Italy for the expedition to Egypt caused a major problem for the French during the War of the Second Coalition. Moreover, in less than a year, the French Army of Italy changed commanders six times. The last change occurred during the lead-up to the war when Joubert was replaced by Barthélemy-Louis Scherer.[5]

The lack of quality military leadership in northern Italy was not the only problem for the French in 1799. French exactions, especially in money and artworks, and revolutionary anticlericalism inflamed the common people. The pent-up anger caused a popular and reactionary explosion against the French and their Italian supporters.[6] The entry of the Allies into northern Italy only exacerbated the situation for the French.

In March 1799 the Austrians had more than 60,000 troops in Italy; 50,700 were located near Verona under the Austrian general Paul Kray;[7] Field Marshal Aleksandr Suvorov, with 24,551 Russian troops, moved to join him.[8] Kray was familiar with Lombardy in general and Pavia, Milan, and Mantua in particular, having been stationed in those places from 1763 to 1778.[9] Scherer, who had recently taken command, received from the Directory on 22 March a plan of attack—along with the 12 March French declaration of war on the emperor of Austria and the duke of Tuscany. Scherer determined to imitate Napoleon's example in 1797 and try to destroy Kray's army before Suvorov could consolidate with it. It was Scherer whom Bonaparte had replaced as commander of the Army of Italy in 1796, and since that time Scherer had not improved as an army commander. He marched toward Verona on 26 March to attack the Austrians.[10] In his advance, the Army of Italy clashed with the Austrian force at Magnano, south of Verona. The French had 34,000 infantry and 7,000 cavalry in the field while the Austrians had nearly

40,000 troops with an additional 5,000 cavalry. Before nightfall, Scherer was defeated; he moved his tattered forces west, taking with them 2,000 prisoners and several cannon—a poor showing for his loss of 4,000 killed and wounded and an additional 4,000 taken prisoner. Magnano was one of the most glorious victories yet for the Austrian crown, and it foreshadowed the fate of the French in the coming operations in northern Italy. After Magnano, the French suffered defeat at Villafranca, followed by one disaster after another until they were driven back across the Maritime Alps. The Austrian victory demonstrated the importance of interior lines and central position as the Austrians held the fortresses of Verona and Legnago, from which they were able to conduct their operations.[11] The Austrians did not, however, follow up their success with a ruthless pursuit. It was a full eight days after the battle before they crossed the Mincio and established themselves at Castellaro. The delay occurred when Kray detached ten battalions of troops and eight squadrons of cavalry to observe Mantua and sent two battalions of infantry with one hundred cavalry to invest Peschiera.[12]

According to Bonaparte, Scherer should only have drawn back to the Mincio, the river guarded by the fortress of Mantua, and remained there to defend the river line. Or if he abandoned this defense, he should have established himself in the Serraglio just south of Mantua and waited there for reinforcements while protected by the Po and the Mincio.[13] Bonaparte, who had experienced the effects of fever on his army around Mantua in 1796 and 1797, was careful about selecting healthy ground. He later stated that the fever season around the fortress began at the end of June and that if the Russians had come up before General Jacques Macdonald's Army of Naples could join Scherer, the French commander should have marched south to meet Macdonald. But instead, an intimidated Scherer ordered a rapid retreat. General Jean-Victor Moreau, on the other hand, proposed to Scherer that the French army should defend a line along the Oglio River and that a halt of several days would allow the troops time to rest and reorganize. Scherer ignored that advice; he was determined not to halt his retreat until he had reached the Adda. So he retired, weakening his army by reinforcing garrisons in his path. Scherer, realizing that Mantua could not be abandoned because of the importance of its geographical location, added 6,600 men to its garrison which brought its strength up to 12,000.[14] His failure to hold the Mincio, however, gave the Austrians the opportunity to begin the investment of Mantua.[15]

Overwhelmed, Scherer wrote to the Directory on 7 April:

> More than half of the regiments of this army are from the old Army of the Rhine, and they repose their entire trust in General Moreau who has always led them to victory. They do not know me, and they have no confidence in me at all. Soldiers identify themselves with successful generals, and Moreau is one of those . . . Citizen Directors, with the fate of the army in mind I beg you to find some excuse to recall me or send me wherever you like—as long as it is not to command an army—and that you give this command to General Moreau.[16]

On 25 April Scherer ordered Moreau to take charge of the headquarters established at Inzago while he went to Milan to plead with the Directory of the Cisalpine Republic to not abandon their capital. At Milan he learned that Moreau indeed replaced him.[17] Moreau was informed of his appointment at Lodi on the evening of 26 April and wasted no time in dispatching orders to his various units to concentrate their forces.[18] In the first review of his divisions, Moreau was greeted with cheers of "*Vive* Moreau! *Vive* the savior of the Army of Italy."[19]

Moreau's position as the new commander of the French Army of Italy put him in a peculiar situation. He had some 27,000 dispirited men facing Suvorov who had combined his Russian troops with the Austrian forces, bringing their total to 90,000 troops.[20]

On 28 April General Michael Melas, the new Austrian commander, and Suvorov entered Milan. The French, meanwhile, retired into the Ligurian Alps, their numbers reduced to some 20,000–25,000 by losses in battle and by the manning of garrisons to reinforce Mantua, Peschiera, and the citadels of Milan and Turin.[21] Kray had been assigned to besiege Peschiera. His batteries opened fire on the city on 4 May, and the bombardment continued until the 7th when the 1,000-man French garrison surrendered under the condition that they receive the honors of war and agree not to serve against the coalition for six months. Kray took seventy-five cannon, eight gunboats, and three larger boats. He was then able to use this flotilla to move his cannons down the Mincio to Mantua to begin the investment of the fortress.[22]

With the Allies in Milan, the capital city of the Cisalpine Republic, a popular revolt broke out against the French in Piedmont and

Lombardy. Still the rebels hardly interfered with the operations of the retreating French army. The rebellion consisted largely of reprisals against those local citizens who collaborated with the French.

In pursuit of Moreau, Suvorov entered Novi by 10 May and drove the French farther west, after some fighting around Marengo and Valenza.[23] The Allies besieged the citadel of Milan on the night of 21–22 May with sixty cannon and mortars. It surrendered in three days under the terms that the garrison would not serve against the Allies for a year. The surrender gave the Austrians 119 pieces of artillery and freed the entire division under Prince Friedrich Hohenzollern to reinforce the besieging army at Mantua. After being informed of Moreau's retreat, Suvorov occupied Valenza, sent a detachment to invest Alessandria, and led his army toward Turin. The Austrian general Vukassovich, who commanded Suvorov's advance guard, seized one of the gates of Turin on 27 May, aided by the local inhabitants, and was able to compel the French, Piedmontese, and Swiss units, commanded by Fiorella, to retreat into the citadel. A formal siege was then undertaken by Lieutenant General Konrad Valentin von Kaim with 5,740 Austrian troops, with Piedmontese auxiliaries and 100 pieces of artillery. When Fiorella capitulated on 20 June, the Austrians captured 374 cannon, 184 mortars, sixty howitzers, and tons of gunpowder as well as a large quantity of military stores that had been accumulating in the city since Bonaparte first conquered it in 1796. The resistance, in 1799, of the fortified cities of Lombardy, which fell quickly to the Allies, displayed little effort or determination. These actions left Moreau and Macdonald in dire straits, for want of military resources.[24] In Turin, much to the Austrian chancellor Baron Franz von Thugut's annoyance, Suvorov proclaimed the restoration of the House of Savoy in the person of Charles Emmanuel IV. The Austrian vision for the future of Piedmont, as perceived by Thugut, was quite different than that of Suvorov, and thus the first crack in the allied coalition started to appear between the Austrian government and the Russian marshal.[25] Suvorov wanted to reestablish the monarchies in the liberated territory, while the Austrians wanted to reassert their control throughout northern Italy.

Piedmont's future was not the only source of friction developing between Suvorov and the Austrian government. Suvorov would have pressed his victories had he been given that flexibility, but his decision was overruled by the cautious policy of the Aulic Council. Above all things, the council wanted to secure the Quadrilateral fortresses of Verona, Legnago, Peschiera, and Mantua to protect Austrian Venetia. They compelled the Russian marshal, against his will, to halt his pursuit and formally besiege Mantua. On 27 May Suvorov wrote to the Russian ambassador at Vienna:

> Your highness well knows that in the instructions I received on leaving Vienna, it is said with respect to Mantua that it shall be besieged or blockaded, as I think best. The latter was done, and Kray and Klenau, after effecting it, proceeded with the rest of their troops to join Ott, in order to obviate all danger to Mantua from the union of Montrichard and Gauthier with Macdonald. They were, however, suddenly recalled by the council of war, to besiege Mantua, without my having received the slightest intimation on the subject—so you see I am not wanted here. This decree disturbs the connection of all my operations, and in consequence I must prolong my stay at this place. . . . I could garrison towns with the best of them, and with the troops they would liberate, act freely in the field; but now, garrisons take half our men. Was not this the grand rule of the French in their rapid conquests?[26]

The same day that Suvorov sent his complaint, he informed Kray to be obedient to his orders from Austria and press the siege of Mantua with all his energy and means and told him that Hohenzollern would be sent from Milan to join him at Mantua, which would raise his force to 32,000 men.[27] Although the Austrians could have gained some advantage by capturing Mantua, that would have been dwarfed by what they stood to gain by controlling all of northern Italy— an outcome that would have been possible had the Aulic Council not restricted Suvorov's initiative. Thus the working relationship between the Russian commander and the Austrian leaders in Vienna became even more strained.

On 9 June Suvorov came to the conclusion that the gathering French forces would attack in the direction of Alessandria. To some degree, this decision was based on the failure of his spies to inform him of the actual French positions. In addition, Moreau had spread false reports that Macdonald would join his forces by sea and that they would both attack from the Riviera. Suvorov called on the Austrian commanders to concentrate their forces with his Russian army. He even explicitly asked Kray at Mantua to send any available cavalry as they would not be as useful during a siege; however, following the policies of the Aulic Council, Kray did not detach the otherwise requested infantry, artillery, or engineer soldiers away from the siege operations.[28]

Modena, Ferrara, Bologna, and Ravenna fell to the Allies, but their advance was limited farther southeast because of French strength in the Rimini area and the forces of Giuseppe Lahoz. Lahoz had defected from the French during the growing discord between the Cisalpine officials and the French Directory. His defection from the French, however, did not carry him to the side of the Allies; rather, he became one of the first ardent Italian nationalists. He and his troops fought the French and Austrians alike in an interesting three-sided war in the Marches that lasted until October.[29]

Macdonald, who came up from southern Italy, easily drove back the Austrian advance troops near Modena.[30] But then instead of moving quickly by the most direct road to join Moreau somewhere to the northeast of Genoa, he thought he saw a chance of smashing the coalition forces by crossing the Po and attacking their lines of communication, possibly relieving Mantua.[31]

Suvorov had already left Turin by 2:00 A.M. on 10 June to move toward Alessandria in preparation for battle. He had 34,000 men under his immediate command, and Vukassovich was on his way with 4,400 more. With reinforcements from Generals Ott and Hohenzollern, Suvorov hoped to have as many as 50,000 men to engage Macdonald.[32] Although Suvorov thought the French would attack from Genoa, once he received word of Macdonald's true position in Tuscany, he quickly notified one of his commanders: "Latest news: The French like bees, and almost from all places, are moving toward Mantua. We must hurry after them. Wherever this reaches you, after resting as much as necessary, hurry to join us. They are strong; God be with us."[33] Suvorov adopted the same energetic resolution by which Bonaparte had repulsed the attack of General Wurmser to relieve Mantua in August 1796. All of his advance posts in Piedmont were recalled and ordered to concentrate at Asti. Suvorov rapidly started reassembling his army on 15 June and ordered Kray to raise the siege of Mantua and dispatch his artillery to Peschiera and Verona and to unite all his available forces with the main army in the vicinity of Piacenza.[34] Kray moved his besieging artillery east to the Adige as directed, but his troops from Mantua failed to join the rest of Suvorov's army.[35] The Austrian emperor had placed so much importance on Mantua that he signed an order to Kray stating that the acquisition of that fortress was of greater importance to him than any other imperial consideration. Suvorov, therefore, had to deal not only with Moreau and Macdonald but also with the restraints placed upon him by the Austrian authorities.[36]

Moreau and Macdonald, now in open communication, decided to unite their forces on the Lower Po, in order to threaten the communications of the Allies, drive the allied forces away from Mantua, and push them off the Lombardy plain. Kray, who commanded all of the Austrian forces on the Lower Po, had 24,000 men, of whom 12,000 were conducting siege operations at Mantua while 5,000, under Hohenzollern, had been dispatched to cover Modena and 6,000 under Ott to guard the lateral valleys of the Taro and the Trebbia.[37] Though a good fighting general, Macdonald was no Bonaparte. As he marched north to Piacenza, Macdonald was met on the Trebbia by Suvorov, whom Moreau had failed to pin down. The desperate battle that followed along the Trebbia lasted for three bitter days (17–19 June), and Macdonald was soundly beaten. The Austrians lost 254 killed, 1,903 wounded, and 500 missing while the Russians lost 681 killed, 2,073 wounded and an indefinite number of missing for a total of about 6,000 in Allied casualties. The only verifiable figures related to French losses are those of the 7,183 nontransportable wounded found by the Allies at Piacenza and the 200 found at Parma. Forced to retreat west over poor roads across the Apennines to the coast, Macdonald arrived with only 20,000 exhausted and demoralized men on the Ligurian Riviera. The French had now lost all of Italy, save the coastal strip on both sides of Genoa, and their casualties had been disastrously heavy.[38]

Fortunately for Macdonald and the French, Suvorov received positive orders from the Aulic Council not to attempt any operations beyond the Apennines until the fortresses of Lombardy were reduced. In addition, he received a letter from the Austrian emperor reminding him of the vital importance of the capture of Mantua, the key to holding the Quadrilateral fortifications and the Lower Po. Consequently, Suvorov was compelled to remain inactive on the Orba River while Macdonald's tattered army moved through Tuscany into Genoese territory. Pressured by the council, Suvorov realized that the only way to resume the offensive was to capture Mantua. He reinforced Kray, bringing the combined Austro-Russian siege force to 32,100 men, not including the thousands of peasants employed in the operations.[39] Kray resumed the difficult task of besieging Mantua and again brought up his heavy artillery, which had been sent as far east as the Adige earlier as a precaution in the face of the expected arrival of Macdonald's forces. Two reserves of heavy Austrian and Russian artillery were united and added, which meant more than six hundred cannon were available to hasten the surrender.[40]

With this powerful siege force, Kray circled the fortress with artillery and entrenchments and conducted the second siege of Mantua. The fortress fell on 30 July 1799, which allowed Kray and his forces to participate in the Battle of Novi on 15 August. The two Austrian corps under Kray and Melas and the Russian corps under General Vilim Kristoforovich Derfelden defeated the French under Joubert, who was slain during the battle.[41]

With the Lombardy plain cleared of French forces, Thugut now wanted the Russians out of Italy as well so that Austria could reestablish its imperial control. As the quickest means of removing the Russians from Italy, and concurrently advancing Austrian interests in Alsace and Lorraine, Thugut transferred Archduke Charles and his army from Switzerland to the middle Rhine and brought Suvorov and his troops from Italy to replace him at Zurich as the commander of the allied forces there. In the meantime Thugut replaced Archduke Charles's troops in Switzerland with a corps of Austrians and 30,000 Russians under General Alexander Korsakov. Although the redeployment of the Russians to Switzerland was contrary to the principle of "mass," considering that the French had yet to be completely defeated, Suvorov received orders to march north on 27 August, less than a month after the fall of Mantua.[42]

Shortly after the fall of Mantua, Bonaparte, in Egypt, received word through the British newspapers that Mantua was being besieged. From his headquarters in Cairo, he informed General Louis Charles Antoine Desaix that France had declared war on 13 March against the Emperor of Austria. Giving some indication that his services would be needed on the Continent, he explained to Desaix that several battles had taken place; that Jourdan had been beaten at Feldkirch, in the Black Forest; that Scherer, who was entrusted with the Army of Italy, was beaten in Rivoli by Kray; and that the enemy had passed the Mincio and Oglio Rivers. He also pointed out that the defeats of the French had occurred before the Russians had arrived in Italy.[43] On 22 August Bonaparte ordered General Jean Baptiste Kléber to assume command of the Army of the Orient, and informed him that he was taking with him Berthier,

Lannes, Murat, Andréossy, and Marmont. In his dispatch, Bonaparte included British and Frankfurt newspapers printed through 10 June stating that Italy was lost by the French. Not knowing that Mantua had already fallen, Bonaparte explained to Kléber that Mantua, Turin, and Tortona were besieged, but that he had reason to hope Mantua would hold out until the end of November, long before which he expected to reach Europe.[44] Given the amount of effort that Bonaparte had devoted to the defense of Mantua, with provisions to sustain a garrison of 36,000 men for one year, he expected the garrison to resist for at least seven and a half months, especially considering that Canto d'Yrles and Wurmser defended the fortress for eight months without forcing the Mantuans to provision themselves as Bonaparte had done.[45] Bonaparte stated in a letter to his finance administrator, Jean Baptiste Etienne Poussielgue, that because of the critical events that occurred in Europe between 15 March and 15 June, he felt a pressing duty to return as quickly as possible. With good fortune, he hoped to arrive while Mantua was still in French hands.[46] Thus, in this letter Bonaparte's primary reason for returning to Europe was to arrive in time to relieve Mantua. Unknown to Bonaparte, Mantua had already fallen twenty-five days before he wrote the letter. En route to France, while in Ajaccio, he learned about the continued reverses in Italy—the Battles of Novi and Trebbia and the capitulation of Mantua.[47]

Because of the continued decline of the Army of Italy and the outbreak of the War of the Second Coalition, the Austrians and their Russian allies were able to capture most of northern Italy. The allocation of troops to besiege Mantua caused problems between the Austrian and Russian forces since the two sides had opposing views on how best to carry out the war. The Austrians pursued their own interests in Lombardy, while Suvorov was concerned with the coalition goals of expelling the French from Italy. When Suvorov agreed to support Kray with the siege, Mantua fell quickly, before Bonaparte even received word of its investment.

CHAPTER 10

FOISSAC-LATOUR AND THE DEFENSE OF 1799

"Enter Mantua at all costs."

FRANCIS II TO SUVOROV

"In order to be honorable, a capitulation must stipulate hard conditions for the garrison. There is always an unfavorable presumption against the garrison which marches out of a place over a bridge of gold."

NAPOLEON BONAPARTE

By late March 1799, it was clear to General Scherer that Mantua would soon be surrounded. From his headquarters in Mantua on 21 March, he sent an order to General François Philippe Foissac-Latour at Lucca to come and take command immediately of the fortress and garrison.[1] By the same courier, Foissac-Latour responded with a lengthy letter informing Scherer that he was flattered to have been given command of the fortress, but that he did not think it could effectively resist unless the proper fortifications were constructed. A grand defense, he argued, should not be undertaken just for the sake of glory; he demanded men and matériel if he were to hold the position.[2] Much confidence was placed in Latour to make a vigorous defense of Mantua, but as a fortress commander, he turned out to be an utter failure for the French.

Latour had been an army engineer his entire career. He entered the French army as a cadet on 1 January 1765, was promoted to captain in the Engineer Corps in 1777, and served in the American Revolutionary War. He was made chief of engineers at Phalsbourg in 1785, a post he held for six years. In 1791 he was knighted in the Order of Saint Louis, and the next year he was promoted to the position of adjutant general lieutenant colonel (a senior staff officer) and served in the Army of the North. In 1793 General Auguste

Picot de Dampierre named him provisional general of brigade, but Latour shortly afterward was suspended and arrested. His royal ties were suspect. He was later freed, confirmed as general of brigade, and reassigned to the Army of the North. He was relieved once again on 30 July 1793 and imprisoned. After again gaining his freedom with the end of the Reign of Terror and the fall of Robespierre, he was promoted to general of division in June 1795 and served in the Army of the Coast of Cherbourg. In October of the same year, he was suspended a third time—this time under the pretext that his brother-in-law was an émigré. He was once again reinstated and then appointed French ambassador to Sweden in January 1796, but he never assumed the post. Instead he took command of the camp at Grenelle in the Army of the Interior. He was subsequently assigned to the Army of Germany in October 1797 but was immediately reassigned at his request to the Army of Italy.[3]

Latour was a prolific writer on engineering and fortifications. In 1789 he helped write a book on the military and political importance of fortification systems. The same year he also published his own two-volume work on the theory and practice of entrenchments.[4] He later republished with commentary the three major works of Marshal Sébastien Vauban on mines and on the attack and defense of fortifications.[5]

Latour, an ardent anti-Semite, also wrote pamphlets against the Jews denouncing them as a threat to his city and country. In one of his many pamphlets, titled "Observations on the Writing in Favor of the Jews of Alsace" (1790), Latour responded to a pro-Jewish pamphlet thus "My reflections are addressed directly to you, Mr. Advocate of the tribe of Judas."[6] In one of his lengthier (109-page) anti-Jewish screeds, he denounced those in his home province of Alsace, while in another, shorter (26-page) pamphlet, he vilified the Jews in Metz.[7] Latour also produced other political writings and a collection of patriotic poems.[8]

Foissac-Latour's reputation as a fortification systems expert prompted the Directory to select him, on 29 March 1798, to survey a line of demarcation with the Austrians and to supervise the refurbishment of Mantua and the construction of other fortresses along that frontier. Scherer, then minister of war, added additional instructions to the survey assignment and forwarded the order to Latour.[9] Latour seemed to be the perfect match for the job: he was a renowned engineer and he was stationed in Italy. In addition, his fluency in the German language would complement his interactions with the Austrians in surveying the demarcation line. Latour completed an initial assessment, and by the end of June 1798 he sent his report to Scherer. Latour noted that the line of demarcation was impossible to determine wherever it did not follow the course of the rivers owing to the differing interpretations of the Treaty of Campo Formio, differences which would have to be resolved at the Congress of Rastadt. With respect to the fortifications at Mantua, Latour pointed out that work had been suspended because of a lack of funds, which he was in the process of demanding from the Cisalpine Republic.[10] Latour was only able to procure 100,000 francs for all of the Cisalpine military frontier fortifications but was promised 2 million more. Still he told Scherer that in reality the promised funds would amount to no more than 500,000 francs and that the money would have to be spent on the new fortresses, specifically the one at Rocca d'Anfo, according to article 13 of the treaty of alliance with the Cisalpine Republic.[11] He thought that Bonaparte, Chasseloup, and Berthier had perhaps too hastily agreed to new fortification projects, which became codified in the treaty, and queried whether the agreement could be modified. While disagreeing with Bonaparte concerning fortification priorities, Latour—in the same dispatch to Scherer—castigated Dabon, the commander of engineers for the Army of Italy, for deviating from his priorities of construction.[12] After the siege Latour would claim that he was convinced Mantua could not endure a regular siege because the defenders could not provide protective fire beyond the front curtain of the Pradella hornwork, thus making Porta Pradella the weakest point of the fortress.[13]

By the time hostilities began in 1799, Latour was commanding at Lucca. He assumed his new command at Mantua on 29 March 1799 and immediately ordered the commissary of war, the chief of artillery, and the chief of engineers to report on the status of their areas of responsibility.[14] On the 31st he started a stream of requests to Scherer to send men and money for the defense of Mantua.[15] Scherer, however, was too busy trying to hold back the Austrian advance led by Kray to worry about Latour's concerns. And Latour was indeed concerned. In early April his spies delivered to him an anonymous poem written by one of the locals indicating the sentiment of the people:

The French shudder
The Cisalpines putter
The high patriots die
Long live the Emperor[16]

On 6 April, the day after the Battle of Magnano, where the French were defeated by Kray, the French abandoned Villafranca and Isola della Scala. Scherer moved his headquarters to Roverbella and concentrated his army. He did not consider his forces to be strong enough to defend the Mincio River, even with the support of Mantua. On the 7th he crossed the Mincio while General Johann Von Klenau's Austrian Corps took the principal towns south of Mantua and carried off hundreds of prisoners and 18,000 muskets intended for the defense of Mantua.[17] In response to these developments, Latour began preparing for a blockade and siege by improving his defenses.[18] To ensure accountability of all his troops, he had to sort out his assigned French garrison soldiers from the other French units that had taken refuge from the Austrians as well as other French troops who were simply loitering at Mantua. On 8 April Latour ordered all nongarrison active-duty soldiers and detachments to leave Mantua immediately and return to their respective units. The noncommissioned officers and soldiers who did not leave within an hour of the order were to be arrested and tried as deserters, and the commissioned officers were to be relieved of command.[19] The military magazines were well supplied, but Latour was frantic to collect more supplies for the fortress to sustain its population. The same day he informed the inhabitants that the customs office would relax the tax for goods being brought into the city so that the people could gather as many provisions as possible from the countryside.[20]

On 11 April Scherer's army marched into Mantua over the Ponte Molina and San Giorgio causeways. Scherer left a 10,000-man garrison of French, Polish, Cisalpine, Swiss, and Piedmontese soldiers in the fortress when the main French army exited Mantua through the Pradella gate and moved on to Bozzolo.[21] The main body of the French troops consisted of the 26th and 29th *Légère*; the 31st, 45th, 56th, and 93rd Line; the 6th Artillery and 7th Dragoons, while that of the Cisalpine was the 1st Light as well as sappers and artillery. The Swiss provided the 1st and 2nd Legions, and Piedmont contributed the 2nd Line and a squadron of carabineers.[22]

The Polish soldiers were members of the Polish Auxiliary Legion of the Cisalpine Republic. Before entering Mantua the legion commandant, General Jozef Wielhorski, tried to convince Scherer not to use the Poles to defend the fortress since they came to Italy expecting to fight in open battle and, more importantly, because many of the Polish privates were deserters from the Austrian lines who had been forced into the Austrian army. Wielhorski knew these soldiers could expect the most severe punishment if the fortress were taken by the Austrians. According to one Polish chronicler, Scherer, who did not like the Poles, should have appreciated having had the Poles to guard the French army's retreat after the Battle of Magnano, instead of arguing that the Polish Legion was intended to defend the important fortress of Mantua and that assigning it this role was demonstrative proof of France's highest trust.[23] The day before Scherer ordered the Poles to Mantua, Latour proclaimed a state of siege of the fortress (see fig. 3).[24]

Strangely enough, Latour made his proclamation of a state of siege before Peschiera fell. Mantua was not even surrounded. But Latour used the pretext of being under siege to begin his consolidation of power. He suppressed the Municipalitá and the Central Administration of the Department of the Mincio; abolished all authorities and laws; and, aided by the most ardent Republicans, formed two commissions: an administrative commission under Teodoro Somenzari for civil and financial functions, and a police commission under Ferdinando Arrivabene. Both executive authorities answered only to Latour.[25]

Meanwhile, General Melas arrived on 8 April to take command of the Austrian army from Kray. Melas sent his advance troops to the Mincio while Klenau pushed on to Mantua.[26] Melas would have crossed the Mincio immediately had the French troops not occupied Mantua and Peschiera on his flanks. Even though his troops outnumbered the enemy's, he could not blockade both fortresses. On 13 April the first Russian columns arrived at Verona, and the next day Melas crossed the Mincio with all his forces. On the 16th Marshal Suvorov took command of the two allied armies, which numbered about 60,000 men. Suvorov left between 18,000 and 20,000 men under the command of Kray to blockade both Peschiera and Mantua, then pushed forward.[27]

Inside Mantua Latour continued to consolidate power and prepare for the siege. On 24 April he issued an order to the citizens that regardless of their status, the people living in the city, the Citadel, and the suburb of San Giorgio would not be allowed to keep any military item or ammunition in their homes. Those who accepted military goods as a gift, including clothing, were to be shackled with irons and sentenced to life imprisonment. Inspectors were deployed to ensure compliance. Anyone found with military weapons or equipment was to be executed for stealing from the military depot.[28] He sought to disarm the populace to prevent rebellion. Already the people of Mantua were disaffected with the French because of two years' worth of relentless requisitions. Latour demanded more.[29]

When Latour arrived in Mantua, he set up a special treasury for the defense of Mantua.[30] The day after his disarmament notice, he called in all debts to the government and imposed a higher tax on the debt. The 25 April avviso stated that the debts had to be paid within ten days; any debtors without available assets had five days to show documentation why they had been unable to sell sufficient assets to discharge their debts. Consequently, the 10 percent tax on the debt was raised to 20 percent. The payment of this tax was intended for Latour's new defense fund.[31] He also confiscated the property of the bishop and imposed new taxes to increase defense resources.[32] In addition, he established at his quarters three separate accounts to manage the funds.[33]

On 4 May, in an effort to try to appease the people, Latour published a fifteen-page proclamation guaranteeing personal liberty and religious freedom as well as protection for the priests and rabbis.[34] At the same time, he demanded a list of the wealthiest people of Mantua in anticipation of a forced loan. Latour personally wrote in the margin next to each Hebrew name: "Jew—he will pay." Members of the administrative commission complained about such fierce anti-Semitism especially given his proclamation of equality. To Somenzari Latour responded, "I do not like the Israelites because they have money, and I have not been given the means to pay the cost of the siege."[35] Countering this, Somenzari argued that they, like everyone else, had paid enormous taxes and offered to Bonaparte 100,000 lire for the notable 11 February 1798 loan. But Latour did not budge.[36] In addition to new heavy taxes on the Jews, he mandated additional payments from business owners and other wealthy individuals. He also levied an enormous tax on religious foundations, churches, and the synagogue, showing his earlier goodwill gesture of personal protections to be empty.[37]

These exactions led Luigi Maria Predaval, head of the chamber of commerce, to consider Latour a type of Nero. He described Latour as one who robbed from the people and destroyed households. Latour ousted Predaval in order to set up his own financial system. Then, only four days after his proclamation guaranteeing personal liberty, he ordered Ferdinando Porro, the police chief, to arrest fourteen members of the administration—honest and respected men all—who had not fully embraced the Jacobin ideas. Although a person's house was declared sacred asylum in the Cisalpine constitution, Porro and his police, in the middle of the night of 7–8 May, broke into the homes of those to be arrested, including Predaval and Leopoldo Camillo Volta. The police took them to the antechamber of the Committee of Police and then brought them to the prison.[38] The fourteen officials were horrified by the illegal procedures. At two o'clock in the morning, they were brought to Latour's quarters, where they spent three hours without being interrogated.[39] Finally, after a cursory examination, the police put them in two prison carts and brought them to the Porta Pradella as the Austrians were launching a counterattack at that location. Up to that point, they thought they were condemned to death. While the French cannon on the fortress walls blasted away during the early morning engagement, the fourteen officials were taken to the external works of the fortress, where they learned that they were condemned as aristocrats to the pain of deportation. Amid French and Austrian musket fire and cannonballs filling the air and with corpses covering the ground, they made their way to the Austrian line, but not before being relieved of their pocket watches and money by two French cavalrymen with drawn sabers. This arbitrary punishment weighed heavily on these Cisalpine officials, but especially on the wives and children they were forced to leave behind, inside the besieged fortress. The family members did not know if their loved ones were taken away and shot or if they were alive.[40]

The resentment of the people increased when Latour introduced new coinage (see fig. 4). The forced loan and special taxes—on Jews, merchants, and the wealthy—ran their course as Latour sought to get enough silver, copper, and bronze for the two mints in Mantua. Two unfortunate fish vendors were summoned to pay 1,500 Mantuan lire each. They wrote to Latour for relief, explaining that their business was modest, and during a siege nonexistent, and that they had no way of coming up with the money. Latour responded on the back of their note: "I cannot judge the truth of this tale, but if merchants would prefer that I make paper siege notes instead of silver money, I wish to serve. This is the time of sacrifice, the requisitions will be refunded and, in the final analysis, it is better to lose a small amount than jeopardize the entire fortune."[41]

Although Bonaparte had already stripped the silverware from the churches, Latour scoured them again. After having suppressed many additional religious communities, Latour mandated that they too had to give all of their silver to be made into coins. He also had the silver statue of St. Anselmo, the patron saint of the city, taken down and melted. This was the third time this silver statue had been confiscated by the French in as many years. It was confiscated in March 1797 by the administrative commission, but Marois Duboscq sold it back to the people for 6,000 lire. It was ransomed again in July 1798. There was an indignant reaction in the city when Latour removed the statue from the cathedral to the siege treasury in May 1799.[42] He told the people that he could not postpone the present circumstances for ridiculous and idolatrous devotion and that if they produced the same amount of silver equal to the weight of the statue in coin and ingot, he would preserve this "*Merveille*, that has attracted the devout homage of the blind."[43] With all church silver being confiscated, little was left to meet Latour's demand. Those who wanted to preserve the statue did not trust Latour's words and refused to turn over any more silver. The statue was taken to the Virgiliana Mint and melted.[44]

After Latour deported Volta, the Cisalpine director of the Virgiliana Academy, he seized that institution's vast collection of 1,000 silver and 442 gold medallions with a value of 10,452 lire. In response to the protest of 28 May by the academy's president, Petrozzani, and his colleagues, Latour mocked: "Medallions with an effigy of a monarch are ridiculous, if not a vile adulation, and are at the very least incompatible with a free country since their presence transmits merit to the monarch."[45]

Latour used the collected silver to produce the new 5- and 10-soldi coins at the Virgiliana Mint. Curiously he also decided that in order to demonstrate the intrinsic value of the new silver 5-soldi Republican coins he would also use the old Austrian Imperial dies and mint the 5-soldi coin dated 1758 with the image of Maria Theresa— directly contradicting his letter to the academy condemning medals with an image of the monarch. In fact, the majority of the newly minted silver coins were of the 1758 Austrian pattern: 193,601.5 lire's worth were produced, compared to only a scant 10,800.15 lire's worth of the Republican 5-soldi coins (see fig. 4).[46] Latour issued a proclamation on 18 June stating that the Austrian money with the image of Maria Theresa was repugnant to him, but he thought it necessary to preserve the sense of value of 5 soldi with those holding old opinions. Anyone refusing to accept the new money and anyone caught forging the money would be put to death. Moreover, he threatened that "anyone who depreciated its value would be considered a usurer, a disturber of the public order, and as such would be tried by court martial and condemned to five years in prison."[47]

Latour also requisitioned the church bells in the immediate countryside and the city to melt them with cannon metal to produce the Republican 1-soldo coin at the Spartana Mint.[48] At the Virgiliana Mint he also reproduced the old Austrian 1/2-soldo coin with the year 1777 on it—yet another coin with monarchical symbols. These 1/2-soldo coins were made from one-fifth requisitioned copper and four-fifths cannon metal. Of all the money produced by the two Mantuan mints, 123,099.15 lire went into Latour's hands, while the remaining 130,981.1 lire went into the siege account, in order to pay various debts. When the Austrians arrived in the city at the end of the siege, they found no funds in the siege account.[49] Latour conveniently left his proclamation of 18 June out of his 635-page book written in defense of his actions at Mantua. The confiscations and the many other methods that Latour employed to mint and circulate the new coins intensified the people's hatred of him, his supporters, and everything French and Republican.[50]

Latour not only took advantage of the local population to increase the wealth of the siege fund; he also exploited his own troops. Only a few days after deporting the fourteen officials from the city, he reduced the soldiers' pay to one-third of their current salary until the end of the siege.[51] He assured them that he would invest the two-thirds remaining so that when the soldiers left the military and returned home they would have some money to live on. Sacrifices would have to be made, he argued, so that France could achieve a victory at Mantua. Girardelet, the commander of the 3rd Battalion of the 26th *Légère*, informed Latour that his troops accepted the measure wholeheartedly, and that he could take their money for the public good since frugality was good for a soldier.[52] Colonel Borthon, the commander of the artillery of the fortress, told Latour that the artillerymen of the four nations under his orders happily agreed to receive one-third of their pay and that they were grateful for the wise measure he was taking to improve their lives.[53] Some commanders used the request as an opportunity to try to get additional supplies for their men. The squadron commander for the Piedmontese Carabineers informed Latour that they accepted the one-third pay but requested better rations because the wine and meat they had been issued was so bad they had to throw it out for fear of getting sick.[54] Jouardet, the commander of the 1st Battalion of the 29th *Légère*, reported that his men would take the one-third pay until the end of the siege but they kindly requested a raise so they could buy soap. He also reminded Latour that the shoes issued to them were so poorly made that they lasted only eight days.[55] Although these commanders sent glowing reports to Latour, the soldiers were disgruntled. After the siege Latour was charged with issuing poor rations to the troops and then selling them the good bread from the magazines located in the Citadel.[56] The deprivations were too much for the discouraged troops to take and some deserted.[57] Latour imposed a draconian rule on his officers and men. He ordered officers without commands to take up the musket and fight beside the soldiers. He rejected soldiers' complaints and quelled three successive troop revolts with summary executions.[58]

Latour was even less successful with the actual conduct of the siege than with winning over the population of the city of Mantua or inspiring his troops. Although he understood and wrote many books about the theory of fortress defenses, he was unable to organize an effective defense. In the first days of April, when the French army had given up the line of the Mincio, Latour ordered General Louis Claude Monnet to guard the Citadel with approximately 1,000 infantrymen; entrusted General Jean Baptiste Meyer to hold San Giorgio with 1,400 men; ordered Polish general Wielhorski to hold the Migliaretto with 1,300; and assigned Colonel César Balleydier with his 29th *Légère* of 500 men to protect the Pradella works.[59] On the evening of 13 April, the Austrians, having passed Mantua, advanced east from Bozzolo to Curtatone, a village on the southwestern shore of the Upper Lake. The next day, the garrison made a sortie that repulsed the Austrians as they tried to advance farther east along the road from Curtatone to Mantua. Meanwhile, the French worked feverishly to build batteries to defend the Pajolo dam along the southeast side of the fortress, to replace the palisades, repair the covered ways, and prepare the Pradella works and the Citadel. On 16 April the Austrians sent reconnaissance forces to observe the Citadel and Cerese. The next day the Austrians continued to probe to the north and south of Mantua, while a deserter from their force announced the approach of an army sent to invest the city with eighteen infantry battalions and four cavalry squadrons.[60]

On 18 April the Austrians approached Mantua from all sides and prevented the peasants in the countryside from communicating with the city. They tried a second time to take Cerese—this time with a cannon and a howitzer—but they failed in this endeavor. The next day the garrison launched a sortie from San Giorgio to drive away the Austrians who had collected 1,800–2,000 soldiers around Mantua. The French sortie drove the Austrians back two miles, killing and wounding several Austrians, while the 56th demibrigade lost two grenadiers. On the 20th the Austrians returned, and just beyond French artillery range they cut off the roads leading to San Giorgio. The next day Latour launched another sortie from San Giorgio, again pushing the Austrians back with losses. The sortie was not as effective as hoped for because some peasants compromised the plan for the attack. From that day until 8 May the garrison continued to launch small sorties to keep the Austrians as far as possible from the city. Yet Kray's forces continued to advance their outposts.[61]

After Peschiera fell to Kray on 7 May, he quickly moved his siege force to Mantua. He was able to move his siege guns, as well as French guns captured at Peschiera, on the Mincio River aboard the seized French flotilla.[62] He began the investment of Mantua with 11,971 troops, and his force continued to grow, especially when Hohenzollern arrived after the citadel of Milan fell and Suvorov diverted Russian troops there.[63]

Latour decided that on 8 May he would send a large sortie against the massive Austrian troop buildup. He launched the assault at 2:00 A.M., which no doubt explains the three-hour delay preceding his short examination of the fourteen Cisalpine officials Police Chief Porro had arrested and brought to his quarters just as the sortie got under way. The massive sortie went out from the four major gates of the fortress: the Citadel, San Giorgio, Pradella, and Cerese. From the Citadel Colonel Bartès of the 1st Swiss Legion commanded three columns comprising seven hundred men. The first column, commanded by *Chef de Bataillon* Baron with his 1st Battalion of the 31st Line, consisted of three hundred infantry, twenty-five dragoons, fifteen sappers, and two 4-pounder cannon. Baron marched on the road leading to Verona and protected the columns assaulting Marmirolo from the Austrians at Favorita. *Chef de Bataillon* Jayet, commander of the 2nd Swiss Legion, led the second column, made up of two companies of the grenadiers from the 1st Swiss Legion, fifty fusiliers of the 2nd Swiss Legion, ten Frenchmen, and eight dragoons; it was ordered to attack along the road to Marmirolo. At the village of Mantovana, they were met head on by Austrians from the Freiherr Wilhelm Schröder Regiment as well as hussars. The third column, led by *Chef de Bataillon* Abyberg of the 1st Swiss Legion, had twenty-five Swiss grenadiers, 160 Swiss fusiliers, thirty Frenchmen, forty dragoons, a howitzer with its caisson, an additional caisson filled with cartridges for the infantry, an artillery officer, and an engineer officer along with fifteen sappers. As the overall commander, Bartès was with this column, which was to take Marmirolo. It succeeded in getting to the edge of the village but was then fired upon from both flanks. In the end each column was repulsed by a strong force.[64]

The San Giorgio sortie under General Meyer was larger and consisted of four columns. The column on the road to Governolo, which had close to three hundred infantry, two hundred dragoons, and two artillery pieces, attacked the advance posts of the Austrians. The second column, on the road to Roncoferraro, was led by *Chef de Bataillon* Jouardet and was composed of five companies of the 29th *Légère* and the 12th Dragoons. *Chef de Bataillon* Lelmy commanded the third column, which took the Castellarrio road with 250 infantry, sixty dragoons, and two cannon. The fourth column, led by Captain Leloup of the 93rd Line, was to march on the road to Due Castelli. In total, the San Giorgio sortie lost five soldiers killed, fifteen wounded, and sixteen taken as prisoners.[65]

The sortie exiting from the Pradella gate was led by Colonel Balleydier. The goals of this sortie were to collect straw for fodder and to push back an Austrian battalion that had come up from Borgoforte.[66] *Chef de Bataillon* Girard led an advance guard column to drive the Austrians out of Curtatone. His column consisted of six hundred men from his 2nd Battalion of the 31st Line along with twenty-five dragoons, a cannon, and a howitzer. Marching along the road on the bank of the Upper Lake, his troops received cannon fire from Captain François Pagés's flotilla at Angioli, which mistook them for Austrians. Girard dispatched a dragoon to go tell the French navy to stop firing on his column. At the bridge at Curtatone he overcame a detachment of hussars, fifty infantrymen, and a single cannon section, and his advance guards continued as far as two miles past Madonna delle Grazie.[67] *Chef de Bataillon* Obert commanded another advance guard column that took the road to Montanara. It was made up of his three-hundred-man 2nd Battalion of the 29th *Légère* in addition to twenty-five dragoons and two cannon. Balleydier's main column had 120 carabineers from the 29th *Légère*, seventy grenadiers from the 31st Line, 140 grenadiers and 470 fusiliers from the Polish Legion, twenty-five dragoons, fifty Piedmontese Carabineers, and thirty sappers. This column of just over 900 men also moved upon the road toward Montanara. Balleydier arrived with the lead battalion of 250 men at Montanara, but he could not capture it. According to the French plan, he was to move toward Cerese to support the main attack led by the Poles, by advancing on the rear of the Austrian formation that would be counterattacking the Polish forces assigned to take Pietole. He moved his force east to San Silvestro then marched to the road between Cerese and Borgoforte and held there briefly until his column was overwhelmed.[68]

The column launched from Cerese consisted of four hundred Polish infantry, fifty dragoons, a detachment of the French 31st Line, two artillery pieces, thirty sappers, and five miners, all commanded by General Wielhorski. He sent Colonel Louis Dembowski with a strong detachment to Pietole to drive the Austrians toward San Benedetto and then attract the Austrians from Cerese so that Balleydier could hit them in the rear. Dembowski, his forces outnumbered, took Pietole twice, but Balleydier arrived too late to take advantage of the exposed rear of the Austrian column counterattacking Pietole. In that detachment alone the legion lost six officers and men killed, ten officers and fifty-nine soldiers wounded, and nineteen soldiers taken prisoner. In his evening report that day, Wielhorski justly praised the valor of the troops under his orders.[69]

The navy and pontoniers also assisted in the sortie. On the Upper Lake, Pagés embarked at 2:00 A.M. with six gunboats on which he transported one hundred men of the 31st Line. He went upstream to Angioli, where he mistakenly fired two or three rounds on Girard's fellow 31st Line troops. Pagés's marines stopped firing because there was no response from what they thought were Austrian troops in the dark of the night. They then went farther upstream about two hundred yards and fired again, this time receiving a volley of musketry. Pagés ordered the fleet to prepare for action just as the leading gunboat *Mérope* was summoned by Frenchmen on the bank who informed the sailors that the 31st Line was in that position. When dawn finally came, Austrians on the Citadel side of the Mincio fired on the fleet. Pagés detached the *Bonaparte* and *Minerva* to attack their position. The fleet could not deliver effective fire against the scattered skirmishers. The wind became violent and Pagés could not sail up to Madonna delle Grazie. Seeing no enemy on the south bank, he disembarked the infantry at Angioli and ordered the fleet back to Mantua.[70] In preparation for the sorties, Pagés ordered the pontonier captain, Jean Baptiste Chapuis, to assist on the Lower Lake. Chapuis took six sloops and seventy infantrymen downstream to the village of Pietole. Chapuis was instructed not to land the soldiers unless he was perfectly sure the Austrians were turned by the Cerese sortie. He was afraid to disembark the conscript infantry, which he deemed incapable of performing under cannon fire. At the Virgil pyramid, near Pietole, he fired a volley of grapeshot at the Austrian outposts, who withdrew immediately.[71] He then docked and disembarked the infantry. Soon the Austrians began an intense cannonade. The heavy wind limited Chapuis's ability to maneuver his sloops effectively, which greatly reduced the accuracy of his cannon. With his boats riddled by twelve cannonball holes—four in his sloop alone—he decided to return to port. During the withdrawal he tried to protect the retreating San Giorgio column with a few cannon shots.[72]

After an all-morning fight, the great sortie ended with Latour's forces returning inside the fortress walls. The French took 290 prisoners but suffered 350 casualties. They failed to push back the massing Austrian troops adequately. That failure was coupled with the discouraging news from a prisoner that Peschiera had capitulated the day before.[73]

That was the last major sortie by Latour. A few more limited sorties were launched to little effect, and the civilian commissary Michel Leclerc attributed the lack of success to General Kray's asking Latour not to send out any more sorties because they only produced a useless effusion of human blood and would not decide the fate of Mantua. In return, and in a chivalric gesture toward the French suffering for want of wood, Kray allowed them to exit freely to cut trees outside of San Giorgio, up to certain marked-out limits.[74]

Latour was certainly feeling the pressure as he learned about French reverses in Italy. On 1 June Kray informed Latour that he received the letter Latour's son delivered but did not see the young man at his headquarters in Roverbella because he was "out enjoying the view of their [the Austrians'] new conquests: Ferrara and its citadel and Ravenna." He also stated that the Austro-Russian forces reached Turin on 25 May.[75]

On 15 June Kray received the order from Suvorov to suspend siege operations, maintain only a blockade, and send a strong detachment to confront General Jacques Macdonald's army. Macdonald suffered a shocking defeat in the resulting Battle of the Trebbia on 17–19 June. The next week Kray sent General Zach into the fortress to meet with Latour and inform him that on 26 June his army would be celebrating with musket and cannon fire the news of some recent victories.[76] The following morning Latour had notices affixed at the standard locations stating that the Austrian celebrations were for the "supposed" victories but that soon the French would celebrate the "real" victories.[77]

After the interruption to Kray's siege plan with the Battle of the Trebbia, Suvorov assisted Kray in pressing the siege by reinforcing him with Ott's division, a strong detachment from General Maxim Rehbinder's Russian division, and later by the garrison troops from Ferrara, Bologna, Parma, and other cities. All together, there were thirty-nine battalion-size units in the siege force, including four grenadier battalions and six squadrons of cavalry. In addition, Kray had the support of engineer, miner, pioneer, and artillery units that included three hundred Russian artillerymen. From Turin, Suvorov sent sixteen 24-pounders. In total, Kray had at his disposal approximately 40,000 men and six hundred artillery pieces.[78]

Kray invested the entire city, but he did not intend to attack from all points with the same effort. Instead, he planned to attack the south side in force with a coup de main. He observed that the south side of Mantua had the weakest defenses and that the waters were narrowest on that side.[79] Kray was determined to attack the face of the weak Pradella hornwork, dominated by the heights of Belfiore, because the main fortress wall behind it was protected only by the San Alessio bastion and the Pradella ravelin (just in front of the Pradella gate), with a 745-yard curtain between them. There were only two redoubts in front of the curtain and this was the area that concerned Latour.[80]

In order to begin entrenching near Belfiore, it was necessary for the Austrians to drive the French away from the Pajolo dam, behind which they had built a battery of four cannon (see map 7: A). They also had to force the French out of Cerese, also armed with four cannon, which covered the road to Borgoforte and protected the locks of the Pajolo canal. Kray decided to encamp the siege corps between Certosa on the shore of the Upper Lake and Capilupa to the southeast and dig the contravallation line from Angioli, through Palazzino, Dosso del Corso, and Chiesa Nova, to Casa Rossa (see maps 4 & 7). Each one of these points would have 200 to 300 men to cut communication from Mantua, supported by light troops who would establish outposts. On the night of 5–6 July, the Allies started to dig at Simeone and Valle (see map 7: 13 & 14) to establish two batteries to fire against the French guns behind the dam opposite Belfiore. During the next night they worked near Casa Rossa to build another battery to fire against the battery behind the dam. When the French soldiers realized what was happening, they unleashed an intense fire on the Allies, which forced them to suspend work. Nevertheless, on the day of 7 July, the Allies raised four more batteries between the vicinity of Cerese and Pietole, to fire at the Cerese tower and the batteries on the Cerese dam (see map 7: 17–20).[81]

Kray knew he would have to take the tower. Once his batteries were established, Colonel Riedt attacked the tower on 10 July with two battalions of infantry preceded by chasseurs. He opened his attack with twenty-four cannon blasting at 5:00 A.M. The artillery battered the tower and destroyed the French batteries. Fifty volunteers then led follow-on troops in an assault on the tower, the bridge, the mill, and the sluice with such impetuosity that Latour's forces abandoned the Cerese mill for the defensive works of the Te. In their retreat, they abandoned two cannon near the tower. Encouraged by this success, the Austrians tried to press the attack further but were stopped by French and Polish grapeshot as they attempted to cross the Pajolo basin along the road on the top of the dam. The Austrians took shelter near the dam but quickly repaired the bridge, despite a withering fire from the French muskets, and then silenced the French soldiers firing at them. The white-coated Austrians established artillery batteries near the sluice they had just captured. The next day the Russians completed their batteries at Simeone and Sparavera (see map 7: 13 & 15), and the Allies improved the batteries. The Allies then demolished the tower and, by controlling the sluice gate, began to drain off water in order to open an extensive direct approach to the city.[82]

In the early afternoon of Latour's birthday, 11 July, Kray's emissary General Zach visited Latour a second time. He stayed all afternoon in the city and then had a two-hour private meeting with Latour conducted in absolute secrecy. Latour allowed no other officer in the room—not even to dismiss the appearance to his staff of impropriety and thus some became suspicious. Zach spent most of the day at Mantua, but Latour did not call the war council together to hear what Zach had to say. Zach finally departed at ten o'clock that evening.[83] During his lengthy visit he delivered a letter from Kray detailing the many French reverses in Italy—the destruction of Macdonald's army on the Trebbia, Moreau's misfortunes on the Bormida River and his retreat, and the arrival of the Russian corps in Borgoforte on the 7th. Kray offered Latour the advantage of a capitulation: "General Zach, my chief of staff, who has my full confidence, is the bearer of this letter; he can give you even more details, *and you can entrust to him all your resolutions,* [even those] *only you think about taking.*"[84] Immediately after Zach departed, Latour called a council of war.[85] Latour recorded the minutes of his war councils in the book he wrote exonerating himself of treason, but this particular war council is not even mentioned. It was, however, an important meeting and must have continued well past midnight, as Latour departed Mantua at 3:00 A.M.through the Pradella gate—the gate leading to Castellucchio, where Kray was headquartered. This is the only known time that Latour himself left the fortress during the siege, and there is no other mention of this particular episode.[86] He normally sent one or both of his sons, Henri and Victor, to deliver messages to Kray.[87] Latour's activities outside the Pradella gate that night are unknown. However, he definitely sent a delegation a few hours later in the early morning to ask for a one-day armistice for 14 July so that his troops could celebrate Bastille Day. It is this armistice, which effectively allowed the Austrians to gain an advantage, that was the focal point of the allegation of treason against Latour as the mechanism for delivering the fortress to the Austrians. In an 11 July letter, Latour wrote to Kray detailing his intentions for celebrating Bastille Day: "A general artillery volley from three places will occur around 5:00 A.M.; a second one, made of shots fired one by one, at just before 5:30 A.M., and a third one, with rolling fire, just before 6:00 A.M. in order to avoid the hottest part of the day. This feast will be celebrated for the dual reason of July 14th *and some good news I received.*"[88]

Even considering the eighteenth-century ideas of honor associated with an armistice, Latour certainly understood the risk that such a proposal would offer his attacker an advantage at this point in the siege as the first parallel had not yet been marked out on the ground. Of anyone in Europe at the time, Latour was perhaps the most knowledgeable on this subject given his many publications on fortifications and sieges, and especially his book *Traité de la Défense des Places*. His actions are inexcusable for someone of his expertise.

During the same morning of Latour's early departure out of the Pradella gate, 12 July, he sent his adjutant general Jean Baptiste Gastine, one of his sons, and a trumpeter to Kray's headquarters for a parley.[89] Gastine delivered a second letter, also written on 11 July, from Latour informing Kray that he told Zach that he has too high an opinion of Kray to accept the proposed capitulation, and that were Kray in his position he would do the same. Latour went on to say that on 12 July he would send Gastine "accompanied by two officers for another purpose."[90] That unstated "purpose" was apparently to get an agreement for the armistice on 14 July; Mantuan, French, Austrian, and Russian chroniclers all state that as the reason for Gastine's visit. It is clear that Latour's decision to request the 14 July armistice took place immediately after his secret meeting with Zach on 11 July since he mentioned the meeting with Zach when he wrote the letter late that night.[91] Even though the record of the late evening council of war led by Latour on 11 July no longer exists, the decision for an armistice was made at that time. Leclerc states that the war council was simply Latour's gathering of a few of his officers to read to them some "complementary" letters he intended to send to Kray.[92] Latour was accused of going through with the armistice even though Borthon protested against it. Latour defended his actions by stating that Borthon did not "protest," but simply disagreed with having a celebration that would waste good powder by firing ceremonial salvos from the fortress cannon.[93] If Latour did indeed commit treason, as alleged, the face-to-face deal was struck with Zach during the meeting on 11 July or with Kray in person that night—or a combination of the two.

Kray agreed to the one-day armistice and also notified Suvorov of his great fortune in receiving Latour's proposal. In Kray's letter to Suvorov, he noted that Gastine arrived with a proposal for the celebration and quotes the proposal as being "in friendship and in ceremony" with "in friendship and" written in German ("in Freundschaft und") and "in ceremony" written in French ("en-ceremonie").[94] Indeed, the three-day advance notice was quite friendly. Kray used the three days to collect 1,200 peasants from the countryside for the project of opening the first parallel during the French festival. The Austrians planned to guard the workers with four battalions of infantry and two squadrons of cavalry.[95]

During the night of 11–12 July, the Russians improved all of their fortifications so that on the day of the 12th they had three batteries of four cannon each directed against the Citadel. During the night of 13–14 July and the following day, the fire slowed down on both sides, and the Austrians prepared to open the trenches.[96]

Meanwhile, in the fortress Latour and the administration prepared for the big celebration.[97] Even before the immediate preparations, some ridiculous use of manpower was diverted away from building defense works. Of 1,200 workers employed to fortify San Giorgio, Latour and Gastine sent 300 to Piazza Argine to demolish houses near the hospital and the hospice in order to make room for a promenade.[98] Free from fear of any attack on the 14th, the French ceased all work to celebrate their national holiday. As planned, they fired cannon with salvos in a spirit of festivity. In the renovated Piazza Argine, soldiers conducted a military parade that was followed by grandiose speeches by Latour and Gastine commemorating the tenth anniversary of the Revolution. In his first of two speeches, Latour noted Louis XVI's betrayal of the constitution, proclaimed great victories in Germany, encouraged his troops, and ended his lengthy talk with "Repeat with me: *Je le jure! . . . Vive la Republique!*" (I swear it! . . . Long live the Republic!)[99] The participants feasted and imbibed, and many became drunk. At Latour's quarters a civic dinner was held for 150 guests at which orators thundered against the kings of Europe. The celebration included a free comedy production at the theater, which was illuminated the entire evening; a concert with Republican airs; and a free ball in the National Palace (the French name for the old Gonzaga Ducal Palace). The *Declaration of the Rights of Man* was posted throughout the city. The festivities took up not only the whole day but also the greater part of the night.[100]

During the night of 14 July, the Austrians used the opportunity to open the first parallel unopposed. They began digging at 10:00

that evening with 3,300 military workers and the 1,200 local peasants gathered the days before.[101] It was only on the morning of the
15th, after the Austrians already had dug to a depth sufficient to provide cover, that the fortress artillery started to fire on the workers.
During the night of 15–16 July, the parallel was completed and the
cannon fire from the fortress decreased considerably. The next night
the Austrians began work on the second parallel between Osteria
Alta and Belfiore.[102] The cannon fire from the fortress increased in
intensity, but it did not delay the work of those digging the trench.
On the 18th this second parallel was improved while the French
kept up an intense cannonade. Two cannon were placed on the edge
of the Upper Lake by Latour to try to enfilade the trenches, but the
distance was too great. On the 19th, after having widened the two
parallels with the 3,300 military workers and now 1,500 peasants,
the Austrians connected them with a communications trench. They
also opened several other communication trenches to the various
artillery batteries. The following day they improved the second parallel and prepared to move the guns into the batteries. On the 21st
and 22nd they lengthened it by 104 yards and completed the connecting trenches.[103]

Kray was pleased with the work. On 22 July he wrote to his
brother: "Tomorrow night I will begin to welcome Mantua from 100
cannon and mortars."[104] That night the Austrians brought up the
artillery and the munitions for emplacement. They spent the following day and night arming the batteries (see map 7: 2–10).[105] Around
4:00 A.M. on 24 July the Austrians unleashed an intense bombardment with 110 cannon from nine batteries—all directed on the San
Alessio bastion, the Te crownwork, and the Pradella ravelin. The
constant fire from the Austrians silenced the French guns after only
a few hours because the guns covering the curtain between the San
Alessio bastion and the Pradella ravelin totaled only about thirty
cannon. That day the Allies fired 8,000–9,000 solid shot and more
than 1,000 bombs and shells into the fortifications and the city. The
batteries at Cerese continued to pound the San Carlo fleches and the
Pajolo dam, while on the other side of the Mincio the Russians doubled their fire against the Citadel. Only a few homes in Mantua were
destroyed, but a fodder magazine caught fire along with the three
bridges leading to the Pradella work. The loss of the wooden bridges
was especially detrimental to the French because of the shortage of
firewood in the fortress.[106]

During the night of 24–25 July, Kray made a strong attack against the Migliaretto and Te fortifications. His intention was to seize the fortified camp on the island of the Te and perhaps even capture Mantua with this blow. When his troops entered the works, Latour's men were forced to withdraw from the Pusterla and Cerese gates of the main fortress wall. For this attack Kray sent two columns of approximately six hundred men each. One, commanded by Colonel Schmidt, departed from the south end of the second parallel against the French battery across the stream (see map 7: A); the other, commanded by Colonel Riedt, moved against the French batteries along the Cerese road on both ends of the Pajolo dam (see map 7: E & F). The Austrian attack began at 11:00 P.M. The column led by Colonel Riedt started the attack at Cerese, seizing the battery there without firing a shot (see map 7: F). Schmidt's column, made up of volunteers, emerged from the second parallel and attacked the Pajolo battery (see map 7: A). Some grenadier companies advanced between the two columns to support them. Riedt's column crossed the marsh and forded the Pajolo stream near the dam with the help of small footbridges. The Russian artillery captain Martinov gathered several artillerymen to join Riedt's attacking column, and they were the first ones into the Pajolo canal and first to reach the French guns. After Riedt's column pushed Latour's forces back to the Migliaretto bastion over the Cerese road, the Russians seized and turned the French guns around. At the same time, the column to the west side, skirting the island of the Te, arrived at the barrier opposite the San Alessio bastion. The resistance of the bastion gave the defenders time to bring up their reserves. Three Polish grenadier companies repulsed the attackers at the sharp corner of the road in front of the bastion, forcing that column to retreat. Latour's intention was to recapture the Cerese and Pajolo batteries, but his attempt failed owing to the effort by the Russian troops to restructure the captured batteries to open fire against the French. Latour made another attempt with the 1st Cisalpine Light Infantry Regiment. The Austrians and Russians, after almost capturing the works, were driven back. That day the Austrians lost 330 officers and men captured, dead, or wounded.[107]

The attack seemed to cause Latour concern. At 5:00 P.M. the same day, 25 July, he convened a council of war. Maubert, the engineer corps commander, was not present due to illness, and Latour raised questions about the value of the demilune at the Pradella hornwork, the Pajolo battery, and the San Giorgio bridgehead.

Latour's opinion influenced the officers at the council; they agreed that the evacuation of the demilune and these locations would not involve the immediate surrender of the fortress. He decided to withdraw General Meyer's troops from San Giorgio to put them in the main hornwork at Pradella. He also planned to spike the guns in the Pradella demilune and emplace a large explosive mine in the works with a timed fuse set to explode once the Austrians occupied the demilune. The council also decided to evacuate the Pajolo battery, which had its flank exposed to the fire of the Allies.[108]

The officers had little time to prepare a plan to evacuate San Giorgio with its four 24-pounder cannon, two 12-pounder cannon, and two 12-inch mortars. Meyer led the French and Polish soldiers out from San Giorgio that night (25–26 July) taking one cannon with them after attempting to damage the others as best they could. During the evacuation the soldiers could see in the distance two flares shooting into the sky. (One officer would later accuse Latour of shooting the flares as a signal to the enemy to occupy San Giorgio.) Afterward Colonel Count Balfy with a squadron of the Kavanagh Regiment occupied the works finding the five abandoned iron cannon. At dawn a battalion from the Jellachich Regiment entered San Giorgio as well.[109] Once again, officers and soldiers murmured that Latour was not behaving like a determined defender. The soldiers that had to evacuate San Giorgio spewed curses of betrayal at being sold out to the enemy.[110]

Meanwhile, the Austrians working on the third parallel, to the west of the Pradella hornwork, had dug to within feet of the fortification.[111] The morning of 26 July, Borthon wrote Latour asking why the infantry from the San Giorgio evacuation was used to reinforce the garrison and not support the cannoneers.[112] Latour replied at length, then used Borthon's letter as the reason to call another council of war at 1:00 P.M. To Latour the reinforcements from San Giorgio were not sufficient to prolong his defense of the main Pradella hornwork, which he thereby sought to evacuate. He immediately adopted a plan designed by Maubert, who was unable to attend the council, to make a cut in the dam between the city and the Pradella hornwork to flood the Pajolo basin along with the Austrian and Russian artillery batteries. The dam served as a bridge between the hornwork and the city and was used to channel water from the Upper Lake around the demilune and the Pradella hornwork itself. The plan called for partially closing the gate that controlled the water of the moat around the Citadel and the gate that controlled the Rio, which flowed through the center of the city, while simultaneously a mine would be exploded in the dam. The partially closed gates would raise the Upper Lake water level, forcing more water through the cut.[113] This operation, by flooding the Pajolo basin and destroying all the small bridges that the Allies had built, would preserve the Te and Migliaretto fortifications and wipe out all of the Allied works established in the basin. Consequently, the French spent that evening digging a place for the mine. As the Austrians increased their fire on the fortress, around 11:00 P.M. Balleydier silently moved his soldiers out of the demilune and the hornwork after spiking all the cannon. Fortunately for the Austrians, the French lit the fuse to both mines too early and the exploding mine on the demilune did not cause any harm to them, although it did destroy the works. The mine in the dam blew, but instead of producing a watery inundation to delay the attackers, the explosion created a hole that provided very useful cover for the besiegers. The senior French officers were highly discouraged because the effort resulted only in the premature evacuation of the Pradella fortifications. The Austrians immediately occupied the demilune and the hornwork; they established a lodgment there and that night opened a communications trench to their third parallel. During the rest of the night and early morning the Austrians quickly built breach batteries and set up mortars in the hornwork, from which they could fire on the Pradella gate fortifications.[114]

After a strong four-hour cannonade directed against the ravelin in front of the Pradella gate the morning of 27 July, the Austrians opened a breach by ten o'clock, threatening an immediate assault.[115] Kray sent an engineer, Lieutenant Colonel Franz Orlandini, under a flag of truce, to ask for surrender. Latour agreed to the proposed truce of three hours.[116] Latour called another council of war. Once again Maubert was absent (he had been sick), and Latour opened the meeting by reading a letter from his chief engineer stating the necessity to defend the breach in the Pradella ravelin. Latour asked for the commanders to give an account of their available soldiers to form a column to defend the breach. He then made a bizarre analysis. He assessed that, after subtracting from his garrison of about 10,300 men, the marines, officers, engineers, artillerymen, musicians, drummers, and the sick and wounded, as well as those working in the hospitals, he had only 3,661 men fit for service to contain the breach. Of these, he calculated that 1,500 men were needed to defend the Migliaretto and Te works, 1,000 were needed to police the city, and 900 were needed as a reserve. That left him with 261 soldiers to plug the breach just in front of the main fortress wall. He then took a vote of the other forty-four officers present for continuing the defense. Six officers—General Monnet, the artillery chief Borthon, the artillery *chef de bataillon* Labadie, the commandant of the city Soulier, Captain Pagés, and Captain Chapuis—all voted to continue defending while the remaining thirty-eight replied in the negative. With that issue decided, Latour gave deference to the six officers and put to vote a second question: Should they continue to defend for two or three days? Thus Latour presented the options as "surrender now" or "surrender in a few days." Borthon, Labadie, Pagés, and Chapuis were the only ones who voted to continue to defend Mantua.[117]

The above description of this council of war relies on two books written by Latour as he prepared for an impending court-martial for treason. The Poles, however, gave a slightly different version of what took place at that meeting. In his work *Dzieje Legionow Polskich* (The Second Polish Legion), Schnur-Popławaski maintains that when the Pradella ravelin was completely destroyed and only the brave legionnaire Czachowski kept guard in that quarter by responding with his few remaining guns to the voluminous fire from the enemy's batteries, Latour called another council of war to decide Mantua's fate. Knowing that the subordinate officers were in the habit of voting for surrender, he invited the *chefs de bataillon* to vote as well—which gave him the required majority he apparently wanted. Surrender was strongly protested by Borthon, the artillery commander, and the naval and engineer chiefs. They insisted the fortress could hold out another month. Borthon reminded the council that the water sluices that controlled the flooding of the fortress trenches were still in the garrison's hands and that the enemy had not made even a tiny break in the internal walls of the fortress. Ultimately there was the Citadel to which the army could retire as well. The Poles' situation was critical at that time. The officers were hesitating on the decision between the glory of fighting on and the ignominy of capitulation. The capitulation, despite Polish protest, would have been accepted by the majority, so the Polish officers decided to follow the majority. But the Poles participating in the council—Kosinski, Dembowski, Krolikiewicz, Mosiecki, and

Wolinski—firmly stated that if the Legion was forgotten at the capitulation, they would have rather blown themselves up than wait for the enemy's mercy.[118] The Polish version is corroborated not only by the Frenchman Leclerc, the secretary of the council, but also an Italian chronicler in 1799 who stated that "during the great debate, the Polish General and the other brigade commanders did not want to give up the city."[119]

With the vote taken, Latour then read in German and translated into French a letter written by Kray that declared the place no longer defendable, and that enjoined Latour "to prevent the bloodshed of the garrison and the inhabitants of Mantua, which could result from the disorder of the inevitable storming." He then declared that the decision of the council authorized a capitulation, one that would be painful but necessary.[120] Latour, seeking an honorable surrender, initially asked Kray for the same terms that Bonaparte had offered to Wurmser in 1797, which would have allowed the entire garrison to return to France. Latour sent General Monnet to Castellucchio with the letter to negotiate with Kray. Negotiations took place throughout the night, and Monnet returned in the morning of 28 July with Kray's answer: he would not agree to the terms offered and insisted that the entire garrison be made prisoners of war.[121]

The Polish sources say that the response annoyed the defenders who would have rather agreed to bury themselves in the fortress than accept such humiliating conditions, and that "Latour pushed toward surrender with a strange stubbornness."[122] That certainly seems to be the case. At 11:00 A.M. Latour called another council of war, but this time Borthon, Pagés, and Chapuis, who had previously voted to continue fighting, were not invited. Latour proposed new terms whereby only the officers of the garrison would be taken prisoner while the soldiers would be able to return to the active French army operating on the coast of Genoa.[123] A vote was taken and all agreed to the capitulation adding this ultimatum: if the conditions were not approved by Kray, the fortress would be defended to the very last.[124]

Latour, Maubert, and Borthon went to Castellucchio to sign the capitulation on 28 July. Earlier Latour ordered Borthon to sign the capitulation document or else be relieved of command.[125] Borthon agreed, but in the end he refused to sign the actual capitulation document; the statement "Borthon refuses to sign for personal reasons" was entered in place of his signature (see appendix B). That day Kray wrote to his brother Alexander describing this "lucky case" of the fortress.[126] Thus Mantua fell after only fourteen days of open trenches. Two hours after the capitulation was signed, water from the Upper Lake broke through more than sixty feet of the dam, weakened by the mine, and flooded the Pajolo basin to such a depth that, had Latour decided to continue his defense, he would have been able to do so for much longer since the attackers would have had to attack across the water using rafts.[127]

Latour's forces marched out of the fortress toward the French border on 30 July; 7,691 noncommissioned officers and soldiers (6,622 French, 602 Cisalpines, and 467 Swiss). These 7,691 soldiers were a far cry from the 261 soldiers Latour calculated he had to hold the Pradella.[128] Nearly 1,000 officers, including six generals, were sent to Austria. Remaining in Mantua were 1,220 sick and wounded and about 1,000 Poles.[129] A procession was led by six field guns followed by the French, Italian, and Swiss soldiers, who, after passing through the rows of Austrian troops lining both sides of the road, placed their guns on the glacis of the Citadel. After those troops were disarmed, Latour ordered the Poles to leave the Citadel, and upon seeing them, the Austrian soldiers tightened their rows and began to separate officers from soldiers with musket butt-ends, cursing and violently shoving them into the nearest houses. When Kosinski saw this, he turned to Kray and Latour, who stood by, and called for their intervention. Simultaneously Krolikiewicz grasped the reins of Kray's stallion and demanded an explanation of his soldiers' behavior. In response, Kray showed the Polish generals an additional paragraph of the surrender, to their astonishment: the secret article agreed to by Latour stated: "the Austrian deserters are to return to their respective regiments and battalions. The imperial commanding general promises that their lives will be preserved" (see appendix B). Latour had thus resigned Mantua's bravest defenders to the enemy's revenge since most legionnaires were in fact fugitives from the Austrian army. Covered with disgrace Latour withdrew from his subordinates' sight. Kray, influenced by the Polish generals, ordered that the violent treatment be stopped and that the Polish privates, who did not come from the Austrian-owned Polish lands, be returned to the garrison command to depart with the French soldiers. Former Polish-Austrian sergeants, who had become officers in the Polish Legion, were punished by demotion to private in the emperor's army. Captain Jackowski and Korniszewski of the 3rd

Battalion were among those. After the whole event, Aksamitowski took only 150 legionnaires back to Lyon, France. A few privates, in their civilian clothes, were taken along by the French soldiers as well. The wounded Poles were laid out in front of a hotel and placed under guard. They followed the soldier column toward France but without medical treatment and only in carriages paid for at their own expense. The pay due them was only received once they made it back to France alive. The legion's senior generals, Wielhorski and Kosinski, were placed at the monastery in Léoben, along with the French officers, where they remained until regaining their freedom after the Battle of Marengo.[130]

On the day the French departed, the townspeople, who were furious against the supporters of the French—or the *patrioti*, as they called them—went to their houses to expel them from the city. Girolamo Coddè, one of the most able and fervent partisans of Revolutionary ideas, was beaten; others locked themselves in their houses but the agitated crowd threw the banners and Republican emblems of the French and Cisalpine government through their windows.[131] About two hundred Jacobins took the uniforms of sick soldiers and exited with the French army. Among them was Somenzari, Latour's puppet city administrator.[132] Some of the Austrians who reestablished the royal government had defended the city during the 1796–97 siege. Count Josef Radetzky, now a lieutenant colonel, was among them.[133] The people were jubilant as the Austrians marched in. For four consecutive evenings the people illuminated the city.[134] The value of the various currencies was quickly set by the Austrians, and the value of the cedola was restored.[135] Soon the Austrian government was fully functioning.

Inside the fortress the Allies captured six hundred cannon (see appendix E) and provisions for more than six months. They also seized Pagés's beautiful flotilla of fifteen gunboats. The premature capture of Mantua allowed Kray to reinforce Suvorov with 18,000 to 20,000 men who arrived at the Bormida River in time to meet Joubert on the plain of Novi. Had Latour delayed signing the capitulation, the flooded Pajolo basin could have helped him extend his defense leaving Kray's forces unavailable to help Suvorov win the Battle of Novi.[136]

Moreau, the new French field army commander, received orders from the minister of war to try General Latour by a court-martial—and with good reason. In addition to the despicable secret article concerning the Poles, a look at some of the other articles of the capitulation (see appendix B) will indicate Latour's demeanor with regard to his surrender. In the first article, Latour requested that he and his officers be sent to the nearest Austrian-held territory as hostages for the noncommissioned officers and men who would return to France. The officers would remain hostages until the soldiers were exchanged. Kray decided to hold them only three months, and before releasing them, he obtained their pledge not to fight against Austria again until they were properly exchanged. Other requests included the following:

> Request [Article III]: "Three covered wagons shall be allowed the Commandant for the carriage of his papers, baggage, and personal property. Those wagons shall not be examined, and shall be subject to his orders only."—Granted.

Significantly, no evidence has surfaced as to what happened to the pay that Latour withheld for his soldiers who were on their way to France while he was on his way to Austria with his three wagons of "personal property." Possibly, the soldiers' pay and much of the taxes and requisitions collected by Latour were carted away by him. Stealing funds from the three separate official accounts that he kept at his quarters was one of the thirty-two offenses Latour was to be charged with under the court-martial.[137]

> Request [Article IV]: "The chief of the staff, and the other chiefs of departments shall have the power of taking with them all papers relating to their own concerns, and shall have the sole charge of the wagons destined for that purpose, and for the carriage of their personal property."—Granted.

In this way personal records of the siege were retained by Latour, Gastine, and Maubert; however, the official French journal for the conduct of the siege was carried back to Vienna by Kray's son along with six captured flags.[138]

> Request [Article X]: "All doubts that may arise out of the present capitulation, shall be explained in favor of the garrison, consistent with the laws of equity."—Granted.[139]

Another provision allowed that a pair of colors be granted to Latour in consideration of the energy of his defense. This language was standard in a capitulation agreement, but many of Latour's own officers did not think Latour put up a determined defense. Latour was also accused by his commissary of war, Michel Leclerc, of informing the enemy as to when and where his sorties were to be launched as well as of abandoning San Giorgio to allow the Austrians to capture it without a fight.[140] The questionable actions of Latour aroused suspicions in the French army, and it quickly received Bonaparte's attention after he became the First Consul. Remembering his many sacrifices in the eight months of siege to capture Mantua in 1796 and 1797, Bonaparte stopped the court-martial investigation and relieved Latour with a blistering denunciation.[141] Although he was only obligated to stay in Austria three months according to the capitulation, he was still there a year later, in July 1800. With Latour still in Austria, Bonaparte told his minister of war that Latour was to return from Austria in dishonor carrying his uniform and that he would not be permitted to wear any French military uniform whatsoever. Bonaparte made it clear in his letter to Carnot that the French government wanted nothing spoken about the "disgraceful siege which will long be a stain on the French army."[142]

Unlike most French commanders, who were promoted to their positions because of merit and out of a sense of duty and loyalty, Latour had gained his place as a fortification specialist. When he surrendered the fortress prematurely, with many months of provisions and ammunition on hand—not to mention the nine-hundred-man reserve that he never employed—questions obviously arose as to his qualifications as a military commander. The inner defenses were still intact, and the Citadel could have served as a defensive position for the garrison.[143] Nevertheless, Latour based his decisions on his theoretical knowledge. Since he had predicted in 1798 that Mantua would need at least 20,000 soldiers to be defended properly, he felt justified in his surrender. Others might regard him as incompetent, a coward, or even a thief, especially when comparing his efforts to those of Wurmser, who held out until all the grain was consumed and the garrison was surviving on horsemeat. In addition, Latour did not put up the gallant defense Bonaparte expected of the Army of Italy. In contrast, Masséna, at Genoa in 1800, held out until his men were reduced to eating horses, dogs, cats, rats, bats, and worms.[144]

General François Philippe Foissac-Latour was one of the foremost theorists of fortifications and defenses during his time—albeit a miserable soldier. He looked at the defense of a fortress from a scientific point of view. Upon receiving command of the fortress at Mantua, he worked hard to prepare it to withstand an attack. Initially he sent out sorties aggressively to hold back the Austrians as long as possible, but Kray was able to build up a 40,000-man siege force. Because of his theoretical approach to siege warfare, Latour felt it was pointless to continue to defend the fortress after the Pradella ravelin had been breached. He could have consolidated his forces, withdrawn to the Citadel, and resisted total capitulation for several more months.[145] If he had only held out a few more weeks, he could have kept Kray from reinforcing Suvorov and thus the disastrous outcome for Joubert and the French at Novi might have been prevented and the War of the Second Coalition may have ended with a quite different outcome. As a military leader Latour ignored the welfare of his troops by issuing them moldy bread and then selling them the healthy rations he had available. When they revolted, he instituted summary executions. He took two-thirds of their pay to "invest it" for them, but they never saw him nor their money again after the surrender. As for his Polish troops, he outright betrayed them with a secret article in the capitulation. He took advantage of his position as commander of the garrison to exploit financially the people of the city as he did his own soldiers. He was accused by many of treason for his brief defense of the powerful fortress. In the end, Latour's performance at the second siege of Mantua in 1799 was one of the most dishonorable and reprehensible acts in French military history.

CONCLUSION

BONAPARTE AND FOISSAC-LATOUR AT MANTUA

Throughout its history, Mantua had stood as an important fortress for the security of empires struggling for dominance in northern Italy. Although the Austrians occupied the fortress from 1708 to 1796, they made only minor modifications to the old *trace italienne* fortifications and the Citadel. The siege that was conducted in June and July 1796 and the blockade that followed were typical of the way siege warfare had been conducted since the time of Sébastien Vauban. Even though the Austrians were able to hold out for eight months, that did not prevent Bonaparte from crushing four Austrian armies sent to relieve the fortress—successes that catapulted him to prominence as a military leader. He contained the Austrian garrison with a minimal number of troops so that he could concentrate and mass his remaining forces to defeat the attacking Austrian armies. Clausewitz argued that although Bonaparte defeated Wurmser's army at Castiglione, the Austrian garrison at Mantua remained in place and Bonaparte's victory came at the price of losing only his siege train there. The fortress likely would have fallen sooner had he maintained the siege, but his field army probably would not have had the numbers to win the great victories at Castiglione, Arcole, and Rivoli.[1] Ultimately, Wurmser held out until the last sack of grain was consumed, the majority of the horses were eaten, and his men were on the verge of starvation. Under Canto d'Yrles, the garrison made four sorties to keep the French at a distance before the first siege was lifted by Bonaparte in July 1796. He continued to launch limited sorties when the French returned to invest the city again. Later, Wurmser conducted several powerful sorties to destroy the French siege works, capture cannon, and collect forage. His largest sortie, on 23 November 1796, numbered some 8,000 men. Wurmser's efforts achieved limited objectives such as capturing prisoners for information and temporarily destroying some of the French siege works. His most disastrous sortie was his final one, which was intended to unite with Provera outside of the Citadel. It was only after the Austrians' fourth attempt to relieve the fortress and Provera's failure at San Giorgio in mid-January 1797 that Wurmser and his exhausted garrison reluctantly came to terms with Bonaparte and Sérurier. It was quite appropriate that he and his gallant defenders were granted the honors of war by the French.

The period between 1797 and 1799 witnessed the establishment of a new republican form of government in Mantua. The events that took place in the city were typical of what the French revolutionaries did when they captured towns in northern Italy. The Jews were freed from the ghetto, satellite republics were established, war contributions were collected, goods were requisitioned, and anticlerical policies were adopted. Mantua had first Sérurier and then Miollis as the fortress commander, both of whom enacted requisition policies typical of Revolutionary occupation forces. Jacques Chambarlhac, the next governor, was unable to stop the soldiers' rebellion, and he was replaced by François Philippe Foissac-Latour, who used his position for personal gain. Latour imposed special taxes and enforced conscription, which led to increasing hostility toward the French.

The 1799 defense of Mantua was assigned to Latour, who was given command as the French were being driven from northern Italy. Initially, Latour conducted a spirited defense launching three limited sorties in April 1799 to obstruct the Austrian approach to the fortress. The sortie launched from San Giorgio was the most effective; it kept the Austrians outside of cannon range for several days. On 8 May he launched his largest sortie of around 3,000 men from all of the major sally ports. This sortie accomplished little more than the capture of a number of prisoners with whom the French were able to conduct prisoner exchanges.[2] Afterward Latour conducted only a few minor demonstrations, and he began to make mistakes that even at the time appeared treasonous. His worst decision was his request for a truce to celebrate Bastille Day, during which he enabled Kray to open the first parallel trench near the Pradella works. After only fourteen days of open trenches, Latour surrendered. Although the Austrians successfully breached the Pradella ravelin, they never breached the inner walls of the fortress. The defenders could have held out for several more months by moving all of their forces in the city to the Citadel, where the food magazines were located and the defensive fortifications were the strongest. The Russian contributions to the siege were significant, despite Austrian historiographical efforts to minimize them, since they held the majority of the fortified positions around the fortress while the Austrians concentrated on the Pradella works.[3] Latour voluntarily evacuated the fortified suburb of San Giorgio and the Pradella hornwork and later used his position to manipulate a council of war into capitulating after the Pradella ravelin was breached.

The results of the second siege stunned the French. Latour surrendered after a three-month defense. He had the resources to resist for a year, thanks to Bonaparte's foresight. Unlike the Austrians, who had allowed the fortifications to deteriorate throughout their occupation, the French had prepared the fortress for a siege of at least a year; nevertheless, Latour decided to surrender with the excuse that the fortress was indefensible according to his scientific analysis. Given Latour's engineering background and field command experience, his defense of the fortress was appalling. In contrast, the Austrians held out for eight months and exhausted all resources before they even considered surrender. Because of Latour's disgraceful leadership during the siege, General Jean Baptiste Bernadotte, France's minister of war, initiated a court-martial.[4] It was never completed because Bonaparte halted the proceedings and relieved Latour from duty in the French military.[5] Yet, in preparation for his court-martial, Latour wrote a lengthy book describing and exonerating his defense of Mantua. He argued, by citing Pommereul's book *Campagne du Général Buonaparte*, published in 1797, that had Bonaparte not lifted the siege at the end of July 1796, Mantua would have fallen in a couple of weeks, just as he was forced to capitulate after two weeks of open trenches.[6] He offered other reasons for the hasty surrender, but the focus of his book was to defend himself against the thirty-two charges being prepared against him in a pending court-martial.

The explanation Latour offered deserves further analysis—particularly in terms of the qualities of leadership offered by the respective commanders. Wurmser surrendered 13,266 officers and men not counting the 6,000 remaining in the hospitals of Mantua. Latour surrendered 9,690 officers and men plus 1,220 in the hospitals. While Latour had to employ 1,000 of his own troops to police the city during the siege, Wurmser was able to utilize the local Mantuan militia for that purpose. Wurmser was more successful in winning the support of the local elite, while Latour alienated them. The importance the two defenders placed on capitulation terms was also quite different. Wurmser wanted to ensure honorable terms including that his army be allowed to return to Austria; the French acquiesced in recognition of his gallant defense. In contrast, Latour did not appear to be concerned about his Polish subordinates. He agreed to a secret article regarding the fate of the Polish soldiers, most of whom were Austrian deserters fighting for the French, to be traitorously turned over to the Austrians. He also pursued his own personal interests in the capitulation terms to ensure that he would be provided with three baggage wagons. In all likelihood, these wagons carried the pay of his soldiers, which he had previously promised to "invest" for them. To make matters worse, he was in a position to negotiate better terms, whereas Wurmser was not.

For the attackers, Bonaparte and Suvorov both proved that the fortress could be bypassed. Suvorov wanted to mirror Bonaparte's tactics of 1796–97. However, he was forced by the Aulic Council in 1799 to divert forces to capture Mantua before continuing his operations; as a result, Kray's capture of the city produced a hollow victory. The Austrians garrisoned the city in 1799 and began to reestablish the pre-1797 government, but the Austrian army under Melas was decisively defeated by the French at Marengo. The Russians, disgusted with Viennese meddling and self-interest, eventually withdrew from the coalition, accelerating its collapse.

During the Austrian reoccupation in 1799, a sympathetic government was reestablished. Within two years, the special taxes levied on the Jewish community by Latour were abolished and any semblance of representative government was eliminated. However, because of the impact of the French reforms, the Austrians could not revert to the pre-1797 government entirely.[7]

The third capture of Mantua during the Revolutionary period was not a result of starvation, as in the first siege, or of a breach in the fortifications, as in the second siege. Instead, Mantua was blockaded briefly and surrendered to the French in 1801, following negotiations at Lunéville. After Bonaparte's victory over the Austrians at Marengo on 14 June 1800, Melas and Berthier signed a convention between Austria and France at Alessandria two days later. The agreement stipulated that there would be a suspension of hostilities between the French and the Austrians, but French successes in late 1800 forced the Austrians to surrender Mantua as a condition of ending the war. Francis II was forced to comply at the Treaty of Lunéville, on 9 February 1801, and Mantua was turned over to the French.[8] The Cisalpine Republic was restored in 1802 and incorporated into the Italian Republic. After Napoleon became Emperor of the French in May 1804, he transformed the Italian republic into a kingdom, ruled by himself, on 15 March 1805. The French retained control of Mantua until 23 April 1814, when a convention signed at Mantua returned the city to the Austrians.[9]

The Austrians' strategy for northern Italy was based on their control of Mantua. The French Directory also felt it was vital for their policies in the region. As a result, extraordinary resources were expended by both sides to control it. At the same time the fortress became a focal point that played a unique role in Bonaparte's rise to power. During the War of the Second Coalition, it remained a vital element in both French and Austrian strategy. Its unexpected capitulation under Foissac-Latour left the French with no presence in northern Italy except at Genoa on the coast.

This study of the two sieges of Mantua helps illuminate the study of siege warfare during the Revolutionary period in northern Italy. It details the respective efforts of France and the Austrian Empire to capture and/or defend this vital fortress and demonstrates how a powerful fortification such as Mantua could have a monumental impact on a campaign, and even on the strategy of a nation or alliance. In addition, this study presents important insights into changes of urban government in northern Italy as well as human behavior and different military leadership styles—the determined, energetic, and prudent leadership of Bonaparte; the obedient and persistent qualities of Wurmser; the focused but relenting characteristics of Suvorov; and the theoretical yet inferior attributes of Foissac-Latour.

EPILOGUE

"Never say that name again."

NAPOLEON BONAPARTE, REFERRING TO FOISSAC-LATOUR

In the thirty-two volumes of Napoleon's *Correspondance*, Foissac-Latour is mentioned only twice. The first time is in a letter of 24 July 1800 in which Bonaparte cashiers him out of the army upon learning that he was planning to return from Austria still wearing the French uniform, which Bonaparte thought disgraceful. Bonaparte wrote to Minister of War Carnot: "Let him know that he ceased to belong to the service of the Republic the day he cowardly surrendered the fortress of Mantua, and expressly forbid him from wearing the uniform. His conduct at Mantua is more accountable to public opinion than to the courts. Moreover, the intention of the Government is to never hear again about that disgraceful siege which will long be a stain on the French army. Citizen Foissac-Latour will find that public contempt is the greatest punishment that can be inflicted upon a Frenchman."[1] The second mention of Foissac-Latour in the *Correspondance de Napoléon* was on 25 August 1801 in a *"Décision"* by Bonaparte, who mandated "Never say that name again" when the issue of Latour's request for a military pension came to his attention.[2] Bonaparte's two edicts had a far-reaching effect. Foissac-Latour's dossier concerning Mantua at the French Military Archive contains only fourteen pages for his entire career in Italy, and documents at the archive on the 1799 siege in general consist of a mere three items: a manuscript by Maubert with handwritten annotations by Latour, a December 1799 letter from Maubert at Léoben to Berthier, and a Vienna newspaper of four pages covering the siege.[3]

Bonaparte's two mandates were essentially fulfilled. The loss of Mantua in 1799 raised his indignation to such a level that whenever the subject was mentioned Bonaparte was at a loss for words to express his rage. When he stopped the investigation for the court-martial and issued his cashiering decree against Latour, many general officers became extremely concerned because Latour's culpability had not been proven. High-ranking French officers everywhere spoke about this seemingly arbitrary decision and were worried that they, too, could be in danger of losing the privilege of being tried by their peers if they displeased the First Consul, Bonaparte.[4] Louis Antoine Fauvelet de Bourrienne, Bonaparte's private secretary, maintained that the decree was highly regrettable and that he himself was concerned about the consequences. A few days after the First Consul issued the decree, Bourrienne ventured to point out to Bonaparte that he thought the decree imposed undue severity and he emphasized the statements made in Latour's favor.[5] According to Bourrienne, he told Bonaparte that "in a country like France, where honor stands above everything, it is impossible that Foissac can escape condemnation if he is culpable."[6] Bonaparte responded, "Bourrienne, perhaps you are right, but the decree is given; the blow is struck. I have given the same explanation to everyone. I cannot retrace my steps so quickly. To step back is to lose. I do not wish to be wrong. I will see later what can be done. Time will bring leniency and pardon. Right now it would be premature."[7] Such is Bourrienne's account, but oddly enough, within a year, he himself would fall from grace with Bonaparte for his immoderate love of money and the taking of public funds.[8]

Seven days after Bonaparte's first decree, the anonymous correspondent to Bonaparte, known simply as Héléodore, wrote a lengthy letter regarding the First Consul's actions against Latour. Héléodore stated: "

> Thus by your expressing only the public opinion on Foissac-Latour, and supposing he is forgiven yet no longer employed, it is as if you are saying to him: You are a soldier who in the current circumstances, did not show enough firmness; the nation wants more character than you have and it cannot employ you. Will he request a retirement? The law is there; it owes it to him after thirty years of service. . . . However the letter is written. What will you do First Consul, with the first request of Foissac-Latour? He will return to face a court-martial. It is better to do the right thing immediately than try to consolidate a measure that, after an examination, may appear illegal.[9]

Such was the unresolved state of affairs concerning Foissac-Latour in July 1800, one year after his surrender of Mantua.

While at St. Helena, Napoleon reflected on the decree: "It was an illegal and tyrannical act, but still was a necessary evil. It was the fault of the law. He was 100, nay, 1,000 times guilty and yet it was doubtful whether he would be condemned. We therefore assailed him with the shafts of honor and public opinion. Yet I repeat it was a tyrannical act, and one of those violent measures which are at times necessary in great nations and in extraordinary circumstances."[10] On another occasion at St. Helena, Napoleon stated that "when General Foissac-Latour, who commanded at Mantua, so basely surrendered that place, Field Marshal Kray presented him with a flag, passing many encomiums on his valor. The praises of an enemy are suspicious—they cannot flatter a man of honor, until after the cessation of hostilities."[11] Bonaparte certainly had reason to suspect Latour from the beginning. With Bonaparte's network of informants and spies, he would likely have been privy to insights long lost to recorded history.

Others suspected Latour as well. On 28 August, at the Council of Ancients in Paris, Moreau de l'Yonne gave a blistering condemnation of Foissac-Latour as a traitor, even calling him the "assassin" of General Joubert, who fell at Novi.[12] A week earlier, the famous historian Carlo Botta, a longtime acquaintance of Bonaparte, wrote to a friend saying, "The mythical Republicans do not know how to punish the despicable traitors, that one after the other steal the hope of the country. Foissac-Latour, praised by Kray, long accused by the friends of freedom, will likely not be punished because during these particular times, which are as they say 'the times of the regeneration of man,' whoever is rich cannot be guilty."[13]

The French minister of war, Bernadotte, did not fit Botta's mold as a "mythical Republican" with respect to dealing with perceived "despicable traitors." The day before Botta's letter, 20 August 1799, Bernadotte wrote to the commanding general in Italy: "The newspapers, Citizen General, some days back, published the rumor of the surrender of Mantua. Such news is too extraordinary to find credence from those who know French valor. If, contrary to all probability, that surrender has taken place, whatever be the conditions, it must have been the result of treason. I order you, in the name of the Republic and of its interests and glory, to bring General Foissac-Latour and all of his staff without delay before a court-martial."[14] The following day, 21 August, Bernadotte's order for a court-martial of Foissac-Latour made the headlines in *Le Publiciste* in Paris.[15]

For others who were at Mantua, it was simply clear that Latour was guilty. Colonel Borthon, who refused to sign the capitulation at Castellucchio, later accused Latour of selling the fortress for 1.8 million francs. He also claimed that the fortress was capable of being defended for another twenty-two months and that it was well provisioned. Borthon also stated that Latour was in constant communication with King Charles Emmanuel IV's sister, the royalist Maria Theresa of Savoy, the Comtesse d'Artois.[16] Borthon published these accusations on 26 May 1800 with an article in a Munich newspaper, the *Gazzette de la Haute Allemagne*.[17] It did not bode well for Latour's position that the Comtesse d'Artois was living in Klangenfurt as was he. She had fled there during the 1799 French occupation of Turin.[18] Latour even admitted to a relationship with the Comtesse d'Artois while at Klangenfurt but dismissed it as no more than being kind to a woman so as not to insult her misfortune.[19] Latour spent his "imprisonment" at Klangenfurt while the majority of his officers were held on the island of Léoben. Ironically, in June 1800 Latour moved to Turin and wrote *Le Général de Division Foissac La Tour à la France, à ses armées, à l'Europe*, which was published there on 9 July. The pamphlet defended his actions at Mantua. By 31 July he published *Supplement A L'Appel* there as well. The supplement contains a letter written on his behalf by his relative Henry Wimpffen, a second lieutenant. The letter from the young officer, which assists Latour in denouncing one of his many detractors, seems circumspect. Latour's royalist mother was Dorothée de Wimpffen, and Latour explained that the Austrians knew that Henry Wimpffen was a relative, and therefore, they passed information through Henry.[20] Later, in 1800, Latour would use another statement by Wimpffen and two other company-grade officers that read:

> We the undersigned officers of the garrison of Mantua declare that our Austrian escort officer, Honiéde, said for us to be wary of the artillery officer Borthon because he said that he will propose to have General Foissac guillotined upon his arrival in France for having sold the fortress of Mantua and that he (Borthon) was the only faithful man in the place since he was the only one who did not sign the capitulation.[21]

Latour's notoriety reached as far south as Naples, where Colonel Joseph Méjean sold the fortress of Sant'Elmo for 150,000 ducats

(800,000 francs) to the Allies in July 1799. Francesco Lomonaco wrote a letter to Carnot stating that Méjean, known as "the merchant," was "educated in the school of Foissac-Latour."[22]

Suspicion of Latour was justified given the terms of surrender (see appendix B). Upon Michel Leclerc's return to France, General-in-Chief Etienne Championnet ordered him, on 5 September 1799, to write an account of what took place at Mantua in preparation for Latour's pending court-martial.[23] On 17 September 1799 in Grenoble, Michel Leclerc published his pamphlet *Observations du Commissaire des guerres Leclerc, sur la conduit du Général Foissac-Latour, ayant commandé à Mantuoue, et du Général Gastine, chef d'état-major dans cette place* concerning the improprieties of Foissac-Latour and General Gastine. Leclerc, a *commissaire des guerres* employed as an *ordonnateur* at Mantua, was a civilian official responsible for the army's administrative and logistical functions with authority to order disbursements. Given the position of this very knowledgeable man of about thirty-one years of age, he was the logical choice to recount the actions of the leadership throughout the siege.[24] He maintained that he completed his work without ostentation or passion.[25] The pamphlet was, however, very damning of Latour and his chief of staff, Gastine, and pointed out Latour's greatest failings were greed and trying to convince everyone that he had only 261 soldiers to defend the wall at Pradella when in fact he had 3,661 capable and available soldiers under arms out of the 10,000 soldiers present.[26]

Leclerc's pamphlet initiated a "War of the Pens" (see appendix G). Responding from Klangenfurt, Latour wrote *Mémoire du général de division Foissac-Latour, ayant commandé la place de Mantoue, aux citoyens Consuls de la République française* on 23 October 1799, a fifty-seven-page book published in Paris. Maubert, from his prison in Léoben, wrote *Exposé de ce qui s'est passé pendant le blocus et le siège de Mantoue et des causes qui ont le plus contribué a sa Reddition*, which Latour edited; it was also completed on 23 October and published in Paris as *Relation du Blocus et du Siége de Mantoue*. The printed version of Maubert's work differed from his original manuscript with additional "facts" presented. It is unclear how Foissac-Latour edited Maubert's work given they were at different prisons. Given that Latour's entire staff was under a pending investigation for a court-martial, both Latour and Maubert had a vested interest in ensuring the two accounts matched before both were published. Latour, who was familiar with publishing, most likely made the arrangements for publication. Latour's publication also had variations in the official letters used as evidence from the surviving original letters as written. These alterations always cast Latour in a better light. During the "War of the Pens" that ensued, an anonymous author with the initials "P.L." published a sixteen-page denouncement of Latour and Gastine that stated unequivocally, "There is no doubt that the treacherous general, by a secret deal, sacrificed the brave Republicans." This pamphlet focused on the plight of the artillery at Mantua and gave specific details about Borthon, Labadie, and the "brave Poles." It was most likely written by *Chef de Bataillon* Labadie, of the 6th Artillery Regiment, who refused to surrender the fortress.[27]

After a brief stay in Verona, Latour moved to Turin to write another pamphlet, denouncing Borthon, and to respond once more to Leclerc as well as to Pagés. Latour admitted that he had not seen the new work by Pagés, and had only heard about it, but went on to say that Pagés could not read and certainly could not write and that therefore his work must have been that of a paid "Mercenary Pen."[28] The daily reports from Pagés to Latour, concerning his fleet and movements of the Austrians, prove Latour wrong about Pagés's level of literacy.[29] Latour's pamphlet accuses Pagés of taking a boat at night and hiding in the reeds on the enemy bank to meet with some correspondents of his who paid him forty gold coins for the surrender of his fleet, adding that someone wishing to denounce the actions was kept silent with a portion of the money.[30] Yet, according to Latour's own accounts, Pagés was one of the ardent few who always voted to continue fighting during the war councils.

The 24 July 1800 decree by Bonaparte upset Latour and his two sons greatly. When in Turin, Victor, Latour's younger fifteen-year-old son, publicly vented in the military coffeehouse, bitterly denouncing "the Corsican Upstart" to many assembled officers. Victor Latour suggested that Bonaparte was trying to minimize his own shame by disgracing the most ancient French families.[31]

Latour eventually returned to Paris, where he published yet another defense of his actions, *Précis, ou Journal Historique et Raisonné des Opérations Militaires et Administratives qui on eu lieu dans la Place de Mantoue depuis le 9 germinal jusqu'an 10 thermidor de l'an 7 de la République française.* In this massive, two-part book, Latour took pains to exonerate himself in detail and attempted systematically to refute the charges he was to face in his court-martial. The book is full of errors and "changes" to documents that survived in Poland and Italy. In some cases, whole paragraphs are missing in the *Précis* version of the letters.[32] Throughout the book he condemns Leclerc, Borthon, Pagés, and the officers who refused to surrender the fortress. Leclerc responded with a short, thirty-six-page pamphlet titled *Foissac-Latour Dévoile*, which he likens to the young Hebrew boy David, who did not fear to fight against the giant Goliath—meaning Latour's tome.[33] He acknowledged Bonaparte's statement that the French government wanted to hear no more about the siege, but felt he was justified in writing a response to Latour's defense. Leclerc pointed out Latour's violation of the old proverb "One who lies must have a good memory," explaining that he was not present in Mantua early enough to have done some of the things Latour accused him of doing.[34] He expounded on the third article of surrender concerning the three covered wagons destined to depart with Foissac-Latour, noting that hidden in them were a woman attached to Gastine's general staff, and two guards— all "under the protection of the massive silver statue of St. Anselmo, removed from Mantua with the [442] gold medals of the Academy [of Virgiliana], and thus led to Austria irreligiously as a prisoner of war although he [St. Anselmo] had been a noncombatant at Mantua."[35] According to Édouard Gachot, a customs inspector at Villach found only papers and clothing in the wagons.[36] Latour must have been separated from the wagons, as his personal papers did eventually arrive, after him, in Klangenfurt, where he remained for a year, although only obligated to stay three months according to the capitulation. Leclerc condemned Latour for proclaiming a celebration of the fall of the Bastille in order to bring about the fall of Mantua.[37]

The ongoing literary skirmish became quite heated, even causing Latour's older son, Henri, to fight a pistol duel with a superior officer—*Chef de Bataillon* Leclerc, brother of the civilian *ordonnateur* Michel—a month after Bonaparte's pronouncement never to say Foissac-Latour's name again. On 29 September 1801 in the forest of Boulogne, Henri was slightly wounded during the duel, which he fought to rectify the dishonor brought upon his father by Michel Leclerc's writings.[38]

One of the last episodes of the "War of the Pens" was a letter from *Chef de Bataillon* Leclerc, written 10 June 1802, to an undisclosed general in Paris asking him to read the short answer to the nonsense printed against his brother Michel by the ex-general Foissac-Latour. He went on: "You will find in these writings details of the siege of Mantua and the operations of this commander which I think will make you reconsider some of your ideas regarding my brother whom the government has always treated with distinction and no one should judge without reading or hearing his side." The letter was enclosed with Michel Leclerc's two pamphlets bound in a small red booklet.[39]

Yet matters concerning Latour himself seem to have been resolved by then. Earlier, in 1801, Latour purchased a massive estate at Acqueville along the Seine River that he and his two sons refurbished. Latour initially lived at Acqueville under a "forced residence," whereby he was under constant surveillance by the state police. Even before the end of the literary controversy in 1802, and despite Bonaparte's *décision* never to say his name again, when the subject of retirement came up on 25 August 1801, Latour was rehabilitated and admitted into retirement that same month.[40] Time brought leniency as Bonaparte had predicted. Latour remained at Acqueville until he died on 11 February 1804. He left the estate to his two sons.[41]

His son Henri, ironically, eventually served on Napoleon's staff. At Waterloo, however, he stayed loyal to King Louis XVIII. Henri Foissac-Latour became a baron and later *vicomte* for the Comte d'Artois, who became King Charles X in 1824 upon the death of his brother Louis.[42] But by this time all memory of the allegations of Henri's father's involvement with the Comtesse d'Artois in selling the fortress was forgotten—or at least not mentioned. In 1830 Henri was selected by Charles X (d'Artois) to deliver the act of abdication to the Duc d'Orléans, Louis Philippe.[43] For his service, his name was inscribed on the 19th column of the Arc de Triomphe. Thus "Mantoue" (1796–97) and "Foissac-Latour" (Henri) are both inscribed on the Arc, which could cause confusion to an onlooker if these were mistaken for the siege of "Mantoue" in 1799 and its ignoble commander, François Philippe Foissac-Latour.

Back in Mantua, tales of the cruelty of Foissac-Latour abounded. The siege of 1799 provided rich material for playwrights and authors. Anselmo Belloni wrote a three-act comedy about the siege. In the play Somenzari was called *Sicofanti* (the Sycophant), Porro was *Ferro* (the Tool), and Coddé was *Fantastici* (the Fantastic). The comedy is filled with allusions to the rapacity of Foissac-Latour, the indignities committed by the Jacobins, and the persecutions suffered by the people.[44]

The Poles never forgave Latour for his betrayal of more than a thousand of their countrymen, which General Jan Henri Dombrowski had left under his command at Mantua. Today's Polish national anthem has a stanza describing the Polish Legion in Italy and the birth of the Polish nation, conjuring images of Dombrowski's soldiers. Half of the legionnaires entered Mantua against their will and were later "sacrificed" by Latour. In 1902–3 the famous Polish novelist Stefan Żeromski wrote *Popioły* (Ashes), which includes a scene of the Polish soldiers exiting Mantua after laying down their arms and then being beaten by Austrian soldiers—and only then finding out about the secret article in the capitulation document that treated them as deserters.[45] In 1965 Polish director Andrzej Wajda's popular film based on the novel was released; it, too, depicts this humiliating incident.[46]

The family of Foissac-Latour continued to live at Acqueville until 1877 when the property passed to the family of Courthial de Lassuchette. Later, the château fell into disrepair, until recently when it was purchased and eventually renovated into a four-star hotel with eighty suites and apartments.

The papers of Foissac-Latour, which he had at Klangenfurt, never entered the Archives de la Guerre in Paris. In 1999 a large portion of the papers were acquired by Libreria Antiquaria Scriptorium in Mantua, a bookshop that deals with antique books and manuscripts, particularly about the history of Mantua. The proprietor, Mansueto Bassi, with whom I became acquainted while researching the 1796–97 siege, contacted me, and thus began my search, in earnest, to find out what happened in Mantua in 1799. I hope this book has filled that gap as well as presented a comprehensive account of the 1796–97 siege and the transitional government.

I could not find conclusive evidence that Foissac-Latour sold, or attempted to sell, the fortress, although much evidence and many circumstances point to that conclusion. If he was in fact engaged in treason, then his erratic behavior during the defense begins to make sense. If he did not sell or attempt to sell the fortress, then his actions during the defense of Mantua are all the same inexplicable and reprehensible as he was the leading French theorist of the day, among the engineers, with respect to defending and attacking fortresses.

In retrospect, the story of the two sieges of Mantua, like any military history, is largely a story of people, personalities, and decisions. The analyses offered here of the different approaches taken by Bonaparte, Canto d'Yrles, Wurmser, Foissac-Latour, Kray, and Suvorov in attacking and/or defending the fortress comprise the real value of this study. Bonaparte and Latour represent perhaps the best and worst of what the French Revolutionary army had to offer with respect to generalship. Ironically, the association between the two commanders and their respective struggles at Mantua caused the former to try to suppress any mention of the latter's experience at that highly significant fortress city.

Appendix A

Terms of the Capitulation of Mantua,
2 February 1797

Between His Excellency Marshal Wurmser, commander to the army of His Majesty Emperor and King, and General of Division Sérurier, commanding the troops of the French Republic at Mantua.

San Antonio 14 pluviôse an V (2 February 1797)

Article I. The imperial garrison of Mantua and the Citadel shall go out through the main gate of the Citadel, with the honors of war, with drums beating, colors flying, and matches lit: taking with them two 6-pounders, two 12-pounders and two howitzers, with their ammunition wagons, and a proportionate quantity of military stores. The garrison shall form at the causeway that leads from Marmirolo to Mantua, shall not lay down their arms, but shall continue prisoners of war until an exchange takes place, with the exception of those made mention of in the second article.

Answer. Agreed to, with the exception that the garrison, once outside the town, shall lay down their arms, colors, standards, and every military appendage belonging to them.

Article II. Marshal-Count Wurmser and his suite shall not be made prisoners of war: to wit, the adjutant generals Auer and Bauloht, and aide-de-camp, Captain Count Degenfeld; the generals and aides-de-camp of the army, two hundred cavalrymen and their respective officers, besides five hundred individuals whom his Excellency, the marshal, may choose to select. The suite shall be accompanied with the six pieces of cannon mentioned in article I, their gunners, and ammunition.

Capitulation, 2 February 1797, FM/K 1139, 1797.2.16, OSK.

Answer. Granted with regard to what concerns personally his excellency marshal Wurmser, as well the cavalrymen, officers, and five hundred individuals that he may think proper to select; the artillery comprised in article I, the general officers of the army, those of the headquarters, and whatever other persons he may wish to annex to his suite.

Article III. All officers shall retain their swords, horses, and equipage; the soldiers their knapsacks, and the civil officers their effects.

Answer. The officers shall keep their swords, and pursuant to their rank, the number of horses stipulated respectively:

Lieutenant generals	16
Major generals	10
Colonels	8
Lieutenant colonels and majors	7
Captains of cavalry	3
Captains of infantry	2
Lieutenants of cavalry	2
Lieutenants and ensigns of infantry	2

The commissioners of war shall be treated equivalently to the rank they hold with officers of the army. Subalterns, who before had more than one horse, shall now retain one.

Article IV. I demand the parole of honor for the officers included under this capitulation, and pledge my word that no individual of the army shall carry away with him any effects but those which are his private property. Every soldier shall take with him his knapsack, and every cavalryman his portmanteau.
The imperial garrison shall be conducted by the nearest road toward Gorizia in the Friuli and shall claim the preference of being the first among those who shall be exchanged for French prisoners of war.

Answer. The troops shall march in a direction through Porto Legnago, Padua, and Treviso: an exchange of prisoners shall be made as speedily as possible: and the seven hundred men submitted to the choice of Field Marshal Wurmser, shall promise not to serve against the French army three months from this date.

Article V. The march of the troops shall be regulated by French commissioners, divided into two columns, and shall not advance more than four French miles in one day, the garrison having been subject to fatigue and enfeebled by disease. The commissioners shall supply the requisite aids of provision and forage and provide vehicles for the accommodation of those whom sickness may overtake in the prosecution of their march.

Answer. Not to levy contributions on the country through which the imperial army will necessarily pass, and to afford a more abundant supply of provisions to the troops, several days shall be taken to prepare for the departure of the columns: each of which shall be composed of a thousand men; and they shall begin their march the 4th of February, or the 16th of pluviôse, French style. Carriages shall accompany the columns for the convenience of the sick, or of those who eventually may become sick, and provisions and forage shall be provided for the subsistence of the men and the horses.

Article VI. The convoy-wagons carrying the treasury of the army, as well as the war chest, forming collectively twenty-nine wagons of which twenty-five are drawn by two horses, and four with four horses, shall be suffered to join the garrison and repair to Gorizia.

Answer. Refused. A commissioner shall be appointed to inspect the registers and other papers of the treasury which, should they be found of no utility to the French republic, shall be transported to the place of destination.

Article VII. The sick and wounded shall be treated humanely. Surgeons and attendants shall be left in the hospital to minister them assistance, and after their recovery, they shall receive, in common with other soldiers, the privileges granted by the capitulation. Those whom circumstances may keep them at Mantua shall be indulged with passports when their business is finished.

Answer. Granted without the least exception.

Article VIII. All the civil officers in the service of his imperial majesty shall be permitted freely to depart with their bureaus and treasury, and shall be accommodated with carriages for the transportation of their effects.

Answer. Individuals shall be suffered freely to depart: but the bureaus and treasury of commissioners shall be examined and if it is judged necessary, remain in possession of the French army.

Article IX. The city shall be supported in all its rights and privileges; the people and the religion of the people shall be respected: and no citizen shall be called to an account for any services that he may have rendered to his lawful sovereign.

Answer. Granted.

Article X. Whatever citizen or inhabitant of the city may be inclined to retire from Mantua, with his effects, into the dominions of his imperial majesty, shall be allowed a year to dispose of his lands or possessions, and shall be indulged with passports whenever he shall demand them.

Answer. Granted.

Article XI. The gunners of the city who served on the ramparts against the French army shall not undergo questioning about their position, having only performed their duty, founded upon the constitution of the Dukedom of Mantua. They shall return quietly to their families.

Answer. Granted.

Article XII. If any doubtful article is found in the capitulation, that may give rise to contest or dispute, it shall be explained in favor of the garrison.

Answer. It shall be discussed and interpreted pursuant to the rules of justice.

Article XIII. Three hours after the signing of the capitulation, the French troops shall remove from the Citadel to the nearest drawbridge, and the French commissioners only shall be allowed to enter into the Citadel, or those who may be sent there by the French commander of the blockade. The French army shall not enter into the Citadel until it is evacuated by the imperial garrison.

Answer. The Citadel shall be wholly given up three hours after the signing of the capitulation but should that happen at a late hour, it shall be postponed until the following morning. All communication shall be prevented between the troops of the respective powers, and the French troops shall occupy the advance posts of the city. None but French commissioners, officers of artillery, and those appointed to take plans and charts shall enter into the Citadel.

Article XIV. An officer shall be sent to His Majesty the emperor and another to the chief general of the imperial army in Tyrol with a copy of the capitulation.

Answer. Granted. The commissioner general shall be provided with a passport to traverse the territory of His Imperial Majesty.

Appendix B

Terms of the Capitulation of Mantua by Foissac-Latour, 28 July 1799

At the Headquarters at Mantua 10 thermidor an 7 [28 July 1799] of the French Republic, one and indivisible.

Foissac-Latour, general of division and commander of Mantua and the Citadel,

Propose, to Baron Kray, general of artillery and commander of His Majesty, the Emperor's, troops at Mantua, to surrender the city, under the following conditions, deliberated by the defense's Council of War.

1. The garrison of Mantua will depart 12 thermidor an 7 [30 July 1799], through the Citadel of Mantua at noon, with the honors of war and six field artillery pieces at the front.

The garrison shall be prisoners of war. To avoid the disgrace and misery of confinement, the commanding general, the other generals under his orders, the officers of the staff, and all the officers of the garrison, consent to remain prisoners in the nearest Hereditary German land where they will serve as hostages for the noncommissioned officers and soldiers, who shall be sent back to France by the shortest road, and shall not serve against the troops of the Emperor or his allies until after their exchange.

Accordingly, when they arrive at the glacis of the Citadel, the garrison will lay down their arms. The officers will keep their swords, their equipment, and their assigned number of horses according to their grade.

The noncombatants will also return to France; the generals will keep their secretaries, and all of the officers their servants.

It is agreed that colors will go to general of division Foissac-la-Tour, in consideration of the energy of his defense.

Capitulation, Article 15, section 1*3, Service Historique.

Answer—Granted in the fullest extent, and in addition, in consideration of the French manner, brave and loyal, covering the garrison of Mantua's conduct, attributed to the commander, the staff, and the military officers of the garrison, after having remained three months in the Hereditary States, will return to their respective countries upon their word of honor not to take up arms against His Royal Imperial Majesty and his allies until reciprocally exchanged. The three months shall begin from the day the capitulation is signed.

2. The Cisalpine, Swiss, Polish, and Piedmontese troops will be considered and treated under all the terms as the troops of the French Republic.

Answer—Granted.

3. It is granted to the commanding general three covered wagons for his baggage, papers, and other personal property objects. The wagons will not be inspected and the destination and disposition of them will be as his orders.

Answer—Granted.

4. The chief of staff and the other chiefs of departments will be able to take with them all of the papers relating to the administration, and shall have the charge of the wagons destined for that purpose and for the transportation of their personal effects. The commissioners are responsible to remove the objects that, by their nature, belong to the fortress.

Answer—Granted.

5. Trusting to the fairness and generosity of the Austrian government, the citizens employed by the Cisalpine government can rest assured that the Emperor formally recognized the peace treaty of Campo Formio, as well as those there who manifested Republican opinions. The commissioners and the civil artillery will be treated the same as with the noble capitulation made by Bonaparte and General Wurmser.

Answer—Agreed.

6. There will be named the officers, from those of engineers and of artillery, who will receive instructions where to deliver the objects belonging to their branch of service.

Answer—Agreed.

7. Equally, there will be named, from the commissioners of war and of supplies, one to make the delivery of the magazines that are found in the fortress.

Answer—Agreed.

8. The sick and wounded that are not able to be transported will continue to receive all of the necessary treatment from the garrison. The French surgeons and medics will remain to do this. The commanding general will name an official that will keep watch and will look after their transportation and furnish all the means necessary for the army to be exchanged, or for the return to France or Germany under the same conditions according to their respective grade.

Answer—Agreed.

9. There will be furnished, by the Austrian troops, escorts expedient and sufficient to guarantee all of the individuals that comprise the present capitulation, against all abuses where the population will riot. The commanders of the escorts are particularly responsible [for this guarantee].

Answer—Granted.

10. All doubts that may arise out of the present capitulation shall be explained in favor of the garrison, consistent with the laws of equity.

Answer—Agreed.

11. After the signature of the present capitulation, hostages will be mutually exchanged; by the French, a brigade commander and a captain, and from the Austrians, a colonel and a captain.

Answer—Agreed.

12. Until the signature and the exchange of the hostages, there will be a flawless armistice by both sides.

Answer—Agreed.

13. The Migliaretto will be occupied by a battalion of Austrians who will detach fifty men to occupy the exterior portion of the Cerese gate. The two armies will not communicate with each other with the exception of the leaders and those that receive permission from the respective generals.

Answer—Agreed.

14. The executive commissioners of provisions and the inspector general of police of the Cisalpine Republic at Mantua will be free to leave the city to go wherever they please.

Answer—Agreed.

15. Two wagons will be allowed for the people of the suite of the general and to those others that have received the orders to follow the departure of the garrison.

Answer—Granted.

16. There will be allowed the number of wagons necessary for the transportation of effects of the officers and of the entire garrison of the French army, as many as those that they do not have to leave anything in the city.

Answer—Granted.

17. The generals and other officers that want to return to France may send a portion of their belongings with the column of soldiers, unless General Kray, who always acts like a man of the highest honor and liberality, consents that the officers should share the same fortune of the troops, and be permitted to return to France as prisoners under their word of honor.

Answer—As outlined in the first article.

Additional Article. The Austrian deserters are to return to their respective regiments and battalions. The Imperial Commanding General promises that their lives will be preserved.

General Headquarters at Castelucchio,
28 July 1799.

Signed:

General of Division Foissac-Latour

Maubert, *Chef de Brigade*, Commander in Chief of Engineers.

Borthon, Commander of Artillery.

Refuses to sign for personal reasons.

Appendix C

Military Stores Captured by the Austrians, 1 August 1796

Cannon	No.	Howitzers	No.	Mortars	No.
2-pounder	4	7-pounder	1	22 pounder	3
2 1/4-pounder	1	9 1/2-pounder	1	30-pounder	2
2 1/2-pounder	2	12-pounder	1	40-pounder	1
3 1/4-pounder	2			42-pounder	2
5 1/4-pounder	1			44-pounder	2
6-pounder	3			64-pounder	2
8-pounder	6			66 1/2-pounder	1
8 1/2-pounder	5			67-pounder	3
9-pounder	2			67 1/2-pounder	4
9 1/2-pounder	1			68 2/3-pounder	1
10-pounder	3			70-pounder	3
12-pounder	13			75-pounder	3
12 1/2-pounder	5			78-pounder	2
15-pounder	4			86-pounder	1
15 1/2-pounder	2				
16-pounder	12				
17-pounder	2				
18-pounder	28				
19-pounder	2				
21-pounder	1				
24-pounder	9				
25-pounder	7				
26-pounder	12				
36-pounder	16				
Column totals	**143**		3		30
TOTAL STORES CAPTURED 176					

In his journal, Baldassare Scorza gives a detailed account of exactly what took place and what the Austrians captured on 1 August 1796.[1]

In addition to the cannon the Austrians seized 79 *doppel-stutzen*, 1,500 new muskets, 516 used muskets, 120 repaired muskets, 98 nonusable muskets, 45,825 cannonballs of various calibers, 5,450 mortar shells of various calibers, 900 howitzer shells, 641 grapeshot canisters, 610 incendiary projectiles, 3,760 hand grenades, 14,900 shell and grenade fuses, 1,026 pounds of incendiary material for shells, 7,500 musket flints, 492,000 fixed cartridges, 67,800 sandbags, 5,420 shovels (2,094 of which did not have handles), many other entrenching implements, artillery and siege materials, 249 powder bags, and tons of lead.[2]

APPENDIX D

MILITARY STORES CAPTURED BY THE FRENCH, 2 FEBRUARY 1797

	Bronze Cannon	
126	cannon	16- to 36-pounders
175	cannon	15-pounders
56	mortars	
2	bronze mortars that fire stones	
40	small bronze grenade mortars	
7	cannon fitted for boats	

	Iron Cannon	
21	cannon	from 6- to 12-pounders
16	Howitzers	
4	iron cannon that fire stones	

	Field Artillery	
26	cannon	3-pounders
6	cannon	6-pounders
2	cannon	12-pounders
4	howitzers	7-inch

485 total artillery pieces

	Field Artillery Ammunition	
5,736	fixed cartridges	3-pounder
1,836	fixed cartridges	6-pounder
540	fixed cartridges	12-pounder
1,200	canister shot	3-pounder
340	canister shot	6-pounder
164	canister shot	12-pounder
184	ammunition wagons and other covered wagons	

A considerable quantity of harnesses for the field artillery

---

5 February 1797, B³39, Service Historique.

Fortress Ammunition

14,746	fixed cartridges
2,093	howitzer shells
187,319	iron cannonballs of various sizes
14,502	bombs of various sizes
3,828	canister shot of different sizes
82+ tons	iron shot of different sizes

Vast quantity of combustible material for illuminating rounds

Small Arms and Small Arms Ammunition

17,115	infantry muskets and cavalry carbines	(5,000 of which are usable)
4,484	pistols	(2,500 of which are usable)
1,214,000	musket cartridges	
160,228	cavalry cartridges	

Miscellaneous

Equipment for 25 Pontoons

264 tons	powder
80 tons	lead (in pigs)
80+ tons	new bar iron

Fuses for the artillery and pioneers

Timber for gunstocks

APPENDIX E

MILITARY STORES CAPTURED BY THE AUSTRIANS AND RUSSIANS, 28 JULY 1799

Bronze Cannon

243	cannon
27	light and medium howitzers
51	mortars

Iron Cannon

256	cannon
3	mortars

20 other artillery pieces

600	**total artillery pieces**

Small Arms

12,959	muskets
70	*doppelhaken*
1,260	pistols

Also in the magazines the Austrians captured vast quantities of foodstuffs, cloth, canvas, leather, medicines, and wine.

Stutterheim, "Geschichte des Feldzugs," 9.

Appendix F

Royal Governing Giunta

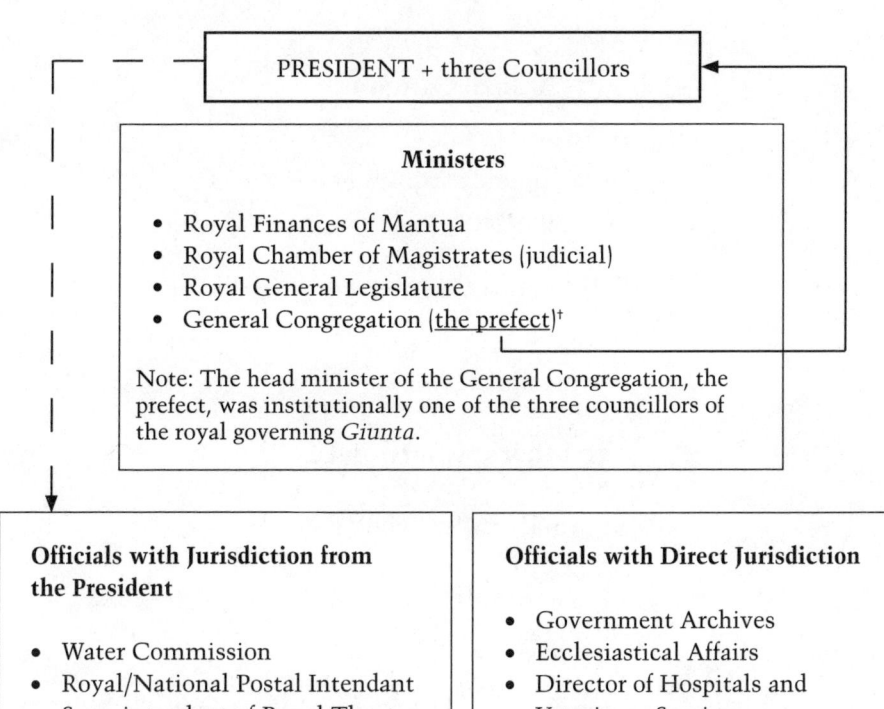

PRESIDENT + three Councillors

Ministers

- Royal Finances of Mantua
- Royal Chamber of Magistrates (judicial)
- Royal General Legislature
- General Congregation (<u>the prefect</u>)[†]

Note: The head minister of the General Congregation, the prefect, was institutionally one of the three councillors of the royal governing *Giunta*.

Officials with Jurisdiction from the President

- Water Commission
- Royal/National Postal Intendant
- Superintendent of Royal Theaters

Note: These officials needed approval from the president of the *Giunta* for major policy changes.

Officials with Direct Jurisdiction

- Government Archives
- Ecclesiastical Affairs
- Director of Hospitals and Veterinary Services
- Royal Academy of Science

Note: These officials were autonomous.

[†] The Ministry of the General Congregation consisted of 100 property owners: thirty nobles, fifteen lawyers and judges, fifteen merchants, and forty landed gentry. The landed gentry comprised thirty members who represented the fifteen districts of the Mantovano and ten who represented the district of the city of Mantua. The sixteen districts of the Mantovano were Mantua, Ostiglia, Roverbella, Goito, Castiglione delle Stiviere, Castelgoffredo, Canneto, Marcaria, Borgoforte, Bozzolo, Sabbioneta, Viadana, Suzzara, Gonzaga, Revere, and Sermide.

Appendix G

War of the Pens

29 July 1799	Latour writes positive letter commemorating Citizen Michel Leclerc.
28–30 July 1799	Surrender of Mantua.
22 Aug. 1799	The *Moniteur* publishes (1) an article with a letter from Bernadotte accusing Foissac-Latour of treason and (2) Bernadotte's order to the general commanding forces in Italy to bring General Foissac-Latour and all his staff before a court-martial.
17 Sept. 1799	Leclerc writes *Observations du commissaire des guerres Leclerc, sur la conduite du Général Foissac-Latour, ayant commandé à Mantoue, et du Général Gastine, chef d'état-major dans cette place* at Grenoble, 1 complementaire an 7.
23 Oct. 1799	Foissac-Latour writes *Mémoire du général de division Foissac-Latour, ayant commandé la place de Mantoue, aux citoyens Consuls de la République française* at Klangenfurt, 1 brumaire an 8 (published in Paris).
23 Oct. 1799	Maubert writes *Relation du Blocus et du Siége de Mantoue et expose des causes qui ont contribute a sa Reddition* at Léoben, 1 brumaire an 8 (published in Paris).
26 May 1800	Borthon publishes an article in the *Gazette de la Haute-Allemagne* of Munich accusing Foissac-Latour of selling the fortress of Mantua for 1.8 million francs.

9 July 1800	Foissac-Latour writes *Le Général de Division Foissac La Tour à la France, à ses armées, a l'Europe* at Turin, 20 messidor an 8.
24 July 1800	Foissac-Latour is stripped of his rank by letter from the consuls; Bonaparte orders Foissac-Latour to return to France and no longer wear his uniform. Bonaparte states that he did not want to hear any more about the disgraceful siege that woud be forever a stain on the French military.
31 July 1800	Foissac-Latour writes *Supplement a L'Appel* at Turin, 12 thermidor an 8.
1800–1801	Foissac-Latour writes *Précis, ou Journal Historique et Raisonné des Opérations Militaires et Administratives qui on eu lieu dans la Place de Mantoue depuis le 9 germinal jusqu'an 10 thermidor de l'an 7 de la République française* (published in Paris, an 9).
1800–1801	Leclerc writes *Foissac-Latour dévoilé, ou, Notice sur la conduite de cet ex-général dans le Conseil de defense et l'administration militaire de la place de Mantoue* at Genoa, an 9.
25 Aug. 1801	Bonaparte issues his edict to never say Foissac-Latour's name again.
29 Sept. 1801	Henri Latour fights a duel with *Chef de Bataillon* Leclerc (brother of Michel Leclerc), 8 vendémiaire an 10.
10 June 1802	*Chef de Bataillon* Leclerc's brother writes a letter and sends Michel Leclerc's book to a general in Paris, 21 prairial an 10.
11 Feb. 1804	Foissac-Latour dies.

Appendix H

Historiography of the Sieges

Although a multitude of works have been produced on the northern Italian campaigns of the Wars of the First and Second Coalitions, the vast majority of these center on the classical dramatic battles and operational maneuvering—not the sieges that took place. In both wars, however, it was the struggle to hold or take Mantua that greatly influenced the conduct and outcome of the maneuver battles surrounding the fortress city. For the 1796–97 campaign, almost all the books and articles published that concern the siege of Mantua center on Bonaparte's victories over the Austrians at Castiglione in August 1796, Bassano in September, Arcole in November, and Rivoli in January 1797—all of which occurred during the Austrians' attempt to relieve the fortress. Some military historians have criticized Bonaparte saying that he should have masked Mantua in 1796 and followed Beaulieu into to the Tyrol.[1] Because of the diminished attention given to the eight-month siege, the historiographical emphasis on the pitched battles perpetuates a misconception that Bonaparte should have bypassed Mantua. But Bonaparte was intent on capturing Mantua from the very beginning, and he, like the Austrians, placed a special emphasis on controlling the fortress.

One possible reason for the paucity of writing about the 1799 siege, at least in French, is that so little material is available in the French military archives on this siege and its French commander owing to Bonaparte's declaration in July 1800 that he "wanted to hear no more about this disgraceful siege."[2] Hence few primary source documents have been available for historians to research. The 1799 siege deserves considerable attention as the French ruled Mantua for two years (1797–99), during which they continued to improve its fortifications; clearly, they could have held out much longer.

Besides the French and Austrian military journalists and diarists who recorded the events of the first siege, a member of the town Giunta, Don Baldassare Scorza, wrote a day-by-day account of the entire event.[3] Scorza's manuscript was edited, condensed, and published in Mantua in 1883 by Attilio Portioli under the title *Le Vicende di Mantova nel 1796*. Portioli supplemented Scorza's memoir with information that he obtained from two other local diarists. One of the diarists, Giuseppe Lattanzi, was elected to the municipal government when the French took over in February 1797. His early writings about Mantua were published under the titles *Istoria del Blocco e dell'Assedio della Città e Fortezza di Mantova* and *Giornale di Quanto è Succeduto in Mantova Durante il di lei Secondo Assedio* around 1797. Although the title of the latter work translates to "Journal of What Happened in Mantua during the Second Siege," Lattanzi has in mind the period after the Battle of Castiglione in August 1796 when the French returned to renew the siege. The "first" siege had to be temporarily lifted so that Bonaparte could use most of the besieging force at Castiglione. Lattanzi did not give his name in either of the publications but instead indicated his authorship thus: "written by a citizen who witnessed it." Both works were printed in Cremona. The other diary Portioli used was published in 1797, again anonymously, as *Giornale dei Due Assedi della Città di Mantova Diviso in Tre Parti Contenente i Fatti d'Armi Accaduti dai Primi di Giugno 1796 Sino alla Conclusione della Pace nel 1797*. The author of this "Journal of the Two Sieges of the City of Mantua . . . ," who remains unknown, described himself as "a Mantuan and a friend in Rome." Lattanzi's view was pro-French, while the "Journal of the Two Sieges of the City of Mantua" was written by a pro-Austrian author who was self-exiled in Rome. Portioli relied primarily on the Scorza manuscript but greatly condensed it.[4] In 1974 Luigi Pescasio edited and republished Portioli's work with the title *Cronaca Vissuta del Duplice Assedio di Mantova degli Anni 1796 e 1797*.[5] Later Pescasio expanded this book, including many of the *avvisi*, or notices, that were posted by both Austrian and French administrations. This revision, entitled *Mantova Assediata 1796–1797* and published in Mantua in 1989, still relied primarily on Portioli's treatment of the Scorza manuscript.

Another chronicler who played an important role was Leopoldo Camillo Volta.[6] He established the first public library in Mantua and served on the municipal council under the French in 1797. His massive undertaking, a work on the city's history, appeared under the title *Compendio Cronologico-Critico della Storia di Mantova*

(Chronological and critical compendium of the history of Mantua)—
but was left unfinished. Volta died in 1823 having published only
the first volume of the history in 1807.[7] Using Volta as his pen
name, Giuseppe Arrivabene worked with Volta's notes to complete
the manuscripts and published the four remaining volumes of the
Compendio by 1838.[8]

There have been many works in French covering the northern
Italian campaign of 1796–97 that also demonstrate the importance
of the fortress of Mantua. Most of these works relied on French eye-
witnesses, Napoleon's correspondence, and reports of French army
officers to describe the events surrounding the blockade of Mantua.
The earliest well-known French book that covers many aspects of
the siege of Mantua, but still focuses mainly on Bonaparte's campaigns in northern Italy, is General François René Jean Pommereul's
Campagne du Général Buonaparte en Italie.[9] This work was published in 1797 in Paris. In 1798 it was translated into English by John
Davis and published in New York; in 1799 it was likewise translated
into English by T. E. Ritchie and published in London. In 1798 the
famous work was even translated into Italian, German, and Dutch.[10]
In 1808 Father Piuma, a chaplain in the Austrian army, published
a refutation of certain arguments in Pommereul's book in London.
This response to Pommereul's work, though printed in England,
was written in French, and a second edition was published in Paris
in 1814.[11] Another work in French in 1797 that was quickly translated to English is *The History of the Campaign of 1796 in Germany
and Italy.*[12] This work is very interesting in that both its original
publication and its translation were anonymous. It seems prudent
that the French author, sometimes noted to be Baron de Pomp,
remained anonymous since he was very critical of Bonaparte's 1796
campaign. The English translation (often attributed to Thomas
Graham), printed in 1797, is probably the first complete work published in English on the northern Italian campaign with some detail
concerning the events at Mantua. Ironically, the English translation
of this work was translated back into French by the French play-
wright Maurin de Pompigny and published in Paris in 1817—safely
after the second restoration of the French monarchy. Still wishing to
remain somewhat anonymous, however, the translator was given as
"M***" in the series.[13]

There are many other works in French covering the overall campaign that were published after the Napoleonic Wars. However,

none of these contains a thorough analysis of the siege itself even though Antoine-Henri Jomini vividly described the sieges of 1796–97 and 1799 in his enormous work *Histoire Critique et Militaire des Guerres de la Révolution* and Abel Hugo did the same in his lengthy *Histoire des Armées Françaises de Terre et de Mer de 1792 a 1833*.[14] Another multivolume work that addresses both sieges of Mantua is *Victoires, Conquêtes, Désastres, Revers et Guerres Civiles des Français de 1789 a 1815*, edited by Charles Beauvais de Preau. This twenty-seven-volume work was compiled between 1817 and 1821 by many of the officers who participated in the campaigns. Several aspects of the French experience during the two sieges are described in this work.[15] Another work, similar to Jomini's and Beauvais's, that focuses on the Italian Campaigns, discusses the role of Mantua in 1796, and relies mainly on French sources was published by the Didot firm in Paris in 1859 under the title *Guerres des Français en Italie Depuis 1794 jusqu'à 1814*. In 1899 Louis Tuetey published a biography of General Jean Mathieu Sérurier with two chapters concerning his activities during his command of the siege of Mantua. In these chapters, Tuetey used French sources exclusively, relying heavily on the Archives de la Guerre, the *Correspondance de Napoléon*, Pommereul, Jomini, and the memoirs of General Alexandre Dumas.[16] There are, however, important works in French published at the turn of the nineteenth century in which the authors consulted Italian and Austrian documents as well as private French sources for their research concerning the northern Italian campaigns. Édouard Gachot, in his *Histoire Militaire de Masséna: La Premiere Campagne d'Italie (1795–1798)*, published in Paris in 1901, vividly describes the actions around Mantua in which General André Masséna was involved. Gachot consulted Attilio Portioli's *Le Vicende di Mantova nel 1796*, as well as the archives of Mantua and Vienna.[17] The edited memoirs of Masséna by General J. B. F. Koch also give some detail about the first siege of Mantua.[18]

Some of the extremely detailed works in French concerning the Italian campaign only cover the earliest portion of the campaign and never discuss the siege of Mantua. Félix Bouvier's *Bonaparte en Italie, 1796*, for example, is a well-researched 745-page account of the campaign, but his volume ends when Bonaparte establishes the government in Milan in May 1796. In this work, published in Paris in 1899, Bouvier examined documents and manuscripts from the French Archives de la Guerre, Archives Nationales, and various Italian archives in Milan and Turin as well as the works of Napoleon, Pommereul, Piuma, Jomini, and Clausewitz. Although he used many Austrian sources, he did not use the Austrian archives. Unfortunately for our purposes, this massive project about Bonaparte in Italy in 1796 ends before the French soldiers march on Mantua. Similarly, the three-volume project by Gabriel Joseph Fabry, *Histoire de L'Armée d'Italie 1796–1797*, in which he compiled the correspondence between the various French generals, only reaches March 1796—just before Bonaparte took command of the Army of Italy.[19] The works of Bouvier and Fabry do, however, give a detailed description of the French army and its commanders that would ultimately besiege Mantua in 1796–97.

Just as the French, Austrian, and Italian chroniclers documented the history of the sieges as they were taking place, there was also an Englishman in Mantua who recorded his experiences. Colonel Thomas Graham of the British 90th Light Infantry, a military observer serving with Field Marshal Dagobert Siegmund Wurmser, was locked up inside the fortress during the Battle of San Giorgio in September 1796. His letters to Lord William Grenville in London immediately after his escape give an interesting "outsider's" look at the siege of Mantua during his four months within the walls of the city. This celebrated colonel is the person given credit for the anonymous 1797 English translation of Pomp's history of the 1796 campaign.[20]

The first complete treatment of the siege published in German was compiled by Johann Schels in the *Österreichische Militärische Zeitschrift* in 1830–1832. He used the vast collection of documents in the Austrian military archives, the 1821 publication of Napoleon's early *Correspondance*, Napoleon's memoirs, and Jomini's history to complete his work. The detail of Schels's work is equaled only by Baldassare Scorza's manuscript in terms of its treatment of Austrian activity during the sieges. In 1903 Viktor Hortig published *Bonaparte vor Mantua, Ende Juli 1796*, which covers the history of the Quadrilateral fortresses of Verona, Legnago, Mantua, and Peschiera from May until August 1796. Hortig relied heavily on Schels's work but also utilized the 1858 edition of the *Correspondance de Napoléon* and the dispatches of Colonel Graham for his study of the campaign.[21] At Vienna in 1908 Erwin Honig published *Die Kämpfe um Mantua*, which utilized some Austrian archival documents, but this work concerned only the events that took place between August and September 1796.

There are many other works that discuss Mantua, but they focus mainly on the campaigns and battles of the relief armies trying to rescue the Mantua garrison. A complete treatment of the siege of 1796 does not exist in English, and studies of General Bonaparte's efforts to capture the city are limited.

The French held Mantua for more than two years after they captured it. There are only a few works in Italian that discuss the French administration of Mantua from 1797 to 1799, and there are no works in French, German, or English on this topic. The two main Italian works concerning this subject are simply compilations of newspaper articles and published notices by the French during their administration. Very little analysis is given in either work; nevertheless, they do provide an interesting perspective on life in a northern Italian city under French domination.[22] Francesca Fantini D'Onofrio, who was an assistant director of the Archivio di Stato di Mantova, published an article in 1996 about the Mantua archives and their treasure of primary sources on this topic. Her work focuses on the material available in the archive concerning the French administration of 1797–99.[23] The director of the archives, Daniela Ferrari, published *Mantova nelle Stampe* (Mantua's prints) in 1985, which gives contemporary views of the combat around Mantua in the 1790s, and later she produced *La Città Fortificata* (The fortified city) in 2000, an excellent presentation of the fortification developments at Mantua before, during, and after French rule that makes use of maps from the Kriegsarchiv in Vienna.[24]

There are few works that mention the 1799 siege of Mantua. Most volumes that treat the war in 1799 are concerned with Bonaparte's campaign in Egypt or Masséna's operations in Switzerland. One exception is Édouard Gachot's *Souvarow en Italie*, published in Paris in 1903, which has a chapter dedicated to the 1799 siege. The most complete work concerning this siege, albeit from the French commander's point of view, is Foissac-Latour's *Précis*.[25] Michel Leclerc was tasked with writing an account of the siege that was, in essence, a condemnation of Latour in preparation for the latter's trial for treason.[26] Latour's massive work complemented some of his previous writings that also defended his actions. Latour's chief engineer, Maubert, was quick to produce a small book supporting the French defense of Mantua when Bernadotte ordered Latour and all of his staff to be brought up on charges.[27] Leclerc later wrote yet another piece further condemning Latour.[28] Latour's letters that were used to produce his 635-page book are no longer available, although they were most certainly in Paris to type-set for his publication. His registry of letters and his papers are not to be found in the Archives de la Guerre in Paris.[29] However, some of these materials have recently surfaced at the Libreria Antiquaria Scriptorium, an antique bookshop in Mantua, after the owner, Mansueto Bassi, purchased them from another antique book dealer in Paris.[30]

Another work that gives an adequate description of the 1799 siege—this time from the Allies' perspective—is that of Dmitrij Alekseevich Miljutin. In volume 2 of his four-volume work on the history of Suvorov during the War of the Second Coalition, Miljutin devotes an entire chapter to the siege of Mantua. His work is complete with a large map of the siege works and the placement of Russian artillery batteries.[31] This work has been translated from Russian to German, but it has yet to appear in English. In Italian, Luigi Pescasio published *Mantova 1799: Un Nuovo Assedio*, which is an edited version of the contemporary account of the siege by Luigi Maria Predaval, who was head of the Mantua chamber of commerce in 1799.[32] In the work, Pescasio inserts avvisi at the appropriate places in the chronology. In Polish, the chronicler Cyprian Godebski wrote *Pamie.tnik Oble.z´enia Mantui* (Diary of the siege of Mantua), which Kniaziewicz put to use in his work commemorating the Polish defense of Mantua. Schnur-Popławski in turn used Kniaziewicz's and Godebski's works to complete a history of the Second Polish Legion.[33] In German, besides the accounts already named, there is a primary source titled *Briefe über Italien geschrieben in den Jahren 1798 und 1799 vom Verfasser der vertraulichen Briefe über Frankreich und Paris*, written by the officer Carl Friedrich Woyda, who fought on the side of the French.[34] Another important primary source in German is the collection of Kray's letters published in 1909 by the Austrian War Archives.[35] Using the vast resources of this same collection, Joseph Stutterheim published a detailed account of the 1799 siege focusing on the Austrian perspective.[36]

There are several additional works that address the sieges of Mantua, but their focus is on the many battles and campaigns of the Wars of the First and Second Coalition and their analysis of the sieges of Mantua is minimal. Colonel Ramsay Weston Phipps's five-volume work, *The Armies of the French Republic;* Yorck von

Wartenburg's *Napoleon as a General;* Spenser Wilkinson's *Rise of General Bonaparte;* Elijah Adlow's *Napoleon in Italy 1796–1797;* Guglielmo Ferrero's *Aventure: Bonaparte en Italie (1796–1797),* George Hooper's *The Italian Campaigns of General Bonaparte in 1796–7 and 1800;* and more recently, Martin Boycott-Brown's fascinating and detailed *Road to Rivoli* all fall into this category.[37] Until now, a complete analysis of these sieges has not been made in English, and treatments of the two sieges of Mantua in other languages are limited. It was the goal of this study to provide a comprehensive and analytical study of the sieges, to examine the experience of those living in the city during the ordeals, and to determine the tactical and strategic importance of the events at Mantua and their actual impact on the Italian campaigns of the late 1790s.

Notes

Prologue

1. The practice of selling fish at this location was an old tradition even before the French arrived in 1796, as the ancient name of the bridge itself suggests: "Bridge of Fish Vendors."
2. Italy was not a unified polity until much later but I will use the term in this study for convenience.
3. Unlike Captain Napoleon Bonaparte, the first names of some of the officers mentioned in this study could not be determined. For those officers, only their rank and last name is presented.
4. The Austrians in Mantua were besieged by the French in 1703 during the War of the Spanish Succession and in 1735 during the War of the Polish Succession, and the French in Mantua were besieged by the Austrians and Russians in 1799 during the War of the Second Coalition. Several of the regular French battalions, which formed the core of the amalgamated demibrigades participating in the 1796–97 siege, had taken part in the American siege at Yorktown, and most took part in the siege of Toulon. Some of the demibrigades participating in the siege in 1796–97 also had their colors present during the 1703 and 1735 sieges around the same "island" fortress. In 1796 the French army planners and engineers studied how the French army had besieged Mantua in 1735 just as that army in 1735 had studied the French siege documents of 1703 to learn how to conquer the city. Article 15, section 3*1, Sièges Des Places Etrangères; MR 1831, Notes Brahaut, dossier 11ᵉ, 12ᵉ, 13ᵉ; MR 1834, Notes Brahaut, dossier 30ᵉ—all in Château de Vincennes, Archives de la Guerre, Service Historique de l'armée de Terre (hereafter cited as Service Historique); Reinhard, *Avec Bonaparte in Italie*, 115.

Introduction

1. Napoleon Bonaparte spelled his name with the Italian spelling using the "u" (Buonaparte) until he took command of the Army of Italy in 1796, after which he signed it "Bonaparte," which I have used throughout this work. Bonaparte's first use of this style of signing his name is found in a letter dated 24 March 1796. I reserve the name "Napoleon" to refer to him only after he becomes emperor. Bonaparte to L'Administration Municipale de Morseille, 24 March 1796, *Correspondance de Napoléon Ier*, no. 90, 1:118.
2. Boycott-Brown, *Road to Rivoli*, 20.
3. Ibid., 21.
4. Ibid., 62–63.
5. Chandler, *Campaigns of Napoleon*, 10, 13.

6. Herold, *Age of Napoleon*, 35.

7. Ibid., 45. For the use of "Germany" in this paragraph and elsewhere, see page 238, note 20.

8. "Plan Pour la Seconde Opération Préparatoire a L'Overture de la Campagne de Piédmont," 21 May 1794, *Correspondance de Napoléon Ier*, no. 27, 1:28–38; Bonaparte, *Letters and Documents*, 9.

9. "Plan Pour la Seconde Opération Préparatoire a L'Ouverture de la Campagne du Piédmont," 20 June 1794, *Correspondance de Napoléon Ier*, no. 30, 1:41–51.

10. Buonaparte to Multedo, 23 September 1794, *Correspondance de Napoléon Ier*, no. 37, 1:54–57; Bonaparte, *Letters and Documents*, 9–10.

11. Bonaparte, *Letters and Documents*, 10.

12. In three of the five letters concerning the Army of Italy, Bonaparte spoke of the importance of taking Mantua in order to make a rapid advance through Lombardy and the Trent valley. "Mémoire sur l'Armée d'Italie," "Mémoire Militaire sur l'Armée d'Italie," "Instructions," "Instruction Militaire," and "Instruction," July 1795, *Correspondance de Napoléon Ier*, nos. 49, 50, 51, 52, and 53, 1:65–83.

13. "Mémoire Militaire sur l'Armée d'Italie," July 1795, *Correspondance de Napoléon Ier*, no. 50, 1:70–73; see also Bonaparte, *Letters and Documents*, 54–56.

14. Ibid. The Tyrol is an alpine region in western Austria that borders Italy to the south and Germany to the north.

15. In Bonaparte's mind the capture of Mantua must have been the foremost objective south of Trent since the other three fortresses of the Quadrilateral were not mentioned in his writings on the Army of Italy. "Mémoire sur l'Armée d'Italie," "Mémoire Militaire sur l'Armée d'Italie," "Instructions," "Instruction Militaire," and "Instruction," July 1795, *Correspondance de Napoléon Ier*, nos. 49, 50, 51, 52, and 53, 1:65–83.

16. Buonaparte to Joseph, 20 August 1795, *Correspondance de Napoléon Ier*, no. 56, 1:85.

17. "Note sur la Direction que l'on doit donner a l'Armée d'Italie," 12 October 1795, and "Note sur l'Armée d'Italie," 19 January 1796, *Correspondance de Napoléon Ier*, nos. 75 and 83, 1:103–104, 113–14.

18. "Note sur l'Armée d'Italie," 19 January 1796, *Correspondance de Napoléon Ier*, no. 83, 1:113–14.

19. Barthélemy-Louis Scherer was born in 1747 and entered military service at the age of thirteen. The same year, 1760, he was wounded at Torgau. During the early part of the Revolution he fought along the Rhine. Six, *Dictionnaire Biographique*, 2:433.

20. Bonaparte to Directory, 24 April 1796, *Correspondance de Napoléon Ier*, no. 222, 1:211.

21. Bonaparte to Carnot, 29 April 1796, *Correspondance de Napoléon Ier*, no. 267, 1:244–45. Bonaparte knew the value of force ratios, as he continued to urge Carnot: "mainly [in reference to the reinforcements] so I can engage the enemy in battle while they are weak."

1. The Importance of Mantua to Austria and France

Epigraph. Graham to Grenville, 22 May 1796, in Rose, "Despatches of Colonel Thomas Graham," 113.

1. Mantua would remain strategically significant during the nineteenth century, as evidenced by the emphasis that Marshal Radetsky placed on holding the fortress during the insurrection of 1848.

2. Faustino, *Compendio degli Assedi e Blocchi di Mantova*, 8.

3. Ibid., 12–14, 20, 26, 34.

4. Schels, "Die Verteidigung von Mantua," 85. The Fossetta, Sortita, San Nicolo, San Giovanni, and Sapetto are some of the smaller sally ports. [Graham], *History of the Campaign of 1796*, 259–60; and *History of the Campaign of 1799*, map on 183.

5. Francesco Pogliani, *Storia della Fondazione di Mantova e suo Ducato con le Operazioni fatte da' Francesi, ed i fatti più importanti seguiti durante l'assedio di detta Città* (Milan, 1796), 17.

6. A hornwork is an outwork composed of two half bastions and a curtain, with two long sides. Hogg, *Fortress*, 61.

7. A crownwork is much larger than a hornwork. It is less common as well but can be likened to a hornwork increased in size as to include a bastion on its front, thus forming a structure that resembles a crown. The resulting face of the embattlement thus has two fronts of fortification. Ibid.

8. A fleche is a small outwork, with the appearance of an arrowhead, consisting of a trench and a parapet that is placed in the salient angle of the glacis and usually connected to the covered way with a short passage. Ibid., 155.

9. Schels, "Die Verteidigung von Mantua," 84–85.

10. Volta, *Compendio Cronologico-Critico della Storia di Mantova*, 5:337–38 (hereafter cited as *Storia di Mantova*), Archivio di Stato di Mantova (hereafter cited as ASM); *Avviso Pastorale*, 2 May 1796, Gridario Bastía 37, document 139, ASM; *Gazzetta di Mantova*, 6 May 1796, 4.

11. *Le Moniteur Universel*, 24 May 1796, no. 245.

12. General Johann Peter Beaulieu was born in Belgium in 1725 and entered the army in 1743. He served as a company-grade officer in the Seven Years' War, and in 1789 he became a brigade commander in the Austrian army. He became a division commander in 1790 and served against the French in Belgium from 1792 to 1795. He took command of the Austrian army in Italy on 4 March, or seventeen days before Bonaparte left Paris for Italy. Johann Schels, *Neue Militärische Zeitschrift* 3 (1813), in Rose, "Despatches of Colonel Thomas Graham," 114; Fiebeger, *Campaigns of Napoleon*, 18.

13. Bonaparte to Carnot, 11 May 1796, *Correspondance de Napoléon Ier*, no. 383, 1:314–15. A *décade* is ten days on the French Revolutionary Calendar. In this letter Bonaparte demonstrated his strategic understanding in addition to his operational mastery of the situation. He went on to say:

Could you coordinate my operations with that of the two armies there? [in Germany] I imagine that by now there is fighting on the Rhine. If this armistice were to continue, the Army of Italy would be destroyed. If the two armies on the Rhine take the field, please let me know their position and what you hope they will be able to do, so I can decide whether to enter the Tyrol or remain on the Adige.

14. Carnot to Bonaparte, 31 May 1796, AF III, 374, carton 160, Archives Nationales, Paris (hereafter cited as AN), in *Recueil des Acts du Directoire Exécutif*, 2:513. See also Bonaparte, *Memoirs at Saint Helena*, 3:466–68.

15. Bonaparte to Faypoult, and "Extrait de l'Ordre du Jour," 13 May 1796, *Correspondance de Napoléon Ier*, nos. 417 and 418, 1:332–33.

16. Bonaparte to Directory, 14 May 1796, *Correspondance de Napoléon Ier*, no. 420, 1:334. In this same letter Bonaparte quickly got to his main point—that of contesting their decision to split his army in half and give part of it to General François Étienne Kellermann to command. He made a convincing argument that two good generals were worse than one bad general, thus demonstrating his grasp of the concept of unity of command.

17. "Campagnes d'Italie," *Correspondance de Napoléon Ier*, 29:123.

18. Bonaparte to Communes de la Lombardie, 16 May 1796, *Correspondance de Napoléon Ier*, no. 427, 1:339.

19. Bonaparte to Lallement, 17 May 1796, *Correspondance de Napoléon Ier*, no. 441, 1:351.

20. Although Germany did not exist as a political state at the time, I will use the term anachronistically for convenience.

21. Bonaparte to Barthélemy, 20 May 1796, *Correspondance de Napoléon Ier*, no. 468, 1:375.

22. Ibid.

23. Avviso, 20 May 1796, Gridario Bastía 37, document 151, ASM.

24. *Gazzetta di Mantova*, 20 May 1796, 4; Volta, *Storia di Mantova*, 5:334.

25. Jean Mathieu Sérurier was born in Laon in 1742 and entered the Laon militia as a lieutenant in 1755. He served in Germany from 1758 till 1760 when he was wounded at Warbourg. In 1762 he participated in an expedition to Portugal, and in 1770 he went to Corsica, where he stayed until 1774. In 1793 he was promoted to general of brigade, and in 1794 he was assigned to the Army of the Alps and was promoted to general of division. The next year he took command of a division in the Army of Italy. Six, *Dictionnaire Biographique*, 2:452–53.

26. Volta, *Storia di Mantova*, 5:335.

27. Hortig, *Bonaparte vor Mantua*, 25.

28. Graf Joseph Canto d'Yrles was born in Vienna in 1731, and at age fourteen he became an officer candidate. During the Seven Years' War, he was promoted to captain (1758). He fought in the battles of Prague, Breslau, Neisse, Strehlen, and Wittenberg. He distinguished himself at Teplitz in 1762. In 1768 he was promoted to major; in 1773 he served as lieutenant colonel and commander of a grenadier battalion; and in

1779 he was made a colonel. During the Austro-Turkish War of 1788–91, he was in Bucovina, where he was commemorated for bravery at Rohatyn Pass. While fighting at the siege of Chocim during that war, Canto d'Yrles was promoted to major general, and when Chocim fell in 1789, Prince Coberg made him commander of the occupied fortress. Wurzbach, *Biographisches Lexikon des Kaiserthums Österreich*, 2:268–69.

29. *Gazzetta di Mantova*, 27 March 1795 and 24 April 1795.

30. A curtain is that part of the rampart lying between two bastions and joining their flanks.

31. The large number of animals would rapidly consume stores of fodder. When the fortress was cut off, the *Fuhrwesen*, or transport and wagon section, had eighty-one men and 235 horses. In addition to these draft horses, there were 432 cavalry and 323 officers' horses in the fortress consuming the small amount of fodder available for these animals. Schels, "Die Verteidigung von Mantua," 93.

32. Instructions to commanders, 16 May 1796, and Cocastelle to Beaulieu, 23 May 1796, Festung Mantua [FM], Karton [K] 1121, 1796.5.14 and 1796.5.35, Österreichisches Staatsarchiv, Kriegsarchiv (hereafter cited as OSK); Bonaparte to the Directory, 14 May 1796, *Correspondance de Napoléon Ier*, no. 420, 1:334–35; Schels, "Die Verteidigung von Mantua," 86–87.

33. Beaulieu to Canto d'Yrles, 16 May 1796, FM/K 1121, 1796.5.18½, OSK. These signals would indicate how many times a cannon or battery of cannon was to fire, as well as the length of time in-between shots.

34. This figure includes *extrabrachen*, the Austrian term for artillery, engineer, and other combat support troops. Schels, "Die Verteidigung von Mantua," 87. Thomas Graham, who accompanied Beaulieu at his headquarters, put the number of men going into the fortress at 8,000. Graham to Grenville, 19 May 1796, in Rose, "Despatches of Colonel Thomas Graham," 112.

35. Schels, "Die Verteidigung von Mantua," 87.

36. Michele Angelo Alessandro Colli-Marchei was born in Piedmont in 1738 and entered the Austrian army in 1756. He was a company-grade officer until 1768, held field-grade rank until 1787, and was promoted to division commander in 1793. He served with the Army of Piedmont from 1793 to 1796 and later served in the Papal and Neapolitian armies. He died in 1808. Fiebeger, *Campaigns of Napoleon*, 18.

37. Schels, "Die Verteidigung von Mantua," 89.

38. Graham to Grenville, 22 May 1796, in Rose, "Despatches of Colonel Thomas Graham," 113.

39. This would be the second time that Wurmser would replace Beaulieu within the year. Wurmser had taken command of the Upper Rhine Army from Beaulieu in August 1795. Dagobert Siegmund Wurmser was born in Schlettstadt, Alsace, on 22 September 1724 and entered the French army in 1741. (The *Allgemeine Deutsche Biographie* gives his birthday as 7 May.) He served with the Bercheny Hussars and participated

in the War of the Austrian Succession and the Seven Years' War during which he was promoted to colonel. In 1762 he joined the Austrian army and the next year was promoted to major general. During the War of the Bavarian Succession (1778–79), Wurmser was promoted to lieutenant field marshal and received the Commander's Cross of the Order of Maria Theresa. He was made a division commander in 1779 and a corps commander in 1787. He also served in the Turkish War of 1788–91. He served with distinction on the Rhine from 1793 to 1796. Wurzbach, *Biographisches Lexicon des Kaiserthums Österreich*, 59:1–7; *Allgemeine Deutsche Biographie*, 44:338–40; Hortig, *Bonaparte vor Mantua*, 25–26, 30.

40. Francis II to Wurmser, 29 May 1796, in Vivenot, *Thugut, Clerfayt and Wurmser*, 447–52. The original letter is in French. In the same letter, Francis informed Wurmser that the court in London had designated Colonel Graham to follow the Austrian commander's headquarters and keep contact with the English fleet in the Mediterranean and English ambassadors at the various Italian courts so that the army could continue to operate as circumstances dictate. In addition, a postscript from Francis stated that he was giving Colonel Klenau to work as Wurmser's adjutant because Francis wanted General Vacquant of the general staff to remain in Germany with the Army of the Rhine.

41. "Arrêté," 19 May 1796, *Correspondance de Napoléon Ier*, no. 454, 1:361–63. The new government was outlined in this 19 May decree signed by Bonaparte and Salicetti. The sixteen members composing the municipal government of Milan were the Marquis Francesco Visconti-Ajmi; Duke Giovanni Galeazzo Serbelloni; the bankers Carlo Bignami and Carlo Ciani; the lawyers Antonio Corbetta, Fedele Sopransi, Cesare Pellegata and Giuseppe Pioltini; Giovanni-Batista Sommariva, a lawyer from Lodi; Count Cajetano Porro, the future minister of police for the Cisalpine Republic; Count Pietro Verri, a renowned historian; the chemist Paolo Sangiorgio; Doctor Antonio Crespi, a physician and great friend of Porro; the engineers Carlo Parea and Antonio Caccianino; and the priest Felice Lattuada. Bouvier, *Bonaparte en Italie*, 612–13.

42. Wurzbach, *Biographisches Lexicon des Kaiserthums Österreich*, 59:3; *Allgemeine Deutsche Biographie*, 44:339–40.

2. Bonaparte's Investment of Mantua

Epigraph. Bonaparte to Josephine, 18 July 1796, *Napoleon's Letters to Josephine, 1796–1812*, no. 3, 20.

1. General André Masséna was born in Nice in 1758 and enlisted in the infantry in 1775. Having reached the rank of noncommissioned officer, he left the service in 1789. He later entered with the volunteers and was elected *chef de bataillon* in 1792. He served with the Army of Italy from 1792 to 1797. In 1793 he attained the rank of general of brigade and then general of division. In 1804 he became a marshal of France. Six, *Dictionnaire Biographique*, 2:164–65.

General Pierre François Augereau was born in Paris in 1757. He enlisted in the Neapolitan cavalry and later in 1792 returned to France to enter service with the volunteers. He rose in rank rapidly and in 1794 was promoted to general of division. In 1804 he was made a marshal of France. Ibid., 1:28–29.

2. Bonaparte to Masséna, Sérurier, and Augereau, 31 May, 1 June, and 3 June 1796, *Correspondance de Napoléon Ier*, nos. 534, 542, and 564, 1:418, 428, 442.

3. Schels, "Die Verteidigung von Mantua," 88–89.

4. Citadel strength report, 14 May 1796, FM/K 1121, 1796.5.4, OSK.

5. General Mathias Ruckavina was born in Croatia in 1737. An officer's son, he joined the army in 1755 and fought in the Seven Years' War. Later, he gained experience fighting against the Turks, and in 1794 he was sent to Italy. In 1795 he was promoted to major general. *Biographisches Lexikon des Kaiserthums Österreich*, 27:251.

6. Schels, "Die Verteidigung von Mantua," 91–92. Sturioni's and Salisch's first names are not known.

7. Bonaparte to Augereau and Bonaparte to Sérurier, 1 June 1796, *Correspondance de Napoléon Ier*, nos. 541 and 542, 1:427–28.

8. The two engineer officers captured were Captains Bertrand and Baillet. Captain Bertrand was General Sérurier's adjutant. Sérurier to Canto d'Yrles and Canto d'Yrles to Sérurier, 5 June 1796, FM/K 1121, 1796.6.8, OSK.

   Castiglione Mantovano, located ten kilometers north of the Citadel, should not be confused with Castiglione delle Stiviere, after which the famous 5 August 1796 battle was named.

9. Bonaparte to Masséna, 1 June 1796, *Correspondance de Napoléon Ier*, no. 544, 1:429–30; "Table de l'Emplacement des Quartiers Généraux du Général Bonaparte," 9.

10. Bonaparte to Lambert, 2 June 1796, *Correspondance de Napoléon Ier*, no. 555, 1:438. In an earlier message in the *Correspondance*, Lambert was identified as the *commissaire ordonnateur en chef* in April 1796: Bonaparte to Lambert, 7 April 1796, no. 125, 1:143.

    General Andréossy was born in 1761. He joined the French artillery corps and in 1781 was commissioned a second lieutenant at Auxonne. He served in Holland where he was captured by the Prussians in 1787. He was freed in a prisoner exchange and promoted to captain in 1788. In 1792 and 1793 he was the director of the artillery park of the advance guard of the Army of Italy. In 1795 he was promoted to battalion commander, and the following year Bonaparte made him assistant director of the pontoon and bridge train personnel for the Army of Italy. Six, *Dictionnaire Biographique*, 1:15.

11. Captain Comte Pierre Baste was born in Bordeaux on 21 November 1768. He had plenty of experience with the blue-water navy having served in the merchant marines on the *Le Pactole* at Saint Domingue in 1781–82 and along the eastern coast of Africa and the Atlantic. He went back to Saint Domingue in 1791. In 1793 he traveled to the United States, embarking at Baltimore as an auxiliary ensign on the *Petit Jacobin* and serving along the U.S. coast up to New York until 1794 as the second captain on the three-mast *La Pucelle*. He returned to

France and was captured by the British in 1795 near Toulon. After being released, he departed to complete his service with Bonaparte along the Mincio. Six, *Dictionnaire Biographique*, 1:59–60. After Mantua, Baste was sent to Venice to oversee the transport of the four bronze Horses of St. Mark's to Paris. Balteau, *Dictionnaire de biographie française*, 5:781–82.

12. The Serraglio is the strip of land between the Po to the south, the Mincio to the north and east, and the Gambari to the west. It can also be identified as the area between Curtatone, Governolo, Borgoforte, and the village of Serraglio. Schels, "Die Verteidigung von Mantua," 90. Joseph Philipp Vukassovich was born in 1755. He joined the service in 1778 and from 1788 to 1789 took part in the Austro-Turkish War. In the Italian campaigns he fought at Voltri and Dego. Wurzbach, *Biographisches Lexikon des Kaiserthums Österreich*, 52:22–23.

13. Scorza, "Memorie sul Blocca ed Assedio di Mantova," 13–14.

14. Schels refers to this weapon, the Austrian Models 1768 and 1769 over-under rifle/shotgun, as "Doppelhaken" (though *doppel-stutzen* is its more common name). The M 1768 had the top barrel rifled to 15.2 mm for accurate musket fire; the bottom barrel fired a shotgun load. The M 1769's top rifle barrel was 14.8 mm. Rothenberg, *Napoleon's Great Adversaries*, 52; Posio, "Castiglione delle Stiviere," 109.

15. Schels, "Die Verteidigung von Mantua," 91.

16. Ibid., 93. Later the *Mantuanischen Landmiliz* would serve on the cannon at San Giorgio Castle. Canto d'Yrles was probably concerned, at this early stage, about their training and preferred Austrians to man the guns. In addition, it was logical for the fortress commander to use this militia as a police force since they were citizens of the town and no doubt familiar with the city's vast road network and the populace.

17. An order was given to change these every day at 3:00 A.M. In case of alarm, the troops not on rampart duty would gather in four places: near the Porta Pradella, Porta Pusterla, the cattle market, and St. Peter's Square in the city center. Schels, "Die Verteidigung von Mantua," 94.

18. The artillerymen had to prepare ammunition for 3-, 3 1/4-, 3 -, 5-, 5 1/2-, 6-, 6 3/4-, 12-, 18-, 22-, 23-, 24-, 25-, and 26-pounders. Schels, "Die Verteidigung von Mantua," 94. Fixed ammunition is prepackaged ammunition containing a powder charge, a wooden sabot, and a cannonball or canister containing iron shot.

19. A fascine is a bundle of sticks tied together that is used to revet or reinforce an earthen wall by staking it into the vertical side of the breastwork, or parapet. A gabion is an open-ended cylinder, generally of woven vines or brushwood, that was filled with dirt and used to revet or reinforce the sides of excavations, especially in fieldworks, to prevent trenches or ditches from caving in.

20. Portioli, *Vicende di Mantova nel 1796*, 11–12.

21. Bonaparte to Sérurier, 3 June 1796, *Correspondance de Napoléon Ier*, no. 561, 1:441.

22. Bonaparte to Masséna, 3 June 1796, *Correspondance de Napoléon Ier*, no. 562, 1:441–42.

23. General Comte François Chasseloup-Laubat was born on 18 August 1754 at Saint-Sornin (Charente-Inférieure). He joined the engineers as a second lieutenant in 1778 and became a captain in 1791. He was a *chef de bataillon* of engineers by 1793, and he served at the siege of Maestricht in 1794 and became *chef de brigade* of engineers on 8 November the same year. He served at the siege of Mayence in 1795 and was assigned to the Army of Italy on 3 March 1796. Six, *Dictionnaire Biographique*, 1:229.

General Baron Claude Dallemagne was born at Peyrieu (Ain) on 8 November 1754. In 1773 he volunteered for the Hainaut Infantry Regiment, which later became the 50th Infantry Regiment in 1791. He became a sergeant by 1779 and served in the American Revolutionary War from 1778 to 1783, participating in the siege of Savannah. By 1786 he was a sergeant major, and in 1791 he became a second lieutenant of grenadiers. He was named general of brigade in the Army of the Pyrénées-Orientales in 1793. The next year he was assigned to the Army of Italy. Ibid., 1:281.

24. Bonaparte to Augereau, to Andréossy and Chasseloup, and to Dallemagne and Sérurier, 3 June 1796, *Correspondance de Napoléon Ier*, nos. 564, 565, and 566, 1:442–44.

25. Bonaparte to Directory, 8 June 1796, *Correspondance de Napoléon Ier*, no. 587, 1:461–63.

26. In the short defense the Austrians lost five dead, one wounded and four missing. Schels, "Die Verteidigung von Mantua," 95. Bonaparte reported to the Directory that the Austrians lost one hundred men killed and taken prisoner and that he had lost two hundred men. Bonaparte to Directory, 8 June 1796, *Correspondance de Napoléon Ier*, no. 587, 1:461–63.

27. Baldassare Scorza states there were 230 Mantuan militiamen manning the cannon that drove the French off the dam. Scorza, "Memorie sul Blocca ed Assedio di Mantova," 16. Bonaparte reported to the Directory that the soldiers on the dam intended to take Mantua by assault and that they claimed that there were many more cannon on the bridge than at Lodi. Bonaparte, however, decided to call off the attack because the conditions were not the same as at Lodi. Bonaparte to Directory, 8 June 1796, *Correspondence de Napoléon Ier*, no. 587, 1:461–63.

28. "Plan de Mantoue et de ses Attaques," map drawn by Chasseloup and his engineers on 9 October 1796, in Article 15, section 3*1, Sièges Des Places Etrangères, Service Historique.

29. Schels, "Die Verteidigung von Mantua," 96–97.

30. Bonaparte to Sugny, 4 June 1796, Bonaparte, *Correspondance de Napoléon Ier*, no. 569, 1:445.

31. Schels, "Die Verteidigung von Mantua," 97.

32. Bonaparte to Directory, 8 June 1796, *Correspondance de Napoléon Ier*, no. 587, 1:461–63.

33. Schels, "Die Verteidigung von Mantua," 97.

34. Sérurier to Canto d'Yrles and Canto d'Yrles to Sérurier, 5 June 1796, FM/K 1121, 1796.6.8, OSK; Scorza, "Memorie sul Blocca ed Assedio di Mantova," 16–17.

35. Schels, "Die Verteidigung von Mantua," 98.
36. Bonaparte to Sérurier, 5 June 1796, *Correspondance de Napoléon Ier*, no. 579, 1:454–55.
37. General Alexandre Berthier was born in 1753 and entered the general staff in 1770. He served as chief of staff of several different Revolutionary armies before becoming chief of staff of the Army of Italy. Six, *Dictionnaire Biographique*, 1:87–88.
38. Schels, "Die Verteidigung von Mantua," 99–100.
39. "Campagnes d'Italie," *Correspondance de Napoléon Ier*, 29:141. A flying column is a strong detachment that can move quickly and that normally operates apart from the main force.
40. Schels, "Die Verteidigung von Mantua," 115.
41. Bonaparte then went on to say that Brescia and Verona should be able to provide the needed supplies. Bonaparte to Lambert, 8 June 1796, *Correspondance de Napoléon Ier*, no. 593, 1:467.
42. "Order of the Day," 8 June 1796, *Correspondance de Napoléon Ier*, no. 595, 1:468–69.
43. Bonaparte to Kellermann, 9 June 1796, *Correspondance de Napoléon Ier*, no. 599, 1:471.
44. Bonaparte to Sérurier, 10 June 1796, *Correspondance de Napoléon Ier*, no. 609, 1:476.
45. Bonaparte to Chasseloup, 10 June 1796, *Correspondance de Napoléon Ier*, no. 603, 1:473.
46. Bonaparte to Augereau and Sérurier, 12 June 1796, *Correspondance de Napoléon Ier*, nos. 619 and 620, 1:482–84.
47. Schels, "Die Verteidigung von Mantua," 115.
48. Avviso, 6 June 1796, Gridario Bastía 37, document 159, ASM.
49. Schels, "Die Verteidigung von Mantua," 115.
50. Avviso, 13 June 1796, Gridario Bastía 37, document 168, ASM.
51. Avviso, 21 May 1796, Gridario Bastía 37, document 152, ASM.
52. Schels, "Die Verteidigung von Mantua," 116.
53. Beaulieu to Canto d'Yrles, 13 and 14 June 1796, FM/K 1121, 1796.6.13 and 1796.6.14, OSK.
54. Michael Melas was born in 1735. At seventeen years of age he joined the army and attained the rank of captain during the Seven Years' War. In 1793 he commanded a brigade on the Sambre River. In 1796 he was transferred to Beaulieu's command in Italy. Later, at the Battle of San Giorgio, he was locked up inside Mantua with Wurmser. Wurzbach, *Biographisches Lexikon des Kaiserthums Österreich*, 17:322–23.
55. Francis II to Wurmser, 16 June 1796, Berichte/K 1135, 1796.6.8, OSK; Melas to Canto d'Yrles (two messages), 23 June 1796, FM/K 1121, 1796.6.19, OSK.
56. The signals established between the fortress commander and the field army became very complex, and this complexity often led to confusion between the two forces. This particular signal is probably one of the best signals arranged for transmitting an affirmative message since the signal would take place over the space of an hour with six salvos being fired at ten-minute intervals, commencing at a time not likely to

be clouded with the report of cannon from normal fighting. The major problem with this signal, however, was that if Canto d'Yrles recognized the approach of the field army in the morning, it would be many hours before the field army commander could be informed.

57. Major Franz Orlandini was a count as well as the garrison engineer officer. He was born in Italy and attended the Engineer Academy in Vienna before taking part in the Austro-Turkish War of 1788–91 as a lieutenant in the Engineer Corps. At Mantua he wanted Canto d'Yrles to occupy the land between and immediately in front of the Pradella gate, the Te crownwork, and the Migliaretto works. Schels, "Die Verteidigung von Mantua," 116–17; Wurzbach, *Biographisches Lexikon des Kaiserthums Österreich*, 21:99.

58. Schels, "Die Verteidigung von Mantua," 116.

59. On 16 June 1796 the garrison report listed the strength at 13,691 serviceable and 1,528 nonserviceable soldiers, of which 882 were carried as sick and 646 as footsore. Ibid.

60. Ibid., 117.

61. Bonaparte, *Memoirs at Saint Helena*, 3:218–19, 226.

62. Schels, "Die Verteidigung von Mantua," 118.

63. Bonaparte to Directory, 21 June 1796, *Correspondance de Napoléon Ier*, no. 664, 1:518.

64. Canister is a load of small iron balls that turn a cannon essentially into a giant shotgun.

65. Sugny outlined his plan as follows:
   1. Attack the Citadel's central Holy Trinity bastion with two batteries of five guns, two batteries of four guns, two batteries of three guns, and three additional mortars.
   2. Attack the fortress itself in the following locations:
      • To the right of the Cerese dam: with one battery of eight guns, one battery of six guns, one battery of four guns, and four mortars.
      • Near Casa Michelli: with twelve guns and six mortars.
      • Near the Casa Zampoli (another house near Casa Zipata): with six mortars.

The total amounted to eleven batteries with fifty-four guns and twenty-two mortars. In addition to the guns included in Sugny's plan, Sérurier demanded a proportionate reserve artillery in order to be able to replace any pieces damaged by the Austrian cannon. To carry out a coordinated attack, Sérurier asked for 1,084 artillerymen, to allow for replacements every twenty-four hours; 20,000–25,000 infantry; and 1,000 cavalry. Since there was not enough artillery to meet Sugny's plan, the attack on the Citadel was canceled. Sérurier to Bonaparte, 28 June 1796, and Sugny to Bonaparte, 29 June 1796, *Correspondance Inédite*, 1:303–304, 307–308.

66. Schels, "Die Verteidigung von Mantua," 121–22.

67. Avvisi, 13, 26, and 27 June 1796, Gridario Bastía 37, documents 168, 169, 170, ASM; The day of the census the numbers of Austrian soldiers were recorded as 13,448 serviceable and 1,849 nonserviceable. Of the

hospitalized, the sick accounted for the majority, with nineteen officers and 1,109 rank and file; the rest were either wounded or footsore. Schels, "Die Verteidigung von Mantua," 122.

68. Portioli, *Vicende di Mantova nel 1796*, xiii; Pescasio, *Cronaca Vissuta del Duplice Assedio di Mantova*, 74.

69. The sortie consisted of the following:
    1. For the attack on the enemy sentries and the covering of the forage party: one officer, thirty rifles in the advance guard, three officers and one hundred men of the 39th Nadasdy Regiment, three officers and one hundred men of the 43rd Thurn Regiment.
    2. For the forage party: one officer to direct sixty men with scythes and one officer to direct one hundred men to carry the grass cuttings.
    3. Additionally, all the carpenters of Roselmini's brigade garrisoning the Citadel were ordered to follow the sally and cut down as many trees as possible.
    Schels, "Die Verteidigung von Mantua," 122–23.

70. Chasseloup, "Journal du Siège de Mantoue," 6 July 1796, 4, Article 15, section 3*1, Sièges Des Places Etrangères, Service Historique. The Austrians lost two dead and eighteen wounded in this action. In such sorties it was common for both sides to overestimate how many of the enemy forces they killed. Bonaparte put the Austrian loss at about fifty. He did not mention French losses in his report. Scorza, "Memorie sul Blocca ed Assedio di Mantova," 31; Bonaparte to Directory, 6 July 1796, *Correspondence de Napoléon Ier*, no. 725, 1:568–70.

71. Bonaparte to Directory, 6 July 1796, *Correspondence de Napoléon Ier*, no. 725, 1:568–70.

72. Chasseloup, "Journal du Siège de Mantoue," 8–9 and 9 July 1796, 4–5, Article 15, section 3*1, Sièges Des Places Etrangères, Service Historique. The Casa Zipata Battery is also referred to as the Casa Zampoli Battery because that house is also near it. Likewise, the Casa Michelli Battery (see map 6, H) is sometimes referred to as the Belfiore Battery.

73. Wurmser to Canto d'Yrles, 6 July 1796, FM/K 1121, 1796.7.5, OSK.

74. A 1780 treatise on artillery by John Muller explains how to make various types of "light balls to discover the enemy's works." Some are made of coarse flax or hemp dipped into a composition of sulfur, pitch, rosin, and turpentine and worked into a ball. Others take a ball of stone or iron that is covered by this same composition with the last coat being granular powder. Muller, *Treatise of Artillery*, 206.

75. Scorza, "Memoire sul Blocca ed Assedio di Mantova," 34.

76. Chasseloup, "Journal du Siege de Mantoue," 10, 10–11, and 12 July 1796, 6, Article 15, section 3*1, Sièges Des Places Etrangères, Service Historique. The attack for the evening of the 10th was planned by Bonaparte on 7 July. It was to be made on the gate at Cerese by the 19th demibrigade well supported by artillery. Bonaparte warned Sérurier to keep this attack secret. Bonaparte to Sérurier, 7 July 1796, *Correspondance de Napoléon Ier*, no. 731, 1:575.

77. Andréossy to Bonaparte, 6 July 1796, *Correspondance Inédite*, 1:365–68.
78. Andréossy to Bonaparte, 7 July 1796, *Correspondance Inédite*, 1:368–69.
79. Scorza, "Memorie sul Blocca ed Assedio di Mantova," 38; In the middle of July, before the attack, the number of sick on both sides began to increase rapidly. On 15 July the garrison numbered 12,905 fit for service and 2,309 noneffectives, of whom 43 officers and 1,475 men were sick. Schels, "Die Verteidigung von Mantua," 127–28. Bonaparte reported to the Directory on 12 July that "the number of sick in the army was beginning to increase although not one soldier had died. The heat was excessive and the air around Mantua was plague-stricken." Bonaparte to Directory, 12 July 1796, *Correspondance de Napoléon Ier*, no. 755, 1:592.
80. Bonaparte to Directory, and Orders to Generals Murat, Sérurier, and Dellemagne, for the attack on 16–17 July, 12 and 16 July 1796, *Correspondance de Napoléon Ier*, nos. 755 and 764, 1:591, 597–98; Bonaparte, *Memoirs at Saint Helena*, 3:229.
81. Schels, "Die Verteidigung von Mantua," 128–29.
82. General of Brigade Pascal Antoine Fiorella was born in Ajaccio in 1752. He joined the Royal Corsican Infantry in 1770 and rose to the rank of lieutenant colonel before the Revolution. He served in the Army of Italy from 1794 to 1799. Six, *Dictionnaire Biographique*, 1:451–52.
83. During the actions on 16 July, the Austrians lost two officers and 68 men killed, ten officers and 320 men wounded, and one officer and 63 men missing. Vukassovich to Canto d'Yrles (Früh Rapport), 18 July 1796, FM/K 1121, 1796.7.18; Früh Rapport, 15 July 1796, FM/K 1121, 1796.7.9; Captain Gelber, "Feldzug 1796 in Italian," in K MS-kg 86, V, 114—all in OSK; Pommereul, *Campagne du Général Buonaparte*, 92; Schels, "Die Verteidigung von Mantua," 129–30; Chasseloup, "Journal du Siège de Mantoue," 15–16 July 1796, 8, Article 15, section 3*1, Sièges Des Places Etrangères, Service Historique.
84. Chasseloup, "Journal du Siège de Mantoue," 16 July 1796, 9, Article 15, section 3*1, Sièges Des Places Etrangères, Service Historique.
85. Canto d'Yrles to Wurmser, 17 July 1796, FM/K 1121, 1796.7.11, OSK.
86. Hacked shot is a musket ball that is carved so that it will expand upon contact, thereby inflicting a gaping wound. It is similar to the dumdum bullets that were outlawed before World War I. Canto d'Yrles to Fiorella, 16 July 1796, FM/K 1121, 1796.7.12ad, OSK.
87. Fiorella to Canto d'Yrles, 16 July 1796, FM/K 1121, 1796.7.12; Sérurier to Canto d'Yrles, 17 July 1796, FM/K 1121, 1796.7.15; Canto d'Yrles to Sérurier, 17 July 1796, FM/K 1121, 1796.7.15ad—all in OSK. Masséna explained that the alleged bullets that Canto d'Yrles thought were hacked shot were no more than some musket balls that had been scarred after ricocheting. Koch, *Mémoires de Masséna*, 2:107.
88. Bonaparte to Directory, 22 July 1796, *Correspondance de Napoléon Ier*, no. 783, 1:613–15.
89. Ibid.; Schels, "Die Verteidigung von Mantua," 135–36; Bonaparte, *Memoirs at Saint Helena*, 3:229.

90. Bonaparte to Josephine, 18 July 1796, in Bonaparte, *Napoleon's Letters to Josephine*, no. 3, 20–21.
91. Bonaparte to Sérurier and Murat, 18 July 1796, *Correspondance de Napoléon Ier*, nos. 765 and 766, 1:598–99; Chasseloup, "Journal du Siège de Mantoue," 17–18 July 1796, 9, Article 15, section 3*1, Sièges Des Places Etrangères, Service Historique.
92. Chasseloup, "Journal du Siege de Mantoue," 18 July 1796, 9–10, Article 15, section 3*1, Sièges Des Places Etrangères, Service Historique.
93. Scorza, "Memorie sul Blocca ed Assedio di Mantova," 47; Pommereul, *Campagne du Général Buonaparte*, 92; Schels, "Die Verteidigung von Mantua," 134.
    General Martin Vignolle was born in 1763. He volunteered in the Barrois Infantry Regiment in 1779. In December 1794 he was made adjutant general of brigade by the Representatives on Mission of the Army of Italy, and his position was confirmed by the Committee of Public Safety. Six, *Dictionnaire Biographique*, 2:552.
94. Chasseloup, "Journal du Siège de Mantoue," 18–19 July 1796, 10–11, Article 15, section 3*1, Sièges Des Places Etrangères, Service Historique; Pommereul, *Campagne du Général Buonaparte*, 92.
95. Grapeshot is a fixed cannon charge consisting of several small cannonballs. The charge is often wrapped with canvas and tied with cord, which gives it the charge the appearance of a cluster of grapes.
96. Bonaparte, *Memoirs at Saint Helena*, 3:229–30; After the fight, fourteen dead and six seriously wounded French troops lay in the covered way. One French officer and seven grenadiers had been taken prisoner. In his report, Canto d'Yrles put the French losses at 900. The Austrian garrison lost one officer, seven men dead, thirty-two men wounded and eight men missing for a total of forty-eight casualties. Schels, "Die Verteidigung von Mantua," 134–36.

3. A City on Fire, a City at Peace

Epigraph. Bonaparte to Josephine, 19 July 1796, *Napoleon's Letters to Josephine*, no. 4, 21–22.

1. Volta, *Storia di Mantova*, 346–49; Arrivabene, "Memorie Storiche di Mantova del Secolo XVIII," 377; Scorza, "Memorie sul Blocca ed Assedio di Mantova," 48–53. Canto d'Yrles moved his headquarters from Amorotti Palace to Arrigoni Palace, which was bombarded with hot-shot on 23 July 1796. *Gazzetta di Mantova*, 5 August 1796.
2. Chasseloup, "Journal du Siège de Mantoue," 18–19 July 1796, 10, Article 15, section 3*1, Sièges Des Places Etrangères, Service Historique.
3. The bombardment continued until 7:00 A.M. on 19 July with about 500 shells as well as hot-shot hitting the town. Scorza, "Memorie sul Blocca ed Assedio di Mantova," 52–53; Schels, "Die Verteidigung von Mantua," 137.
4. "Journal du Siège de Mantoue," 19 July 1796, B³29, Service Historique. Note there are two documents titled "Journal du Siège de Mantoue" in the archive at Vincennes, each of which emphasizes different details during the construction of the trenches and batteries.

5. Bonaparte to Josephine, 19 July 1796, *Napoleon's Letters to Josephine,* no. 4, 21–22. The first parallel was surveyed the night of 18–19 July when the digging started and it was "opened" the following night.

6. Wurmser to Canto d'Yrles, 16 July 1796, FM/K 1121, 1796.7.10, OSK; Volta, *Storia di Mantova,* 348.

7. "Journal du Siège de Mantoue," 19–20 July 1796, B^{3}29, Service Historique; Schels, "Die Verteidigung von Mantua," 138–39.

8. "Journal du Siège de Mantoue," 20 July 1796, B^{3}29, Service Historique.

9. In the forty-eight hours beginning 12:00 A.M. 19 July, the fortress artillery fired no fewer than 12,298 salvos of round shot and canister and 179 bombs, and used at least 389 grenades. Schels, "Die Verteidigung von Mantua," 139.

10. Berthier to Canto d'Yrles, 19 July 1796, FM/K 1121, 1796.7.23; Canto d'Yrles to Bonaparte, 20 July 1796, FM/K 1121, 17996.7.ad23—both in OSK. Pommereul states that Berthier wrote the letter to Canto d'Yrles on 18 July, before the initial bombardment began, in order to give the fortress commander a chance to avoid further bloodshed. Pommereul, *Campagne du Général Buonaparte,* 94.

11. Bonaparte to Commissaire Ordonnateur en Chef, 20 July 1796, *Correspondance de Napoléon Ier,* no. 767, 1:599–600.

12. Bonaparte to Denniée, 20 July 1796, *Correspondance de Napoléon Ier,* no. 775, 1:607.

13. Bonaparte to Sanson, 20 July 1796, *Correspondance de Napoléon Ier,* no. 768, 1:600.

14. "Journal du Siège de Mantoue," 20–21 July 1796, B^{3}29, Service Historique; Koch, *Mémoirs de Masséna,* 2:111; Schels, "Die Verteidigung von Mantua," 140.

15. Schels, "Die Verteidigung von Mantua," 141.

16. "Journal du Siège de Mantoue," 21 July 1796, B^{3}29, Service Historique.

17. Ibid., 21–22 July 1796; Schels, "Die Verteidigung von Mantua," 141.

18. "Journal du Siège de Mantoue," 22 July 1796, B^{3}29, Service Historique. A sap is a trench, normally in a zigzag pattern, that extends from a parallel with the purpose of constructing a new parallel closer to the besieged fortress or to form a starting point for an assault. A sap roller is used to protect the men digging a sap. It is made by tightly weaving sticks and vines into a tubelike structure long enough to protect the width of the trench and usually three to six feet in diameter. The sappers would roll the device in front of the approach trench they were digging to protect them from enemy fire. The dirt from the trench was always shoveled to the side closest to the enemy for additional protection.

19. Ibid., 23 July 1796; Schels, "Die Verteidigung von Mantua," 141–42.

20. These messages, usually measuring no larger than 1" × 3" and written on thin paper with a fine point, were rolled up and placed in a capsule that would be coated with wax. If need be, the messenger would swallow the capsule to avoid getting caught in the French lines with Austrian military correspondence. Spies were hired to carry messages in and out of the fortress. The highest premium paid was 50 *zecchino,* Venetian

gold coins, to accomplish the mission. The risk matched the handsome price paid to deliver these messages, as the French had proclaimed in all the churches surrounding Mantua that orders were given to fire on anybody approaching the Lake of Mantua. Thomas Graham to Lord William Grenville, 6 January 1797, in Rose, "Dispatches of Thomas Graham" (April 1899), 321; Wurmser to Canto d'Yrles, 20 and 21 July (three letters), 25 and 31 July 1796, FM/K 1121, 1796.7.34, 1796.7.41, 1796.7.64, 1796.7.65, 1796.7.66, and 1796.7.102, OSK.

21. John Trevor to Thomas Graham, 20 July 1796, in Aspinall-Oglander, *Freshly Remembered*, 93.

22. Schels, "Die Verteidigung von Mantua," 143-44.

23. Ibid., 144.

24. "Journal du Siège de Mantoue," 26 July 1796, B^{3}29, Service Historique; Schels, "Die Verteidigung von Mantua," 144.

25. Schels, "Die Verteidigung von Mantua," 144-46.

26. Scorza, "Memorie sul Blocca ed Assedio di Mantova," 71-73; Volta, *Storia di Mantova*, 5:350; Schels, "Die Verteidigung von Mantua," 146-47; Pescasio, *Mantova Assediata 1796-1797*, 54-55.

27. Schels, "Die Verteidigung von Mantua," 147-48.

28. Hortig, *Bonaparte vor Mantua*, 114.

29. Scorza, "Memorie sul Blocca ed Assedio di Mantova," 77-78.

30. Hortig, *Bonaparte vor Mantua*, 115. Johann Meszaros was born in Hungary in 1737. He joined a hussar regiment and fought with distinction during the Austro-Turkish War of 1788-91 and in the Rhine campaigns. Later he was forced to take refuge in Mantua with Wurmser's army. Wurzbach, *Biographisches Lexikon des Kaiserthums Österreich*, 17:456-59.

31. Bonaparte to Sérurier, 31 July 1796, *Correspondance de Napoléon Ier*, no. 813, 1:633-34.

32. According to an Austrian report, between 19 and 31 July the French had fired at the fortress 4,000 mortar bombs, 2,000 exploding shells, and 6,000 hot-shot—not counting the cold round shot. The garrison had lost 372 dead from disease; two officers and 118 men killed in combat; fourteen officers and 381 men wounded; seventy-three persons taken prisoner or missing; and thirteen deserters. Schels, "Die Verteidigung von Mantua," 149, 152.

33. Bonaparte to Sérurier, 31 July 1796, *Correspondance de Napoléon Ier*, no. 813, 1:633-34; Wurmser to Canto d'Yrles, 31 July 1796, FM/K 1121, 1796.7.102, OSK; Schels, "Die Verteidigung von Mantua," 149.

34. The actual number of battalions was given as 4 2/3 and squadrons as 41/2. The Austrians often used fractions to indicate companies of infantry and troops of cavalry (a battalion would normally consist of three companies; a squadron would normally consist of two troops). In this case, the two-thirds battalion would represent two companies of infantry; the half squadron would represent one cavalry troop.

35. Hortig, *Bonaparte vor Mantua*, 116. General Karl Funk was born in Ansbach, Bavaria, in 1744. He joined the Austrian army at an early age

and took part in the Seven Years' War. At age twenty he was made a captain. Wurzbach, *Biographisches Lexikon des Kaiserthums Österreich*, 5:35.

General Franz Lauer was born in 1735 to a military family. He entered an engineer academy as a cadet in 1755. In 1795 he fought at Mannheim, where he distinguished himself, winning a promotion and the Commander's Cross of the Order of Maria Theresa. In July 1796 he was sent to Italy. Ibid., 14:214–15.

36. In his memoirs, Colonel Thomas Graham of the British 90th Light Infantry claimed that he and the Austrian Colonel Vincent were the first to enter Mantua on 1 August to give Canto d'Yrles "positive information concerning what had occasioned this very unexpected movement, and the sacrifice of all the heavy artillery, amounting to over 200 pieces of cannon, which were about to be placed in the batteries, then nearly ready for their reception." Memoirs of Thomas Graham, in Delavoye, *Life of Thomas Graham*, 123.

37. San Michele del Bosco is six miles southeast of Marcaria on the Oglio where Sérurier's division was gathering. Scorza, "Memorie sul Blocca ed Assedio di Mantova," 94; Schels, "Die Verteidigung von Mantua," 150.

38. Of the twenty-six prisoners there were two inspectors, two secretaries, two adjutants, and twenty soldiers. Scorza, "Memorie sul Blocca ed Assedio di Mantova," 94.

39. Ibid.; Schels, "Die Verteidigung von Mantua," 150. Schels listed "5,000" in the French column (undoubtably a typographical error); Scorza has the number at 500 in his manuscript.

40. In his journal, Baldassare Scorza gives a detailed account of exactly what took place and what the Austrians captured on 1 August 1796. The various gun calibers in appendix C show that the guns were in fact Austrian made; that is, by this time the French had already converted to the standard sizes of the Gribeauval system. Scorza, "Memorie sul Blocca ed Assedio di Mantova," 89–94.

41. On 1 August the Austrians took as prisoners 28 officers, among whom were Colonel Giraut and Lieutenant Colonel Raynard, 4 surgeons, and 743 men for a total of 775 personnel. Schels, "Die Verteidigung von Mantua," 150.

42. Scorza, "Memorie sul Blocca ed Assedio di Mantova," 91–95.

43. Canto d'Yrles to Wurmser, 1 August 1796; Wurmser to Francis II, 2 August 1796—both in Vivenot, *Thugut, Clerfayt und Wurmser*, 475–77 and 474–75, respectively. Wurmser forwarded Canto d'Yrles's letter and his own letter to the emperor from Valeggio. This should not be confused with the report he sent to the emperor later that day after he actually visited Mantua.

44. Francis to Wurmser, 11 August 1796, in Vivenot, *Thugut, Clerfayt und Wurmser*, 478–90; *Gazzetta di Mantova*, 26 August 1796.

45. Pommereul, *Campagne du Général Buonaparte*, 117–18. Pius VI was born Giovanni Angelo Braschi of a noble but poor family in Cesena, in

northern Italy, in 1717. He established the first diocese in the United States at Baltimore with John Carroll as its bishop on 6 November 1789. In two briefs in 1791 he condemned the French Civil Constitution of the Clergy, which obliged the French clergy to take an oath of complete obedience to the state enacted by the French National Assembly in July 1790. Later when Bonaparte discovered the pope was secretly negotiating with Austria, he invaded the Papal States and forced Pius VI to sign the Treaty of Tolentino on 19 Febraury 1797. The following year, French troops entered Rome and when Pius VI refused to renounce his temporal power he was taken under custody and eventually moved to Valence, in southern France, where he died on August 29, 1799. *Catholic Encyclopedia*, 8:467–69.

46. Suspension of Hostilities, 23 June 1796, in Anderson, *Constitutions and Documents of France*, 255–56.

47. Heriot, *The French in Italy*, 100–101.

48. Hortig, *Bonaparte vor Mantua*, 120. Hortig also states that Canto d'Yrles argued that Ruckavina could not go to Goito since he had fallen sick and had gone to Padua that day. Scorza reports, however, that Ruckavina went that very day to meet Wurmser. Scorza, "Memorie sul Blocca ed Assedio di Mantova," 99.

49. Ibid., 99–100.

50. Hortig, *Bonaparte vor Mantua*, 131. Most descriptions in French, and in English translations that rely on these French sources, do not account for Wurmser's visit to Mantua the afternoon of 2 August. For example, Ramsey Phipps, in his work *The Armies of the First French Republic*, states: "It is just possible that Wurmser may have gone himself to Mantua, but, if so, it must have been after hearing that the siege was raised, and so against all light" (4:66). Austrian and Italian accounts, understandably, record his visit. Jomini, however, states that Wurmser went into Mantua on the 1st; but this would have been highly unlikely given Wurmser's dispatches, his locations on the 1st, and Scorza's account of Wurmser's reception on the second. Jomini, *Histoire des Guerres*, 8:317.

51. Scorza, "Memorie sul Blocca ed Assedio di Mantova," 100–101; Hortig, *Bonaparte vor Mantua*, 120.

52. Voykowitsch, *Castiglione*, 69.

53. Bonaparte to Salicetti, 2 August 1796, *Correspondance de Napoléon Ier*, no. 820, 1:638–39.

54. "Campagnes d'Italie," *Correspondance de Napoléon Ier*, 29:161–62.

55. Baron Joseph Alvintzy was born in Transylvania in 1735. At age fifteen, he joined the Austrian army. He distinguished himself in the Seven Years' War and later was made colonel of the 19th Infantry Regiment. Under Laudon he commanded during the Austro-Turkish War of 1788–91. From 1792 to 1796 he served with distinction in the Netherlands and on the Rhine. In 1808 he was made a field marshal. He died in 1810. Wurzbach, *Biographisches Lexikon des Kaiserthums Österreich*, 1:22.

56. Alvintzy to Canto d'Yrles, 6 August 1796, FM/K 1121, 1796.8.16, OSK; Scorza, "Memorie sul Blocca ed Assedio di Mantova," 101.

57. Wurmser to Canto d'Yrles, 5 August 1796, FM/K 1121, 1796.8.11, OSK; Schels, "Die zweite Einschließung Mantuas," 254, 257; Hortig, *Bonaparte vor Mantua*, 177; Voykowitsch, *Castiglione*, 84. Fiebeger, *Campaigns of Napoleon*, 24.

Peter Vitus von Quosdanovich (1738–1802) entered military service in 1752 at fourteen years of age. He fought in the Seven Years' War and in 1773 was made a first lieutenant and commander of the Karlstädter *Gränzers*. He fought in the War of the Bavarian Succession (1778–79) and was promoted to colonel and decorated with the Knight's Cross of the Order of Maria Theresa. In 1788 he fought in the Austro-Turkish War. In 1792 he was made field marshal-lieutenant. For his efforts in the 1796–97 campaigns, he received the Commander's Cross of the Order of Maria Theresa. Wurzbach, *Biographisches Lexikon des Kaiserthums Österreich*, 24:153–54.

58. General Karl Spiegel had been a colonel with the 42nd Infantry Regiment since 1790. He was promoted to major general in 1796. Later he would be forced inside of Mantua with Wurmser. He retired in 1798 and died in 1805. Voykowitsch, *Castiglione*, 25.

General Ferdinand Minkwitz was the commanding colonel of the 24th Infantry Regiment. Like Spiegel, he too was promoted to major general in 1796. After the Battle of Castiglione, he was sent into Mantua, where he remained until February 1797. In the War of the Second Coalition he fought at Megnano and was assigned command of Mantua after the fortress had been retaken by the Austrians in July 1799. Ibid., 25–26.

59. A total of 5,047 men went into the fortress, raising the number to more than what it had been when the detachments first departed in answer to Wurmser's call for reinforcements. There were 14,942 in the fortress on 1 August, 10,788 on 5 August, and 15,513 on 7 August. Of this latter total, 3,533 were in the hospital or otherwise unfit for service. Früh Rapport, 1, 5, and 7 August 1796, FM/K 1121, 1796.8.1, 1796.8.13, and 1796.8.17, OSK.

60. Scorza, "Memorie sul Blocca ed Assedio di Mantova," 104–105.

61. Bonaparte to Fiorella and Augereau, 6 August 1796, *Correspondance de Napoléon Ier*, nos. 847 and 849, 1:658–59.

62. "Campagnes d'Italie," *Correspondance de Napoléon Ier*, 29:162.

63. Hortig, *Bonaparte vor Mantua*, 177.

64. Schels, "Die zweite Einschließung Mantuas," 259, 262.

65. Jean Joseph Sahuguet was born in 1756. He entered the French army as a lieutenant and was promoted to captain in 1784. He was made lieutenant colonel of dragoons in 1791, general of brigade in 1792, and general of division in 1793. He served in the Army of the Pyrenees and then the Army of Italy. For the early part of September 1796 he was charged with the renewed investment of Mantua. That winter he would later serve as governor of conquered provinces. He died in 1803. Fiebeger, *Campaigns of Napoleon*, 38.

66. Bonaparte to Sahuguet, 10 August 1796, *Correspondance de Napoléon Ier*, no. 866, 1:671.

67. Bonaparte to Directory, 14 August 1796, *Correspondance de Napoléon Ier*, no. 889, 1:685. The *Correspondance* has a typographical error in this passage, where "38th" is inserted for "18th" for the demibrigade of light infantry. General Pommereul used the same letter from Bonaparte to the Directory in his book, and there it is the 18th that Masséna applauded for its action on the field. According to Masséna's memoirs and Jomini, there was no "38th" under Masséna's command or in the Army of Italy. Pommereul, *Campagne du Général Buonaparte*, 122; Jomini, *Histoire des Guerres*, 8:320. On 25 July 1796 the 18th demibrigade had 2,784 men. Jomini, *Histoire des Guerres*, 8:305; Koch, *Mémoires de Masséna*, 2:531–32.

68. Bonaparte to Sahuguet, 15 August 1796, *Correspondance de Napoléon Ier*, no. 897, 1:691.

69. Avviso, 7 August 1796, Gridario Bastía 37, document 179, ASM.

70. Avviso, 12 August 1796, Gridario Bastía 37, document 183, ASM.

71. Pommereul, *Campagne du Général Buonaparte*, 123.

72. Bonaparte to Directory, 16 August 1796, *Correspondance de Napoléon Ier*, no. 925, 1:708.

73. In his memoirs Napoleon states he "did not attempt to form a second siege train, since it could not have been ready before new enemies would have exposed him to the chance of losing it as he had lost the former, by forcing him to raise the siege a second time." This may have been the seed that historians cultivated into the myth of Napoleon's using Mantua to lure in the Austrian forces. The simple fact remains that Bonaparte had no choice in organizing a second siege train because all the heavy guns in northern Italy that he had at one time captured and shipped to Borgoforte were now in Austrian hands. Bonaparte, *Memoirs at Saint Helena*, 3:251–52; Fiebeger, *Campaigns of Napoleon*, 29.

4. The Second Austrian Attempt to Relieve Mantua

Epigraph. Berthier to Wurmser, 16 October 1796, *Correspondance de Napoléon Ier*, no. 1092, 2:70.

1. Früh Rapport, 13 September 1796, FM/K 1121, 1796.9.9, OSK.

2. Avviso, 5 September 1796, Gridario Bastía 37, document 187, ASM.

3. Bonaparte to Commissaire Ordonnateur en Chef, 1 September 1796, *Correspondance de Napoléon Ier*, no. 951, 1:731–32. Bonaparte also ordered the commissariat to not send the sick soldiers from Mantua to Brescia probably because the hospitals in Brescia were already overflowing with both Austrian and French wounded.

4. *Gazzetta di Mantova*, 9 September 1796, 5–6.

5. Directory to Moreau, 12 August 1796, AF III, 394, dossier 2088, AN, in *Recueil des Acts du Directoire Exécutif*, 3:336–37; Schels, "Die zweite Einschließung Mantuas," 277.

6. Directory to Bonaparte, 12 August 1796, AF III, 394, dossier 2088, AN, in *Recueil des Acts du Directoire Exécutif*, 3:332–34.

7. General Johann Ludwig Loudon was born in 1762 into an Irish family in Riga and entered the Russian army. In 1789, at the rank of captain in

the Russian army, he was called to Austria by his uncle Field Marshal Gideon Ernst von Loudon. Later he would command with distinction at Novi. He died near Vienna in 1822. Wurzbach, *Biographisches Lexikon des Kaiserthums Österreich*, 16:92.

8. General Baron Paul Davidovich was born in 1737 in Hungary. He joined the army in 1757 and served throughout the Seven Years' War. In 1796 he commanded the bulk of Wurmser's army at Castiglione. Later he served at Novi in 1799 and at Caldiero in 1805. He died in Komorn in 1814. Voykowitsch, *Castiglione*, 23.

9. Wurmser to Francis II, 1 September 1796, in Vivenot, *Thugut, Clerfayt und Wurmser*, no. 198, 486–89; Schels, "Die zweite Einschließung Mantuas," 280.

10. General Charles-Henri Vaubois was born in 1748. He was a captain of artillery at the beginning of the French Revolution. He was made a general of division in 1795. In 1798 he was appointed as commander of the island of Malta, which he successfully defended for two years. He was elected as a senator and made a count in 1808. He died in 1839. Six, *Dictionnaire Biographique*, 2:534.

11. General Charles Edward (Edouard) Kilmaine was born in Dublin, Ireland, in 1751. In 1774 he entered the army to serve with the Royal Dragoons. In 1778 he was adjutant of the *Volontaires etrangeres de la marine*. He served in North America from 1780 to 1783 under Rochambeau. He fought at Jemappes, and in December 1792 he was made lieutenant colonel. In January 1793 he was made colonel, and in March of the same year he was promoted to general of brigade. He died in 1798. Ibid., 2:6–7.

12. Fiebeger, *Campaigns of Napoleon*, 32.

13. Bonaparte to Directory, 31 August 1796, and Bonaparte to Moreau, 31 August 1796, *Correspondance de Napoléon Ier*, nos. 944 and 945, 1:724–25.

14. Vaubois's division consisted of the 22nd and 27th demibrigades of light infantry and the 25th and 39th demibrigades of line infantry. Guieu's brigade was composed of the 17th demibrigade of light infantry and the 85th Line. Bonaparte to Vaubois, 31 August 1796, *Correspondance de Napoléon Ier*, no. 947, 1:726–28.

   Jean Joseph Guieu was born on 30 September 1758 in Champcella (Hautes-Alpes). He enlisted in the artillery in 1780 and was made *chef de bataillon* in 1792 and both *chef de brigade* and provisional general of brigade in 1793. He was named general of division by the Directory on 6 December 1796. On 14 January 1797 he was ordered to take command of Augereau's division during the latter's absence. Guieu retired in 1803 and died in 1817. Six, *Dictionnaire Biographique*, 1:541–42.

15. The cavalry brigade consisted of the 22nd Chasseurs, the 7th Hussars, and the 20th Dragoons. Bonaparte to Berthier, 1 September 1796, *Correspondance de Napoléon Ier*, no. 954, 1:733–35.

16. That Bonaparte detailed more instructions to Sahuguet than to Masséna, Augereau, Dubois, Kilmaine, and Guieu combined, at this critical moment in the campaign, could also be attributed to the fact

that Sahuguet was new to the command of the siege, that Bonaparte trusted the other commanders' experience and initiative, and that most of the directions to the field commanders were simply movement orders.

17. The order to Sahuguet was made the morning of 2 September while the previous orders to the other generals were made the night of 1 September. Bonaparte to Berthier, 2 September 1796, *Correspondance de Napoléon Ier*, no. 955, 1:735–38.

18. All French historical accounts refer to the town as Roveredo. Today it is called Rovereto.

19. Bonaparte to Directory, 6 September 1796, *Correspondance de Napoléon Ier*, no. 967, 1:744–48.

20. *Arrêté portant règlement pour l'administration de la ville de Trente*, 6 September 1796, *Correspondance de Napoléon Ier*, no. 970, 1:750–51.

21. Bonaparte to Vaubois, 6 September 1796, *Correspondance de Napoléon Ier*, no. 971, 1:751–52.

22. Scorza, "Memorie sul Blocca ed Assedio di Mantova," 120–28.

23. Kilmaine to Bonaparte, 6 September 1796, B³29, Service Historique.

24. Bonaparte to Directory, 6 September 1796, *Correspondance de Napoléon Ier*, no. 968, 1:748–49.

25. Pommereul, *Campagne du Général Buonaparte*, 137.

26. Scorza, "Memorie sul Blocca ed Assedio di Mantova," 128.

27. Pommereul, *Campagne du Général Buonaparte*, 139–41.

28. Bonaparte to Directory, 9 September 1796, *Correspondance de Napoléon Ier*, no. 978, 1:756–58.

29. Bonaparte to Josephine, 10 September 1796, *Letters to Josephine*, no. 10, 27; Fiebeger, *Campaigns of Napoleon*, 34.

30. Sahuguet to Bonaparte, 10 September 1796, B³29, Service Historique.

31. Bonaparte to Directory, 16 September 1796, *Correspondance de Napoléon Ier*, no. 1000, 1:773. Castellarrio is now called Castel d'Ario.

32. Bonaparte to Kilmaine, 12 September 1796, *Correspondance de Napoléon Ier*, no. 990, 1:776.

33. Bonaparte to Masséna, Bonaparte to Augereau, and Bonaparte to Directory, 12 September (two letters) and 16 September 1796, *Correspondance de Napoléon Ier*, nos. 987, 991, and 1000, 1:764, 766, 773. Bonaparte explained to the Directory that these orders to Masséna and Sahuguet were given on the 11th. The orders given on 12 September to Masséna were dispatched at 5:00 A.M., and the orders to Augereau were also given on the morning of the 12th.

34. Fiebeger, *Campaigns of Napoleon*, 35.

35. On 10 September Bonaparte ordered Sahuguet to unite all of his forces at Goito and prepare to march. Bonaparte to Sahuguet, 10 September 1796, *Correspondance de Napoléon Ier*, no. 984, 1:761; Bonaparte, *Memoirs at Saint Helena*, 3:270; Fiebeger, *Campaigns of Napoleon*, 35.

36. Bonaparte, *Memoirs at Saint Helena*, 3:270–71; Fiebeger, *Campaigns of Napoleon*, 35.

37. Augereau to Bonaparte, 12 September 1796, B³29, Service Historique.

38. Pommereul, *Campagne du Général Buonaparte*, 144.
39. Augereau to Bonaparte, 12 September 1796, B³29, Service Historique.
40. General Louis-André Bon was born at Romans (Drôme) on 25 October 1758. He enlisted in the Bourbon Infantry Regiment on 1 June 1776. He served at the siege of Toulon in December 1793. He served under Augereau at the Battle of Saint-Laurent-de-la-Mouga and was wounded there 13 August 1794. He was wounded again at the Battle of Montagne Noire on 20 November 1794. He was named provisional general of brigade by the representatives of the people four days later and was assigned to Augereau's division in Italy to which he reported in July 1795. Six, *Dictionnaire Biographique*, 1:115–16.
41. Bonaparte to Directory, 16 September 1796, *Correspondance de Napoléon Ier*, no. 1000, 1:772–74; Bonaparte, *Memoirs at Saint Helena*, 3:271–72.
42. Fabry, *Rapports Historiques*, 54.
43. Koch, *Mémoires de Masséna*, 2:194.
44. Gachot, *Histoire Militaire de Masséna*, 180–82. Bonaparte stated in his memoirs that the French troops "were excessively fatigued, and their duty began to be negligently performed." Bonaparte, *Memoirs at Saint Helena*, 3:271. Indeed, the French soldiers must have been fatigued. The distance from Rivoli to Lavis is sixty miles; from Lavis to Cittadella, seventy miles, and from Cittadella to Mantua, through Ronco, seventy miles. Thus the divisions of Masséna and Augereau marched an average of fifteen miles a day from 2 to 13 September inclusive, besides fighting the Austrians almost daily. Fiebeger, *Campaigns of Napoleon*, 36.
45. Bonaparte to Sahuguet, 14 September 1796, *Correspondance de Napoléon Ier*, no. 998, 1:770.
46. After seven hours of combat in front of the Citadel, the 12th Line lost seven men killed as well as three lieutenants and thirty-six soldiers wounded. The 6th Line lost eight killed and seventy-seven wounded. Fabry, *Rapports Historiques*, 54, 37–38.
47. Bonaparte to Directory, 16 September 1796, *Correspondance de Napoléon Ier*, no. 1000, 1:772–77; Bonaparte, *Memoirs at Saint Helena*, 3:272–73; Koch, *Mémoires de Masséna*, 2:196–98; Gachot, *Histoire Militaire de Masséna*, 183–86.
48. Bonaparte, *Memoirs at Saint Helena*, 3:273; Schels, "Die Begebenheiten in und um Mantua," 163.
49. Rothenberg, *Napoleon's Great Adversaries*, 46.
50. Früh Rapport, 17 September 1796, FM/K 1121, OSK.
51. Masséna to Bonaparte, 16 September 1796, in Koch, *Mémoires de Masséna*, no. 20, 2:501–503.
52. Bonaparte to Directory, 16 September 1796, *Correspondance de Napoléon Ier*, no. 1000, 1:772–77.
53. Masséna to Bonaparte, n.d., in Koch, *Mémoires de Masséna*, 2:199.
54. In order to conduct the blockade, Kilmaine was given the following demibrigades of line infantry: 5th, 6th, 11th, 12th, 19th, 45th, and 69th. The 12th *Légère* was also attached until the Serraglio was retaken, after which it was to return to move to Roverbella. The 1st Brigade of Cavalry

under General Beaumont would be given the 1st and 5th Regiments of Cavalry, the 8th and 20th Dragoons, the 1st Hussars, and the 24th and 25th Chasseurs. Bonaparte to Berthier and Bonaparte to Kilmaine, 16 September 1796 (two letters), *Correspondance de Napoléon Ier*, nos. 1001 and 1002, 1:778–82.

55. *Giornale dei Due Assedi della Città di Mantova*, pt. 1, 29–31.
56. Six, *Dictionnaire Biographique*, 1:59.
57. Scorza, "Memorie sul Blocca ed Assedio di Mantova," 143.
58. Before 22 September the Austrians would bring into Mantua at least 430 wagons loaded with provisions. Ibid., 143–44; Bonaparte states that Wurmser threw a bridge over the Po in order to get provisions to Mantua. Schels, however, points out that there was already a bridge at Borgoforte that was not destroyed, which was used by Wurmser. Bonaparte, *Memoirs at Saint Helena*, 3:273; Schels, "Die Begebenheiten in und um Mantua," 165.
59. Pommereul, *Campagne du Général Buonaparte*, 154.
60. *Giornale dei Due Assedi della Città di Mantova*, pt. 2, 34.
61. Schels, "Die Begebenheiten in und um Mantua," 166–67.
62. Scorza, "Memorie sul Blocca ed Assedio di Mantova," 144–45.
63. Ibid.; Lattanzi, *Giornale di Quanto e' Succeduto in Mantova*, 3; *Giornale dei Due Assedi della Città di Mantova*, pt. 2, 36; Pommereul, *Campagne du Général Buonaparte*, 154. In this action the Austrians lost 18 men killed, 3 officers and 110 men wounded, 21 officers and 877 men captured or missing, and 41 horses killed or captured. Schels, "Die Begebenheiten in und um Mantua," 169. Using Bonaparte's letter to the Directory, Pommereul shows that Bonaparte claimed 1,100 prisoners. However, the published *Correspondance* has Bonaparte's claim as 110 men, omitting the last zero (a likely error). Bonaparte to Directory, 1 October 1796, *Correspondance de Napoléon Ier*, no. 1055, 2:31.
64. Avviso, 18 September 1796, Gridario Bastía 37, document 189, ASM.
65. Avviso, 26 September 1796, Gridario Bastía 37, document 192, ASM.
66. Avviso, 24 September 1796, Gridario Bastía 37, document 191, ASM.
67. *Giornale dei Due Assedi della Città di Mantova*, pt. 2, 41.
68. Letter of Sulkowski, in Reinhard, *Avec Bonaparte en Italie*, 124–25. Reinhard edited and published the letters of Joseph Sulkowski.
69. *Giornale dei Due Assedi della Città di Mantova*, pt. 2, 41.
70. Bonaparte to Chasseloup, 28 September 1796, *Correspondance de Napoléon Ier*, no. 1041, 2:20.
71. Ibid.
72. Bonaparte to Berthier, 28 September 1796, *Correspondance de Napoléon Ier*, no. 1039, 2:19.
73. Bonaparte to Lespinasse, 28 September 1796, *Correspondance de Napoléon Ier*, no. 1040, 2:19–20.
74. Six, *Dictionnaire Biographique*, 1:59.
75. Bonaparte to Lespinasse, 30 September 1796, *Correspondance de Napoléon Ier*, no. 1047, 2:23–24. Bonaparte advised Lespinasse to put the 3-pounders in the most advanced positions, hitch up all of the

5- and 11-pounders, and return all of the cannon with French calibers to the artillery park. Bonaparte informed him that he wanted only cannon with foreign calibers firing on Mantua. Bonaparte chose to reserve his standardized French artillery pieces for his mobile field units to facilitate more rapid cannon ammunition distribution.

76. Bonaparte to Directory, 1 October 1796, *Correspondance de Napoléon Ier*, no. 1055, 2:31.

77. Ibid.; Scorza, "Memorie sul Blocca ed Assedio di Mantova," 147–49; *Giornale dei Due Assedi della Città di Mantova*, pt. 2, 41–44; Schels, "Die Begebenheiten in und um Mantua," 169.

78. Bonaparte to Berthier, 30 September 1796, *Correspondance de Napoléon Ier*, no. 1045, 2:22.

79. Bonaparte to Directory, 1 October 1796, *Correspondance de Napoléon Ier*, no. 1055, 2:31.

80. "Table de l'Emplacement des Quartiers Généraux du Général Bonaparte," 14–15.

81. Directory to Bonaparte, 20 September 1796, AF III, 403, dossier 2191, AN, in *Recueil des Acts du Directoire Exécutif*, 3:656–57; Bonaparte to Berthier (two letters), and Bonaparte to Directory, 29 September 1796 (two letters), and 24 October 1796, *Correspondance de Napoléon Ier*, nos. 1043, 1044, and 1106, 2:21–22, 85–86.

82. Directory to *Commissaires* of the Army of Italy and Directory to Bonaparte, 29 September 1796 (two letters), AF III, 405, dossier 2209, AN, in *Recueil des Acts du Directoire Exécutif*, 3:717–18.

83. Bonaparte to Directory, 1 and 2 October 1796, *Correspondance de Napoléon Ier*, nos. 1055 and 1060, 2:31, 40–43.

84. Directory to Bonaparte, 15 October 1796, AF III, 408, dossier 2244, AN, in *Recueil des Acts du Directoire Exécutif*, 4:62–63.

85. Proclamation, 4 October 1796, *Correspondance de Napoléon Ier*, no. 1066, 2:46–47; Pommereul, *Campagne du Général Buonaparte*, 154–55; Heriot, *The French in Italy*, 97.

86. Directory to Bonaparte, 1 October 1796, AF III, 405, dossier 2215, AN, in *Recueil des Acts du Directoire Exécutif*, 3:735.

87. Bonaparte to Francis II, 2 October 1796, *Correspondance de Napoléon Ier*, no. 1061, 2:34–35.

88. Bonaparte to Directory, 1 October 1796, *Correspondance de Napoléon Ier*, no. 1055, 2:31.

89. Delavoye, *Life of Thomas Graham*, 137. Attilio Portioli put the population that had to be maintained in Mantua after Wurmser's field army moved in at 20,000 civilians and 35,000 military. Portioli, *Vicende di Mantova nel 1796*, 70. See also Schels, "Die Begebenheiten in und um Mantua," 163, 169. The number 28,500 was derived from the number of soldiers in Mantua on 16 September minus those lost in the fighting in the Serraglio. Portioli seems to overestimate the number (perhaps by counting French prisoners with his "military" count).

90. Schels, "Die Begebenheiten in und um Mantua," 171. Schels states the first time horseflesh was issued was 2 October 1796. The author

of an Italian journal states that the cattle supply was exhausted by 25 September and that the Austrians began butchering cavalry horses that day. *Giornale dei Due Assedi della Città di Mantova*, pt. 3, 39.

91. Delavoye, *Life of Thomas Graham*, 137–38.

92. On 31 October only 2,120 of the cavalry horses remained. Schels, "Die Begebenheiten in und um Mantua," 185.

93. Pescasio, *Cronaca Vissuta del Duplice Assedio di Mantova*, 33.

94. Delavoye, *Life of Thomas Graham*, 138.

95. Lattanzi, *Giornale di Quanto è Succeduto in Mantova*, 3.

96. By the end of October, the 28,500 men that Wurmser had at the beginning of the month had been reduced to 23,708; of these, only 12,420 were fit for service. Schels, "Die Begebenheiten in und um Mantua," 185; Delavoye, *Life of Thomas Graham*, 138.

97. The "army" was Davidovich and Quasdanovich's combined forces. Francis II to Alvintzy, 24 September 1796, in Vivenot, *Thugut, Clerfayt und Wurmser*, 494–97; Delavoye, *Life of Thomas Graham*, 138.

98. Kilmaine to Canto d'Yrles and Canto d'Yrles to Kilmaine, 3 October 1796, FM/K 1122, 1796.10.15, OSK; Scorza, "Memorie sul Blocca ed Assedio di Mantova," 150.

99. Cocastelli to Wurmser, 4 October 1796, FM/K 1122, 1796.10.19ad, OSK; Avviso, Cocastelli, 14 May, 1796, No 145.

100. Cocastelli to Wurmser, 5, 6, 7, 15, 17, 18, and 21 October 1796, FM/K 1122, 1796.10.21, 1796.10.21ad, 1796.10.25, 1796.10.32, 1796.10.33, 1796.10.36, and 1796.10.42, OSK.

101. Avviso, 6 October 1796, Gridario Bastía, document 195, ASM. To ensure authenticity, each cedola had to be signed by Dr. Luigi Tonni, a Royal Council clerk from the Chamber of Magistrates, and Counselor Don Baldassare Scorza, the Royal Council clerk from the Royal Archives. Scorza is also the author of "Memorie sul Blocca ed Assedio di Mantova." Later Cocastelli issued another avviso authorizing additional persons to sign the promissory notes to speed up the process. Avviso, 24 October 1796, Gridario Bastía, document 200, ASM. This change is understandable considering the vast amount of papers Tonni and Scorza had to sign. The government printed more than 7.5 million lire's worth of cedola promissory notes, which were distributed in the following amounts: 6,000 of 10 soldi; 9,000 of £1; 163,600 of £3; 388,200 of £6; 146,180 of £9; 89,820 of £12; 62,840 of £18; 19,660 of £45; and 2,160 of £135.

102. Scorza, "Memorie sul Blocca ed Assedio di Mantova," 150–51; *Giornale dei Due Assedi della Città di Mantova*, 50–51.

103. Scorza, "Memorie sul Blocca ed Assedio di Mantova," 151–52; *Giornale dei Due Assedi della Città di Mantova*, 52–55; Pommereul, *Campagne du Général Buonaparte*, 155; Schels, "Die Begebenheiten in und um Mantua," 174–75.

104. Scorza, "Memorie sul Blocca ed Assedio di Mantova," 152–53; *Giornale dei Due Assedi della Città di Mantova*, 56–59; Lattanzi, *Giornale di Quanto é Succeduto in Mantova*, 5; Pommereul, *Campagne du Général Buonaparte*, 155.

105. Berthier to Wurmser, 16 October 1796, *Correspondance de Napoléon Ier*, no. 1092, 2:70.
106. Scorza, "Memorie sul Blocca ed Assedio di Mantova," 168.
107. Alvintzy to Wurmser and Wurmser to Alvintzy, 12 and 24 October 1796, FM/K 1122, 1796.10.35½ and 1796.10.45, OSK.
108. Moreau commanded the Army of the Rhine and Jourdan the Army of the Sambre and Meuse. In September Archduke Charles concentrated his forces against Jourdan and defeated him at Amberg and Altenkirchen.
109. *Giornale dei Due Assedi della Città di Mantova*, 71–74.
110. Scorza, "Memorie sul Blocca ed Assedio di Mantova," 169–70; Schels, "Die Begebenheiten in und um Mantua," 179–82.
111. Schels, "Die Begebenheiten in und um Mantua," 183.

5. Alvintzy and the Third Attempt to Relieve Mantua

Epigraph 1. Francis II to Alvintzy, 5 December 1796, in Vivenot, *Thugut, Clerfayt und Wurmser*, no. 215, 524–28.
Epigraph 2. Bonaparte to Directory, 6 December 1796, *Correspondance de Napoléon Ier*, no. 1233, 2:177–78.
  1. Roider, *Baron Thugut*, 226.
  2. Giovanni Marchese di Provera was born to a noble family in Lombardy. He joined the Austrian army and advanced rapidly in rank by the time of the war with France. He fought in the Seven Years' War and the Austro-Turkish War. By 1796 he was made field marshal-lieutenant and named a marchese. For his efforts in the 1796–97 campaigns he received the Knight's Cross of the Order of Maria Theresa. Wurzbach, *Biographisches Lexikon des Kaiserthums Österreich*, 24:22–23. Provera controlled the brigades commanded by Major Generals Anton Lipthay, Adolph von Brabeck, and Anton von Schubirz.
  3. Kircheisen, *Napoleons feldzug in Italien und Österreich*, 225. Quosdanovich's subordinate brigade commanders were Major Generals Prince von Hohenzollern (vanguard), Philipp Pittoni, Fürst Roselmini, Lipthay, Schubirz, and Brabeck.
  4. Bonaparte to Carnot, 25 October 1796, *Correspondance de Napoleon Ier*, no. 1111, 2:92–93.
  5. Bonaparte to Masséna, 2 November 1796, *Correspondance de Napoleon Ier*, no. 1144, 2:114.
  6. *Guerres des Français en Italie*, 1:211; Fiebeger, *Campaigns of Napoleon*, 41.
  7. Scorza, "Memorie sul Blocca ed Assedio di Mantova," 171; *Giornale dei Due Assedi della Città di Mantova*, pt. 2, 2:3.
  8. Avviso, Cocastelli, 14 May 1796, Gridario Bastía 37, document 145, ASM.
  9. Scorza, "Memorie sul Blocca ed Assedio di Mantova," 171–72; *Giornale dei Due Assedi della Città di Mantova*, pt. 2, 2:3–4.
 10. Wine was strictly controlled with different prices for new, middle-aged, and older wines. *Giornale dei Due Assedi della Città di Mantova*, pt. 2, 2:4–5.

11. Ibid., 2:6.
12. Alvintzy to Wurmser, 29 October 1796, in Schels, "Die Begebenheiten in und um Mantua," 185. On the day Alvintzy crossed the Adige, he planned to give the signal between 6:00 and 7:00 P.M. with eight 12-pounders firing three volleys at five-minute intervals.
13. *Giornale dei Due Assedi della Città di Mantova*. pt. 2, 2:6.
14. Ibid., 2:7.
15. Proclamation, 11 November 1796, *Correspondance de Napoleon Ier*, no. 1180, 2:135–36.
16. Bonaparte to Directory, 13 November 1796, *Correspondance de Napoleon Ier*, no. 1182, 2:136–40.
17. Francis II to Alvintzy and Thugut to Alvintzy, 9 and 12 November, in Vivenot, *Thugut, Clerfayt und Wurmser*, nos. 209 and 210, 510–17.
18. Directory to Francis II, 14 November 1796, AF III, 415, AN, in *Recueil des Acts du Directoire Exécutif*, 4:281–83.
19. *Délibération secrète du 25 Brumaire an V*, 15 November 1796, AF III, 20, AN, in *Recueil des Acts du Directoire Exécutif*, 4:28.
20. Berthier to Alvintzy, 29 November 1796, AF III, 59, no. 1, AN; Alvintzy to Berthier, 3 December 1796, AF III, 59, no. 2, AN; Alison, *History of Europe*, 1:416.
21. Scorza, "Memorie sul Blocca ed Assedio di Mantova," 172; *Giornale dei Due Assedi della Città di Mantova*, pt. 2, 2:8–9; *Guerres des Français en Italie*, 219–22.
22. Bonaparte to Directory, 19 November 1796, *Correspondance de Napoleon Ier*, no. 1196, 2:150; Schels, "Die Begebenheiten in und um Mantua," 186.
23. Alison, *History of Europe*, 1:417.
24. Scorza, "Memorie sul Blocca ed Assedio di Mantova," 173–74; Schels, "Die Begebenheiten in und um Mantua," 187.
25. Scorza, "Memorie sul Blocca ed Assedio di Mantova," 174; Delavoye, *Life of Thomas Graham*, 138.
26. Bonaparte to Josephine, 19 November 1796, *Napoleon's Letters to Josephine*, no. 15, 31.
27. Bonaparte to Directory, 19 November 1796, *Correspondance de Napoléon Ier*, no. 1196, 2:150. This letter was also published on the first page of *Le Moniteur Universel* on 2 December 1796, no. 72. A letter from Berthier also written on 19 November 1796 echoes Bonaparte's prediction of the imminent fall of Mantua. Berthier wrote: "The army of Alvintzy became separated and ineffective, and will be no obstruction to our obtaining Mantua, which we estimate will belong to us in about fifteen days." *Le Moniteur Universel*, 3 December 1796, no. 73.
28. Bonaparte to Carnot, 19 November 1796, *Correspondance de Napoléon Ier*, no. 1197, 2:151.
29. *Le Moniteur Universel*, 4 December 1796, no. 74.
30. Fiebeger, *Campaigns of Napoleon*, 47.
31. Scorza, "Memorie sul Blocca ed Assedio di Mantova," 176; *Giornale dei Due Assedi della Città di Mantova*, pt. 2, 2:13–15; Schels, "Die Begebenheiten in und um Mantua," 188–90.

32. Schels, "Die Begebenheiten in und um Mantua," 189–90.
33. Scorza, "Memorie sul Blocca ed Assedio di Mantova," 176–77; *Giornale dei Due Assedi della Città di Mantova*, pt. 2, 2:15–16; Schels, "Die Begebenheiten in und um Mantua," 190–91.
34. Jomini, *Histoire des Guerres*, 11:231; Schels, "Die Begebenheiten in und um Mantua," 192.
35. Wurmser to Spiegel, to Ott, and to Minkwitz, 23 November 1796, FM/K 1122, 1796.11.23a, 1796.11.23c, and 1796.11.26, OSK; Scorza, "Memorie sul Blocca ed Assedio di Mantova," 176–77; Beauvais, *Victoires, Conquêtes, Désastres*, 4:210.
36. Rapport, 23 November 1796, FM/K 1122, 1796.11.27, OSK.
37. Wurmser to Alvintzy, 25 November 1796, FM/K 1122, 1796.11.28, OSK. In the letter, Wurmser also responded to the last letter he received, which Alvintzy wrote at Montebello on 10 November, indicating that his column would relieve Mantua soon. Alvintzy to Wurmser, 10 November 1796, FM/K 1122, 1796.11.28ad, OSK; *Giornale dei Due Assedi della Città di Mantova*, pt. 2, 2:17.
38. Bonaparte to Directory, 24 November 1796, *Correspondance de Napoléon Ier*, no. 1217, 2:164–65. This letter was also published in Paris in *Le Moniteur Universel*, 7 December 1796, no. 77.
39. Bonaparte to Clarke, 29 November 1796, AF III, 59, no. 5, AN.
40. *Le Moniteur Universel*, 20 December 1796, no. 90.
41. Clarke to Bonaparte, n.d., AF III, 59, no. 6, AN; Bonaparte to Directory, 6 December 1796, *Correspondance de Napoléon Ier*, no. 1232, 2:1176–77.
42. "Campagnes d'Italie," *Correspondance de Napoléon Ier*, 29:245.
43. Bonaparte to Directory, 6 December 1796, *Correspondance de Napoléon Ier*, no. 1233, 2:177–78. The money from Rome that Bonaparte referenced amounted to 30 million livres.
44. Barras to Bonaparte, 18 January 1797, B³37, Service Historique.
45. Directory to Clarke, 7 January 1797, B³37, Service Historique.
46. "Campagnes d'Italie," *Correspondance de Napoléon Ier*, 29:246.
47. Francis II to Alvintzy, 17 December 1796, in Vivenot, *Thugut, Clerfayt und Wurmser*, 534–37.
48. "Campagnes d'Italie," *Correspondance de Napoléon Ier*, 29:246.
49. Bonaparte to Directory and Bonaparte to Carnot, 1 October and 19 November 1796, *Correspondance de Napoléon Ier*, nos. 1055 and 1197, 2:30, 151.
50. Bonaparte promised the Directory to take Mantua in fifteen days and then in another letter told Carnot he would take it in ten days.
51. Dumas's claim to fame would only be to father his more famous son, the author Alexandre Dumas, who wrote *The Three Musketeers* and *The Man in the Iron Mask*. Radetzky would later be known throughout Europe for his leadership in crushing the Piedmontese revolution of 1848 and for the march named after him. Graham's fame came during the British advance into France on the Iberian Peninsula, where he was reportedly the first British general to place the English standard on French soil. Alison, *History of Europe*, 1:148.
52. Gallaher, *General Alexandre Dumas*, 73–74.

53. Dumas to Bonaparte, 25 December 1796, Arch. Guerre, B³118, in Gallaher, *General Alexandre Dumas*, 76, 161.
54. Francis II to Alvintzy, 5 December 1796, in Vivenot, *Thugut, Clerfayt und Wurmser*, 524–28.
55. Dumas, *Mes Mémoires*, 1:74.
56. Thiébault, *Memoirs of Baron Thiébault*, 283–84.
57. Bonaparte to Directory, 28 December 1796, *Correspondance de Napoléon Ier*, no. 1319, 2:259–62. These messages placed in the hazel-nut-sized capsules averaged 2" × 3" in size. The writer would use an extremely fine-tipped pen—perhaps even a pin or needle.
58. *London Times*, 21 February 1796.
59. Alvintzy to Wurmser, 15 December 1796, in Dumas, *Mes Mémoires*, 74–75.
60. Bonaparte to Dumas, 28 December 1796, in Dumas, *Mes Mémoires*, 77–78.
61. Gallaher, *General Alexandre Dumas*, 78.
62. Grenville to Graham, 3 May 1796, *Life of Thomas Graham*, 109.
63. Count Radetzky held the rank of captain and the position of deputy adju-tant general on Beaulieu's staff when he met Graham. Graham's mem-oirs, in Delavoye, *Life of Thomas Graham*, 112; Radetzky, *Radetzky Autobiographische Schriften*, 15.
64. Delavoye, *Life of Thomas Graham*, 138–40; the regiment of Wurmser's Hussars, the marshal's namesake, was commanded by Klenau. In May Radetzky was promoted to major in the engineer corps. Graham main-tains that he was a colonel by December. Wurzbach, *Biographisches Lexikon des Kaiserthums Österreich*, 24:177.
65. Delavoye, *Life of Thomas Graham*, 139–40; *Giornale dei Due Assedi della Città di Mantova*, pt. 2, 2:22.
66. Even with doubling the guards, Dumas was not able to keep messengers and spies from getting into and out of the fortress. Wurmser received a letter from Alvintzy on 11 December and several afterward. Four days later Wurmser, in fact, received a second letter from Alvintzy dated 13 December, which helps explain the word that spread throughout the city on 18 December about Alvintzy's imminent relief. The let-ter told Wurmser that the new relief would take place in three weeks or a month. Four days before Graham departed, Wurmser received two more messages from Alvintzy about the army's movements and a note in Italian from local informants about the disposition of French units around Mantua. These messages were very small in size, and were prob-ably smuggled in the usual way using a capsule. Alvintzy to Wurmser, 28 November and 2 December 1796, and note in Italian, n.d., FM/K 1122, OSK; Schels, "Die Begebenheiten in und um Mantua," 269–70.
67. Graham to Lord Cathcart, 27 December 1796, and Graham's memoirs, in Delavoye, *Life of Thomas Graham*, 146–48, 141–45; Aspinall-Oglander, *Freshly Remembered*, 97–98. In a letter to his brother Graham stated that he traveled "about 52 miles in 13 hours" to the Venetian town of "Policella" (i.e., Polesella is no doubt the town he was referring to).

68. Graham to Lord Grenville, 6 January 1797, in Rose, "Dispatches of Thomas Graham," 321.
69. Wurmser to Alvintzy, 30 December 1796, FM/K 1122, 1796.12.132, OSK.

6. The Fourth Attempt to Relieve Mantua

Epigraph. Bonaparte to Directory, 17 January 1796, *Correspondance de Napoléon Ier*, no. 1394, 2:318–20.

1. The consumption of horses had left only 1,819 remaining in the Mantua garrison by 1 January 1797. Schels, "Die Begebenheiten in und um Mantua," 277.
2. Cocastelli reports, 15, 20, 23, and 28 December 1797, FM/K 1122, 1796.12.93a, 1796.12.93b, 1796.12.102, 1796.12.113, and 1796.12.112½, OSK; Scorza, "Memorie sul Blocca ed Assedio di Mantova," 178.
3. Cocastelli to Wurmser, 8 January 1797, FM/K 1139, 1797.1.30½, Matrix, 1797.1.ad30½, OSK.
4. Fiebeger, *Campaigns of Napoleon*, 50–51; Wartenburg, *Napoleon as a General*, 1:94; Atlas accompanying *Napoleon as a General*, 19; Burton, *Napoleon's Campaigns in Italy*, 83.
5. Bonaparte to Berthier, 20 and 21 (two letters) December 1796, *Correspondance de Napoléon Ier*, nos. 1295, 1304, and 1305, 2:229–31, 240–47.
6. Bonaparte to Lespinasse, 25 December 1796, *Correspondance de Napoléon Ier*, no. 1313, 2:253–55.
7. Bonaparte to Lespinasse, 30 and 31 (three letters) December 1796 and 1 (two letters) and 3 January 1797, *Correspondance de Napoléon Ier*, nos. 1332, 1333, 1335, 1337, 1342, 1343, and 1353, 2:274–77, 280–82, 288.
8. Bonaparte to Berthier, 21 December 1796, *Correspondance de Napoléon Ier*, no. 1301, 2:235–37.
9. Bonaparte to Berthier, 21 December 1796 and 7 January 1797, *Correspondance de Napoléon Ier*, nos. 1302 and 1367, 2:237–39, 297–98.
10. General Barthélemy-Catherine Joubert was promoted to general of division on 7 December 1796. Six, *Dictionnaire Biographique*, 1:606.
11. *Guerres des Français en Italie*, 239–40; Fiebeger, *Campaigns of Napoleon*, 51–52. Within the two divisions Sérurier had a total of seven demibrigades *de bataille* under his command—the 5th, 6th, 11th, 17th, 45th, 64th (2 battalions), and 69th—and for cavalry he had the 20th Dragoons and the 22nd and 25th Chasseurs. "Emplacements de Armée," 7–17 January 1797, B³38, Service Historique.
12. Jomini, *Histoire des Guerres*, 11:265.
13. *Guerres des Français en Italie*, 241; Fiebeger, *Campaigns of Napoleon*, 52–53.
14. Bonaparte to Masséna, 12 January 1797, *Correspondance de Napoléon Ier*, no. 1371, 2:300–301.
15. Jomini, *Histoire des Guerres*, 11:266.
16. Ibid., 288.
17. Bonaparte, *Memoirs at Saint Helena*, 3:416.

18. Bonaparte to Masséna, 13 January 1797, *Correspondance de Napoléon Ier*, no. 1381, 2:308–309.

19. Bonaparte to Rey, 13 January 1797, B³37, Service Historique.

20. Bonaparte, *Memoirs at Saint Helena*, 3:416.

21. Pommereul, *Campagne du Général Buonaparte*, 233; Jomini, *Histoire des Guerres*, 11:289.

22. Bonaparte, *Memoirs at Saint Helena*, 3:416; Jomini, *Histoire des Guerres*, 11:287, 290; Koch, *Mémoires de Masséna*, 2:307.

23. Sextius-Alexandre-François Miollis was born in Provence in 1759. As a second lieutenant he participated in the American Revolutionary War under Rochambeau. His experience at the siege of Mantua was not his first exposure to siege warfare. He was wounded by a shell fragment during the siege of Yorktown in 1781. A few weeks after the capture of Mantua, he was made the military governor of the city. Six, *Dictionnaire Biographique*, 2:203.

24. Jomini, *Histoire des Guerres*, 11:290–91.

25. Pommereul, *Campagne du Général Buonaparte*, 233–34, 247.

26. Prince Friedrich Hohenzollern was born near Maastricht in 1757. He belonged to the Hohenzollern-Hechingen side of the Hohenzollern family. He entered the Dutch army at age eighteen. In March 1796 he was made a major general and held commands throughout the 1796 campaign in Italy. He later participated in the 1799 siege of Mantua. He died in Vienna in 1844. Voykowitsch, *Castiglione*, 26.

27. Sérurier to Bonaparte, 16 January 1797, B³37, Service Historique; Scorza, "Memorie sul Blocca ed Assedio di Mantova," 183; "Campagnes d'Italie," *Correspondance de Napoléon Ier*, 29:260; Pommereul, *Campagne du Général Buonaparte*, 247.

28. Volta, *Storia di Mantova*, 5:374.

29. Pommereul, *Campagne du Général Buonaparte*, 248.

30. Sérurier to Bonaparte, 16 January 1797, B³37, Service Historique.

31. Scorza, "Memorie sul Blocca ed Assedio di Mantova," 184–85; Bonaparte to Directory, 17 January 1797, *Correspondance de Napoléon Ier*, no. 1397, 2:326–231; Jomini, *Histoire des Guerres*, 11:291–93; Pommereul, *Campagne du Général Buonaparte*, 247.

32. Bonaparte to Directory, 17 January 1797, *Correspondance de Napoléon Ier*, no. 1394, 2:318–19; Volta, *Storia di Mantova*, 5:375; Koch, *Mémoires de Masséna*, 2:307–309.

33. *Etat de Officier Austriene Prisonnier de Guerre*, 14 to 18 January 1797, B³37, Service Historique.

34. Bonaparte to Alvintzy, 17 January 1797, B³37, Service Historique.

35. Miollis to Bonaparte, 29 January 1797, B³38, Service Historique.

36. Sérurier to Bonaparte, 16 January 1797, B³37, Service Historique.

37. Upon his return to Vienna, Provera was exiled to his estates in Carinthia on the grounds that he overstepped his bounds in advancing against Mantua before he had received intelligence about the progress of Alvintzy. Alison, *History of Europe*, 1:419–20.

38. Bonaparte to Beaumont, 17 January 1797, B³37, Service Historique.

39. Bonaparte to Chabot, 17 January 1797, B³37, Service Historique.
40. Bonaparte to Berthier, 20 January 1797, B³38, Service Historique.
41. Bonaparte to Sérurier, 22 January 1797, B³38, Service Historique.
42. Bonaparte to Sérurier, 27 January 1797, B³38, Service Historique.
43. Bonaparte to Sérurier, 26 January 1797; Bonaparte to Augereau, 26 January 1797—both in B³38, Service Historique.

7. Capitulation and Bonaparte's Rise

Epigraph. Wurmser to Bonaparte, 29 January 1797, in *Bonaparte Letters and Despatches, Secret, Confidential, and Official*, 2:240.

1. Directory to Clarke, 7 January 1797; Directory to Bonaparte, 18 January 1797—both in B³37, Service Historique.
2. Directory to Bonaparte, 19 January 1797, AF III, 428, dossier 2428, AN, in *Recueil des Acts du Directoire Exécutif*, 4:686–87; Directory to Bonaparte, 25 January 1797, AF III, 429, dossier 2443, AN, in *Recueil des Acts du Directoire Exécutif*, 4:722; Directory to Council of 500 and Council of Ancients, 26 January 1797, AF III, 429, dossier 2445, AN, in *Recueil des Acts du Directoire Exécutif*, 4:726; Instructions for General Clarke, 26 January 1797, AF III, 429, dossier 2445, AN, in *Recueil des Acts du Directoire Exécutif*, 4:727; Alison, *History of Europe*, 1:418.
3. Pommereul, *Campagne du Général Buonaparte*, 261.
4. Ibid., 262.
5. Avviso, Cocastelli, 24 January 1797, Gridario Bastía 37, document 213, ASM.
6. Avviso, Wurmser, 25 January 1797, Gridario Bastía 37, document 214, ASM.
7. Cocastelli to Wurmser, 8 January 1797, FM/K 1139, 1797.1.30½, Matrix, 1797.1.ad30½, OSK.
8. Cocastelli to Wurmser, 29 January 1797, Busta 119, document 265, ASM.
9. Wurmser to Commander of the Siege, 29 January 1797, FM/K 1139, 1797.2.4 and 1797.2.5, OSK. A typeset copy of the same letter, made by the *Correspondance de Napoleon Ier* Commission, is also located in the French Army Archives in B³38, Service Historique.
10. "Campagnes d'Italie," *Correspondance de Napoléon Ier*, 29:262.
11. Ibid.
12. Kircheisen, *Napoleons feldzug in Italien und Österreich*, 272. Bonaparte's *Correspondance* has no entries for 30 and 31 January, but he writes again on 1 February in Bologna. There is also a letter in a private collection from Bonaparte to Clarke from Verona on 1 February. In it he states: "Wurmser wrote me to offer me the city and the castle as long as I let the garrison go free. I simply refused granting only the release of 500 men, 200 horses and six cannon while the rest would be made prisoners. Talks are ongoing with General Sérurier whom I sent my instructions." The only evidence of this conversation with Klenau comes from Bonaparte, so it is conceivable that this episode is only a figment of his imagination. His "memory" at St. Helena contradicts his

letter to the Directory on 1 February. In addition, documents concerning negotiations for the capitulation at the Austrian archives in Vienna are all signed by Sérurier. FM/K 1139, 1797.2.11 and 1797.2.12, OSK.

13. Bonaparte to Directory, 1 February 1797, *Correspondance de Napoléon Ier*, no. 1435, 2:373–74; Bonaparte to Clarke, 1 February 1797 (details of this letter, which was sold at public acution on 11 October 2004 and is now in a private collection, are at http://www.auction.fr/UK/sale_books_comic_books_and_autographs/v7097_gros_delettrez/1823104_parlementation_avec_wurmser_sur_la_ville_de_mantoue_lettre_signee_bonaparte.html).

14. Kircheisen, *Napoleons feldzug in Italien und Österreich*, 273.

15. Scorza, "Memorie sul Blocca ed Assedio di Mantova," 187.

16. Sérurier to Bonaparte, 30 January 1797, B³38, Service Historique. This letter is also in *Bonaparte Letters and Despatches, Secret, Confidential, and Official*, 2:243–44.

17. Bonaparte to Directory, 1 February 1797, *Correspondance de Napoléon Ier*, no. 1435, 2:373–74.

18. Bonaparte to Sérurier, 1 February 1797, B³39, Service Historique.

19. Wurmser to Sérurier, [31?] January 1797, FM/K 1139, 1797.2.10, OSK.

20. Sérurier to Wurmser, 1 February 1797, FM/K 1139, 1797.2.12, OSK. Sérurier allowed two howitzers, two 5-pounders, and two 11-pounders with all of their equipment and assigned allotment of ammunition to go out with the Austrian troops. The final surrender terms would indicate two howitzers, two 6-pounders and two 12-pounders, thus changing the calibers slightly. This letter arrived at Roverbella and was returned to Mantua on 1 February 1797.

21. Sérurier made changes to all of the articles except 7, 9, 10, 11, and 14. Capitulation Terms, 2 February 1797, FM/K 1139, 1797.2.14, 1797.2.15 and 1797.2.17, OSK.

22. Scorza, "Memorie sul Blocca ed Assedio di Mantova," 187.

23. Unit List, 2 February 1797, FM/K 1139, 1797.2.18, OSK. This list of five hundred individuals and two hundred cavalrymen was prepared by Adjutant General Auer.

24. Wurmser to Ott, 2 Feburary 1797, FM/K 1139, 1797.2.13, OSK. Wurmser sent a sealed letter and a copy of the original articles to General Ott in the Citadel with an explanation that Klenau was negotiating those particular articles.

25. FM/K 1139, 1797.2.14, OSK.

26. Capitulation, 2 February 1797, FM/K 1139, 1797.2.16, OSK; Pommereul, *Campagne du Général Buonaparte*, 268. The capitulation is also in the *Correspondance*: see 2 February 1797, no. 1443, 2:378–82. In addition, Scorza recorded the capitulation in Italian in his journal: Scorza, "Memorie sul Blocca ed Assedio di Mantova," 190–201.

27. Matrix, 2 February 1797, FM/K 1139, 1797.2.28 and 1797.2.29, OSK.

28. Wurmser to Alvintzy, 30 December 1797, FM/K 1139, 1796.12.132, OSK. If these horses had been slaughtered for the garrison and populace, Wurmser could have resisted for perhaps fifteen more days, but

he then would not have had the ability to transport his army's baggage back to Austria.

29. Pommereul, *Campagne du Général Buonaparte*, 276.
30. Ibid., 281–82. For a complete listing of the weapons captured with the capitulation, see appendix D.
31. Wurmser to Francis II, 3 February 1797, FM/K 1139, 1797.2.20, OSK.
32. Sérurier to Bonaparte, 3 February 1797, B³39, Service Historique.
33. Sérurier to Wurmser, 3 February 1797, FM/K 1139, 1797.2.21, OSK.
34. Karl Philipp Sebottendorf was born into a military family in 1740. In 1758 he graduated from the Vienna *Neustädter* Military Academy. In 1796 he was given divisional command and sent to the Italian theater of operations. Wurzbach, *Biographisches Lexikon des Kaiserthums Österreich*, 33:245–46.
35. March Columns, n.d., FM/K 1139, 1797.2.27, OSK.
36. FM/K 1139, 1797.2.29, OSK.
37. Augereau to Wurmser, 8 February 1797, and Desponai to Wurmser, 9 February 1797, FM/K 1139, 1797.2.45 and 1797.2.47, OSK.
38. Guieu to Bonaparte, 12 February 1797, B³39, Service Historique. Bonaparte in fact sent Augereau to Paris to deliver to the Directory the flags captured at Mantua. Bonaparte to the Minister of War, 8 February 1797, *Correspondance de Napoléon Ier*, no. 1470, 2:406.
39. March table, FM/K 1139, 1797.2.60, OSK. Wurmser used a march table to coordinate the movements to Gorizia.
40. Bonaparte to Directory, 1 February 1797, *Correspondance de Napoléon Ier*, no. 1435, 2:373–74.
41. Bonaparte to Directory, 3 February 1797, *Correspondance de Napoléon Ier*, no. 1448, 2:384–85.
42. Ibid.
43. Bonaparte, *Napoleon's Letters to Josephine*, 222.
44. Capitulation, 2 February 1797, FM/K 1139, 1797.2.16, OSK.
45. Bonaparte to Directory, 10 February 1797, *Correspondance de Napoléon Ier*, no. 1474, 2:408.
46. Pommereul, *Campagne du Général Buonaparte*, 268, 270.
47. Ibid., 270–72.
48. Ibid., 272. For more on Pommereul, see page 288, note 9.
49. Ibid.
50. Ibid., 273.
51. Pierre, *Les Hymnes et Chansons*, 781; Davenson, *Le Livre Des Chansons*, 221–23.
52. *Chanson Poissarde sur la Prise de Mantoue*, B³39, Service Historique.
53. Canzone, *"L'Albero della Liberta"* and *"La Lombardia,"* 14 and 18 February 1797, nos. 244 and 255, Museo del Risorgimento.
54. Bonaparte to Directory, 20 January 1797, *Correspondance de Napoléon Ier*, no. 1403, 2:335.
55. Pommereul, *Campagne du Général Buonaparte*, 282–86.
56. Proclamation to the Army of Italy, 10 March 1797, *Correspondance de Napoléon Ier*, no. 1552, 2:482–84.

8. Bonaparte's Administration and Preparation for War, 1797–1799

Epigraph. Proclamation to the soldiers of the Army of Italy, *Correspondance de Napoleon Ier*, no. 1552, 2:482–84.

1. Faustino, *Compendio degli assedi e blocchi di Mantova*, 55.
2. D'Onofrio, "L'Archivio della Municipalità di Mantova," 121.
3. Busta 119, document 255, ASM; D'Onofrio, "L'Archivio della Municipalità di Mantova," 128–29.
4. D'Onofrio, "L'Archivio della Municipalità di Mantova," 128–29.
5. Ibid., 129.
6. Ibid., 126–27.
7. Busta 119, document 257, ASM. The other seven delegates were councillor Don Angelo Maria Petrozani, lawyer Don Domenico Todeschini, Don Luigi Avigni, lawyer Giulio Bosio, Amadio Basilia, Filippo Mordini, and Dr. Pietro Corradini. For more on Volta, see page 288, notes 6 and 7.
8. D'Onofrio, "L'Archivio della Municipalità di Mantova," 126–27. The French administration of the Mantovano can be divided into three periods: the provisional *Municipalitè* (2 March–19 July 1797); the State Administration (19 July–2 November 1797); and the Department of the Mincio, with the introduction of the Cisalpine Republic (2 November 1797–28 July 1799). Finzi, "Il *Giornale Degli Amici della Libertà Italiana*," 161.
9. Busta 119, ASM; D'Onofrio, "L'Archivio della Municipalità di Mantova," 131. Sérurier decided to meet this delegation at the suggestion of Cocastelli, the Giunta's ex-president.
10. Sérurier to Municipalitè, 3 February 1797, Busta 119, ASM.
11. Volta, *Storia di Mantova*, 5:377.
12. Avviso, 7 February 1797, Gridario Bastía 37, document 224, ASM.
13. Portioli, *La Zecca di Mantova*, 42.
14. D'Onofrio, "L'Archivio della Municipalità di Mantova," 124, 156, 165; Busta 80, documents 93–98. The siteeen Austrian districts of the Mantovano were: Mantua, Ostiglia, Roverbella, Goito, Castiglione delle Stiviere, Castelgoffredo, Canneto, Marcaria, Borgoforte, Bozzolo, Sabbioneta, Viadana, Suzzara, Gonzaga, Revere, and Sermide. The French extended the "Department of the Mincio" eastward and in turn established thirteen districts: Mantua, Governolo, Ostiglia, Isola della Scala, Castellaro, Villafranca, Castiglione delle Stiviere, Goito, Asola, Marcaria, Gonzaga, Revere, and Sermide.
15. D'Onofrio, "L'Archivio della Municipalità di Mantova," 132–33.
16. Bonaparte to Berthier, 4 February 1797, *Correspondance de Napoleon Ier*, no. 1453, 2:389–91.
17. Ibid.
18. Ibid.
19. This is similar to what the Austrians did during the break in siege in August 1796 after Bonaparte raised the siege to fight at Castiglione.
20. Avviso, 6 February 1797, Gridario Bastía 37, document 221, ASM.
21. The metric system, which was introduced in France in 1795, legally made a quintal equal to 100 kilograms. Bonaparte and his commissaries

in 1797, however, were most likely still using the royal unit definition of a quintal: 100 livres (pounds), which equated to 48.95 kilograms, or 107.916 Imperial pounds. Thus Bonaparte's order called for 1,079,160 pounds (or 540 short tons) of corn.

22. Rudolf Emanuel de Haller (1747–1833) was a Swiss financier who had founded a bank in Paris. In 1816 he became bankrupt after losing the large fortune he had acquired by questionable means while working for the French Treasury. Marshall-Cornwall, *Marshal Masséna*, 66.

23. Order, 13 February 1797, *Correspondance de Napoleon Ier*, no. 1491, 2:422–23.

24. Order, 4 February 1797, *Correspondance de Napoleon Ier*, no. 1456, 2:392–93.

25. Bonaparte to Sérurier, 4 February 1797, *Correspondance de Napoleon Ier*, no. 1454, 2:391.

26. Bonaparte to Sérurier, 13 February 1797, *Correspondance de Napoleon Ier*, no. 1490, 2:421.

27. Volta, *Storia di Mantova*, 5:382.

28. Simonsohn, *History of the Jews in the Duchy of Mantua*, 93–96. In the 1770s the Rabbi of Mantua, Jacob Saraval, and the lawyer Giovanni Battista Benedetti of Ferrara debated the same issues as well.

29. *Prospetto di un Foglio Periodico*, Gridario Bastía 37, document 233, ASM.

30. *Giornale degli Amici della Libertà Italiana*, no. 1, 18 Febraury 1797.

31. Ibid., no. 1, 16 March 1798.

32. Ibid., nos. 52–53, 4 April 1799.

33. Avviso, 5 February 1797, Gridario Bastía 37, document 217, ASM.

34. Avviso, 7 and 14 February 1797, Gridario Bastía 37, documents 223, 245, ASM.

35. Avviso, 8 February 1797, Gridario Bastía 37, document 227, ASM.

36. Avviso, 14 February 1797, Gridario Bastía 37, document 243, ASM.

37. Bonaparte to Directory, 19 February 1797, *Correspondance de Napoleon Ier*, no. 1510, 2:442–44. In the interim, Bonaparte's operations in February took him to Bologna, Imola, Faenza, Forli, Rimini, Pasaro, Sinigaglia, Ancona, Loretto, Macerata, and Tolentino.

38. Avviso, 25 February 1797, Gridario Bastía 37, document 266, ASM.

39. Avviso, 1 March 1797, Gridario Bastía 37, document 270, ASM.

40. *Prospetto dell' Illuminazione alla Casa de' Fratelli Coddè nell' arrivo in Mantova del Generale in Capo Bonaparte*, 1 March 1797, Gridario Bastía 37, documents 271, 272, ASM.

41. Simonsohn, *History of the Jews in the Duchy of Mantua*, 96.

42. *Giornale degli Amici della Libertà Italiana*, no. 6, 7 March 1797. Even before Bonaparte arrived, the municipal government started to appropriate a lot of money for these civic events. A payment to Giambatta Ferrari on 28 February for five hundred ribbons for the administrators plus publication of one issue of the avvisi announcing Bonaparte's expected arrival cost the government 268 lire. Busta 108, document 296, ASM.

43. *Giornale degli Amici della Libertà Italiana*, no. 6, 7 March 1797.

44. "Campagnes d'Italie," *Correspondance de Napoleon Ier*, 29:275. The custodian of the ancient Gonzaga ducal palace, Filippo Martignoni, presented a bill for Bonaparte's stay that amounted to 45,271 Mantuan lire. The items he listed as taken by Bonaparte's staff included ninety-four damask pattern napkins, five beautiful paintings, a group of bronze statuettes, and a lot of bedding. Luzio, *Francesi e Giacobini*, 22.

45. Bonaparte to Berthier, 2 March 1797, *Correspondance de Napoleon Ier*, no. 1531, 2:465.

46. Bonaparte to Berthier, 2 March 1797, *Correspondance de Napoleon Ier*, no. 1532, 2:466.

47. Six, *Dictionnaire Biographique*, 2:452.

48. Bonaparte to Berthier, 2 March 1797, *Correspondance de Napoleon Ier*, no. 1532, 2:466.

49. Bonaparte to Berthier, 2 March 1797, *Correspondance de Napoleon Ier*, no. 1533, 2:467.

50. Bonaparte to Administrative Commission of Mantua, 8 March 1797, in Arts & Autographes, *Napoléon et son temps*, 128. Bonaparte departed Mantua on 8 March, so this was one of his last administrative actions while at Mantua. The other half of the property of the abbey was to be divided, with two-thirds going to the French army and one-third to the people of San Benedetto. Any property that the abbey had in the territory of the Cisalpine Republic or in Lombardy was to be forfeited to the army, and the abbey itself was to be made available to establish a military hospital. The monks were to return to a convent in the province where they were born unless they were from Mantua. In that case they would go to convents in Pavia or Milan. The last article dictated that the administrative commission of conquered lands and the Municipalità of Mantua were charged with executing this order.

51. "Campagnes d'Italie," *Correspondance de Napoleon Ier*, 29:275.

52. Bonaparte to Directory, 10 February 1797, *Correspondance de Napoléon Ier*, no. 1474, 2:408.

53. Avviso, 9 March 1797, Gridario Bastía 37, document 294, ASM.

54. Busta 108, document 296, ASM. Commander of Engineers Sanson was given 10,786 lire, 2 soldi, 6 denari to pay for materials and the wages of construction laborers.

55. Maubert, *Exposé de ce qui s'est passé pendant le blocus et le siège de Mantoue et des causes qui ont le plus contribué a sa Reddition*, MR 439, Service Historique.

56. "Campagnes d'Italie," *Correspondance de Napoleon Ier*, 29:275.

57. Bonaparte to Berthier, 2 March 1797, *Correspondance de Napoléon Ier*, no. 1534, 2:467–68.

58. Luzio, *Francesi e Giacobini*, 20.

59. *Giornale degli Amici della Libertà Italiana*, no. 14, 4 April 1797.

60. *Marine Militare*, 8 February 1798, Busta 202, Marina, Archivio di Stato Milano; *Navigazione-Barche*, 5 December 1797, Busta 13, Municipalità, documents 181, 182, ASM. The boats were seized by the French, and the local owners requested reparations.

61. Avviso, 2 March 1797, Gridario Bastía 37, document 273, ASM.
62. Bonaparte to the Municipality of Mantua, 6 March 1797, in Luzio, *Francesi e Giacobini*, 20.
63. Luzio, *Francesi e Giacobini*, 22–23.
64. Bonaparte to Haller, 6 March 1797, *Correspondance de Napoléon Ier*, no. 1547, 2:478–79.
65. Order of the Commander in Chief, *Correspondance de Napoléon Ier*, no. 1548, 2:479–81.
66. Proclamation to the soldiers of the Army of Italy, 10 March 1797, *Correspondance de Napoléon Ier*, no. 1552, 2:482–84.
67. *Giornale degli Amici della Libertà Italiana*, no. 10, 21 March 1797.
68. "Campagnes d'Italie," *Correspondance de Napoleon Ier*, 29:275.
69. The literary works were returned after the wars, but unfortunately for the people of Mantua, the major works of art were lost to them forever. These works included wonderful tapestries and paintings of the Verona countryside. Luzio, *Francesi e Giacobini*, 23.
70. Bonaparte to Berthier, 4 March 1797, *Correspondance de Napoléon Ier*, no. 1540, 2:470.
71. Bonaparte to Berthier, 5 March 1797, *Correspondance de Napoléon Ier*, no. 1542, 2:472. The notice was published in both French and Italian on one sheet and bore the names Bonaparte, Berthier, and Miollis at the bottom of the document. This order, distributed widely throughout the city, was one of the very few notices disseminated with Bonaparte's name, which he had appended to emphasize its importance. Generally, the notices included the name of one or more of the members of the Municipalità. Avviso, 5 March 1797, Gridario Bastía 37, document 279, ASM.
72. Order, 6 March 1797, *Correspondance de Napoléon Ier*, no. 1546, 2:476–78; Avviso, 9 March 1797, Gridario Bastía 37, document 297, ASM. The avviso added an article to Bonaparte's requirements.
73. Order, 6 March 1797, *Correspondance de Napoléon Ier*, no. 1546, 2:476–78.
74. *Giornale degli Amici della Libertà Italiana*, no. 8, 14 March 1797.
75. Ibid., no. 7, 11 March 1797.
76. Ibid., no. 9, 18 March 1797.
77. Giuseppe Lahoz to the Patriots of the Mantovano, 8 March 1797, Gridario Bastía 37, document 292, ASM; Bonaparte to Miollis, 18 June 1797, *Correspondance de Napoléon Ier*, no. 1937, 3:178–79.
78. Bonaparte to Berthier, 14 June and 14 July 1797, *Correspondance de Napoléon Ier*, nos. 1919 and 2013, 3:160–63, 241–42.
79. Smith, *Napoleon's Regiments*, 222.
80. Volta to Bonaparte, 15 June 1797, in D'Onofrio, "L'Archivio della Municipalità di Mantova," 142.
81. Ibid., 143.
82. To the Lombards, Orders, 29 June 1797, *Correspondance de Napoléon Ier*, nos. 1966 and 1967, 3:203–204.
83. Volta, *Storia di Mantova*, 5:385.

84. Haller to Frazzini, 15 July 1797, in D'Onofrio, "L'Archivio della Municipalità di Mantova," 144–45.

85. *Giornale degli Amici della Libertà Italiana*, no. 44, 18 July 1797.

86. Bonaparte to Directory, 10 October 1797, *Correspondance de Napoleon Ier*, no. 2296, 3:495–97.

87. Definitive Treaty of Peace, 17 October 1797, *Correspondance de Napoléon Ier*, no. 2303, 3:502–509.

88. Volta, *Storia di Mantova*, 5:398–400. The famous master better known as Giulio Romano is referred to by Arrivabene as Giulio Pippi.

89. *Giornale degli Amici della Libertà Italiana*, no. 36, 20 June 1797.

90. Luzio, *Francesi e Giacobini*, 104–107.

91. Notice, 17 October 1797, *Correspondance de Napoléon Ier*, no. 2301, 3:500–501.

92. *Giornale degli Amici della Libertà Italiana*, no. 75, 2 November 1797. It is not clear whether Baste made another cannon firing demonstration during this visit as he did for other celebrations. During a mock battle exhibition during the 15 October festival of Virgil, the gunboats *Buonaparte* and *Miollis* fired on the *Berthier*, *Masséna*, and *Dallemagne*, and an accidental shot from a cannon seriously wounded some of the marines. Luzio, *Francesi e Giacobini*, 106–107.

93. To the Cisalpine People, 11 November 1797, *Correspondance de Napoleon Ier*, no. 2351, 3:570–71.

94. Bonaparte to Directory, 12 November 1797, *Correspondance de Napoleon Ier*, no. 2354, 3:573–74.

95. Bonaparte to Directory, 26 November 1797, *Correspondance de Napoleon Ier*, no. 2379, 3:595. Bonaparte departed on the 27th and spent the night at Turin, then continued on to Chambéry.

96. Finzi, *Giornale degli Amici della Libertà Italiana*, 110–12.

97. Volta, *Storia di Mantova*, 5:403.

98. Ibid., 400.

99. Bonaparte to Directory, 27 March 1798, *Correspondance de Napoleon Ier*, no. 2456, 4:35–36; Orders, 29 June 1797, *Correspondance de Napoleon Ier*, no. 1967, 3:204.

100. Volta, *Storia di Mantova*, 5:410. Arivabenne gives the number of the garrison in March 1798 as 25,000 men. One archival source gives the number of effectives at Mantua on 27 January 1798 as 6,774 men. Busta 82, document 301, ASM.

101. Luzio, *Francesi e Giacobini*, 192.

102. Finzi, *Giornale degli Amici della Libertà Italiana*, 139.

103. Volta, *Storia di Mantova*, 5:417; Finzi, *Giornale degli Amici della Libertà Italiana*, 153.

104. Finzi, *Giornale degli Amici della Libertà Italiana*, 153–54. Scherer's assignment allowed the previous commander, Joubert, to lead the French war effort in the German lands. When Joubert visited Mantua on 19 November 1798, the theater and homes of the French supporters were festively illuminated that night.

105. Luzio, *Francesi e Giacobini*, 199.

106. Foissac-Latour, *Précis*, 2:10. (Hereafter cited as *Précis* sans author's name.) Latour divided this work into two parts with the second part consisting of letters and justifications for his actions.

9. Enter Kray and Suvorov

Epigraph. Bonaparte to Kléber, 22 August 1799, *Correspondance de Napoléon Ier*, no. 4374, 5:734–38.

1. Ibid.
2. Decree, 12 April 1798, *Correspondance de Napoléon Ier*, no. 2492, 4:67–68.
3. Order, 22 and 23 June 1798, *Correspondance de Napoléon Ier*, nos. 2705 and 2706, 4:250–52.
4. Order, 27 June 1798, *Correspondance de Napoleon Ier*, no. 2707, 4:253–54.
5. Jomini, *Histoire des Guerres*, 11:150–52.
6. Di Scala, *Italy*, 25.
7. Paul Freiherr von Kray von Krajow was born on 3 February 1735 in Käsmark, Hungary. He died on 19 January 1804, in Pest (now Budapest). In 1754 he joined the Haller Infantry Regiment No. 31. He was made an ensign on 16 April 1757, a second lieutenant by the end of the year, and on 22 May 1759 a first lieutenant. He fought during the Seven Years' War and was severely wounded at the Battle of Liegnitz in 1760. In 1764 he was made a company commander and was promoted to captain on 1 March 1766. He was promoted to major in 1778 and lieutenant colonel in 1783 and then transferred to the 2nd *Székler Grenz* (border) Infantry Regiment. In 1785 he was made a colonel and in 1786 commander of the 1st Wallachian *Grenz* Regiment, which he led during the Austro-Turkish War in 1788. He was promoted to major general in 1790 and awarded the title of baron. He served in the Netherlands in 1791 and continued to serve in Belgium and Germany until 1796 when he was promoted to field marshal lieutenant. Kray, *Briefe des Feldzeugmeisters Paul Freiherrn Kray*, 5; Wurzbach, *Biographisches Lexikon des Kaiserthums Österreich*, 13:161–68.
8. Aleksandr Vasilievich Count Suvorov Rimniesky was born at Moscow on 24 November 1729. His father was a Swede who immigrated to Russia in 1622. He entered the army at a young age and served against the Swedes in Finland and against the Prussians during the Seven Years' War. He was promoted to colonel in 1762 after distinguishing himself in battle. He then served in Poland, participated in the storming of Kraków (1768), and was made a major general. He fought against the Turks in 1773–74. He was made a lieutenant general in 1780 and general of infantry in 1783 after his campaigns in the Crimea and the Caucasus. He won many victories fighting against the Turks once again in 1788–91 and was at Kinburn. With his great victory on the Rimnik in 1788, Catherine II made him a count with the name Rimniksky in addition to his own name, and Emperor Joseph II created

him a count of the Holy Roman Empire. After fighting in Bessarabia in 1790, he was given command of the army that subdued the Poles. He was then made a field marshal and was retained in Poland until 1795. After Catherine died in 1796, her successor, Paul, dismissed Suvorov in disgrace. He retired near Moscow until February 1799, when he was summoned by the czar to take the field again, this time against the French in Italy. *Encyclopaedia Britannica,* 26:172–73.

9. Kray, *Briefe des Feldzeugmeisters Paul Freiherrn Kray,* 10.
10. Di Scala, *Italy,* 254; Jomini, *Histoire des Guerres,* 11:154, 172–76.
11. Jomini, *Histoire des Guerres,* 11:179. In addition to the losses at Magnano, the French lost seven standards, eight cannon, and forty caissons.
12. Ibid., 199.
13. "Des Événements Militaires," *Correspondance de Napoléon Ier,* 30:314–15.
14. Phipps, *Armies of the First French Republic,* 5:258.
15. Beauvais, *Victoires, Conquêtes, Désastres,* 5:413.
16. Scherer to Directory, 7 April 1799, in Gachot, *Souvarow en Italie,* 91.
17. Phipps, *Armies of the First French Republic,* 5:260.
18. Blease, *Suvorof,* 231.
19. Beauvais, *Victoires, Conquêtes, Désastres,* 5:419.
20. Phipps, *Armies of the First French Republic,* 5:262.
21. Rodger, *War of the Second Coalition,* 162.
22. Beauvais, *Victoires, Conquêtes, Désastres,* 5:501–502.
23. Rodger, *War of the Second Coalition,* 162.
24. Duffy, *Eagles over the Alps,* 119–21.
25. Rodger, *War of the Second Coalition,* 162.
26. Suvorov to Rasumowski, 27 May 1799, in Macready, *Sketch of Suwarow,* 95–96.
27. Ibid., 96–97.
28. Blease, *Suvorof,* 244.
29. Heriot, *The French in Italy,* 247. "The Marches" is the region in central Italy on the Adriatic coast around the port city of Ancona.
30. Rodger, *War of the Second Coalition,* 162.
31. Ibid., 163.
32. Miljutin, *Istorija vojny Rossii,* 2:230–31; Blease, *Suvorof,* 245.
33. Suvorov to Rosenberg, 13 June 1799, in Miljutin, *Istorija vojny Rossii,* 2:246.
34. Jomini, *Histoire des Guerres,* 11:350.
35. Macready, *Sketch of Suwarow,* 71.
36. Jomini, *Histoire des Guerres,* 11:386.
37. Macdonald, *Recollections of Marshal Macdonald,* 1:268; Jomini, *Histoire des Guerres,* 11:341–43.
38. Duffy, *Eagles over the Alps,* 110. Duffy estimated that the total French losses at the Battle of the Trebbia may have been as high as 12,000.
39. Francis II to Suvorov, 21 June 1799; Russian Order of Battle (24 June–22 July)—both in Miljutin, *Istorija vojny Rossii,* 2:608–609, 639. Suvorov

also received another letter from the Austrian emperor, written on 10 July, that was focused on his army capturing Mantua. Miljutin, *Istorija vojny Rossii*, 2:610-12.

40. [Graham], *History of the Campaign of 1799,* 183; Botta, *Storia d'Italia dal 1789 al 1814,* 3:332.

41. Duffy, *Eagles over the Alps,* 136-39.

42. Duffy, *Russia's Military Way,* 214.

43. Bonaparte to Desaix, 11 August 1799, *Correspondance de Napoléon Ier,* no. 4341, 5:709-11.

44. Bonaparte to Kléber, 22 August 1799, *Correspondance de Napoléon Ier,* no. 4374, 5:734-38.

45. Bonaparte to Berthier and "Arête," 4 February 17976 and 6 March 1797, *Correspondance de Napoléon Ier,* nos. 1453 and 1546, 2:389-91, 476-78.

46. Bonaparte to Poussielgue, 22 August 1799, *Correspondance de Napoléon Ier,* no. 4378, 5:740. Poussielgue later wrote to Menou stating that he was persuaded that Bonaparte had good reasons to return, but that he would never forgive him for making it a mystery to the men who always shared his confidence, and who were charged with the burden of the government. Poussielgue to Menou, 7 September 1799, in Berthier, *Mémoires du Maréchal Berthier,* no. 9, 1:228-29.

47. *Retour de Général Bonaparte en Europe,* 15 October 1799, *Correspondance de Napoléon Ier,* no. 4383, 5:743-46.

10. Foissac-Latour and the Defense of 1799

Epigraph 1. Gachot, *Soubarow en Italie,* 347.
Epigraph 2. Correspondance Militaire de Napoléon Ier, 10:204.

1. Scherer to Foissac-Latour, 21 March 1799, *Précis,* no. 8, 2:10. The actual selection of Latour to command Mantua, as for all other high commands, was made by the Directory. Jomini, *Histoire des Guerres,* 12:35. The general's last name, Foissac-Latour, is sometimes given as Latour-Foissac. I will refer to him as Latour for convenience.

2. Foissac-Latour to Scherer, 24 March 1799, *Précis,* no. 9, 2:10-12. In his letter to Scherer he did, however, say that he would leave Lucca promptly for Mantua. He stated that he was not idle and had taken from the clergy the necessary funds (500,000 francs) for the fortification and artillery of Lucca but was not clear as to what actually happened to the money. Throughout Latour's time as commander of the fortifications of Lucca and Mantua, he was extremely concerned with finances.

3. Maubert, *Relation du Blocus et du Siége de Mantoue,* 56-57; Six, *Dictionnaire Biographique,* 2:68-69; *Biographie universelle, ancienne et moderne: Supplément* 70:349.

4. Foissac-Latour and Michaud d'Arcon, *Examen détaillé;* Foissac-Latour, *Traité théorie pratique.*

5. Vauban, *Traité de l'attaque des places;* Vauban, *Traité de la défense des places;* Vauban, *Traité des mines.*

6. Foissac-Latour, *Observations sur un écrit en faveur des Juifs d'Alsace,* 1. Other anti-Semitic works by Latour are *Observations sur la*

possibilité et l'utilité de l'admission des Juifs en Alsace aux droits de citoyens and *Plaidoyer contre les Juifs des Évêchés.*

7. Foissac-Latour, *Plaidoyer contre les Juifs des Évêchés;* Foissac-Latour, *Le cri du citoyen contre les Juifs de Metz.*

8. Foissac-Latour, *Discours sur le rétablissement momentané de la Gabelle;* Foissac-Latour, *Ministère de la Police Générale de la République;* Foissac-Latour, *Le Chantre de la liberte, poesies fugitives et patriotiques.*

9. *Le Procès-verbaux du Directoire Exécutif an V–an VIII,* NA; Jomini, *Histoire des Guerres,* 12:36; Foissac-Latour to Scherer, 8 August 1798, *Précis,* no. 3, 2:4; Six, *Dictionnaire Biographique,* 2:69. Six points out that the order was given on 1 April 1798, three days after the Directory selected him for the survey assignment.

10. Foissac-Latour to Scherer, 28 June 1798, *Précis,* no. 1, 2:1–3; Foissac-Latour to Dabon, 6 August 1798, *Précis,* no. 2, 2:3–4.

11. Foissac-Latour to Scherer, 8 August 1798, *Précis,* no. 3, 2:4–5.

12. Foissac-Latour to Scherer, 8 August 1798, *Précis,* nos. 4 and 5, 2:5–7.

13. Jomini, *Histoire des Guerres,* 12:36. Jomini's only acknowledged source was Foissac-Latour's book that was written as a legal justification for the rapid surrendering of the fortress after a breach in the Pradella ravelin just in front of the Pradella gate.

14. Order of the Day, 30 March 1799, *Précis,* no. 10, 2:12–13.

15. Foissac-Latour to Scherer, 31 March 1799, *Précis,* no. 11, 2:13–14.

16. "Rapports des Espions et de la Police," Papers of Foissac-Latour.

17. [Graham], *History of the Campaign of 1799,* 36, 37.

18. "Substance des Lettres du General Foissac La Tour," Papers of Foissac-Latour, 1–18 April 1799, 3.

19. Avviso, 8 April 1799, *Avvisi 1799,* 141, Biblioteca Comunale di Mantova (hereafter cited as BCM).

20. Ibid., 142.

21. *Giornale dei Fatti d'Arme,* 10, 11, BCM.

22. Foissac-Latour, *Mémoire du général de division Foissac-Latour,* 41–46.

23. Schnur-Popławski, *Dzieje Legionow Polskich,* 131. Here Schnur-Popławski uses Kniaziewicz's work.

24. Proclamation, Foissac-Latour, 10 April 1799, Busta 208, document 187, ASM.

25. Busta 160, documents 1–6, ASM; Volta, *Storia di Mantova,* 5:436–37; Luzio, *Francesi e Giacobini,* 201.

26. [Graham], *History of the Campaign of 1799,* 39.

27. Ibid., 39, 40.

28. Avviso, 24 April 1799, *Avvisi 1799,* 155, BCM.

29. Avviso, 25 April 1799, *Avvisi 1799,* 154, BCM.

30. "Finances, situation des caisses," Papers of Foissac-Latour.

31. Avviso, 25 April 1799, *Avvisi 1799,* 154, BCM.

32. "Finances, situation des caisses," Papers of Foissac-Latour.

33. Ibid.; *Précis,* 1:49.

34. *Proclama Soldati Francesi, ed Alleati della Francia del Presidio di Mantova,* 4 May 1799, Opuscolo 5665, ASM.

35. Luzio, *Francesi e Giacobini,* 201.

36. Ibid.
37. "Finances, situation des caisses," Papers of Foissac-Latour.
38. The fourteen officials Porro arrested were Luigi Maria Predaval, head of the Chamber of Commerce; Leopoldo Camillo Volta, the influential lawyer, scholar, and library inspector; Canon Fioratti, a theologian and orator; Giovanni Guardini, vice prefect of waterworks; Gaetano Mancina, official of the confidential archive; Pietro Malagutti, doctor of law; Giuseppe Maria Cerudelli, chancellor for tax payments; Antonio Battaglia, bookkeeper; Francesco Maschera, official of the justice tribunal; Canon Mancina; Abbot Francesco Muti; Francesco Goltara; Giacobbe Basilea; and Pietro Bertazzoni.
39. P[redaval], *Saggio della Rigenerazione*, 23–24; P[redaval], *Supplemento al Saggio della Rigenerazione*, 3–7—both in Opuscolo 5672, ASM.
40. P[redaval], *Supplemento al Saggio della Rigenerazione*, 8–11, Opuscolo 5672, ASM. After the Austrians retook the city, Predaval and Volta would return to Mantua, where Predaval published an account of these events in 1799 and Volta eventually began work on a general history of Mantua.
41. Luzio, *Francesi e Giacobini*, 202.
42. Ibid., 204–205.
43. Antonio Baracchi to Foissac Latour, 10 June 1799, in Portioli, *La Zecca di Mantova*, 42–45.
44. *Giornale dei Fatti d'Arme*, 18, BCM; Portioli, *La Zecca di Mantova*, 45.
45. Busta 179, documents 280, 281; Latour to Virgiliana Academy of Sciences, 1 June 1799, *Précis*, 2:187–88; Luzio, *Francesi e Giacobini*, 202–203.
46. Portioli, *La Zecca di Mantova*, 53.
47. Proclamation, 18 June 1799, in Pescasio, *Mantova 1799*, 58.
48. Portioli, *La Zecca di Mantova*, 44–45.
49. Ibid., 54.
50. The local government needed money to function during the siege. Expenses mounted daily. Some examples of these payments are 60.16.8 Milanese (lire, scudi, denari) to Giacomo Targa for his contract burials of seventy-three soldiers during the month of messidor (19 June to 18 July) and 659.10.8 (lire, scudi, denari) to various workers at the hospital of S. Leonardo. Busta 17, Municipalità, Protocollo Appuntimenti presi della Municipalità, ASM.
51. "Substance des Lettres du General Foissac La Tour," 11 May 1799, 29, Papers of Foissac-Latour.
52. Girardelet to Foissac-Latour, 11 May 1799, "Lettres des officiers Généraux," 5, Papers of Foissac-Latour.
53. Borthon to Foissac-Latour, 12 May 1799, "Lettres des officiers Généraux," 9. The commanders of the 1st demibrigade of Cisalpine troops, the 7th Regiment of Dragoons, the 3rd Battalion of the 15th demibrigade and the 31st demibrigade responded in a similar manner. Eugene to Foissac-Latour, Deslisle to Foissac-Latour, Malbrun to Foissac-Latour, and Fédon to Foissac-Latour, 12 May 1799, "Lettres des officiers Généraux," 4, 6, 10, 3, Papers of Foissac-Latour.

54. Armand-Gros to Foissac-Latour, 12 May 1799, "Lettres des officiers Généraux," 8, Papers of Foissac-Latour.

55. Jouardet to Foissac-Latour, 12 May 1799, "Lettres des officiers Généraux," 7, Papers of Foissac-Latour.

56. *Précis*, 1:43.

57. Report from San Giorgio, 9 June 1799, "Rapports des Espions et de la Police," 10, Papers of Foissac-Latour.

58. Gachot, *Souvarow en Italie*, 324–25.

59. Jomini, *Histoire des Guerres*, 12:37.

60. Maubert, *Relation du Blocus et du Siége de Mantoue*, 9–10. Initially, Maubert, an engineer, was posted at San Giorgio.

61. Ibid., 10.

62. Beauvais, *Victoires, Conquêtes, Désastres*, 5:501–502.

63. Duffy, *Eagles over the Alps*, 123.

64. Report of Bartès and Report of Baron, *Précis*, 2:129–34.

65. Meyer to Latour, 10 May 1799, in Foissac-Latour, *Précis*, 2:127–29.

66. Maubert, *Relation du Blocus et du Siége de Mantoue*, 11.

67. Girard, *Rapport du chef de bataillon Girard, commandant l'avant-garde de droite, sous les ordres du chef de brigade Balleydier, au gènèral en chef*, *Précis*, 2:135–37.

68. Balleydier, 12 May 1799, *Récit historique des opérations militaires de la colonne commandée par le soussigné, chef de la 29.ᵉ légère, sortie le 19 floréal à deux et demie du matin, par la porte Pradella de Mantoue*, *Précis*, 2:134–35. Captain Ferrier of the 7th Dragoons made a daring escape with his unit. For the sortie he commanded his squadron of dragoons along with another squadron of the Piedmontese Carbineers, forming the advance guard of Balleydier's main column. When Balleydier turned to go to the Cerese gate, Captain Ferrier's unit acted as the rear guard. He charged the Austrians, had his horse killed under him, and the main body abandoned him, his artillery, and his wounded. Left to his own defense, he gathered his forces and charged an Austrian column and recaptured the cannon he had recently lost near Cerese. They turned the cannon around and fired at the Austrians. This bolstered the spirits of some nearby French infantrymen, who came to his aid. He gathered his wounded and returned with them through the Pradella gate along with his cannon and some Austrian prisoners. Beauvais, *Victoires, Conquêtes, Désastres*, 5:598–99.

69. Wielhorski, *Rapport du front de Migliaretto*, and Dembowski, *Rapport du chef de brigade Dembowski, commandant en second la colonne sortie par la porte Cerezia, au gènèral Foissac-Latour, commandant en chef*, *Précis*, 2:123–27.

70. François Pagés to Foissac-Latour, 8 May 1799, *Précis*, 2:139.

71. The pyramid was destroyed by the Austrians and Russians when they occupied the area in 1799. Luzio, *Francesi e Giacobini*, 106–107.

72. Chapuis, *Rapport de l'affaire qui a eu lieu au lac inférieur*, *Précis*, 2:140.

73. Maubert, *Relation du Blocus et du Siége de Mantoue*, 11. The Austrian loss of 290 prisoners does not take into account their other casualties (killed and wounded).

74. Leclerc, *Observations*, 12.

75. *Précis*, 2:188–89.

76. Kray to Latour, 25 June, *Précis*, 2:218; *Giornale dei Fatti d'Arme*, 27–28, BCM; Leclerc, *Observations*, 19–20.

77. *Giornale dei Fatti d'Arme*, 28, BCM.

78. Beauvais, *Victoires, Conquêtes, Désastres*, 5:596; Mikaberidze, *Russian Officer Corps*, 321. Magnus (Maxim) Woldemar von Rehbinder was born in 1730 to a noble Westphalian family. He enlisted in 1759 and served in the Russo-Turkish War in 1769–74, earning a reputation as a recklessly courageous officer. In the 1787–91 Russo-Turkish War, he distinguished himself in the Kuban Valley campaign. In 1799 he fought at the Adda and Trebbia Rivers and at Novi.

79. [Graham], *History of the Campaign of 1799*, 183–84.

80. Jomini, *Histoire des Guerres*, 12:37.

81. *Journal Uber Mantuas Belagerung*, 1799.7.3, OSK; Jomini, *Histoire des Guerres*, 7:38; Miljutin, *Istorija vojny Rossii*, 2:391–99.

82. Jomini, *Histoire des Guerres*, 12:39; [Graham], *History of the Campaign of 1799*, 184–85; Chodźko, *Histoire des legions Polonaises*, 201.

83. *Giornale dei Fatti d'Arme*, 31–32, BCM; Leclerc, *Observations*, 19–20.

84. Kray to Latour, 11 July 1799, *Précis*, 2:240–41. Latour added the emphasis and then explained in a note, "I could take this ambiguous sentence in a seductive way: one will see how I knew to respond." This particular note was number 145, in which Latour explained the awkward irregularities during his command. *Précis*, 2:477.

85. *Giornale dei Fatti d'Arme*, 31, BCM.

86. Ibid.

87. *Précis*, 2:144, 188–89; *Giornale dei Fatti d'Arme*, 29, BCM.

88. Latour to Kray, 11 July 1799, *Précis*, 2:240. Latour put *"and some good news I received"* in italics in his book and then stated in an endnote that this has been the source of his "crime." He states that the "good news" he received was from a spy (2:477).

89. *Giornale dei Fatti d'Arme*, 31–32, BCM.

90. *Registre de correspondance du général Foissac-Latour*, 11 July 1799, 5; Latour to Kray, 11 July 1799, *Précis*, 2:241.

91. *Registre de correspondance du général Foissac-Latour*, 11 July 1799, 5; Latour to Kray, 11 July 1799 (two letters), *Précis*, 2:240, 241; *Giornale dei Fatti d'Arme*, 31–32, BCM; Woyda, *Briefe über Italien*, 3:387–88; Leclerc, *Observations*, 19–20; Volta, *Storia di Mantova*, 443–44. Of the two letters Latour wrote on 11 July, one was the negative response to the request for surrender; the other was his request for the 14 July armistice. The letter detailing the planned events of 14 July was delivered by Gastine on the morning of 12 July. There is no account of Gastine, or any officer for that matter, going out of the fortress on 11 July with the exception of Latour himself. Latour's negative response letter, to

the summons for surrender, mentions Zach's visit and also mentions that Gastine would deliver another letter for a "different purpose" on the 12th. This would indicate that both letters were written late on the 11th—after it was impossible to deliver them during the day of the 11th. In Latour's book, there is no indication when either was written. Latour places the armistice request letter in his book before the 11 July letter that Zach delivered to indicate that he made the armistice decision before Zach's visit. This is highly improbable because Zach came early in the day and the letter was not delivered until the following day. It would stand to reason that the armistice request letter was written after the council of war that took place after Zach's visit. This is one of many examples in the accounts in Latour's book where the author tries to put himself in the best light by the way he presents the events.

92. Leclerc, *Observations*, 19–20.

93. *Précis*, 1:43–44.

94. Kray to Suvorov, n.d., in Miljutin, *Istorija vojny Rossii*, no. 231, 2:639 (referenced on 399).

95. *Journal Uber Mantuas Belagerung*, 1799.7.3.f, 1799.7.3.g, and 1799.7.3.h, OSK.

96. Miljutin, *Istorija vojny Rossii*, 2:399; Jomini, *Histoire des Guerres*, 12:39.

97. Busta 17, Municipalità, Protocollo Appuntimenti presi della Municipalità, ASM.

98. Ibid.; Leclerc, *Observations*, 13. Latour had decided to build a nice promenade on 8 June. *Précis*, 2:197.

99. Woyda, *Briefe über Italien*, 3:389; *Précis*, 2:265–70. Latour made two speeches and Gastine made one.

100. Volta, *Storia di Mantova*, 5:444; Woyda, *Briefe über Italien*, 3:389; *Giornale dei Fatti d'Arme*, 32, BCM; Miljutin, *Istorija vojny Rossii*, 2:399; Gachot, *Souvarow en Italie*, 341; P. L[abadie?]., *Détail Circonstancié*, 11 (Labadie's first name is unknown); Maubert, *Relation du Blocus et du Siége de Mantoue*, 16; Busta 17, Municipalità, Protocollo Appuntimenti presi della Municipalità, ASM.

101. *Journal Uber Mantuas Belagerung*, 1799.7.3.f, 1799.7.3.g, and 1799.7.3.h, OSK.

102. Miljutin, *Istorija vojny Rossii*, 2:400.

103. *Journal Uber Mantuas Belagerung*, 1799.7.3.i, 1799.7.3.k, 1799.7.3.l, and 1799.7.3.m, OSK; Jomini, *Histoire des Guerres*, 12:40.

104. Paul Kray to Alexander Kray, 22 July 1799, in Kray, *Briefe des Feldzeugmeisters Paul Freiherrn Kray*, 259.

105. *Journal Uber Mantuas Belagerung*, 1799.7.3.m, OSK.

106. Ibid.; Maubert, *Relation du Blocus et du Siége de Mantoue*, 17–19; Jomini, *Histoire des Guerres*, 12:41.

107. Jomini, *Histoire des Guerres*, 12:41–42; Miljutin, *Istorija vojny Rossii*, 2:400–401; Maubert, *Relation du Blocus et du Siége de Mantoue*, 20; *Journal Uber Mantuas Belagerung*, 1799.7.ad2, 1799.7.3.m, 1799.7.3.n, and 1799.7.3.o, OSK.

108. *Procès-verbal de la sèance du conseil de guerre de défense de la place de Mantoue*, du 7 thermidor, *Précis*, 2:338–40.

109. *Journal Uber Mantuas Belagerung*, 1799.7.3.0, OSK; *Journal de l'armèe assiègeants*, *Précis*, 2:342; P. L[abadie?], *Détail Circonstancié*, 7, 9–10.

110. Woyda, *Briefe über Italien*, 3:387, 389; P. L[abadie?], *Détail Circonstancié*, 9–10.

111. *Journal Uber Mantuas Belagerung*, 1799.7.3.0, OSK; *Journal de l'armèe assiègeants*, *Précis*, 2:342; P. L[abadie?], *Détail Circonstancié*, 7, 9–10.

112. Borthon to Latour, 26 July 1799, *Précis*, 2:345–46.

113. *Procès-verbal de la sèance du conseil de guerre de dèfense*, du 8 thermidor, *Précis*, 2:347–49.

114. Jomini, *Histoire des Guerres*, 12:45–46; *Journal Uber Mantuas Belagerung*, 1799.7.3.p, OSK.

115. *Giornale dei Fatti d'Arme*, 39, BCM; *Journal Uber Mantuas Belagerung*, 1799.7.3.q, OSK.

116. Kray to Foissac-Latour, 28 July 1799, *Précis*, no. 408, 2:373; [Graham], *History of the Campaign of 1799*, 189; *Giornale dei Fatti d'Arme*, 39, BCM. Two years earlier Orlandini was with the Austrian forces inside Mantua when the French besieged the city.

117. Maubert, *Relation du Blocus et du Siége de Mantoue*, 7; Latour, *Mémoire du général de division Foissac-Latour*, 40–44; *Précis*, 2:364–68. The version of this council of war (*Mémoire, Séance du 9 thermidor, an 7 de la république française, une et indivisible*) in Latour's first book, *Mémoire du général de division Foissac-Latour*, varies slightly from that in *Précis*.

118. Schnur-Popławski, *Dzieje Legionow Polskich*, 136–37. Here Schnur-Popławski uses Kniaziewicz's work.

119. *Giornale dei Fatti d'Arme*, 39, BCM.

120. Latour, *Mémoire du général de division Foissac-Latour*, 40–44; *Précis*, 2:364–68.

121. *Précis*, 2:369–71; *Journal Uber Mantuas Belagerung*, 1799.7.3.q, OSK.

122. Schnur-Popławski, *Dzieje Legionow Polskich*, 137.

123. *Précis*, 2:372–73.

124. Schnur-Popławski, *Dzieje Legionow Polskich*, 137.

125. Leclerc, *Observations*, 8.

126. See Paul Kray to Alexander Kray, 24 August 1799, in Kray, *Briefe des Feldzeugmeisters Paul Freiherrn Kray*, 260. In this letter, Kray states that he hopes Alexander received his letter from Mantua on 28 July in which he describes the "lucky case" of this fortress. Unfortunately, as Just notes, this particular letter was missing from the collection of letters to his brother Alexander that was held at the Kriegsarchiv in 1909 when it was published.

127. Jomini, *Histoire des Guerres*, 12:46.

128. *Précis*, 1:72; Jomini, *Histoire des Guerres*, 12:47–48.

129. Jomini, *Histoire des Guerres*, 12:47.

130. Schnur-Popławski, *Dzieje Legionow Polskich*, 138–40.

131. Portioli, *La Zecca di Mantova*, 41.
132. Gachot, *Souvarow en Italie*, 347.
133. Avviso, 31 July 1799, in Pescasio, *Mantova 1799*, 110. Radetzky wasted no time in posting an avviso in the city calling for artisans, carpenters, wheelwrights, builders, blacksmiths, masons, miners, and those with similar skills to join his pioneer corps.
134. Cantù, *Grande Illustration*, 377.
135. Avviso, 1 August 1799, in Pescasio, *Mantova 1799*, 106.
136. Jomini, *Histoire des Guerres*, 12:47–48.
137. "Finances, situation des caisses," Papers of Foissac-Latour; Leclerc, *Observations*, 10–11; *Précis*, 1:49–50.
138. *Précis*, 1:72.
139. Capitulation, Article 15, section 3*1, Service Historique.
140. Ibid.; *Précis*, 1:49–50.
141. Bourrienne, *Mémoirs de M. de Bourrienne*, 3:247; [Graham], *History of the Campaign of 1799*, 193.
142. Bonaparte to Carnot, 24 July 1800, *Correspondance de Napoléon Ier*, no. 5019, 6:529–30.
143. [Graham], *History of the Campaign of 1799*, 190–91. Latour had at least six months' worth of provisions in the magazines, which the Austrians, upon their entry into Mantua, claimed could have lasted for a year. Stutterheim, "Geschiechte des Feldzugs," 9, Österreichisches Staatsarchiv, Kriegs Bibliothek.
144. Botta, *History of Italy during the Consulate and Empire*, 1:50, 51.
145. The flight of two thousand Austrians from Milan into the citadel of Milan on 9 May 1796—where they held out until 29 June—provides a good historical example of what Latour might have accomplished at Mantua.

Conclusion

1. Clausewitz, *On War*, 162.
2. Kray to Latour, 14 and 15 May 1799, "Correspondance des officers genereaux Austrichiens et autres officers de l'Empereur," Papers of Foissac-Latour. Several prisoner exchanges took place in mid-May after the 8 May sortie. Both sides took more than two hundred prisoners.
3. This significant Russian contribution is diminished by the account of Jomini and the works of Joseph Sutterheim, both of whom give the Russian participation short shrift, merely acknowledging their presence.
4. Bernadotte to Council in Genoa, 22 August 1799, *Précis*, ix–x.
5. Bonaparte to Carnot, 24 July 1800, *Correspondance de Napoleon Ier*, no. 5019, 6:529–30. Bonaparte halted the court-martial proceedings because he felt that the premature surrender of Mantua was more an affair of honor than a legal question. He stated that he did not want to hear any more about the disgraceful siege that would be forever a stain on the French military. Bonaparte ordered that Latour was no longer allowed to wear the uniform of the French.

6. *Précis*, 1:25. *Précis* contains 32 pages of introduction and then part 1 with 103 pages in which Latour discusses in detail the thirty-two charges brought against him. Part 2 includes a text of 500 pages of Latour's defense with supporting documentation, two large foldout maps, and several charts.

7. Simonsohn, *History of the Jews in the Duchy of Mantua*, 328. During the period of French rule, the *patrioti* abolished the special rights of the Jewish community and replaced the "University of the Jews." During the Austrian return, the "university" was reinstated for some time, but was then abolished completely when the French took over again in 1801. Some French changes lingered in other areas. The coins minted by Latour were not abolished until 28 December 1799. Portioli, *La Zecca di Mantova*, 55.

8. *Recueil des Principaux Traités*, 2nd ed., 7:71, in Parry, *Consolidated Treaty Series*, 55:477–82.

9. Rath, *Provisional Austrian Regime in Lombardy-Venetia*, 5.

Epilogue

1. Bonaparte to Carnot, 24 July 1800, *Correspondance de Napoléon Ier*, no. 5019, 6:529–30.

2. Bonaparte, *Décision*, 25 August 1801, *Correspondance de Napoléon Ier*, no. 5703, 7:295.

3. Maubert, *Exposé de ce qui s'est passé pendant le blocus et le siège de Mantoue*, MR 439; "Opérations politiques et Militaires de Foissac-Latour," MR 440—both in Service Historique.

4. Bourrienne, *Mémoires de M. de Bourrienne*, 3:247–48.

5. Ibid., 248.

6. Ibid.

7. Ibid.

8. Bourrienne, *Memoirs of Napoleon Bonaparte*, 1:xi. Bourrienne's memoirs often reflect his bitter resentment toward Bonaparte for the loss of the close relationship. Marmont said that when Bourrienne "speaks of others, his work is only an assemblage of gratuitous suppositions and of false facts put forward for special purposes." Marmont (ii, 224) as quoted in Bourrienne, *Memoirs of Napoleon Bonaparte*, 1:xviii.

9. Héléodore to Bonaparte, 31 July 1800, in *Lettres de Héléodore*, 1:13–14.

10. Bonaparte, *Le Mémorial de Sainte-Hélène*, 2:154.

11. Bonaparte, *Memoirs at Saint Helena*, 1:243.

12. Moreau (de l'Yonne), *Discours Prononcé par Moreau (de l'Yonne), Sur la mort du général Joubert*, Séance, 28 August 1799.

13. Carlo Botta to Pico, 21 August 1799, *Lettere Inedite di Carlo Botta*, 161. Decades later, Botta would complete his history of Italy during the Napoleonic Wars and drastically, even suspiciously, change his view to say that Latour was thought falsely accused and that his surrender was caused neither by cowardice nor by avarice. Botta, *Storia d'Italia dal 1789 al 1814*, 3:338. Ironically, Botta was accused much later of being influenced monetarily in his presentation of history.

14. *Précis,* ix, x.
15. *Le Publiciste,* 4 fructidor an 7 (21 August 1799). In addition to the head-line, an article in the paper stated that official news about the surrender of Mantua was received in Paris on 20 August. The Leyde newspaper on 20 August published the same information in copying news received in a letter from Vienna written on 3 August stating that the Aulic Council received word that Kray accepted the surrender of Mantua on 28 July. *Supplement Aux Nouvelles Politiques Publiées à Leyde,* 20 August 1799.
16. *Précis,* 1:33–34.
17. Ibid., 1:33.
18. *Biographie universelle, ancienne et moderne, Supplément,* 61:132.
19. *Précis,* 1:36.
20. Ibid., 1:100; see also Foissac-Latour, *Foissac La Tour à la France, à ses armées, à l'Europe,* and *Supplement A L'Appel.*
21. *Précis,* 1:99, 100. This letter, written at Léoben on 7 October 1799 by Captain Békly, Second Lieutenant Wimpffen, and Staff Captain J. Bissien, was duplicated as a "certificate" in Latour's final work of exoneration.
22. Francesco Lomonaco to Carnot, in Lomonaco, *Rapporto Al Cittadino Carnot,* 3–5.
23. Leclerc, *Foissac-Latour dévoilé,* 13.
24. Foissac-Latour, *Supplement A L'Appel,* 5.
25. Leclerc, *Foissac-Latour dévoilé,* 3.
26. Leclerc, *Observations,* 18, 33.
27. P. L[abadie?], *Détail Circonstancié,* 16.
28. Foissac-Latour, *Supplement A L'Appel,* 21.
29. "Marine," Papers of Foissac-Latour.
30. Foissac-Latour, *Supplement A L'Appel,* 22.
31. Bronson, *Select Reviews,* 2:112.
32. Papers of Foissac-Latour; Willaume, "Lettres Inédites du Général Foissac La Tour," 163–76.
33. Leclerc, *Foissac-Latour dévoilé,* 5.
34. Ibid., vi, 4.
35. Ibid., 31; Luzio, *Francesi e Giacobini,* 202–203.
36. Gachot, *Souvarow en Italie,* 348.
37. Leclerc, *Foissac-Latour dévoilé,* 19.
38. *Le Journal de Débats,* 8 vendémiaire an 10 (30 September 1801).
39. *Chef de Bataillon* Leclerc to "General" in Paris, 10 June 1802, author's private collection.
40. Six, *Dictionnaire Biographique,* 2:69.
41. Ibid.
42. Ibid.
43. Williams, *Princess of Adventure,* 274.
44. Luzio, *Francesi e Giacobini,* 216.
45. Żeromski, *Popioły,* 1, see chapter 17.
46. Wajda's black-and-white, critically acclaimed film (*The Ashes,* 1965) was even translated into Russian.

Appendix C

1. The various gun calibers show that the captured French artillery was in fact predominantly Austrian made since the French had already converted to the standard sizes of the Gribeauval system. The total number of cannon for which Scorza describes the caliber is 143; however, he gives 144 as the total. Scorza, "Memorie sul Blocca ed Assedio di Mantova," 89–94.

2. Ibid., 91–95.

Appendix H

1. Theodore Dodge, a lieutenant colonel in the United States Army, published a work on Napoleon in 1904 in which he examined the art of war. He does not criticize Napoleon for spending the time and resources to lay siege to Mantua. He simply states: "It has been suggested by some military critics that Bonaparte should have at once masked Mantua and followed up Beaulieu." Dodge, Napoleon, 1:255. Napoleon himself reflected, "Some eloquent writers have blamed me for not having masked Mantua and pursued Beaulieu into the Tyrol." Jomini, Life of Napoleon, 109.

2. Bonaparte to Carnot, 24 July 1800, Correspondance de Napoléon Ier, no. 5019, 6:529–30.

3. See Scorza, "Memorie sul Blocca ed Assedio di Mantova" (manuscript at Museo del Risorgimento, Milan).

4. Giuseppe Lattanzi was born near Rome on Lake Nemi around 1762. He was expelled from Rome for theft in 1786 and sent to Mantua, where, despite the accusation against him, Léopold II named him the secretary of the academy, owing to the charm of his wife. But upon the death of Léopold, Archduke Ferdinand relieved him of this job. Lattanzi was made deputy of the Legislative Corps of the Cisalpine Republic, served General Jean Etienne Championnet in Naples, and was made a member of the Consulate of Lyon in 1801. With his wife he founded Le Courrier des Dames, a fashion journal that was published for many years. He was repatriated to Rome, where he died in 1822. Bouvier, Bonaparte en Italie, 678–79. Portioli, Vicende di Mantova nel 1796; [Lattanzi], Istoria del Blocco e dell'Assedio della Città e Fortezza di Mantova; [Lattanzi], Giornale di Quanto è Succeduto in Mantova; Giornale dei Due Assedi della Città di Mantova.

5. Each time Scorza's manuscript was edited, first by Portioli and then in Pescasio's editing of Portioli, many details were omitted. Pescasio apparently did not see the original manuscript, which is now located in Milan at the Museo del Risorgimento. It was donated to the museum in 1925 by Dr. Achille Bertarelli, who had a large private collection of Risorgimento manuscripts and books. Before him, Dr. Luigi Ratti of Milan owned the manuscript, as indicated by a paper nameplate glued to its cover. Pescasio explains that maybe the reason Portioli said the provenance was anonymous was that its authorship "may not have been indicated in the manuscript." The actual manuscript does in fact

say that Baldassare Scorza compiled it, but Portioli was being cautious since the handwritten note on the front of the manuscript seems to be written by a different hand. Portioli did state that he is certain Scorza was the author, and he goes on to give proof why. It is quite possible that Portioli actually wrote the note on the front of the manuscript explaining that Scorza was the author. Scorza, "Memorie sul Blocca ed Assedio di Mantova," cover page; Portioli, *Vicende di Mantova nel 1796*, vii; Pescasio, *Cronaca Vissuta del Duplice Assedio di Mantova*, 5.

6. Volta was born in Mantua in 1751. At an early age, he applied himself to writing and painting. Later he started to study law. After receiving his doctorate in law in 1776, he went to Vienna to study science. He made many friends in the imperial court, and in 1779 he was made a prefect. The imperial court gave him the job of erecting and organizing a library for the Mantovano. In Mantua, Volta was the eminent intellectual of the city. He was elected to the municipal court for the Cisalpine Republic. Faccioli, *Mantova: Le Lettere*, 3:164.

7. Leopoldo Camillo (often spelled Cammillo) Volta is entombed in the Basilica of Saint Andrew in Mantua. His bust and a painting of him are prominently displayed in the Biblioteca Comunale of Mantua along with the avviso, dated 29 March 1780, proclaiming the creation of the Biblioteca Comunale, the first public library in Mantua.

8. Arrivabene to a "friend in Mantua," 22 September 1840, Arrivabene manuscript, Academiae Vergiliane. The last manuscript of Arrivabene's work on the *Compendio Cronologico-Critico della Storia di Mantova* is located in the Academiae Vergiliane, and the letter is bound between the cover and the first page. The rest of Arrivabene's manuscripts are in the Archivio di Stato di Mantova. Volume 5 of the Compendium deals with the siege of Mantua. Arrivabene, "Memorie Storiche di Mantova del Secolo XVIII," Parti d'Arco no. 176, Academiae Vergiliane; Volta, *Storia di Mantova*, ASM.

9. Pommereul entered service in the French artillery in 1764 at age 19. In 1787 he received permission to leave the French service to serve in the artillery of the king of Naples. In October 1796 he returned to the French army with the rank of general of brigade. The next month, on 13 November, he was made a member of the central committee of artillery, and on 16 November he was promoted to general of division. See Six, *Dictionnaire Biographique*, 2:322.

10. The translations of Pommereul's work include the following: Davis, *Campaign of General Buonaparte in Italy*; Ritchie, *Buonaparte's Campaign in Italy*; *Campagna del Gen. Buonaparte in Italia*; Frey, *Feldzug des Gen. Bonaparte in Italien*; and *Veldtocht van den generaal Buonaparte in Italien*.

11. See Piuma (Le père), *Examen de la Campagne de Buonaparte*.

12. See [Graham], *History of the Campaign of 1796*.

13. The original anonymous French author, sometimes noted as Baron de Pomp, continued to write about each of campaigns in Italy, Germany, and Switzerland in 1797, 1798, and 1799. In 1800 another English

edition was published in London, a five-volume work titled *The History of the Campaigns 1796–1799* that included all the previous French editions. It, too, was published anonymously, as was the original translation, but both English editions are often attributed to Thomas Graham. This English work was translated back into French in 1817 as M[aurin de Pompigny], *Histoire des Campagnes*.

14. See Jomini, *Histoire des Guerres*, vols. 8-11; and Hugo, *Histoire des Armées Françaises*, vols. 2–3.

15. The first edition of Beauvais's *Victoires, Conquêtes, Désastres*, which had seventeen volumes, was completed in 1807.

16. See Tuetey, *Un Général de L'Armée d'Italie*.

17. Eugène Trolard's book *De Montenotte au Pont D'Arcole* also relies heavily on Austrian and Italian sources; however, Trolard does not give much detail concerning the blockade of Mantua.

18. See Koch, *Mémoires de Masséna*, vol. 2.

19. Fabry, *Histoire de L'Armée d'Italie*. Fabry also published a book containing the written reports of each of the units of the Army of Italy, some of which served at Mantua. See Fabry, *Rapports Historiques*.

20. Colonel Thomas Graham's memoirs covering his time at Mantua were published, along with some of his correspondence to Lord Grenville, in 1880 by Alex M. Delavoye, a captain who previously served with the 90th Light Infantry. Delavoye, *Life of Thomas Graham*. Many of Graham's letters were also published in 1899; see Rose, "Despatches of Colonel Thomas Graham," *English Historical Review* 14, nos. 53–54, pp. 111–24, 321–31. J. Holland Rose, who wrote this article, also published the two-volume account *The Life of Napoleon I*, which contains a chapter titled "The Fights for Mantua" but again emphasizes only the battles surrounding Mantua—not the siege itself.

21. Schels, "Die Verteidigung von Mantua," 83–100, 115–52; Schels, "Die zweite Einschließung Mantuas," 251–95; Schels, "Die Begebenbeiten in und um Mantua," 161–93, 254–77; 115–44, 239–67; 167–203; Hortig, *Bonaparte vor Mantua*. Austrian Johann Baptist Schels wrote prolifically in the 1820s on the campaigns in Italy during the War of the First Coalition. He was born on 9 November 1780 in Brünn, Moravia. He entered the Austrian service in 1800 as an ensign. In 1805 he was caught in the Austrian disaster at Ulm. Later he served in Hungary, and in February 1809 he was made a captain in the pioneer corps. He was wounded three times in May during the fighting near Warsaw. From 1810 on he served on various general staffs and ended up on Swartzenberg's staff in 1815. He became the major contributor to *Östreichische Militärische Zeitschrift*, a very important journal of military history. Wurzbach, *Biographisches Lexikon des Kaiserthums Österreich*, 29:191–95.

22. See Luzio, *Francesi e Giacobini*; Finzi, *Giornale degli Amici della Libertà Italiana*.

23. D'Onofrio, "L'Archivio della Municipalità di Mantova," 121–66.

24. See Ferrari, *La Città Fortificata*.

25. Foissac-Latour arrived in Mantua on 29 March 1799. A biographical sketch of Latour is found in chapter 10. It is interesting to note that Latour used Pommereul's book in this work. See *Précis*, 1:25, 2:12.

26. See Leclerc, *Observations*.

27. See Maubert, *Relation du Blocus et du Siége de Mantoue*.

28. Leclerc, *Foissac-Latour dévoilé*.

29. There is at the French Archives de la Guerre one carton concerning Foissac-Latour and the siege in 1799, which contains only fourteen pages; see "Opérations politiques et Militaires de Foissac-Latour, général commandant à Mantoue," Carton MR 440, Service Historique.

30. This small collection has only about three hundred letters, none of which are in his book. Several of the charts, tables, and lists in this collection are, however, printed in his book verbatim, including the changes to the original documents written in another hand and with a different pen.

31. See Miljutin, *Istorija vojny Rossii*. A biographical sketch of Suvorov is found in chapter 9 notes.

32. See Pescasio, *Mantova 1799*.

33. See Godebski, *Pamiętnik Oblężenia Mantui*; and Schnür-Popławski, *Dzieje Legionów Polskich*.

34. See Woyda, *Briefe über Italien*, vol. 3.

35. See Kray, *Briefe des Feldzeugmeisters Paul Freiherrn Kray*, vol. 6.

36. See Stutterheim, "Geschichte des Feldzugs."

37. See Phipps, *Armies of the French Republic*; Wartenburg, *Napoleon as a General*; Wilkinson, *Rise of General Bonaparte*; Adlow, *Napoleon in Italy*; Ferrero, *Aventure (The Gamble)*; and Boycott-Brown, *Road to Rivoli*.

Bibliography

Manuscripts and Archival Sources
Mantua, Italy
Academiae Vergiliane

Arrivabene, Giuseppe. "Memorie Storiche di Mantova."
Faustino, Curti. *Compendio degli assedi e blocchi di Mantova.* Mantua:
Stab. Tip. Lit. Mondovi, 1889.

Archivio di Stato di Mantova (ASM)

Arrivabene, Giuseppe. "Memorie Storiche di Mantova del Secolo XVIII."
n.d., Patri d'Arco N° 176.
Busta 13, Municipalità, Navigazione-Barche.
Busta 17, Municipalità, Protocollo Appuntimenti presi della Municipalità.
Busta 82, Municipalità, Militare: Approvvigionamento d'Assedio.
Busta 108, Municipalità, Tesoreria-Crediti.
Busta 119, Municipalità, Affari di Massima.
Busta 208, Municipalità, Polizia, Giustizia e Militare.
Busta 80, Amministrazione di Stato, Amministrazione Centrale del
Dipartimento del Mincio e Commissione Amministrativa.
Busta 160, Amministrazione di Stato, Amministrazione Centrale del
Dipartimento del Mincio e Commissione Amministrativa.
Busta 179, Amministrazione di Stato, Amministrazione Centrale del
Dipartimento del Mincio e Commissione Amministrativa.
Foissac-Latour, François Philippe. *Proclama Soldati Francesi, ed Alleati
della Francia del Presidio di Mantova.* 14 May 1799. Opuscolo 5665.
Gridario Bastía 37.
P[redaval], L[uigi] M[aria]. *Saggio della Rigenerazione apportata dai
Francesi all'Italia.* Mantua: Giuseppe Braglia, 1799. Opuscolo 5672.
———. *Supplemento al Saggio della Rigenerazione apportata dai Francesi
all' Italia di L. M. P., Mantovano Contenente la Deportazione di
Quattordici Cittadini durante l'Assedio di Mantova.* Mantua:
Giuseppe Braglia, 1799. Opuscolo 5672.
Volta, Leopoldo Cam[m]illo [Giuseppe Arrivabene]. *Compendio
Cronologico-Critico della Storia di Mantova.* Vol. 5. Mantua:
Stampatore della R. Accademia, 1838.

Biblioteca Comunale di Mantova (BCM)

Avvisi 1799.
Avviso, 29 March 1780.
*Giornale dei Fatti d'Arme, e delle Operazioni Accadute Sotto Mantova
e nell'Assedio di essa dal di 26 Marzo 1799, sino al 28 Luglio dello
stess'anno.* Anon. Milan, 1799.

Milan
Archivio di Stato Milano

Busta 202, Marina.

Museo del Risorgimento

Canzone—a collection of songs and odes of 1796 and 1797.
Lattanzi, Giuseppe. *Istoria del Blocco e dell' Assedio della Città e Fortezza di Mantova.* Cremona, 1797[?]. H. 208.
———. *Giornale di Quanto è Succeduto in Mantova Durante il di lei Secondo Assedio.* Cremona, 1797[?]. Opuscolo 4333.
Scorza, Baldassare. "Memorie sul Blocca ed Assedio di Mantova." Dott. Archille Bertarelli Collection. N.d. Vol. 50. 15.
Storia della Fondazione di Mantova e suo Ducato. Milan: Presso Francesco Pogliani, 1796.

Biblioteca Nazionale Braidense

Giornale dei Due Assedi della Città di Mantova diviso in tre parti Contene i fatti d'Armi Accaduti dai Primi di Giugno 1796 sino alla Conclusione della Pace nel 1797. N.p., 1797[?]. "Written by a Mantuan and a friend in Rome." C.V. 7,678.
Map of Mantua with French Batteries, July 1796. *Carte Topografiche e Quasi Topografiche.* Vol. 1. Serie Atlan. P. 66.

Vienna
Österreichisches Staatsarchiv, Kriegsarchiv (OSK)

Berichte Erzherzog Carl, Wallis, Colli, etc., Karton 1135. January–May 1796.
Festung Mantua, Karton 1121. May through September 1796.
Festung Mantua, Karton 1122. September through December 1796.
Festung Mantua, Karton 1139. January through February 1797.
Festung Mantua, Karton 1256. 1799.
Journal Uber Mantuas Belagerung. 1799.
Karton MS-kg 86. Italien 1792 bis 1799.

Österreichisches Staatsarchiv, Kriegs Bibliothek

Buonapartes Feldzüge in Italien aus dem Französichen des Bürges Pommereul Generaloffiziers der französischen Armee. Leipzig, 1898.
Schels, Johann. "Die Begebenbeiten in und um Mantua vom 16 September 1796 bis 4 Februar 1797; nebst der Schlacht von Rivoli." *Österreichische Militärische Zeitschrift* 2 (1832): 161–93, 254–77; 3 (1832): 115–44, 239–67; 4 (1832): 167–203.
———. "Die Verteidigung von Mantua im Juni und Juli 1796." *Österreichische Militärische Zeitschrift* 1 (1830): 83–100, 115–52.
———. "Die zweite Einschließung Mantuas im August 1796 und gleichzeitige Ereignisse bei dem k. k. Heere unter dem FM. Grafen Wurmser in Tirol und Vorarlberg." *Österreichische Militärische Zeitschrift* 4 (1831): 251–95.

Stutterheim, Joseph. "Geschichte des Feldzugs der k.k. Oesterreichischen Armee in Italien im Jahre 1799," in *Oesterreichische Militaerische Zeitschrift* (Vienna, 1812).

Paris
Archives Nationales (AN)

Carton AF III, 59.
Le Procès-verbaux du Directoire Exécutif an V–an VIII 5, 20. 2006 ed. http://www.archivesnationales.culture.gouv.fr/chan/chan/pdf/sm/ PV5.pdf.

Château de Vincennes, Archives de la Guerre, Service Historique de l'armée de Terre (Service Historique)

Carton B³29.
"Journal du Siège de Mantoue." Anonymous.
Carton B³37.
Carton B³38.
Carton B³39.
Carton MR 439. *Exposé de ce qui s'est passé pendant le blocus et le siège de Mantoue et des causes qui ont le plus contribué a sa Reddition."* By André Etienne Constantin Maubert.
Carton MR 440. "Opérations politiques et Militaires de Foissac-Latour, général commandant à Mantoue."
Carton MR 1831. Notes Brahaut.
Carton MR 1834. Notes Brahaut.
Série V, génie, Carton Article 15, section 3*1. Sièges Des Places Etrangères. Capitulation.
   Chasseloup-Laubat, François. "Journal du Siège de Mantoue."
   "Plan de Mantoue et de ses Attaques." Map drawn by Chasseloup and his engineers on 9 October 1796.

Author's Private Collection

Leclerc, *Chef de Bataillon, aide-de-camp* (Michel's brother). Letter to General officer dated 10 June 1802.
Papers of Foissac-Latour. The 253 documents in this collection concerning the 1799 siege of Mantua are contained in seven folders categorized as follows: Latour's registry of letters, the army finances, reports of the police and spies, the artillery, the marine, letters from the Austrian generals, and letters from Latour's general officers and others.
   "Substance des Lettres du General Foissac La Tour."
   "Lettres des officiers généreaux et autres."
   "Finances, situation des caisses."
   "Rapports des Espions et de la Police."
   "Artillerie."
   "Marine."
   "Correspondance des officers genereaux Austrichiens et autres officers de l'Empereur."

Books and Articles

Adlow, Elijah. *Napoleon in Italy 1796–1797*. Boston: William J. Rochfort, 1948.

Alison, Archibald. *History of Europe from the Commencement of the French Revolution in 1789 to the Restoration of the Bourbons*. London: William Blackwood and Sons, 1847.

Allgemeine Deutsche Biographie. Vol. 44. Leipzig: Verlag von Dunder & Humbolt, 1898.

Anderson, Frank Meloy. *Constitutions and Documents Illustrative of the History of France, 1789–1907*. Minneapolis: B. W. Wilson Company, 1908.

Anonymous [Pomp, Baron de]. Translated [by Thomas Graham]. *The History of the Campaign of 1796 in Germany and Italy*. London: Stationers Hall, 1797.

———. *The History of the Campaign of 1799 in Italy*. Vol. 4 of *The History of the Campaigns 1796–1799*. London: J. Barfield, 1800.

Anonymous. Translated from the English [Graham] by M[aurin de Pompigny]. *Histoire des Campagnes d'Allemagne, d'Italie, de Suisse, etc. pendant les années 1796, 1797, 1798 et 1799*. 4 vols. Paris: Fournier, 1817.

Arts & Autographes. *Napoléon et son temps*. Vol. 9. Paris, 2012.

Aspinall-Oglander, Cecil. *Freshly Remembered: The Story of Thomas Graham, Lord Lynedock*. London: Hogarth Press, 1956.

Balteau, J. *Dictionnaire de biographie française*. Paris: Letouzey et Ané, 1933.

Beauvais de Preau, Charles, ed. *Victoires, Conquêtes, Désastres, Revers et Guerres Civiles des Français de 1789 a 1815*. 27 vols. Paris: C. L. F. Panckoucke, 1817–21, 1834–36.

Berthier, Louis Alexandre. *Mémoires du Maréchal Berthier*. Paris: Baudouin Frères, Éditeurs, 1827.

Biographie universelle, ancienne et moderne. Supplément. Vols. 61 and 70. Paris: Chez L.-G. Michaud, 1836, 1842.

Blease, Lyon. *Suvorof*. London: Constable and Company, 1920.

Bonaparte, Napoleon. *The Bonaparte Letters and Despatches, Secret, Confidential, and Official; from the Originals in His Private Cabinet*. Vol. 2. London: Saunders and Otley, 1846.

———. *Correspondance de Napoléon Ier publiée par ordre de l'Empereur Napoléon III*. Paris, 1858. Vols. 1–7, 10, and 29.

———. *Correspondance militaire de Napoléon Ier, extraite de la correspondance générale et publiée par ordre du ministre de la guerre*. Vol. 10. Paris: Plon, 1897.

———. *Letters and Documents of Napoleon*. Selected and translated by John Eldred Howard. New York: Oxford University Press, 1961.

———. *Memoirs of the History of France during the Reign of Napoleon, Dictated by the Emperor at Saint Helena to the Generals Who Shared His Captivity, and Published from the Original Manuscripts Corrected by Himself*. Vols. 1, 3. London: Henry Colburn and Co., 1823.

———. *Le Mémorial de Sainte-Héléne par le Comte de Las Cases*. Edited by Emmanuel Las Cases. Vol. 2. Paris, 1831.

———. *Napoleon's Letters to Josephine 1796–1813*. Translated by Henry Foljambe Hall. London: J. M. Dent & Co., 1901.

Botta, Carlo. *History of Italy during the Consulate and Empire of Napoleon Buonaparte*. Vol. 1. London: Baldwin and Cradock, 1828.

———. *Lettere Inedite di Carlo Botta*. Notes by Paolo Pavesio. Faenza, Italy: Ditta Tipografica Pietro Conti, 1875.

———. *Storia d'Italia dal 1789 al 1814*. Vol. 3. Livorno, Italy: Vignozzi, 1824.

Bourrienne, Louis Antoine Fauvelet de. *Mémoires de M. de Bourrienne Ministre d'état sur Napoléon*. Vol. 3. Paris: Chez Ladvocat, 1829.

———. *Memoirs of Napoleon Bonaparte*. Edited by R.W. Phipps. Vol. 1. London: Richard Bentley, 1885.

Bouvier, Félix. *Bonaparte en Italie, 1796*. Paris: Librairie Léopold Cerf, 1899.

Boycott-Brown, Martin. *The Road to Rivoli: Napoleon's First Campaign*. London: Cassell & Co., 2001.

Bronson, E. *Select Reviews and Spirit of the Foreign Magazines*. Vol. 2. Philadelphia, 1809.

Burton, Reginald George. *Napoleon's Campaigns in Italy*. London: G. Allen & Company, 1912.

Cantù, Cesare. *Grande Illustration del Lombardo-Veneto*. Vol. 5. Milan: Corona e Caimi, 1859.

Catholic Encyclopedia for School and Home. Vol. 8. New York: McGraw-Hill, 1965.

Chodźko, Léonard. *Histoire des legions Polonaises*. Paris, 1829.

Davenson, Henri. *Le Livre Des Chansons*. Paris: Baconnière, 1944.

Delavoye, Alex M. *The Life of Thomas Graham, Lord Lynedoch*. London: Richardson & Co., 1880.

Di Scala, Spenser. *Italy: From Revolution to Republic*. Boulder, CO: Westview Press, 1995.

Dodge, Theodore Ayrault. *Napoleon*. Vol. 1. Boston: Riverside Press, 1904.

D'Onofrio, Francesca Fantini, "L'Archivio della Municipalità di Mantova: Testimonianze dell'Amministrazione Napoleonica nel Mantovano." In *La Battaglia di Castiglione del 5 Agosto 1796: L'Amministrazione Napoleonica dell'Alto Mantovano (1796–1799)*. Mantua: Associazione delle Colline Moreniche Mantovane del Garda, 1997.

Duffy, Christopher. *Eagles over the Alps: Suvorov in Italy and Switzerland, 1799*. Chicago: Emperor's Press, 1999.

———. *Russia's Military Way to the West*. London: Routledge and Kegan Paul, 1981.

Dumas, Alexandre (père). *Mes Mémoires*. 5 vols. Reprint, 1954. Paris: Michel Levy Freres, 1865.

Elting, John R. *Swords around a Throne: Napoleon's Grande Armée*. New York: Free Press, 1988.

Encyclopaedia Britannica. Edited by Hugh Chisholm. 11th ed. Vol. 26. New York: Encyclopaedia Britannica, 1910.

Fabry, Gabriel Joseph. *Histoire de L'Armée d'Italie 1796–1797*. 3 vols. Paris: Librairie Honoré Champion (vols. 1–2) and Librairie Militaire R. Chapelot & Cie (vol. 3), 1900–1901.

———. *Rapports Historiques des Régiments de l'Armée d'Italie Pendant la Campagne de 1796–1797*. Paris: Librairie Militaire R. Chapelot & Cie, 1905.

Faccioli, Emilio. *Mantova: Le Lettere*. Vol. 3. Mantua: Istituto Carlo d'Arco, [1963?].

Ferrari, Daniela. *La Città Fortificata: Mantovanelle mappe ottocentesche del Kriegsarchive di Vienna*. Modena, Italy: Il Bulino edizioni d'arte, 2000.

———. *Mantova nelle Stampe*. Brescia, Italy: Grafo, 1985.

Ferrero, Guglielmo. *Aventure; Bonaparte en Italie (1796–1797)*. Paris: Plon, 1936.

———. *The Gamble: Bonaparte in Italy 1796–1797*. Translated by Bertha Pritchard and Lily C. Freeman. London: G. Bell and Sons, 1939.

Fiebeger, G. J. *The Campaigns of Napoleon Bonaparte of 1796–1797*. West Point, NY: U.S. Military Academy Printing Office, 1911.

Finzi, Gilberto, ed. *Giornale degli Amici della Libertà Italiana (1797–1799)*. Mantua: Tip. Alce, 1962.

———. "Il *Giornale degli Amici della Libertà Italiana* e l'opinione pubblica a Mantova alla fine del '700." *Bollettino Storico Mantovano* 1, no. 3 (1956): 161–201. Mantua.

Foissac-Latour, François Philippe. *Le Chantre de la liberte, poesies fugitives et patriotiques*. N.p., 1794.

———. *Le cri du citoyen contre les Juifs de Metz*. Metz, 1786.

———. *Discours sur le rétablissement momentané de la Gabelle: Adressé au Bataillon de la Milice Nationale de Phalsbourg & lieux circonvoisins*. N.p., n.d.

———. *Le Général de Division Foissac La Tour à la France, à ses armées, à l'Europe*. Turin, 1800.

———. *Mémoire du général de division Foissac-Latour, ayant commandé la place de Mantoue, aux citoyens Consuls de la République française*. Paris, an 8 [1799 or 1800].

———. *Ministère de la Police Générale de la République*. Paris: De L'Imprimerie du Directoire-Exécutif, 1796.

———. *Observations sur la possibilité et l'utilité de l'admission des Juifs en Alsace aux droits de citoyens, addressées à un membre de la Société des amis de la Constitution à Strasbourg*. Strasbourg, 1790.

———. *Observations sur un écrit en faveur des Juifs d'Alsace: Présenté au Comité des amis de la Révolution de Strasbourg*. Phaltzbourg, 1790.

———. *Plaidoyer contre les Juifs des Évêchés, de l'Alsace et de Lorraine*. N.p., 1790[?].

———. *Précis, ou Journal Historique et Raisonné des Opérations Militaires et Administratives qui on eu lieu dans la Place de Mantoue depuis le 9 germinal jusqu'an 10 thermidor de l'an 7 de la République française*. Paris: Chez Magimel, 1800.

————. *Supplement A L'Appel*. Turin, 1800.

————. *Traité théorie-pratique et élémentaire de la guerre des retranche-mens; precede des notions de géométrie et d'un Discours sur l'art de la guerre*. Strasbourg: De l'impr. De Levrault, 1790.

Foissac-Latour, François Philippe, and Jean Claude Michaud d'Arcon. *Examen détaillé: De l'importante question de l'utilité des places fortes et des retranchemens, dans lequel on rapporte toutes les objec-tions militaries et politiques qu'on a faites contre leur usage et leur effet, tant le systême des anciennes guerres, que depuis l'invention des armes à feu*. 2 vols. Amsterdam: De l'Imprimerie de la Socieété de Van-Haering et de Van-Koess, 1789.

Gachot, Édouard. *Histoire Militaire de Masséna: La Premiere Campagne d'Italie (1795–1798)*. Paris: Perrin et Cie, Libraires-Éditeurs, 1901.

————. *Souvarow en Italie*. Paris: Perrin et Cie, Libraires-Éditeurs, 1903.

Gallaher, John G. *General Alexandre Dumas: Soldier of the French Revolution*. Carbondale: Southern Illinois University Press, 1997.

Godebski, Cyprian. *Pamiętnik Oblężenia Mantui*. Lviv, 1864.

Guerres des Français en Italie Depuis 1794 jusqu'à 1814. Paris: Didot, 1859.

Heriot, Angus. *The French in Italy, 1796–1799*. London: Chatto & Windus, 1957.

Herold, Christopher. *The Age of Napoleon*. Boston: Houghton Mifflin, 1963.

Hogg, Ian. *Fortress*. New York: St. Martin's Press, 1975.

Honig, Erwin. *Die Kämpfe um Mantua*. Vienna: Verlagsbuchhandlung C. W. Stern, 1908.

Hooper, George. *The Italian Campaigns of General Bonaparte in 1796–7 and 1800*. London, 1859.

Hortig, Viktor. *Bonaparte vor Mantua, Ende Juli 1796*. Rostock: G. Nusser, 1903.

Hugo, Abel, ed. *Histoire des Armées Françaises de Terre et de Mer de 1792 a 1833*. Vols. 2–3. Paris: Chez Delloye, 1835, 1836.

Jomini, Antoine-Henri. *Histoire Critique et Militaire des Guerres de la Révolution*. Vols. 8–12 and maps. Paris, 1821.

————. *Life of Napoleon*. Translated by Henry W. Halleck. New York: D. Van Nostrand, 1864.

Kircheisen, Friedrich M. *Napoleons Feldzug in Italien und Österreich 1796–1797*. Munich: Georg Müller, 1913.

Koch, J[ean] B[aptiste] F[rederic]. *Mémoires de Masséna*. Vol. 2. Paris: Paulin et Lechevalier, Libraires-Éditeurs, 1848.

Kray, Paul. *Briefe des Feldzeugmeisters Paul Freiherrn Kray de Krajova et Topolya an seinen Bruder Alexander von Kray*. Edited by Dr. Just. Vol. 6. Vienna: Mitteilungen des k. und k. Kriegsarchivs, 1909.

L[abadie?], P. *Détail Circonstancié de ce qui s'est passé pendant le blocus et le siége de la ville de Mantoue*. N.p., 1799[?].

Leclerc, Michel. *Foissac-Latour dévoilé, ou, Notice sur la conduite de cet ex-général dans le Conseil de defense et l'administrtion militaire de la place de Mantoue*. Genoa, an 9 [1800 or 1801].

————. *Observations du commissaire des guerres Leclerc, sur la conduite du Général Foissac-Latour, ayant commandé à Mantoue, et du Général Gastine, chef d'état-major dans cette place.* N.p. [1799?].

Lettres de Héléodore adressées a Napoléon Bonaparte. Paris: Imprimerie de Fleuriot, Au Mans, 1833.

Lomonaco, Francesco. *Rapporto al Cittadino Carnot sulla Catastrofe Napoletana di 1799.* Notes by Mariano D'Ayala. Naples: Tip. Di M. Lombardi, 1861.

Luzio, Alessandro. *Francesi e Giacobini a Mantova dal 1797 al 1799.* Mantua: Stab. Tipografico Eredi Segna, 1890.

Macdonald, Jacques. *Recollections of Marshal Macdonald.* Edited by Camille Rouset. Translated by Stephen Louis Simeon. London: Richard Bently and Son, 1892.

Macready, Edward. *A Sketch of Suwarow, and His Last Campaign.* London: Smith, Elder and Co., 1851.

Marshall-Cornwall, James. *Marshal Massena.* London: Oxford University Press, 1965.

Maubert, [André Etienne Constantin]. *Relation du Blocus et du Siége de Mantoue et expose des causes qui ont contribute a sa Reddition.* Paris: Magimel, an 8 [1799 or 1800].

Mikaberidze, Alexander. *The Russian Officer Corps of the Revolutionary and Napoleonic Wars, 1795–1815.* New York: Savas Beatie, 2005.

Miljutin, D[mitrij]. A[lekseevich]., ed. *Istorija vojny Rossii s' Francieju v' carstvovanije imperatora Pavla I v' 1799 godu* (History of the war of Russia with France in the reign of Emperor Paul I in the year 1799). Vol. 2, pts. 3 and 4. St. Petersburg, 1852.

Moreau (de l'Yonne). *Discours Prononcé par Moreau (de l'Yonne), Sur la mort du général Joubert.* Séance 11 fructidor an 7. Legislative Corps session 28 August 1799 in the Conseil des Anciens. Paris: L'Imprimerie National, 1799.

Muller, John. *Treatise of Artillery.* London: Whitehall, 1780.

Parry, Clive, ed. *The Consolidated Treaty Series, 1648–1919.* Vol. 5. New York: Oceana Publications, 1969.

Pescasio, Luigi. *Cronaca Vissuta del Duplice Assedio di Mantova degli Anni 1796 e 1797.* Mantua: Grassi, 1974.

————. *Mantova Assediata 1796–1797.* Mantua: Edizioni Bottazzi Suzzara, 1989.

————. *Mantova 1799: Un Nuovo Assedio.* Mantua: Edizioni Bottazzi Suzzara, 1990.

Phipps, Ramsey Weston. *The Armies of the First French Republic.* Vols. 4 and 5. 1935, 1939. Reprint, Westport, Conn.: Greenwood Press, 1980.

Pierre, Constant. *Les Hymnes et Chansons de la Révolution.* Paris: Imprimerie Nationale, 1904.

Piuma (Le père). *Examen de la Campagne de Buonaparte en Italie dans les années 1796 et 1797, par un témoin oculaire (le père) Piuma, aumônier des armies autrichiennes.* London: J. G. Peltier, 1808; 2nd ed., Paris, 1814.

Pogliani, Francesco. *Storia della Fondazione di Mantova e suo Ducato con le Operazioni fatte da' Francesi, ed i fatti più importanti seguiti durante l'assedio di detta Città.* Milan, 1796.

Pommereul, F. R. J. *Campagne du Général Buonaparte en Italie pendant les années IVe et Ve de la République Française.* Paris: Plasson, 1797.

———. *Campaign of General Buonaparte in Italy during the Fourth and Fifth Years of the French Republic.* Translated by John Davis. New York, 1798.

———. *Buonaparte's Campaign in Italy in 1796–7.* Translated by T. E. Ritchie. London, 1799.

———. *Campagna del Gen. Buonaparte in Italia negli anni IV e V della Repubblica Francese scritta da un uffizial generale.* Genoa, 1798.

———. *Feldzug des Gen. Bonaparte in Italien währ: Des vierten und fünften Jahres der französ. Republik, 1796–97.* Translated by V. Frey. Leipzig, 1798.

———. *Veldtocht van den generaal Buonaparte in Italien geduurende het vierde en vijfde jaar der Fransche Republiek.* Rotterdam: J. Bronkhorst, 1798.

Portioli, Attilio. *La Zecca di Mantova.* Mantua: Premiato Stab. Tipografico Mondovi, 1882.

———. *Le Vicende di Mantova nel 1796.* Mantua: Stab. Tib. Eredi Segna, 1883.

Posio, Vannozzo. "Castiglione delle Stiviere—5 Agosto 1796 Le Armi dei due Eserciti." In *La Battaglia di Castiglione del 5 Agosto 1796: L'Amministrazione Napoleonica dell'Alto Mantovano (1796–1799).* Mantua: Associazione delle Colline Moreniche Mantovane del Garda, 1997.

Radetzky, Josef. *Radetzky Autobiographische Schriften.* Leipzig, n.d.

Rath, John. *The Provisional Austrian Regime in Lombardy-Venetia 1814–1815.* Austin: University of Texas Press, 1969.

Recueil des Acts du Directoire Exécutif. Vols. 2–4. Paris: Imprimerie Nationale, 1911–17.

Reinhard, Marcel. *Avec Bonaparte en Italie, d'après les lettres inédites de son aide de camp Joseph Sulkowski.* Paris: Librairie Hachette, 1946.

Roider, Karl A., Jr. *Baron Thugut and Austria's Response to the French Revolution.* Princeton, NJ: Princeton University Press, 1987.

Rose, J[ohn] Holland. "The Despatches of Colonel Thomas Graham on the Italian Campaign of 1796–1797." *English Historical Review* 14, nos. 53–54 (January–April 1899): 111–24, 321–31.

———. *The Life of Napoleon I.* 2 vols. London: George Bell and Sons, 1902.

Rothenberg, Gunther E. *Napoleon's Great Adversaries.* London: B. T. Batsford, 1982.

Schechter, Ronald. *Obstinate Hebrews: Representations of Jews in France, 1715–1815.* Berkeley: University of California Press, 2003.

Schnür-Popławski, Stanisław. *Dzieje Legionów Polskich.* Kraków: Spólka Wydawnicza Polska, 1897.

Simonsohn, Shlomo. *History of the Jews in the Duchy of Mantua.* Jerusalem: Kiryath Sepher, 1977.

Six, Georges. *Dictionnaire Biographique des Généraux & Amiraux Français de la Révolution et de l'Empire (1792–1814).* 2 vols. Paris: Librairie Historique et Nobiliaire, 1934.

Smith, Digby George. *Napoleon's Regiments: Battle Histories of the Regiments of the French Army, 1792–1815.* London: Greenhill Books, 2000.

"Table de l'Emplacement des Quartiers Généraux du Général Bonaparte pendant les Campagnes d'Italie et d'Egypte, de 1796 à 1800." N.p., n.d.

Thiébault, Paul Charles. *The Memoirs of Baron Thiébault.* Translated by Arthur John Butler. London, 1896.

Trolard, Eugène. *De Montenotte au Pont D'Arcole.* Paris: A. Savine, 1893.

Tuetey, Louis. *Un Général de L'Armée d'Italie: Serurier 1742–1819.* Paris: Berger-Levrault, 1899.

Vauban, Sébastien. *Traité de l'attaque des places.* Edited by Foissac-Latour. Paris: Chez Magimel, 1795.

———. *Traité de la défense des places.* Edited by Foissac-Latour. Paris: Chez Magimel, 1795.

———. *Traité des mines.* Edited by Foissac-Latour. Paris: Chez Magimel, 1795.

Vivenot, Alfred. *Thugut, Clerfayt und Wurmser.* Vienna: Wilhelm Braumüller, 1869.

Voykowitsch, Bernhard. *Castiglione 1796.* Vienna: Helmet Military Publications, 1998.

Wartenburg, Count Yorck von. *Napoleon as a General.* Edited by Walter H. James. London: Gilbert and Rivington, 1897.

Wilkinson, Spenser. *The Rise of General Bonaparte.* Oxford: Oxford University Press, 1930.

Willaume, Juljusz. "Lettres Inédites du Général Foissac La Tour." In *Revue Des Études Napoléoniennes*, vol. 34. Paris: Librairie Félix Alcan, 1932.

Williams, Hugh Noel. *A Princess of Adventure: Marie Caroline, Duchesse de Berry.* New York, 1911.

Woyda, Carl Friedrich. *Briefe über Italien geschrieben in den Jahren 1798 und 1799 vom Verfasser der vertraulichen Briefe über Frankreich und Paris.* Vol. 3. Leipzig: Pet. Phil. Wolf und Comp., 1802.

Wurzbach, Constant. *Biographisches Lexikon des Kaiserthums Österreich.* 60 vols. Vienna: Typografisch-Literarisch-Artistischen Anstalt, 1856–91.

Żeromski, Stefan. *Popioły.* Warsaw, 1904.

Newspapers

Gazzetta di Mantova
Giornale degli Amici della Libertà Italiana
Le Journal de Débats
Le Moniteur Universel
Le Publiciste
Nouvelles Politiques Publiées à Leyde
Times (London)

Index

References to maps and illustrations are in italic type.